Ezekiel

Giving Birth as a ...

Intercourse as effusion of ...

Sexual coupling indicates fractory of androgenous male, p. 84-85

Yahweh & Elohim as representing androgenous male, p. 87

CIRCLE IN THE SQUARE

p. xii + p. 68, p. 76-77 - sexual symbolism of writing instrument (phallus) letters (semen), tablet (feminine) — Zohar

Ein Sof gendered - p. 77

female part of male - p. 80, p. 91

xiii - male androgeny

p. 102 - confusion of
109 phallus with breasts

Torah = Shekinah p. 16
Torah in general, not just oral Torah, personif as female p. 13

Kabbalistic overflowing as phallic
sefirot or vessels as female) p. 64

Bahir

Unity of Torah & female masculine, Zohar, Cordovero, Luria, p. 20, 22

Zohar & Luria: Creation as a male masturbatory activity (p. 69) + p. 71 - writing

(Another appropriation of Goddess trait!)

God begetting himself (p. 74) - [rather than being born of Goddess!]

Another explanation of why Malkut is called Adonai, p. 105

CIRCLE ◆ IN THE ◆ SQUARE

STUDIES IN THE USE OF
GENDER IN KABBALISTIC SYMBOLISM

Elliot R. Wolfson

State University of New York Press

Published by
State University of New York Press, Albany

Printed in the United States of America

For information, address State University of New York
Press, State University Plaza, Albany, N.Y., 12246

Production by Marilyn P. Semerad
Marketing by Fran Keneston

Library of Congress Cataloging-in-Publication Data

Wolfson, Elliot R.
Circle in the square : studies in the use of gender in Kabbalistic symbolism / Elliot R. Wolfson.
p. cm.
Includes index.
ISBN 0-7914-2405-7 (alk. paper). — ISBN 0-7914-2406-5 (pbk. : alk. paper)
1. Cabala—History. 2. God (Judaism) 3. Masculinity of God. 4. Femininity of God. 5. Zohar. I. Title.
BM526.W64 1995
296.1'6—dc20 94-18316
CIP

10 9 8 7 6 5 4 3 2 1

For
Elijah Gabriel and Josiah Abraham

it will become you; and if you are glad
whatever's living will yourself become.
Girlboys may nothing more than boygirls need

—e. e. cummings

◆ CONTENTS ◆

◆ PREFACE ◆

One of the most engaging issues in the rich body of Jewish mystical literature, especially medieval kabbalistic texts, is the use of gender images to characterize the divine-human encounter as well as the nature of the Godhead itself. To be sure, gender imagery, particularly the erotic interplay of the lover and the beloved, is central to the texture of religious experience as it has been expressed both in the Occident and in the Orient. In this respect, therefore, the kabbalistic tradition is not unique in the history of religions. Moreover, even within the more circumscribed religious history of Judaism, the kabbalistic orientation is not distinctive. That is to say, the use of gender images to depict either the nature of God or the relationship between God and humanity is a phenomenon well attested in other forms of religious expression within Judaism, beginning as far back as certain documents contained in Scripture. However, what is singular about the kabbalistic use of gender to characterize the divine is the explicitness of expression and the extensiveness of application. Elsewhere I have argued that one could chart the history of mystical speculation in Judaism as a transition from an implicit to an explicit phallocentrism connected especially to the visualization of God. The esoteric dimension so central to the various currents of Jewish mysticism is inseparably tied to the question of eroticism. The issue of gender, therefore, goes to the very heart of Jewish mysticism in its different historical and literary configurations. Indeed, to attain the ground whence the way of kabbalistic thinking proceeds one must heed the complex phenomenon of imaging the deity in explicitly gendered terms.

While much of my scholarly work touches upon the problem of gender and the symbolic mythicization of God in kabbalistic sources, the four chapters I have selected for this volume deal with aspects of this problem in essential ways. The first chapter, "Female Imaging of the Torah: From Literary Metaphor to Religious Symbol," deals at length with the evolution of one of the central symbols of the feminine in Judaism. With the exception of only slight revisions from the original essay, I have left the piece as it was originally published in 1989. The significance of the topic, the feminization of the Torah, arguably the central artifact in all forms of religious worship in Judaism, alone justifies the decision to include this chapter in this collection. In terms of my own intellectual development, the reader will sense that at the early stage of my research I was mostly concerned with delineating the exegetical transformations in the midrashic and kabbalistic texts clustered about this fundamental motif that has informed the religious mentality and practice of Jews through the ages.

The second chapter, "Circumcision, Vision of God, and Textual Interpretation: From Midrashic Trope to Religious Mystical Symbol," published in essay form in 1987, deals with the correlation of three seemingly disparate phenomena that are nevertheless intrinsically connected in the Jewish hermeneutical imagination, especially as it is expressed in the classical work of medieval theosophic kabbalah, the *Zohar*. The detailed study of this correlation seeks to bring to light the ecstatic underpinning of the midrashic form of the zoharic life experience. Beyond this concern I have also sought to highlight the deeply erotic nature of esoteric hermeneutics in the *Zohar*, as well as to expose the phallocentric ocularcentrism of this work that informed subsequent developments in Jewish mysticism. Although I had not yet formulated the analytic category that has informed my more recent work on gender symbolism in theosophic kabbalah, namely, the conception of the male androgyne or the androgynous phallus, it will be evident to the circumspect reader that some of the texts that I cited in this piece point in that direction.

The third chapter, "Erasing the Erasure/Gender and the Writing of God's Body in Kabbalistic Symbolism," is a much elaborated version of a study to be published in French in 1995. In this chapter I suggest that the depiction of God as writer as it evolves in theosophic kabbalah is related to the attribution of gender characteristics to the divine. In particular, the activity of writing is valorized in distinctively sexual terms: the instrument of writing is the phallus; the letters that are written are the semen; and the tablet upon which the writing is inscribed is the feminine. As a consequence of the sustained reflection on the convergence of these two central aspects of kabbalistic speculation I have shown that the role of gender is assigned to the upper limits of the divine, to the Ein-Sof itself. The phallocentric interpretation of the act of God writing himself underscores the androcentric core of the engendering myth of theosophic kabbalah. This nexus of ideas attains its fullest expression in some of the Lurianic texts, which depict the initial activity of the Infinite, prior to any creation, as the play of God delighting with himself, a play that I have understood in explicit sexual terms. To be sure, this self-play of God is a way of depicting the mental processes of God, but the point of these texts is to underscore that thought itself is to be understood as erotic play. In a profound transvaluation of sexual mores, the basic act of God is portrayed as precisely that activity that in the human sphere is viewed as the cardinal sin for which the unfolding of history is the gradual rectification.

The final chapter of this volume, "Crossing Gender Boundaries in Kabbalistic Ritual and Myth," is a preliminary essay of an essential motif in the kabbalistic sources that has not been adequately addressed in scholarly literature. I examine the phenomenon of gender transformation in terms of the female becoming male and the male becoming female. Both types of transformation are predicated on the ontological assumption that the female is part of the male and hence the ultimate purpose of unification is to restore the female to the male, to contain the left in the right, to turn the feminine back around so that she stands face-to-face with the masculine front. Although kabbalists clearly describe the divine in terms of male and female, in the final analysis the dualistic posture gives way to a metaphysical monism that can be expressed mythically as the male androgyne; that is, the gender polarity of God is transcended in the singular male form that comprises both masculine and feminine. I argue, moreover, that the ontological status of the female as being part of the male is most vividly articulated in kabbalistic sources in the mythic complex of the androgynous phallus. That is, the locus of gender dimorphism is in the male organ itself. More specifically, the feminine aspect of God in its ontological root is portrayed as the corona of the penis. For the kabbalist, therefore, redemption consists of the restoration of the female to the male, a process that is fundamentally the reconstitution of the male androgyne rather than the unification of two autonomous entities. The secret of unity ultimately involves the merging of the female into the male and not the preservation of their ontic distinctiveness. The point is poignantly expressed by the adaptation in Lurianic kabbalah of the eschatological motif of the righteous sitting in the world-to-come with their crowns on their heads. This image conveys the idea that in the eschaton there is a reconstitution of the androgynous phallus symbolized by the restitution of the female crown to the male organ.

◆ 1 ◆

FEMALE IMAGING OF THE TORAH: FROM LITERARY METAPHOR TO RELIGIOUS SYMBOL

I

It is widely acknowledged that one of the more overtly innovative features of kabbalistic symbolism is its ready utilization of masculine and feminine images to depict aspects of the divine reality. It is the purpose of this study to trace the trajectory of one of the central motifs, the feminine personification of the Torah, from classical midrashic sources to kabbalistic texts. We are dealing not with one image but rather a cluster of images whose formation spans a wide historical range. While it is undeniably true that literary images in religious texts often reflect the social and cultural milieu that, at least in part, helped foster these images, it is also equally true that the evolution of ideas within "traditional" Jewish sources proceeds along an internal axis, with older texts influencing subsequent formulations and generating significant, though at times subtle, semantic transformations.

One may reasonably conjecture that the rabbinic depiction of the Torah in images related to a female personification reflects an older idea found in Jewish sources, both of Palestinian and of Alexandrian provenance, concerning the feminine Sophia or Wisdom.[1] Insofar as the identification of Torah as *Ḥokhmah,* or Sophia, first made explicitly in literary form in the books of Baruch and Ben Sira,[2] became widespread in the classical rabbinic sources,[3] it seems reasonable to suggest that such a conception may underlie the feminine characterization of the Torah. Yet, it seems to me that there is an essential difference between the older speculation on Sophia in the Wisdom and apocalyptic literature and the feminine characterization of Torah in the rabbinic texts. In the latter, unlike the former, it is clear that in most cases the feminine images are meant figuratively and are thus almost always expressed within a parabolic context as literary metaphors. I do not mean to suggest that the Torah was not personified by the rabbis; indeed, for the rabbis the Torah did assume a personality of its own, culminating in the conception of the Torah as the preexistent entity that served as the instrument with which God created the world.[4] Moreover, one occasionally discovers in the rabbinic sources vestiges of an obvious mythical conception of Torah as a feminine entity. Thus, for example, in one aggadic statement attributed to R. Joshua ben Levi, Moses is portrayed as describing the Torah as the "hidden treasure" (*ḥemdah genuzah*) with which God takes delight each day.[5] It is reasonable to assume that this expression, *mishta ͨashe ͨa bah,* "to take delight with her," derived from Proverbs 8:30, suggests a sexual connotation.[6] Underlying this remark is a mythic conception of the female Torah that is involved in an erotic relationship with God.

Although there is a resonance of such mythical depictions in other sources, particularly in liturgical poems, in the majority of rabbinic writings the female images of the Torah are metaphorical in their nuance. In one striking example in the Palestinian Talmud, the following tradition is recorded: "What is [the practice] regarding standing before the Torah-scroll? R. Ḥilqiah [in the name of] R. Simeon said in the name of R. Eleazar: Before her son you stand, how much more so before the Torah herself!"[7] Insofar as the sage is here referred to as "her son,"[8] it is reasonable to assume that the Torah is being characterized metaphorically as a female, specifically, a mother figure. In the parallel version of this passage in the Babylonian Talmud the feminine image is removed, although the basic meaning is left intact: "What is [the practice] regarding standing before the Torah-scroll? R. Ḥilqiah, R. Simeon, and R. Eleazar said: It is an argument *a fortiori,* if we stand before those who study it, how much more so [is it required to stand] before it!"[9]

The figurative characterization of the sage as the son of Torah gives way in the second passage to the more straightforward characterization "those who study it." The second passage in no way alters the meaning of the first passage, but simply renders it in a less metaphorical way. The implied image of the Torah as the mother is obviated by the fact that the one who studies the Torah is not described as the son of Torah. Although other examples could be adduced, suffice it here to conclude from the example that I have given that the figurative depiction of the Torah in feminine terms in no way implies some mythical entity. Indeed, it is correct, following the locution of R. Meyer, to speak in general of a suppression in classical rabbinic thought of the mythological character of the hypostatized *Ḥokhmah* in favor of a "nomistic rationalism."[10] In the course of time, however, the literary tropes did yield in Jewish texts a decidedly mystical and mythical conception of Torah as the divine feminine. One can speak, therefore, of a remythologization of the Torah that results from a literary transference of the images from the realm of metaphor to that of symbol.[11]

II

There are several distinct feminine images of the Torah in the body of classical rabbinic literature. I would like to mention here three of the more salient images: daughter of God, or sometimes expressed as the daughter of the king, the bride, and the mother.[12] With respect to all three the relevant talmudic and midrashic contexts make it clear that we are dealing with figurative expressions, that is, metaphorical characterizations of the Torah, rather than any hypostatic element. In the case of the former, the daughter of God or the king, it is necessary to make a further distinction: this image occurs either in the context of a wedding motif[13] (to be discussed more fully below) or outside that specific context.[14] Moreover, in the case of the bride, it is also possible to make several distinctions: the Torah is characterized respectively as the bride of Israel, God, or even Moses.

The feminine characterization of the Torah as a bride of Israel is connected in several sources, both in the Babylonian Talmud and other collections of scriptural exegeses, with the midrashic reading of the word "heritage," *morashah*, in the expression describing the Torah, "heritage of the congregation of Jacob" (Deut. 33:4), as *meʾorasah*, "betrothed."[15] In *Sifre Deuteronomy*, for example, one reads as follows: "Another interpretation [of 'a heritage of the congregation of Jacob,' *morashah qehillat yaʿaqov*]: Do not read heritage (*morashah*) but betrothed (*meʾorasah*). This teaches that the Torah is betrothed to Israel and [is to be considered] a married woman [that is forbidden] in relation to the nations of the world."[16] The above aggadic notion is even applied in one talmudic context to a legal discussion concerning the position enunciated by R. Yoḥanan that a non-Jew engaged in Torah is deserving of corporal punishment. According to the one who reads the expression *morashah*, heritage, as *meʾorasah*, the betrothed, the non-Jew who is involved with Torah is to be treated like the individual who has relations with a woman who is betrothed to another man, and such an individual receives the punishment of stoning.[17] In still another talmudic context this midrashic reading of Deuteronomy 33:4 serves as a basis for the following homiletical interpretation:

"R. Ḥiyya taught: Whoever is involved in Torah before an ignoramus it is as if he had sexual relations with his bride right in front of him, as it says, 'Moses commanded the Torah to us, as the heritage of the congregation of Jacob.' Do not read heritage (*morashah*) but rather betrothed (*me*ʾ*orasah*)."[18] Whatever the subsequent usages made of this older midrashic reading, the root idea here is the aggadic notion that the Torah is compared to a woman betrothed to the congregation of Jacob, the Jewish people.[19]

This feminine characterization of the Torah is also connected in some texts to the metaphorical depiction of the Sinaitic theophany as a wedding day.[20] In one of the earliest collections of homiletical midrashim, *Pesiqta de-Rav Kahana,* the image is clearly stated: " 'In the third month' (Exod. 19:1). The third month came. [This may be compared] to a king who betrothed a woman, and set a time [for the marriage]. When the time arrived they said, 'It is time to enter the [marriage] canopy.' Similarly, when the time arrived for the Torah to be given, they said, 'It is time for the Torah to be given to Israel.' "[21] In this midrashic comment the event at Sinai is again compared to a wedding; the giving of the Torah is thus likened to entering the marriage canopy. But here, unlike some other early sources,[22] the bridegroom is not God but Israel, and correspondingly the bride is not Israel but the Torah itself. The Sinaitic revelation is thus the wedding of the Jewish people, the groom, to the Torah, the bride. That this interpretation is correct is borne out by a later version of this passage in the thirteenth-century Yemenite collection, *Midrash ha-Gadol,* which reads as follows:

> "In the third month" (Exod. 19:1). The third month came. [This may be compared] to a king who betrothed a woman, and set a time [for the marriage]. When the time arrived they said: "It is time for the woman to enter the [marriage] canopy." Similarly, when the time arrived for the Torah to be given, they said, "It is time for the Torah to be given to Israel."[23]

This view of Torah as the bride informed the midrashic reading attested in several sources of another key verse, Exodus 31:18, "When He finished speaking with him on Mt. Sinai, He gave Moses the two tablets of the pact, stone tablets inscribed with the finger of God." The word *ke-khalloto,* "when He finished," was read in accord with its masorertic defective spelling (without the *waw*) as *ke-khallato,* "as his bride."[24] This reading, then, confirmed the idea that the Torah was given to Israel—through Moses—as a bride. From this were generated, in turn, several homiletical interpretations that compare the scholar himself, or the words of Torah that proceed from his mouth, to a bride.[25] This reading, moreover, served as the basis for the following passage in the medieval collection of moral precepts, *ᵓOrḥot Ḥayyim*, spuriously attributed to R. Eliezer ben Hyrcanus[26]: "Whoever rejoices with the groom it is as if he received the Torah from Sinai, as it says, 'When He finished (*ke-khalloto*) [speaking with him on Mt. Sinai], He gave Moses etc.' It is written, 'as his bride' (*ke-khallato*). The day in which the Torah was given was certainly like the day when the bride enters her bridal canopy."[27] To be sure, the connection between the Sinaitic revelation and an actual wedding underlies earlier teachings, such as the view attributed to R. Joshua ben Levi that one who gladdens the groom with the five voices of joy merits the Torah that was given in five voices.[28] But in the passage from *ᵓOrḥot Ḥayyim* this connection is predicated specifically on the notion that the event at Sinai was itself a wedding between Israel, the groom, and Torah, the bride.

A still further stage in this metaphorical depiction may be gathered from those midrashic passages in which the Torah is parabolically compared to the king's daughter who is given over in marriage to Israel. Thus in *Deuteronomy Rabbah*, whose final stage of redaction is set in the ninth cenutry but which undoubtedly contains earlier material, we find the following parable:

> Another explanation: "The thing is very is close to you" (Deut. 30:14). R. Samuel ben Naḥman said, To what may this be compared? To a princess whom no one knew. The king had a friend who would come to the king all the time, and the princess stood before him. The king said to him: See how much I cherish you, for no one knows my daughter, and she stands before you. Similarly, the Holy One, blessed be He, said to Israel: See how much I cherish you, for no creature in My [celestial] palace knows the Torah, and I have given it to you.[29]

The metaphorical depiction of the Sinaitic revelation as a marriage and the Torah as the king's daughter is highlighted even more in a passage in *Numbers Rabbah*. The relevant remark occurs in the part of the midrash that, although based on much earlier materials, was apparently compiled in the twelfth century in the school of Moses ha-Darhsan, an eleventh-century scholar and aggadist of Narbonne: "To what may this be compared? To a king who married off his daughter and gave her a great wedding celebration . . . Thus did the Holy One, blessed be He, do when He gave the Torah to Israel. . . . This was naught but a wedding celebration."[30] In this text we see again that the event at Sinai is compared to a wedding, *qiddushin*: the bride is the Torah, which is characterized as well as the daughter of the king, that is, God, and the groom is Israel.

A crucial stage in the literary process occurs when the parabolic image of the Torah as bride is subsumed under the image of the king's daughter without any obvious link to the wedding motif. Such a description of the Torah as the king's daughter, *bat melekh*, is to be found in Eleazar Qallir's *silluq* for the Torah reading of the pericope *Sheqalim*. The entire *silluq* is a hymn for the measurements or dimensions of the Torah, indeed in terms often characteristic of the ancient Jewish esoteric *shi*ᶜ*ur qomah* speculation,[31] but in one place in particular it states that "the measure of the king's daughter (*middat bat melekh*)[32] is superior in all, elevated in length, width, depth and height, for there is a limit to every end, but her word expands forever without end."[33] It is fairly obvious that the king's daughter is the Torah whose infinite worth and meaning is here depicted in spatial terms. While it is clear that the image of the king's daughter here has no explicit connection to the metaphorical or parabolic description of the Sinaitic revelation as a wedding, it is not yet obvious that the Torah has assumed a hypostatic status.

Another example of the feminine characterization of the Torah removed from the nuptial context may be gathered from the well-known passage attributed to the second century Tanna, R. Simeon bar Yoḥai, in the *Tanḥuma*ᵓ, a Babylonian-Geonic recension of the Yelammedenu midrash stemming from the seventh century, in which the Torah is compared parabolically to a king's daughter who is set within seven palaces. The king reportedly says: "Whoever enters against[34] my daughter, it is as if he enters against me." The meaning of the parable is immediately rendered in the continuation of the midrash: "The Holy One, blessed be He, says: If a man desecrates my daughter, it is as if he desecrates Me. If a person enters the synagogue and desecrates My Torah, it is as if he rose and desecrated My glory."[35] That this statement may be drawing upon the language of ancient Jewish mystical speculation is supported from the description of the Torah as the princess hidden within seven palaces or *hekhalot*. I am also inclined to believe that the reference to the divine glory at the end of the passage is related to the use of this *terminus technicus* in *merkavah* literature to refer to the anthropomorphic manifestation of the divine. It is thus significant that a link is made between the glory and the Torah.[36] That is, the Torah in the synagogue hidden within the ark is meant to conjure up the image of the *kavod* hidden behind the various palaces in the celestial realm. Hence, the one who rises against the Torah is comparable to one who rises against the *kavod*.[37] Be that as it may, the essential point for the purposes of this analysis is that here the feminine characterization of Torah as God's daughter is affirmed without any conspicuous connection to the Sinaitic theophany or to the wedding imagery.

In still another passage from a work entitled *Midrash ʾAlfaʾ Betot*, one finds an alternative depiction of the wedding motif. Before proceeding to an analysis of the relevant passage, it is necessary to make a preliminary observation about this source. The provenance and subsequent literary history of this text are somewhat obscure. Solomon Wertheimer, who published the text on the basis of only one manuscript, conjectured that this text presumably was a part of the mystically oriented midrash *ʾOtiyyot de-Rabbi ʿAqivaʾ*,[38] a view that has recently been criticized.[39] Admittedly, the lack of a fuller picture regarding the history of this text makes citation from it somewhat suspect, especially in the context of trying to present the development of a motif. Still, it can be argued from the language of the text that it indeed draws heavily from the *merkavah* sources and thus represents an important stage in the literary transmission of Jewish mysticism in Palestine during the seventh and eighth centuries.[40] Even if it cannot be shown conclusively which medieval mystic in particular had this text and was influenced by it, the text itself stands as testimony to a link in the chain of Jewish mystical speculation. At some point some Jewish mystic conceived the Torah in this way, and the conceptual and phenomenological relationship that this view has to other ideas in kabbalistic documents can easily be demonstrated.

In the text of *Midrash ʾAlfaʾ Betot* there is a striking passage that offers a graphic description of the Torah as the royal bride, again without any overt connection to the Sinaitic revelation:

> Another explanation: "Behold it was very good" (Gen. 1:21). The meaning of good is Torah, as it says, "For I give you good instruction, do not forsake My Torah" (Prov. 4:2). This teaches that in that very moment the Torah came from her bridal chamber (*ḥadre ḥupatah*),[41] adorned (*mitqasheṭet*) in all kinds of jewels and in all kinds of royal ornaments. And she stands and dances before the Holy One, blessed be He, and gladdens the heart of the *Shekhinah*. She opens her mouth in wisdom and her tongue with understanding, and praises the name of God with all kinds of praise and all kinds of song.[42]

In this passage we come across two significant elements: first, the Torah is said to emerge from her bridal chamber adorned with jewels and royal ornaments. The only other reference that I am familiar with in the *Hekhalot* corpus to such a motif is to be found in the *Re᾿uyot Yeḥezqel* where it is stated that within the fourth of the seven heavens, *ʿarafel,* is found the "[bridal] canopy of the Torah," *ḥupatah shel Torah.*[43] The assumption of an actual *ḥupah* for the Torah, albeit in the celestial realm, is based on an earlier figurative description of the Torah as the bride in her bridal canopy. Thus, for example, the following exegetical comment is found in the Palestinian Talmud: "It is written, 'Let the bridegroom come out of his chamber, the bride from her canopy' (Joel 2:16). 'Let the bridegroom come out of his chamber' refers to the ark, 'the bride from her canopy' refers to the Torah."[44] In the *Midrash ᾿Alfa᾿ Betot,* as in the *Re᾿uyot Yeḥezqel,* the *ḥupah* is not merely a figure of speech; it refers to an entity that actually exists in the cosmological scheme.

The second point of especial interest in the above passage is that the Torah is depicted as dancing before the Holy One, blessed be He, and gladdening the heart of the divine Presence—significantly, *Shekhinah* is not used interchangeably with the Holy One, blessed be He, but is rather an independent entity, although its exact gender is difficult to ascertain. In several other places in this text the *Shekhinah* is described, together with the throne itself, the glory, and the angels, as standing before God,[45] thereby substantiating the impression that the Presence is not identical with the Holy One, blessed be He. One text, in particular, is noteworthy, for it says that the *Shekhinah* was on the throne of glory from the right side and Moses from the left.[46] Again, it is not clear if this implies an apotheosis of the figure of Moses. In any event, the role of the Torah in the passage cited above is similar to that of the celestial beasts in the *merkavah* texts; that is, the Torah is described as uttering praise and song before God. Even the image of dancing before God—which, I presume, has a sexual connotation[47]—has a parallel in the *merkavah* corpus.[48] Hence, the feminine characterization of the Torah is here abstracted from the particular setting of the Sinaitic theophany. That is, the metaphorical depiction of Torah as the bride is removed from the specific context of a parabolic description of the historical revelation. Moreover, it seems to me that in this text the Torah has already assumed a hypostatic character. We are not simply dealing with the figurative expression of a personified Torah, but with an actual hypostasis of the Torah as a feminine person who emerges from her bridal chamber. This is consistent with the decidedly hypostatic characterization of the *kavod, Shekhinah,* and *kisse᾿ ha-kavod* found in other parts of this text.

In the continuation of the aforecited passage in *Midrash ᾿Alfa᾿ Betot* one finds that the Torah, personified as the daughter of God, is characterized more specifically as the bride of Moses:

> Another explanation: "Behold it was very good" (Gen. 1:21). The word "good" refers to Moses, as it says, "and she saw how good he was" (Exod. 2:2). This teaches that in that very time the Holy One, blessed be He, revealed to the Torah the throne of glory, and He brought forth all the souls of the righteous.[49] . . . And He brought forth the souls of Israel. . . . Afterwards He brought forth the soul of Moses from underneath His throne for he would in the future explain the Torah in seventy languages.[50] God showed him to the Torah and said, "My daughter, take joy and be delighted by this Moses, My servant, for he will be your groom and husband. He will be the one to receive you in the future and to explicate your words to the sixty myriad Israelites."[51]

This comment is an elucidation of a verse in Genesis, suggesting therefore that the setting here is the event of creation. The Sinaitic revelation is only alluded to as a future reference. It is significant that Moses is called the groom of the Torah, for he will be the one to receive the Torah at Sinai and explicate it to the Israelite people. Unlike earlier sources, the wedding at Sinai is not between God and Israel, or Israel and the Torah, but rather Moses and the Torah. The same aggadic tradition is preserved in a comment of Judah ben Barzillai, citing some older source (*nusḥaʾ de-rishonim*). According to the legend mentioned by this authority, at the birth of Abraham God was said to have had the following conversation with the Torah: "He said to her, 'My daughter, come and we will marry you to Abraham, My beloved.' She said to Him: 'No, [I will not marry] until the humble one [i.e., Moses] comes.' "[52] In the continuation of the text we read that God then requested of the *Sefer Yeṣirah* to wed Abraham and, unlike the Torah, it agreed. The purpose of the legend is thus to explain the special connection of *Sefer Yeṣirah* to Abraham as established in the most pervasive traditional attribution of the text. What is of immediate interest for us is the view that Moses would be the one to marry the Torah, the latter personified specifically as the daughter of God. As will be seen later in this analysis, the motif of Moses' being wed to the Torah plays a significant role in the more developed kabbalistic symbolism.

III

The image of the hypostatic crowned Torah served as a basis for the development of one of the key symbols in the incipient kabbalah. Thus, in a critical passage in *Sefer ha-Bahir*, a foundational text in medieval Jewish mysticism, one reads the following depiction of Torah as the king's daughter:

> Whenever a person studies Torah for its own sake, the Torah above (*torah shel maʿalah*) unites with the Holy One, blessed be He. . . . And what is the Torah of which you speak? It is the bride that is adorned and crowned (*mequsheṭet u-meʿuṭeret*), and is comprised[53] in all the commandments (*mukhlelet be-khol ha-miṣwot*), and it is the treasure of the Torah (*ʾoṣar ha-torah*). And she is the one engaged to the Holy One, blessed be He, as it is written, "Moses commanded the Torah to us, as the heritage of the congregation of Jacob" (Deut. 33:4). Do not read heritage (*morashah*) but rather betrothed (*meʾorasah*). How is this possible? When Israel are involved with the Torah for its own sake she is the one engaged to the Holy One, blessed be He, and when she is the one engaged to the Holy One, blessed be He, she is the heritage of Israel.[54]

Here the midrashic image of the Torah as the betrothed of Israel has been transposed into the divine sphere. That is, the Torah below has its reflection in the Torah above, which is joined to the masculine potency of the divine, the Holy One, blessed be He, by means of the study of Torah in the mundane sphere.[55] Furthermore, this supernal Torah, the feminine potency of the divine, is described as the bride that is adorned and crowned and which comprises all the commandments. It is on account of the latter that the supernal Torah is called the *ʾoṣar ha-torah*.[56] A similar expression is employed in yet another passage in which the treasure of the Torah, *ʾoṣarah shel torah*, is identified as the fear of God, *yirʾat yhwh*, based on the verse, "the fear of God was his treasure" (Isa. 33:6). From that context, moreover, it is clear that the fear of God, or the treasure of Torah, refers to the last of the divine potencies as it is presented as the last item in a series of seven cognitive-emotive states that are symbolic referents of God's attributes, that is, wisdom (*ḥokhmah*), understanding (*binah*), counsel (*ʿeṣah*), which corresponds to the attribute of bestowing kindness (*gemilat ḥasadim*), strength (*gevurah*),[57] identified also as the attribute of judgment (*middat ha-din*), knowledge (*daʿat*) or the attribute of truth (*ʾemet*), and the fear of God (*yirʾat yhwh*), which is described as the treasure of Torah (*ʾoṣarah shel ha-torah*).[58] It is fairly obvious, then, that the treasure of the Torah is a technical reference to one of the divine attributes in the same way as the other items in the list; in particular, the attribute to which this phrase refers is the *Shekhinah*, the seventh and last potency enumerated in this series.[59] In the *Bahir*, therefore, one is clearly transferred from the realm of metaphor to that of symbol. That is, in the relevant passages the king's daughter is no longer merely a literary expression used in a metaphorical context; it is rather a living symbol that names one of the divine potencies.[60]

Still other passages in the *Bahir* indicate that the Torah is characterized as a feminine personification. Thus, in one of the opening passages one finds the following complicated sequence: the Torah begins with the letter *bet* of the word *bere'shit,* which stands for blessing (*berakhah*), for the Torah is called "blessing," but blessing in turn is identified as the beginning (*re'shit*), which is nothing but wisdom (*ḥokhmah*).[61] It is further specified there that this is, employing the imagery of 1 Kings 5:26, the wisdom that God gave to Solomon,[62] an event parabolically depicted as the king giving over his daughter[63] in marriage to his son.[64] In another passage, which ostensibly sets out to explain the function of the *bet* at the end of the word *zahav*, "gold," a similar parable is offered:

> This may be compared to a king who had a good, pleasant, beautiful and perfect daughter. He married her to a prince, and he dressed her, crowned and adorned her, and gave her to him for much money. Is it possible for the king to sit outside his house [without being with his daughter]? No! But can he sit all day and be with her constantly? No! What does he do? He places a window between himself and her, and whenever the daughter needs the father or the father the daughter, they join together by means of the window.[65]

In the next paragraph we are given additional information to help us identify the *bet* at the end of the word *zahav*: it is the wisdom with which God will build the house.[66] Hence, the king's daughter, all dressed, adorned, and crowned for her wedding to the prince, is divine wisdom. That the further identification with Torah is here implied may be gathered from the fact that the parable is largely based on a midrashic passage in *Exodus Rabbah* that deals specifically with the Torah[67]:

> The Holy One, blessed be He, said to Israel: "I sold you My Torah, I was sold with it, as it were." . . . This may be compared to a king who had an only daughter. One of the kings came and took her; he desired to go to his land and to take her as a wife. The king said to him: "My daughter whom I have given you is an only child; I cannot separate from her, yet I also cannot tell you not to take her for she is your wife. But do me this favor: in whatever place that you

> go, make a bed-chamber for me so that I may live near you for I cannot leave my daughter." Thus the Holy One, blessed be He, said to Israel: "I gave you My Torah. I cannot separate from it, yet I cannot tell you not to take it. In every place that you go make for Me a house so that I may dwell within it, as it says, 'And make for Me a tabernacle' (Exod. 25:8)."[68]

The bahiric parable is clearly based on the midrashic one, with some significant differences. In the case of the standard midrash, the king's daughter is identified as the Torah given by God to Israel. God's request of Israel to build a tabernacle is understood midrashically in terms of his need to be close to the Torah, which is now in the possession of the Jews. In the *Bahir*, by contrast, the Torah is not mentioned explicitly, though it is implied by the identification of the king's daughter with *Ḥokhmah*. In this case, moreover, there is mention of an actual joining of father and daughter, and not merely the desire to be in proximity to one another.

To be sure, the feminine personification of the Torah is not the only one to be found in the *Bahir*. In one passage, for instance, Torah is identified with the divine attribute of *Ḥesed*, lovingkindness,[69] though in this case, as in some of the passages where Torah is linked with the feminine *Ḥokhmah*, the image of water plays a central role.[70] In still another passage mention is made of the "true Torah," *torat ʾemet*, which is said to be within the divine attribute of Israel.[71] From the next paragraph we learn that the activity of this *torat ʾemet* is within the *Maḥshavah*, "divine thought"; moreover, it is itself one of the ten logoi that establishes all the rest.[72] Although the meaning of this passage is not altogether clear, it strikes me that the *torat ʾemet* is another name for divine thought, the uppermost attribute that establishes the other nine, and which is particularly evident within the attribute of Israel, that is, the attribute that in subsequent kabbalistic texts was most frequently identified with the sixth emanation, *Tifʾeret*. In the list of the ten logoi, the third of these is identified as the quarry of Torah, *meḥaṣev ha-torah*, or the treasure of wisdom, *ʾoṣar ha-ḥokhmah* (reminiscent of the expression *ʾoṣar ha-torah* used in a previous context), for God is said to have hewn the letters of the Torah within this attribute.[73] Finally, the most important alternative conception of the Torah is offered in an elaborate reworking of an earlier aggadic idea concerning the primordial light that was hidden by God for the benefit of the righteous in the world-to-come.[74] According to the *Bahir*, God took a portion from that primordial light, comprised within it the thirty-two paths of wisdom, and then gave it to people of this world.

This light is named the "treasure of the Oral Torah," *ʾoṣarah shel torah she-beʿal peh.* "The Holy One, blessed be He, said: If they observe this attribute in this world, for this attribute is considered part of this world, and it is the Oral Torah, they will merit life of the world-to-come, which is the good hidden for the righteous."[75] From this it follows that the Oral Torah represents a fragment from the primordial divine light that is operative in the mundane realm. The means to attain the full light in the spiritual realm is to observe the commandments of the Torah as mediated through the rabbinic oral tradition. The precise relationship between the Written Torah and the Oral Torah is addressed in a subsequent passage. Interpreting Proverbs 6:23, "For the commandment (*miṣwah*) is a lamp, the Torah a light," the *Bahir* establishes that "commandment" corresponds to the Oral Torah and "Torah" to Scripture.[76] Admittedly, the Written Torah is a much greater light, but the candle of the Oral Torah is necessary to elucidate the meaning of Scripture. This relationship is illuminated by means of a parable: even though it is broad daylight outside, it is sometimes necessary to use a candle in order to see what is hidden in a room in a house.[77]

According to the kabbalistic interpretation of this critical bahiric text that evolved in thirteenth-century Spain, the light or the Written Torah was said to symbolize the masculine potency, usually identified as the sixth emanation, *Tifʾeret,* whereas the Oral Torah or the lamp was said to symbolize the feminine potency, the *Shekhinah.*[78] To be sure, the depiction of the Oral Torah in terms that are applicable to the feminine Presence has a basis in the *Bahir* itself. Notwithstanding this fact, it is evident that such a conception contradicts the other major image found in the *Bahir* according to which the Torah in a generic sense, and not specifically the Oral Torah, was characterized as the feminine potency of God. It is possible that we are dealing with two distinct stages in the literary composition of the *Bahir.* Perhaps at an earlier stage the Torah was simply described in a way that developed organically out of older midrashic sources, whereas at a later stage there developed the unique kabbalistic conception of the dual Torah as corresponding symbolically to the two attributes of God. Support for my conjecture may be found in the subtle shift in terminology from *ʾoṣar ha-torah,* the "treasure of Torah," to *ʾoṣar shel torah she-beʿal peh,* the "treasure of the Oral Torah." That is, in the first passage (§ 196) where Torah is generally described as a feminine potency, it is referred to as the "treasure of Torah," whereas in the second passage (§ 147) where the masculine-feminine duality is introduced, the feminine aspect of Torah is referred to as the "treasure of the Oral Torah." It is, however, difficult to ascertain with any certainty if and when this change may have occurred. What is crucial, however, is that while the correlation of the dual Torah to the male-female polarity within the divine became the norm in kabbalistic documents in thirteenth-century Spain, it can nevertheless be shown that the older mythical-aggadic image did not entirely disappear.

IV

One finds in subsequent kabbalistic texts traces of the identification of the Torah with the feminine potency, particularly the *Shekhinah*.[79] It is significant that a kabbalistic reworking of this motif is found in a relatively early text, Judah ben Yaqar's *Perush ha-Tefillot we-ha-Berakhot.* In the context of commenting on the Friday evening prayer, "You shall sanctify the seventh day," *ʾatah qidashta ʾet yom ha-sheviʿi,* which ben Yaqar interprets in terms of *qiddushin,* a wedding service,[80] he cites the midrashic text from *Deuteronomy Rabbah* mentioned above,[81] in which Moses is described as the scribe who writes the marriage contract (the Torah), Israel is the bride, and God is the groom. Ben Yaqar then cites from the continuation of the same source a comment attributed to Resh Laqish to the effect that the illumination of Moses' face mentioned in Exodus 34:29 could be explained by the fact that in the process of writing the Torah, which was written with black fire on parchment of white fire,[82] Moses wiped the quill with which he was writing in his hair. According to ben Yaqar, the import of this statement is "to say that Moses too betrothed the Torah and she was his bride and portion."[83] Do we have here a cryptic reference to the Torah as the feminine persona of the divine, the *Shekhinah,* who is wedded to Moses, the biblical figure who symbolizes the masculine potency of God? Support for this interpretation may be gathered from a second comment of ben Yaqar on this midrashic passage: " 'A crown of splendor (*kelil tifʾeret*) You placed on his [Moses'] head' . . . a crown of splendor, as it says in *Deuteronomy Rabbah,* he was writing when he was above [i.e., on Mt. Sinai], and he would wipe the quill in his hair and illuminate his face."[84] In the first passage this state of illumination was explained by reference to the idea that Moses was betrothed to the Torah; in the second passage the same idea is expressed by the idea that Moses is crowned by a crown of splendor. The image of Moses' being crowned is equivalent to that of his being wedded to Torah.[85] Moreover, as it can be ascertained from another passage in ben Yaqar, the *Shekhinah* is characterized as the "crown on the head of the king" (*ʿaṭarah be-rosh ha-melekh*),[86] that is, the crown on the head of *Tifʾeret.* It seems to me, therefore, that Moses stands symbolically for *Tifʾeret,* and the crown on his head, as well as the Torah to which he is wedded, for the *Shekhinah.*

A similar kabbalistic usage of this aggadic motif may be found in the writings of one of ben Yaqar's more celebrated students, Naḥmanides (1194–1270). Thus, for example, Naḥmanides returns to this theme in his comments on the very first word of the Pentateuch.[87] After establishing that the opening word of Scripture, *bereʾshit,* refers simultaneously to the emanation of the upper Wisdom, or the "Wisdom of Elohim," symbolized by the heave offering (*terumah*) that is utterly beyond human comprehension, and to the last of the ten emanations, the lower Wisdom, the "Wisdom of Solomon," that is, the *Shekhinah,* symbolized by the *maʿaser,* which is a measure that can be comprehended, Naḥmanides turns his attention to the rabbinic reading that interprets *reʾshit* as a reference to Israel:

> And Israel, who are called the "beginning" (*reʾshit*), refers to the Community of Israel (*keneset yisraʾel*), who is compared in Song of Songs to the bride, and which Scripture calls [by the names] daughter, sister and mother.[88] . . . And thus [the verse] "he saw the beginning for himself" (Deut. 32:21)[89] is spoken with reference to Moses. It is held [by the rabbis][90] that Moses contemplated [the divine] within a speculum that shines, "and he saw the beginning for himself," and thus he merited the Torah. It is all one intention.[91]

For Naḥmanides, then, Moses beheld the vision of the *Shekhinah*—the "beginning" (*reʾshit*) alluded to in Deuteronomy 33:21—through the upper masculine attribute, the speculum that shines, and as a result he merited the Torah.

That the Torah corresponds symbolically to the *Shekhinah* may be gathered from a second comment of Naḥmanides:

> "And this is the offering," *we-zoʾt ha-terumah* (Exod. 25:3). By way of [kabbalistic] truth this is like [the verse] "And the Lord gave wisdom to Solomon" (1 Kings 5: 26). . . . And in *Exodus Rabbah* [it says]: "And this is the offering that you shall take from them" [this refers to] the Community of Israel (*keneset yisraʾel*), which is the offering (*terumah*). . . . The Holy One, blessed be He, said to Israel: I have sold you My Torah and, as it were, I have been sold with her, as it says, "Bring Me an offering" (Exod. 25:2), for the offering is to Me and I am with her.[92]

In this case, in contrast to the one mentioned above, the word *terumah* itself is given the same symbolic valence as *zo't*. Now, insofar as it is clear from other contexts in Naḥmanides' writing that the word *zo't*, the feminine form of the demonstrative pronoun, refers to the *Shekhinah*,[93] we may further infer that in this case *terumah* refers to *Shekhinah*. Moreover, utilizing the midrashic comment from *Exodus Rabbah* already mentioned above, Naḥmanides is able to equate *terumah* and Torah; yet, inasmuch as *terumah* is synonymous with *zo't*, and *zo't* stands for *Shekhinah*, it follows that Torah likewise stands for the *Shekhinah*. This interpretation is corroborated by another brief comment of Naḥmanides: "The word *zo't* alludes to the blessing, which is the Torah, and it is the covenant, as it is written, 'This is my covenant' (*zo't beriti*) (Isa. 59:21)."[94] Hence, *Shekhinah* equals blessing, which equals the Torah and the covenant.

The symbolic nexus that I have described above is preserved as well in the following kabbalistic interpretation of Baḥya ben Asher on the midrashic reading of Deuteronomy 33:4, "do not read heritage (*morashah*) but betrothed (*me'orasah*)":

> By way of kabbalistic explanation (*'al derekh ha-qabbalah*) they had to interpret in this way, for this Torah (*zo't ha-torah*) is betrothed to Jacob, and she is called Rachel. In a time of anger the *Shekhinah* disappears, "Rachel cries over her children, she refuses to be comforted for her children, who are gone" (Jer. 31:14). And in a time of favor Rachel is the wife of Jacob, and this is clear.[95]

According to the kabbalistic interpretation of the midrashic passage, Torah is the *Shekhinah* or Rachel, who is betrothed to *Tif'eret* symbolized by the figure of Jacob. In times of distress the two are separated and Rachel weeps over her children, but in times of mercy they are united in matrimony. Following the tradition of Judah ben Yaqar and Naḥmanides, Baḥya likewise affirms that the Torah is the feminine Presence.

It is, however, in the classical kabbalistic text of this period, the *Zohar*, that the image of the Torah as a woman not only resurfaces but is again elevated to a position of supreme importance. Indeed, one finds that some of the more powerful passages describing Torah in a mystical vein in the *Zohar* draw heavily from the feminine image of the Torah. Specifically, the feminine personification of the Torah is utilized by the author of the *Zohar* to describe the hermeneutical relationship between mystic exegete and Scripture. Thus, for example, in one passage we read the following explanation attributed to R. Isaac for why the Torah begins with the letter *bet*, which is opened on one side and closed on the three other sides: "When a person comes to be united with the Torah, she is open to receive him and to join him. But when a person closes his eyes from her and goes another way, she is closed from another side."[96] In this context, then, it is clear that the author of the *Zohar* upholds the possibility of an individual's uniting with the Torah; indeed, in the continuation of the text, this unification is referred to as joining the Torah face-to-face (*le᾽itḥabber bah ba-᾽oraita᾽ ᾽anpin be-᾽anpin*), an idiom employed in the *Zohar* to connote an intimate sexual union.[97] The Torah is open and closed, depending on the actions and the efforts of the given person. Underlying this suggestive remark is the older feminine personification of the Torah. What is implied in this passage is elaborated upon in greater detail in the famous zoharic parable in which the Torah is likened to a beautiful princess secluded in her palace.[98] From a small opening within her palace the princess reveals herself to her lover, the mystic exegete, showing her face only to him and then immediately concealing it lest others see her. These stages of disclosure correspond metaphorically to the various layers of meaning embedded in the scriptural text. In the final stage, the Torah reveals itself face-to-face with the mystic (*᾽itgali᾽at le-gabe ᾽anpin be-᾽anpin*) and communicates to him all of its inner secrets and esoteric truths. In the moment that the Torah reveals all its secrets to the mystic, the latter is called *ba῾al Torah*[99] or *ma᾽are de-veta᾽* ("master of the house"),[100] two expressions that allude to the fact that the mystic has united with the Torah or *Shekhinah* in a sexual embrace. I have elsewhere dealt at length with the erotic nature of reading that is here suggested.[101] What is critical for this analysis is the obvious characterization of the Torah as a feminine persona. Kabbalistic exegesis is a process of denuding the Torah akin to the disrobing of the princess by her lover.[102] This is stated explicitly by Moses de León (c. 1240–1305), assumed by most modern scholars to be the author of the bulk of the *Zohar*, in his *Mishkan ha-῾Edut* (1293):

> Our holy Torah is a perfect Torah, "all the glory of the royal princess is inward" (Ps. 45:14). But because of our great and evil sins today, "her dress is embroidered with golden mountings" (ibid.). . . . Thus God, blessed be He, laid a "covering of dolphin skin over it" (Num. 4:6) with the visible things [of this world]. And who can see and contemplate the great and awesome light hidden in the Torah except for the supernal and holy ancient ones. They entered her sanctuary, and the great light was revealed to them. . . . They removed the mask from her.[103]

It seems reasonable to suggest, moreover, that this feminine personification of the Torah underlies an oft-repeated theme in the zoharic corpus to the effect that the *Shekhinah,* the feminine presence of God, is immanent in a place where a mystic sage is studying or interpreting the Torah.[104] While the link between Torah study and the dwelling of the *Shekhinah* is clearly affirmed in earlier rabbinic sources,[105] there are two significant differences between the claims of the *Zohar* and those of the classical texts. First, the position of the rabbis is not that study of Torah is a means to bring the divine Presence, but rather that as a natural consequence of fulfilling God's will the *Shekhinah* will be present. In the case of the *Zohar,* by contrast, it is evident that Torah study becomes one of several means to attain the desired result of *devequt,* "cleaving to the divine"; consequently, Torah study is transformed into a decidedly mystical praxis. Second, in the *Zohar* the erotic nature of the unification between the sage and the *Shekhinah* as a result of Torah study is stressed in a way entirely foreign to the classical literature. Of the many examples that could be cited to demonstrate the point, I will mention but one: "Come and see: All those engaged in the [study of] Torah cleave to Holy One, blessed be He, and are crowned in the crowns of Torah . . . how much more so those who are engaged in the [study of] Torah also during the night . . . for they are joined to the *Shekhinah* and they are united as one."[106] Torah study is here upheld as a means for anyone to cleave to God, but the mystics who study Torah during the night are singled out as the ones who are actually united with the *Shekhinah,* a position well attested in many passages in the voluminous corpus of the *Zohar.* That the cleaving to *Shekhinah* as a result of studying Torah is indeed based on a feminine characterization of Torah, as I have suggested, can be supported by the following zoharic passage: "He who is engaged in the [study of] Torah it is as if he were engaged in the palace of the Holy One, blessed be He, for the supernal palace of the Holy One, blessed be He, is the Torah."[107] The meaning of this statement can only be ascertained by noting that the palace of the Holy One, blessed be He, is a standard symbol in the zoharic kabbalah for the *Shekhinah.* Hence, to be occupied with the study of Torah is to be occupied with the *Shekhinah,* for the latter, the supernal palace, is the Torah.

It is of interest to note in passing the following comment on this passage by the kabbalist Ḥayyim Joseph David Azulai (1724–1806):

> It is possible that the Oral Torah corresponds to *Malkhut,* which is called *hekhal* (palace). . . . And this is [the meaning of] what is written, "Whoever is engaged in Torah," for the word engaged (*ʾishtaddel*) for the most part connotes that one is occupied in detailed study (*she-ʿoseq be-ʿiyyun*)

> of the Oral Torah, and by means of this study one causes the unity of the Holy One, blessed be He, and the *Shekhinah*. Therefore one is "engaged in the palace of the Holy One, blessed be He," to unify her with her beloved.[108]

This eighteenth-century kabbalist is compelled to explain the zoharic identification of the palace with the Torah as a reference to the Oral Torah for, on the one hand, it is clear that *palace* refers to *Shekhinah* and, on the other hand, the accepted kabbalistic symbolism is such that *Shekhinah* is the Oral Torah. I have cited Azulai's comment, for it is instructive of the way that a traditional commentator on the *Zohar* is forced to interpret a given text in light of the standard symbolic reference, thereby obscuring the original meaning of the text. In fact, it seems to me that the intent of the author of the *Zohar* is to stress that by means of the kabbalistic study of the Written Torah, one is intimately engaged with the *Shekhinah*, for indeed the *Shekhinah*, or the supernal palace, is the Torah. In this passage, then, the *Zohar* is reverting to the older kabbalistic symbolism that is found in *Sefer ha-Bahir*.

Still other kabbalistic texts indicate that the feminine characterization of Torah played a critical role. Thus, for example, the anonymous author of *Tiqqune Zohar* on several occasions employs this imagery in his kabbalistic discourses. I cite here one striking example of this phenomenon:

> The word *bereʾshit*, this is the Torah (*ʾoraitaʾ*), concerning which it says, "The Lord created me at the beginning (*reʾshit*) of His course" (Prov. 8: 22). And this is the lower *Shekhinah* [the tenth *sefirah*], which is the beginning for the created entities [below the divine realm]. . . . When she takes from *Keter* [the first *sefirah*] she is called "crown of splendor" (*ʿaṭeret tifʾeret*), a crown (*ʿaṭarah*) on the head of every righteous person (*ṣaddiq*),[109] the crown of the Torah scroll (*tagaʾ de-sefer torah*), and on account of her it is written, "He who makes [theurgic] use of the crown (*dishtammash be-tagaʾ*) perishes."[110] When she takes from *Ḥokhmah*, which is the beginning (*reʾshit*), she is called by his name. When she takes from *Binah* she is called by the name *Tevunah*. When she takes from *Ḥesed* she is called the Written Torah, which was given from the right . . . and when she takes from *Gevurah* she is called Oral Torah. . . . And the *Shekhinah* is the Torah of truth (*torat ʾemet*), as it is written, "A proper teaching was in his mouth," *torat ʾemet hayetah be-fihu* (Mal. 2:6).[111]

The author of this text, in conformity with what was by then standard kabbalistic symbolism, depicts the last of the divine emanations, the *Shekhinah*, in multiple ways, depending ultimately on the attribute from which she is said to receive the divine influx. In the moment she receives this influx from the right side, or the attribute of Lovingkindness, the *Shekhinah* is identified as the Written Torah, whereas in the moment she receives from the left side, or the attribute of Judgment, she is identified as the Oral Torah.[112] Hence, in this context, the dual Torah represents two aspects of the *Shekhinah*. Yet, in the beginning and in the end of the passage it is emphasized in a more generic way that the *Shekhinah* is the Torah, or the Torah of truth. Moreover, it is stated that *Shekhinah* is the crown of the Torah, a symbolic image repeated frequently in this book.[113] Utilizing an older kabbalistic symbol, *ʿaṭarah* (crown), for the *Shekhinah*,[114] the author of *Tiqqune Zohar* identifies this crown by several well-established images from the normative Jewish world. That is, the *Shekhinah* is the crown of the Torah, which is also identified with the eschatological crown on the head of the righteous, and, in still other contexts, the crown of Torah is identified with the corona of the *membrum virile* disclosed as part of the circumcision ritual.[115] In one passage in the *Raʿaya᾽ Mehemna᾽* section of the *Zohar*, assumed to have been written by the author of the *Tiqqunim*, the symbolism of the Torah crown is linked specifically to an existing ritual on Simḥat Torah: the Jews crown the Torah, for the Torah "alludes to *Tif᾽eret*" and the "crown of splendor" on the scroll symbolizes the *Shekhinah*.[116] This clearly represents an effort to preserve something of the older symbolism while still affirming the more widely accepted position. That is, the scroll now symbolizes the masculine potency, and the crown, the feminine. Underlying the origin of the crowning ritual was a decidedly feminine characterization of the Torah scroll, but in the case of the kabbalistic explanation the gender of the symbolism has shifted in accord with a new theosophic system. Indeed, the Torah scroll assumes a decidely phallic character in kabbalistic documents,[117] and even the crown should be seen in light of that symbolism. That is, the crown on the Torah scroll symbolically corresponds to the corona of the penis, and both ultimately indicate that the feminine potency is itself ontically part of the male.

There can be no question that in post-zoharic kabbalistic literature the dominant symbolic association was that of the Written Torah with *Tif᾽eret* and the Oral Torah with *Shekhinah*.[118] In that sense, the Torah scroll, the mundane correlate to the supernal Written Torah, was understood in decidedly masculine terminology. Thus, for example, Moses Cordovero (1522–1570) explains the rituals surrounding the taking out of the Torah from the ark in the synagogue in terms of the following symbolism:

> The [mystical] intention in the taking out of the Torah scroll. The reason for this commandment is that the cantor, who corresponds to *Yesod,* goes up from the table, the aspect of *Malkhut,* in the center point of the synagogue, and he goes up to *Binah* . . . to draw forth the secret of the Torah scroll from the supernal ark, i.e., *Tifʾeret* from *Binah* in the secret of the ark wherein is the Torah. *Yesod,* the cantor, goes up from the central aspect in *Malkhut* to *Binah,* the ark, to take out from there the Torah scroll, which is *Tifʾeret,* to draw it forth to *Malkhut,* the center point.[119]

According to Cordovero, then, the taking out of the Torah from the ark symbolically re-enacts the dynamic process in the sefirotic realm whereby the masculine potency of *Tifʾeret* emerges from the supernal palace, *Binah,* in order to unite with the lower, feminine potency, *Shekhinah.* The Torah scroll therefore corresponds to the masculine rather than the feminine aspect of God.[120]

In the more complicated symbolism of the Lurianic kabbalah one can still see very clearly that the Torah scroll is a symbol for a masculine attribute of the divine. Ḥayyim Vital (1543–1620) thus writes that the "Torah scroll is the *Yesod de-ʾAbbaʾ,* which is called the Written Torah, the form of the scroll is like an extended *waw.*"[121] Utilizing this symbolism the eminent disciple of Isaac Luria (1534–1572) thus explained the taking out of the Torah from the ark and the subsequent opening of the scroll as follows:

> The opening of the ark is performed at first, and this is the matter of *Zeʿeir ʾAnpin* itself, which breaks forth to emit the *Yesod de-ʾAbbaʾ,* which is within it, to go out from its body. And the opening of the Torah scroll itself is done afterwards, and this is the secret of the breaking forth of *Yesod de-ʾAbbaʾ,* which is called the Torah scroll, and the [forces of] mercy and judgment that are within it are revealed, and they are called the Written Torah.[122]

Alternatively, Vital offers the following explanation, which he also heard from his teacher, Isaac Luria, and which he considers to be the better one:

> The first breaking forth is that of *Yesod de-ʾImmaʾ* and all the [forces of] mercy within it, which spread forth in *Zeʿeir ʾAnpin,* and they clothe and surround the *Yesod de-ʾAbbaʾ,* which is within them. By means of this breaking forth of

> *Yesod de-ʾImmaʾ*, the light of *Yesod de-ʾAbbaʾ* goes forth, from outside *Yesod de-ʾImmaʾ*, to the body of *Zeʿeir ʾAnpin.* And this breaking forth is the matter of the opening of the ark to take out the Torah scroll, for the ark is the *Yesod de-ʾImmaʾ*, within which is the Torah scroll, which is the *Yesod de-ʾAbbaʾ*. Afterwards comes a second breaking forth, which is that of the *Yesod di-Zeʿeir ʾAnpin* itself, for the light of the *Yesod de-ʾAbbaʾ* goes out. . . . And this breaking forth is the matter of opening the case of the Torah scroll itself, so that the illumination of the Torah, and all that is written within it, will be revealed on the outside to the congregation. Afterwards, when the Torah is read, then the light that is within it goes outside, for this is the Torah itself, which is called light.[123]

The Torah scroll thus symbolizes the aspect of God referred to by the technical expression *Yesod de-ʾAbbaʾ*, the foundation of the divine countenance (*parṣuf*) called by the name Father. The ark in which the scroll is kept symbolizes the aspect of divinity referred to as the *Yesod de-ʾImmaʾ*, the foundation of the divine Mother. When the ark is opened, then the light of *Yesod de-ʾImmaʾ* emerges and shines upon the body of *Zeʿeir ʾAnpin*, the divine son. With the opening of the case of the Torah scroll the light of *Yesod de-ʾAbbaʾ* breaks forth and shines upon the whole congregation. The process of illumination is completed when the portion of the Torah is read, for through the public reading the light that is hidden within the letters of the scroll is released.[124] Vital similarly explains the theurgical significance of "Torah-study for its own sake" in terms of a process of illumination of the masculine upon the feminine; that is, *torah lishmah* is rendered as *torah le-shem heʾ*, which means that through study of Torah the light is released from *Yesod de-ʾAbbaʾ*, the Torah, and shines upon *Binah*, symbolized by the letter *heʾ*.[125] Although the symbolism developed by Vital is significantly more complex than that of Cordovero, both sixteenth-century Safedian kabbalists share the view that the Torah scroll itself symbolizes a masculine aspect of divinity. This, I submit, can be taken as a standard viewpoint in the vast majority of kabbalistic writings.

Only in one very important body of mystical literature does the feminine personification of the Torah reappear to play an instrumental role. I have in mind some of the texts that emerged from the disciples of Israel ben Eliezer, the Baʿal Shem Ṭov (c. 1700–1760), so-called founder of modern Hasidism in eighteenth-century Poland. In a striking passage from the very first published Hasidic text, the *Toledot*

Ya^caqov Yosef of Jacob Joseph of Polonnoye (d. 1782), we again encounter the feminine image of Torah. In this case as well the main concern is the presentation of the Hasidic idea of the study of Torah as a vehicle for mystical union, *devequt,* between the individual and God.[126]

> A person cleaves to the form of the letters of the Torah, which is the bride, and the cleaving of his essence to the inner essence of the letters of the Torah is the true mating (*ha-ziwwug ha-ʾamiti*), "naked without garment"[127] or [any] face, [without] advantage or reward, but rather for its own sake, to love her so as to cleave to her. This is the essence and purpose of everything.[128]

Study of Torah thus involves a technique of cleaving to the letters of the Torah, which serves, in turn, as a means for one to unite with the divine, for, according to the standard kabbalistic symbolism adopted by the Hasidic writers as well, the Torah is identical with God in His manifest form.[129] The person who studies Torah for its own sake—which here assumes the meaning of studying Torah for the sake of cleaving to its letters[130]—acquires knowledge, *yediʿah,* which, as Jacob Joseph further explains, has a decidedly sexual nuance: "The expression knowledge here is like the [usage in the verse] 'And Adam knew (*wa-yedaʿ*) Eve' for he cleaves to God and to His Torah, [a state] which is called knowledge, like the knowledge and communion of physical unification (*ziwwug ha-gashmi*)." Torah study is therefore a form of sexual unification with the divine feminine or the Torah, which is the bride.[131]

The erotically charged significance of the symbol of the feminine Torah is underscored in the following tradition of Dov Baer, the Maggid of Miedzyrzecz (1704–1772) reported by his disciple, Uziel Meisels:

> I have heard from the mouth of my teacher and my master, the genius and the pious, Dov Baer, may the memory of the righteous and saintly one be for a blessing, his soul is in Paradise, with regard to the dictum [on the verse] "When Moses charged us with the Torah as the heritage [of the congregation of Jacob]" (Deut. 33:4), "Do not read heritage (*morashah*) but betrothed (*meʾorasah*)." [The intent here is] to bring the thing close to the matter (*leqarev ha-davar ʾel ha-ʿinyan*), for in the way of the world it is not appropriate for a person who is not honorable to hold on to a princess and to dance with her in a wedding hall. It is not appropriate for such a person to come close to her and certainly not

> to hold on to her and to dance with her. By contrast, when the princess enters into marriage it is customary that the bond is loosened and even the most despised person is permitted to dance with her. So it is with respect to the matter under deliberation: our holy Torah is the princess of the King of kings, the Holy One, blessed be He. Accordingly, it would have been appropriate that whoever wanted should not draw close to her. Nevertheless, it was permitted to us for the Torah is compared to water, and just as water is ownerless so too she is ownerless. . . . In relation to us she is like the princess on the day of her wedding when she is betrothed. This is alluded to in the sweetness of his language, "Do not read heritage but betrothed," that is, in relation to us the Torah is [in the status of] the wedding day when permission is granted to all to dance with her, for we have also been given [permission] to be occupied in Torah.[132]

The view espoused by Jacob Joseph and the Maggid of Miedzyrzecz is reiterated in the *Degel Maḥaneh ʾEfrayim* of Moses Ḥayyim Ephraim of Sudlikov (c. 1737–1800), the gransdon of the Baʿal Shem Ṭov. In the case of this author, the zoharic parable of the Torah as a maiden is used as a basis to characterize the intellectual study and practical fulfillment of Torah as a moment of unification between man and God akin to the sexual unification between husband and wife:

> The Torah and the Holy One, blessed be He, and Israel are all one.[133] For the human person (*ʾadam*) is the Holy One, blessed He, by virtue of the fact that the Tetragrammaton when written out fully equals forty-five, the numerical equivalence of the [word] *ʾadam*. The Torah contains 248 positive commandments and 365 negative commandments, and from there is drawn forth the human person below in the aspect of 248 limbs and 365 inner parts. When a person is occupied with Torah for its own sake . . . he brings his limbs close to their source. . . . He and the Torah become one in unity and perfect oneness (*we-naʿaseh huʾ we-ha-torah ʾeḥad be-yiḥud we-ʾaḥdut gamur*) like the unification of a man and his wife, as it is in the *Sabbaʾ Mishpaṭim* [i.e., the section of *Zohar* containing the parable of the princess]. . . . He becomes one unity with the Torah (*we-naʿaseh ʿim ha-torah be-yiḥudaʾ ḥadaʾ*). "From my flesh I will see God" (Job 19:26)—if with respect to physical unification [it says] "And they will be of one flesh" (Gen. 2:24),

> *a fortiori* with respect to spiritual matters he becomes a perfect unity with the Torah (*she-naʿaseh ʾaḥdut gamur mamash huʾ ʿim ha-torah*).[134]

According to this Hasidic text, then, by being involved in the Torah one mystically unites with the Torah. This merging is likened to the sexual embrace of a man with his wife. Just as the two become one on the physical level, so on the spiritual level the individual unites with, actually becomes one with, the feminine Torah.

As a final example of the female characterization of Torah in the voluminous Hasidic corpus, I will cite one comment of Menaḥem Naḥum of Chernobyl (1730–1797). Commenting on Exodus 31:18, "When He finished speaking with him on Mt. Sinai, He gave Moses the two tablets of the pact, stone tablets inscribed with the finger of God," the rebbe from Chernobyl brought together the midrashic reading of this verse, noted above, and that of Deuteronomy 33:4, "Moses commanded the Torah to us, as the heritage of the congregation of Jacob," also noted above, two of the main loci for the rabbinic notion of the feminine Torah:

> By means of the Torah the groom and bride are united, the Community of Israel [*Shekhinah*] and the Holy One, blessed be He [*Tifʾeret*]. . . . The unification of the groom and bride is always something novel for they have never been united before. Thus must a person unite the Holy One, blessed be He [with the *Shekhinah*] every day anew. . . . And this is [the import of the midrashic teaching of Deut. 33:4] "do not read heritage (*morashah*) but betrothed (*meʾorasah*)." For the Torah is not called heritage but rather betrothed, which is the aspect of the bride, so that the unity will always be new like a bride at her wedding.[135]

The midrashic reading of the word *ke-khalloto* in Exodus 31:18 as *ke-khallato* is here transformed by the Hasidic master in terms of the older kabbalistic symbolism. That is, the Torah is the bride, and by studying Torah one assists in the unification of male and female, the Holy One and the *Shekhinah*.

The Hasidic writers thereby retrieved the older image of the Torah as the bride in their characterization of the ideal of cleaving to God through the Torah. It seems that the ideas and imagery expressed in earlier sources of an aggadic and mystical nature enabled the Hasidic masters to foster once again the feminization of the Torah. This process, in my opinion, attests to the centrality of this motif in Jewish spirituality. Although the alternative kabbalistic model that equated the Written Torah with the masculine potency and the Oral Torah with the feminine is found in the theoretical literature of the Hasidim, it was primarily the image of the Torah as the bride that was revitalized in Hasidic thought.

Let me conclude with a brief analysis of a story by Shmuel Yosef Agnon (1888–1970), *ʾAggadat ha-Sofer* (the "Tale of the Scribe"), which highlights the deep sexual implications of the feminine image of Torah in Judaism. Moving in an almost full circle from the Geonic origins of crowning the scroll on Simḥat Torah based on the aggadic depiction of Torah as the bride,[136] we arrive at Agnon's description of the scene inside the synagogue on the night of Simḥat Torah, which likewise draws largely on this very image. All the people, we are told, were dancing with enthusiasm and were cleaving to the holy Torah; when the young children saw their fathers receive the honor of carrying the Torah they would jump toward them "grasping the scroll, caressing, embracing, kissing it with their pure lips that have not tasted sin."[137] At the seventh, and last, round of the procession around the pulpit the cantor turned to the congregation and summoned all those involved in Torah study to come forth to carry the scrolls. After several of the youth came forward, the cantor again turned to the congregation to summon the scribe, Raphael, to honor him with carrying the Torah and singing a special melody. Here the narrative continues with the description that is most relevant to our concerns:

> Raphael held the scroll in his arm, walking in the lead with all the other youths following him in the procession around the pulpit. At that moment a young girl pushed her way through the legs of the dancers, leaped toward Raphael, sank her red lips into the white mantle of the Torah scroll in Raphael's arm, and kept on kissing the scroll and caressing it with her hands.[138]

In the continuation of the story we learn that the young girl described in this passage was Miriam, who later married Raphael. In the context of the tale, the description of the celebration on Simḥat Torah serves as a flashback, prompted by Raphael's singing the very same melody, as he clutched and danced with the Torah, that he had just written for the memory of Miriam shortly after she had died at a young age. Agnon thus describes the scene of Raphael's celebrating with the Torah scroll after Miriam's death in terms that are meant to echo the past event of Simḥat Torah:

> Raphael came toward Miriam and bowed before her with the Torah scroll in his arm. He could not see her face be-

> cause she was wrapped in her wedding dress . . . Raphael is wrapped in his prayer shawl, a Torah scroll in his arm, and the scroll has the mantle of fine silk on which the name of Miriam the wife of Raphael is embroidered. The house becomes filled with many Torah scrolls, and many elders dancing. . . . They dance without motion . . . and Miriam stands in the center. . . . She approaches Raphael's scroll. She takes off her veil and covers her face with her hands. Suddenly her hands slide down, her face is uncovered, and her lips cling to the mantle of the Torah scroll in Raphael's arms.[139]

The Torah scroll written for Miriam by Raphael, of course, reflects the scroll carried by Raphael on that Simḥat Torah night when they were first brought together. It was through the scroll that the fates of Raphael and Miriam were inextricably linked. Indeed, the Torah is the ritualistic object that binds together the scribe and his wife. The scroll is therefore obviously meant to be an erotic symbol; it functions as the object upon which the sexual passions of both Raphael and Miriam have been displaced. Admittedly, with respect to the gender of the scroll, there is here some equivocation, for it serves as both a masculine object for Miriam and a feminine one for Raphael. Thus Raphael is described in the Simḥat Torah scene as clutching the Torah the way he would his bride, while Miriam keeps kissing the white mantle of the Torah as if it were her groom. Similarly, in the death scene Miriam's lips are said to cling to the mantle of the Torah in Raphael's arms as if she were kissing her husband. Yet, the story ends with a description of Raphael sinking down with his scroll, and "his wife's wedding dress was spread out over him and over his scroll."[140] With the death of Miriam, then, the scroll fully assumes its role as the feminine persona vis-à-vis Raphael the scribe.

Underlying this latter characterization one will readily recognize the mythical motif of the feminine Torah that I have traced in midrashic and kabbalistic sources. For Agnon, however, it is the metaphorical aspect of this motif that again becomes primary, for the Torah, depicted in strikingly effeminate terms, is to be taken in a figurative sense as the object of Raphael's displaced sexual desire. That is, the Torah serves as a substitution for the earthly Miriam, whose own erotic yearnings are symbolized by the fact that her lips are sunk in, or cling to, the mantle of the scroll that is clutched by Raphael. Although Agnon is clearly drawing on the older image of the Torah as a bride, and furthermore reflects actual religious observances that are themselves rooted in that image, it is nevertheless the case that the force of the feminine image of the Torah as a religious symbol is substantially weakened; or, to put the matter in somewhat different terms, in Agnon's story the *Shekhinah*, Miriam, and the Torah all fuse into one image. The symbol, which developed in mystical texts out of a literary metaphor in midrashic sources, has become again in the modern work of fiction a literary metaphor, but one that is intended to characterize the mundane by the sacred rather than the sacred by the mundane.

◆ 2 ◆

CIRCUMCISION, VISION OF GOD, AND TEXTUAL INTERPRETATION: FROM MIDRASHIC TROPE TO MYSTICAL SYMBOL

> Before and after the word comes the sign
> and, in the sign, the void where we grow.
> Only the sign can be seen, being a wound.
> But the eyes lie.
>
> —Edmond Jabès, *The Book of Questions*

The use of sexual imagery to depict religious experience is a well-attested fact in the history of world religions. It should come as no surprise, therefore, to find that the seeing of God, or a God-like presence, is described in religious texts especially by means of language derived from human sexuality. Such formulation, of course, is not strange to any of the major religious traditions in the Occident or in the Orient. It is often the case, moreover, that especially the mystics of particular cultures express themselves precisely in this modality. To experience God involves a state of ecstatic union akin to the union of male and female partners in sexual embrace.

This chapter is a study of one particular motif related to this larger issue in the phenomenology of religious experience. We will examine an idea developed in the *Zohar*, the main sourcebook of thirteenth-century Spanish Jewish mysticism,[1] concerning the correlation between two apparently unrelated phenomena: circumcision and the ability to see the *Shekhinah*, the divine Presence. The causal nexus between these two phenomena is suggested by earlier rabbinic passages but is given an elaborate treatment in the theosophic system of the *Zohar*. As we shall see, implicit in the zoharic discussion is the notion that mystical experience involves a type of sexual union between the initiate and the divine. Beholding the face of the *Shekhinah* becomes in the *Zohar* an actual embrace or penetration of the mystic into the divine feminine. Given the normative halakhic sexual mores, it follows that only one who is circumcised can have such a visionary experience.[2] Circumcision is thus an act of opening that not only ushers the circumcised into the covenantal community of God, but places the individual into an immediate—visual—relationship to the divine.

The phenomenological reciprocity between the opening of circumcision and the visionary experience of God functions in the *Zohar* as a model for divine-human relations in another way, though in this case as well the sexual implications are evident. It is stated explicitly that only the one who is circumcised is permitted to study the Torah.[3] The underlying notion here, as I shall show, is the congruity between textual interpretation and circumcision. Yet, one may well ask, what is it in the nature of hermeneutics that allows the zoharic authorship[4] to link it specifically with circumcision? Or, to invert the question, what is in the nature of circumcision that leads the author of the *Zohar* to limit textual study of the Torah to one who is circumcised? Although a complete answer to this will not be forthcoming until the latter stages of this analysis, we may outline in a preliminary fashion the elements that serve as the basis for this conception.

Circumcision is not simply an incision of the male sex organ;[5] it is an inscription, a notation, a marking.[6] This marking, in turn, is the semiological seal, as it were, that represents the divine imprint on the human body.[7] The physical opening, therefore, is the seal that, in its symbolic valence, corresponds to an ontological opening within God. Hence, circumcision provides the author of the *Zohar* with a typology of writing/reading[8] that is at the same time a typology of mystical experience understood in a sexual vein. The opening of circumcision, in the final analysis, is transformed in the *Zohar* into a symbol for the task of exegesis. The appropriateness of this symbolization lies in the fact that the relation of the visionary to the *Shekhinah* engendered by the opening of the flesh is precisely the relationship of the critic or exegete to the text engendered by the semiological seal. This relationship is simultaneously interpretative and visionary. Through exegesis, that which was concealed, hidden, closed—in a word, esoteric—becomes opened, disclosed, manifest—in a word, exoteric. The uncovering of the phallus is conceptually and structurally parallel to the disclosure of the text. The significance of this dynamic for understanding the literary genesis of the *Zohar* should not be ignored.[9] The closing section of this chapter shall discuss this matter more fully.

I

The nexus between circumcision and the appearance of God is, to my knowledge, first enunciated in the following comment in one of the earliest aggadic compilations,[10] *Genesis Rabbah*, on the verse "The Lord appeared to him [Abraham]" (Gen. 18:1):

> It is written, "This, after my skin will have been peeled off; but I would behold God from my flesh" (Job 19:26). Abraham said, After I circumcised myself many converts came to cleave to this sign. "But I would behold God from my flesh," for had I not done this [i.e., performed the act of circumcision] on what account would the Holy One, blessed be He, have appeared to me? [As it is written] "The Lord appeared to him etc."[11]

The anonymous author of this passage, an astute reader of the biblical text, has noted that the theophany to Abraham at the terebinths of Mamre is preceded in Scripture by the account of Abraham's and Ishmael's being circumcised.[12] The conjunction of these two episodes has forged in the mind of the midrashist a more than casual connection between the act of circumcision and the appearance of God. In disregard of other biblical contexts to the contrary[13] (for example, Gen. 17:1), the author of this comment wishes to state that it is in virtue of the rite of circumcision that God manifests himself to Abraham. "Had I not been circumcised," wonders Abraham, "on what account would God have appeared to me?" That is to say, by means of what deed would he have merited the epiphany of God? The intent of this passage, then, must be seen in light of a standard line emphasized time and again in rabbinic literature: without works there is no reward, or, to invert Paul's locution, one is justified by acts alone.[14] Here, as in many other rabbinic sources, it is particularly the act of circumcision that merits a special favor on the part of God.[15] This interpretation is supported by a similar exegesis of the passage from Job: the first clause refers to the act of circumcision, peeling off the skin (i.e., foreskin), and the second to the vision of God that follows. "But I would behold God from my flesh," that is, from the flesh of the phallus,[16] the organ of circumcision.

It seems reasonable to suggest, therefore, that this is the import of the midrashic statement: by virtue of the merit of circumcision God appeared to Abraham. The divine manifestation demands some prior deed, a *miṣwah,* to create a link between man and God. The rite of circumcision, after all, is the mark of the covenant between God and the (male) children of Israel.[17] Through circumcision, then, one merits to stand in the presence of God, or, to put it differently, the appearance of God is itself the reward for the prior act of fulfilling the divine decree.[18]

There is an additional element alluded to in the above passage from *Genesis Rabbah.* The midrashist asserts that after Abraham was circumcised many converts "came to cleave to this sign,"[19] that is, many desired to convert to the Jewish faith by undergoing the rite of circumcision. We well know from other aggadic sources that Abraham and Sarah were viewed as the first proselytizers for God.[20] It may be suggested, however, that in the present context one can find in the portrayal of Abraham as one who encourages conversion through his circumcision a polemic against the dominant claims of Christianity (following Pauline doctrine) that religious conversion is a matter of faith, not works, and that for newcomers into the covenantal community of God (i.e., the Church) circumcision of the flesh was not a necessary initiation rite.[21] Our midrash emphasizes, to the contrary, that it was precisely Abraham's own circumcision that induced more converts into the faith of Judaism. In opposition to the claims of Christianity, the rabbis maintained that the rite of circumcision was not only still viable as a religious duty but was also the central feature of a proper conversion process.[22] The emphasis on Abraham's circumcision and its drawing forth a horde of potential converts to cleave to that sign can only be seen as a tacit rejection of the Christian position that circumcision of the flesh had been replaced by circumcision of the spirit (enacted in baptism).

That this explanation is indeed plausible is supported by the continuation of this passage in *Genesis Rabbah,* which doubtless was intended by the redactor(s) to drive the point home with ever greater clarity:

> (1) R. Isaac[23] began/opened [his discourse]: "Make for me an altar of earth etc." (Ex. 20:21). R. Isaac said: If I [i.e., God] appear to the one who builds an altar for My name's sake and bless him, how much more so with respect to Abraham who has circumcised himself for My name's sake. [It is thus written] "And the Lord appeared to him etc."
>
> (2) R. Levi began/opened [his discourse]: "An ox and a ram for an offering etc. [for today the Lord will appear to you]" (Lev. 9:4). He said: If I [God] appear to the one who

> sacrifices an ox or ram for My name's sake, how much more so to Abraham who has circumcised himself for My name's sake. "And the Lord appeared to him etc."[24]

The comments attributed to R. Isaac and R. Levi, both third-century Palestinian Amoraim,[25] underscore the intrinsic connection between the meritorious deed of circumcision and the appearance of God. For both, circumcision is to be understood as an act of sacrifice.[26] If one who builds an altar or sacrifices animals merits the approach (and blessing) of the divine, how much more so Abraham whose act of circumcision is likened to an act of self-sacrifice.

The nexus of ideas is reiterated in a later midrashic compilation, *Numbers Rabbah,* but with a strikingly new twist. In addition to viewing circumcision as the deed by means of which one merits the reward of seeing God, this midrashic pericope affirms an even deeper, more intrinsic correlation between circumcision and the visual revelation of God based on the physical purity of the visionary. In this case the matter is not merely deontological, but rather ontological. That is, circumcision effects a change in the very substance of the individual—and not only in his ethicoreligious stature—which prepares him for the visionary experience. It would be in order to cite the passage in full, ostensibly an interpretation of Song of Songs 3:11, "O Maidens of Zion, go forth, And gaze upon King Solomon, wearing the crown that his mother gave him on his wedding day, on his day of bliss." Commenting particularly on the first part of the verse, the anonymous midrashist writes:

> It is speaking about the time when the Presence (*Shekhinah*) rested in the Tabernacle (*mishkan*). "Go forth and gaze," as it is said, "And all the people saw and shouted, and fell on their faces" (Lev. 9:24). "The Maidens of Zion," those [males] who were distinguished (*ha-meṣuyanim*) by circumcision, for if they were uncircumcised, they would not have been able to look upon the Presence. Rather, they would have fallen as Abraham fell, as it is said, "Abram fell on his face, and God spoke to him" (Gen. 17:3).[27] Similarly with respect to Balaam, "[Words of him who hears God's speech, who beholds visions of the Almighty], prostrate, but with eyes unveiled" (Num. 24:4). And thus it says, "Moses said, This is the thing (*zeh ha-davar*) which the Lord has commanded that you do, that the glory of the Lord may appear to you" (Lev. 9:6). What was "this thing"? He told them about [the rite of] circumcision, as it is written, "This is the reason

> [literally, 'this is the thing,' *zeh ha-davar*] why Joshua performed circumcision" (Josh. 5:4). "Which God commanded Abraham to do." This[28] may be compared to a shopkeeper who has a friend who is a priest. He had some unclean thing in his house, and he wanted to bring him [the priest] into the house. The priest said to him: If you want me to go into your house, listen to me and remove that unclean thing from your house. When the shopkeeper knew that there was no unclean thing there, he went and brought the priest into his house. Similarly [with respect to] the Holy One, blessed be He, when He wanted to appear to Abraham, His beloved, the foreskin was hanging from him. When he circumcised himself, immediately [God] was revealed, as it says, "On that very day Abraham was circumcised" (Gen. 17:26), and afterward "The Lord appeared to him" (ibid. 18:1). Therefore Moses said to them, God commanded Abraham, your father, to perform [the act of] circumcision when He wished to appear to him. So in your case, whoever is uncircumcised, let him go out and circumcise himself, "that the glory of the Lord may appear to you" (Lev. 9:6). Thus Solomon said, "O Maidens of Zion, go forth, And gaze upon King Solomon" (Song of Songs 3:11), the King who desires those who are perfect, as it is written, "Walk before Me and be blameless" (Gen. 17:1), for the foreskin is a blemish on the body.[29]

The author of this midrash, in a remarkable reversal of the literal sense of the text, interprets the "Maidens of Zion" as referring to the males marked or "distinguished" (*meṣuyanim*, an obvious play on the word *ṣiyyon*) by circumcision.[30] Clearly, maidens cannot be so distinguished; thus the midrashic reading effectively effaces the literal sense. Even more significant is that the midrashist forges an unambiguous connection between the capablility of beholding the Presence or glory of God and circumcision: he who is uncircumcised will fall on his face—as Abraham himself did prior to his circumcision—in the presence of God's manifestation. The alleged reason for this is given by the midrash itself: the foreskin is a blemish that acts as a barrier separating the individual and God.[31]

In contrast to the earlier midrashic texts that we examined, there is here an essential link between the act of circumcision and the visionary experience of the divine. Circumcision is not simply one good deed amongst many in consequence of which the person merits seeing God. It is precisley and exclusively by means of circumcision that one can see God, for this act removes that potential barrier—symbolized by the cutting of the foreskin[32]—separating human and divine. Circumcision is the vestibule or portal through which one must pass if one is to have a visionary experience of God. The opening of circumcision results in an opening up to God, a receptivity, that enables one to stand in God's presence and to behold the glory.

II

All that is implied in the midrashic passage from *Numbers Rabbah* is made explicit in the *Zohar,* where it is embellished by an intricate theosophic structure. It is quite clear that in the *Zohar* the nexus between circumcision and the vision of God is reaffirmed and given new layers of meaning. The treatment of this midrashic theme in the *Zohar* must be seen in light of a central category in the kabbalistic (especially zoharic) conception of religious perfection: man's relation to God, particularly the *Shekhinah,* the feminine hypostasis of God and the last of the divine emanations (*sefirot*), is viewed in a decidedly sexual manner. One who is uncircumcised cannot see God (or the *Shekhinah*), for seeing involves some sort of intimate contact, touching, immediacy, and only one who is circumcised can have such an experience. The correlation of circumcision and vision is predicated as well on the homologous relation of the eye and the penis, a theme that is expressed in many Jewish sources. In a fundamentally ontological sense, only one who is circumcised has an eye that is open.[33]

The issue of openness/closedness is connected particularly in the *Zohar* with the problem of circumcision and visionary experience. Commenting on Genesis 18:1, "And the Lord appeared to him [Abraham]," R. Abba said: "Before Abraham was circumcised he was closed. When he was circumcised all was revealed and the Presence rested upon him in its completeness."[34] The closure of Abraham, or, more specifically, Abraham's phallus, has an objective correlate: an obscured vision of the divine. That is, before his circumcision Abraham was closed, and hence God was not fully revealed to him. The act of circumcision, on the other hand, is an opening, a removal of closure, which corresponds objectively to a disclosure of God. The relationship of God to a particular man is dependent upon the physical condition of the latter: if closed (uncircumcised), then the vision is obscured; if opened (circumcised), then the vision is complete. It is highly significant that comprehension is here linked especially to the phallus: when Abraham was uncircumcised, and therefore closed, he lacked comprehension of the divine; when he was circumcised, and therefore opened, all was revealed to him. As Moses Cordovero (1522–1570) expressed in his commentary to this passage in the *Zohar*: "Closure brings about the removal of comprehension."[35] (Subsequently, I shall return to the connection between the openness of the phallus and the possibility of comprehension, specifically understood as a hermeneutical mode.)

Even before his circumcision Abraham merited some vision of the divine realm. This is implied in the above passage: "When he was circumcised *all* was revealed to him etc." That is, prior to the circumcision there was, at best, a partial vision of God. This is spelled out in another zoharic passage, attributed to R. Eleazar, which interprets Genesis 18:1, "And the Lord appeared to him," as referring to a time "after Abraham was circumcised. For before Abraham was circumcised [God] did not speak to him except through the lower gradation, and the upper gradations did not stand over that gradation."[36] In yet another passage the zoharic authorship clarifies the difference between Abraham's visionary (prophetic) experience before and after circumcision in more detail:

> "The word of the Lord came to Abram in a vision [*ba-maḥazeh*]" (Gen. 15:1). What is [the meaning of] "in a vision"? This is the vision [or mirror; Aramaic, *ḥeizu*], the gradation in which all images [*deyoqnin*] are seen [*ʾitḥazyan*]. R. Simeon said: Before Abraham was circumcised, one gradation spoke with him. And which one was it? It was the "vision" [*maḥazeh*]. . . . When he was circumcised all the gradations rested on this gradation and then it spoke with him. . . . Before he was circumcised those gradations did not rest upon him to speak [to him].[37]

The divine gradation referred to as the "vision" is the last of the *sefirot*, the *Shekhinah*, so named for this gradation is a prism that reflects all the upper colors or forms. Prior to his circumcision, therefore, God spoke to Abraham through the intermediary of the *Shekhinah*. Indeed, even after the circumcision God continued to speak with Abraham through the *Shekhinah*; however, in the latter case the vision was complete, since all the upper gradations rested upon or stood over the *Shekhinah* in the moment of revelation. While Abraham was uncircumcised, his visionary experience was restricted to the lowest emanation. In a subsequent passage the zoharic authorship returns to this distinction in an effort to clarify further the theophanic transformation undergone by Abraham:

> Come and see: before Abraham was circumcised [God] spoke to him exclusively from within the vision [*maḥazeh*],

> as it is written, "The word of the Lord came to Abram in a vision etc." (Gen. 15:1). In a vision, (i.e.) by means of that vision [*ḥeizu*], the gradation in which all the forms are seen . . . and that vision is the secret of the covenant [*raza᾿ di-verit*]. If you say it is called *maḥazeh* because it is the vision, (i.e.) the gradation in which all the forms are seen, did you also not say at the outset that before Abraham was circumcised no one spoke to him but that gradation when no other gradation rested upon it? Yet, you now say that [the expression] "in a vision" [*ba-maḥazeh*] refers to that vision [or mirror] in which [are seen] the other gradations! Before Abraham was circumcised it is written, "And the Lord spoke to Abram in a vision" (Gen. 15:1). Indeed, that gradation is the vision of all the supernal gradations, and it is fixed in the appearance of the supernal gradations. And even though at that time Abraham was not circumcised, that gradation was in the appearance of the supernal gradations, and she existed in all those [upper] colors . . . for she is the vision of all the upper colors that are over her. And thus in that appearance she stood with Abraham and spoke to him, even though he was not circumcised. When he was circumcised, what is written? "And the Lord appeared to Abram." . . . Thus before Abraham was circumcised that gradation [spoke] to him. When he was circumcised immediately [it says], "The Lord appeared to Abram etc." All the [other] gradations appeared on that gradation, and the latter spoke to him in completeness. And Abraham was bound from gradation to gradation, and entered the holy covenant that appeared in its completeness.[38]

One senses the tension in the mind of the author of the *Zohar*, struggling to clarify the difference in vision accorded to Abraham before and after his circumcision. The biblical term used in connection with God's appearance to Abraham (before the circumcision) is *maḥazeh*, "vision," which is understood kabbalistically to be a symbol for *Shekhinah*, the prism in which all the forms are reflected. Yet the *Zohar* makes the claim that before his circumcision Abraham did not converse with the *Shekhinah* in her fullness, that is, as reflecting all the upper lights. This apparent tension has led various commentaries on the *Zohar* to offer several responses,[39] none of which, in my view, is sufficient. What is clear is that the zoharic authorship is trying to uphold a qualitative distinction in the nature of the vision that Abraham had before and after his circumcision. There is, on the one hand, something about the act of circumcision that effects a change in the individual resulting in a change in his visionary status. On the other hand, as a result of the circumcision there is a change in the nature of the divine itself, particularly the relation of the last gradation to those above her. In the latter respect, it may be said that circumcision includes a theurgical dimension.

In the above passage the nexus between circumcision and theophany is reaffirmed by the introduction of another key concept: the identification of the vision, or *Shekhinah*, as the "secret of the covenant," *raza*ʾ *di-verit*.[40] This should not be construed as an arbitrary or unintentional remark. The biblical term *maḥazeh*, a symbol for the *Shekhinah*, is at the same time the "secret of the covenant." Hence, vision equals Presence equals secret of the covenant: by the principle of transitivity, then, vision equals secret of the covenant. One would therefore not expect this higher gradation to commune with Abraham prior to his circumcision. The symbolic network thus established calls for interpretation.

We may begin to interpret this symbolism by reference to another standard zoharic notion concerning the twofold nature of the *berit*. According to the *Zohar*, the covenant in its totality comprises two aspects, masculine and feminine, the ninth and tenth *sefirot*, *Yesod* ("Foundation") and *Malkhut* ("Kingship") or *Shekhinah*.[41] The "vision" (*maḥazeh*), spoken of as the *raza*ʾ *di-verit*, "secret of the covenant," corresponds to only one of these aspects, the *Shekhinah*. Prior to Abraham's circumcision he could not possibly have merited a complete theophany, but only a partial one related exclusively to the feminine hypostasis of God: the "secret of the covenant," the "vision," the "lowest gradation." After the circumcision, however, Abraham experienced the masculine and feminine aspects of God, for by means of circumcision one enters into both gradations.[42] Only by appropriating the two dimensions could Abraham experience the full theophanic image:

> Come and see: before one is circumcised one is not united to the name of the Holy One, blessed be He; when one is circumcised one enters the name and is united to it.[43] And, if you say that Abraham was united to it before he was circumcised, indeed he was, but not as it is fitting, for out of the supernal love that the Holy One, blessed be He, had for Abraham, He drew him near. Afterward He commanded him to circumcise himself, and gave him the covenant, the bond of all the upper gradations. The covenant: the bond to tie everything together, to contain one in the other; the covenant: the bond in which everything is tied. Therefore, before

> Abraham was circumcised [God] spoke with him only by means of the "vision."[44]

Abraham's bondedness to the sefirotic realm prior to his circumcision was not "proper" or adequate, for it was only out of God's love for him that he was drawn close to the divine. By means of circumcision, however, one properly merits union with the divine; the phallus is the place of the covenant or the knot in which all the upper grades are united. Whereas before the circumcision Abraham was addressed by the "vision," that is, by the *Shekhinah*, after the circumcision he was himself bound to the covenant that binds together the upper forces in the lower grade, that is, the *sefirah* of *Yesod* as united with the *Shekhinah*. In effect, the claim of the *Zohar* is that only one (in this case Abraham) who is circumcised can be united with the *Shekhinah* in her state of fullness and thereby cleave to the upper realm of the *sefirot*.[45]

However, the circumcision of Abraham also has a theurgical dimension, for it effects a change in the nature of the divine: just as in the fulfillment of circumcision one joins the masculine and feminine potencies in oneself, so too one brings about such a unification above. The *Zohar* exegetically connects this mystery to Genesis 18:1 as well:

> Come and see: Before Abraham was circumcised nothing but the [lowest] gradation was upon him, as we have said. After he was circumcised, what is written? "And the Lord appeared to him" (Gen. 18:1). To whom? It is not written, "And the Lord appeared to Abram," for if [God] appeared to Abraham, what more praise is there now than in the beginning, before he was circumcised? For it is written, "And the Lord appeared to Abram" (Gen. 17:1) [i.e., before the circumcision]. This is rather a hidden secret. "And the Lord appeared to him," i.e., to that gradation that spoke with him [Abraham], which did not take place before he was circumcised. For now [after the circumcision] the Voice [i.e., *Tifʾeret*, "Beauty," the sixth emanation, the central pillar in the divine edifice] was revealed and united with the Speech [*Shekhinah*] when the latter spoke to Abraham. "And he sat in the opening of the tent." "And he," [the verse] does not reveal who. The [Torah] here revealed wisdom, for all the gradations [the *sefirot*] rested upon that lower gradation [*Shekhinah*] after Abraham was circumcised.[46]

The secret of the verse alludes to the fact that Abraham's circumcision initiated a change in the *Shekhinah* in relation to the other *sefirot*.

Before Abraham's circumcision, only the *Shekhinah* conversed with him; after his circumcision she was united with her masculine consort, *Tif*ʾ*eret,* and the latter was revealed to Abraham through the *Shekhinah.* This is the mystical meaning of Genesis 18:1, "And the Lord," *Tif*ʾ*eret,* the masculine potency or the attribute of mercy, "appeared to him," that is, to that gradation that spoke to Abraham, the feminine *Shekhinah* or the attribute of judgment. The post-circumcision theophany involved the unification of the Voice (*qol*) and Speech (*dibbur*), the masculine and feminine.[47] At that time, therefore, all the upper grades rested upon the lowest one.

In another context the *Zohar* expresses Abraham's transformation in slightly different terms but in a way that further elucidates the conceptual link between visionary experience and circumcision. "Come and see: when Abraham was circumcised he emerged from the foreskin and entered the holy covenant and was crowned in the holy crown, and entered the foundation upon which the world stands."[48] By circumcising himself Abraham thus departed from the realm of the demonic powers (symbolized by the foreskin) and entered the holy realm.[49] Entrance into the latter comprises two elements: the first gradation is referred to alternatively as the "holy covenant" or the "holy crown," that is, the feminine *Shekhinah;* and the second gradation is referred to as "the foundation upon which the world stands," that is, the masculine *Yesod.* The possibility of seeing God is now understood as being dependent on a transference from the demonic to the sefirotic worlds. Before his circumcision, Abraham could not fully apprehend God because his body was still encased in the demonic shell, the foreskin covering the phallus.

Like the midrashist in *Numbers Rabbah,* the author of the *Zohar* here conceives of circumcision as a removal of the impure obstacle (though in the case of the latter this has become a symbol for a satanic force) that separates man from God and prevents a complete visionary relationship. Moreover, circumcision is an opening up of the human body: "R. Yose said, Why is it written, 'And the Lord will pass over the door (*ha-petaḥ*)' (Ex. 12:23)? . . . 'Over the door,' over that very opening (*ha-petaḥ mamash*), that is, the opening of the body (*petaḥ ha-guf*). And what is the opening of the body? That refers to [the place of] circumcision."[50] The physiological opening, in turn, structurally parallels the opening in the sefirotic realm, the last gradation, *Shekhinah,*[51] through which one enters into relationship with God. The feminine potency is localized in the opening of the penis. This, according to the *Zohar,* is the theosophic significance of the scriptural claim that Abraham—after his circumcision—was "sitting at the opening of the tent (*petaḥ ha-*ʾ*ohel*)" (Gen. 18:1), that is, the *Shekhinah,* "the place that is called covenant, the secret of faith."[52] Circumcision is thus an opening up of the phallus that eventuates in the opening up—the disclosure—of the divine. "Come and see: before Abraham was circumcised he was closed and concealed from every side. When he was circumcised he was opened with respect to everything and was not closed or concealed as before. This is the mystery, as we have taught, 'And he [Abraham] was sittting at the opening of the tent' (Gen. 18:1),' for the *yod* was revealed."[53]

To appreciate fully the import of this passage one must bear in mind that the letter *yod*, in classical midrashic sources,[54] was conceived of as the letter or mark of circumcision imprinted, as it were, on the phallus. In zoharic terms, the letter *yod*, the seal of circumcision, the *ʾot berit*, corresponds to the *sefirah* of *Yesod*.[55] By disclosing the *yod* on one's body, the corona of the phallus, the *yod* in the upper realm is likewise disclosed. The result of this process is alluded to in the end of Genesis 18:1, "And he [Abraham] was sitting at the opening of the tent." Two meanings are implied here: Abraham below sat at the tent's entrance, which itself reflects the condition of openness he achieved by the circumcision. Theosophically, Abraham symbolizes the *sefirah* of *Ḥesed* (Love), and the opening of the tent symbolizes the *Shekhinah*. When the phallic *yod* (*Yesod*) is revealed, then *Ḥesed* is united with the *Shekhinah* and the forces of judgment are ameliorated.[56]

III

The zoharic reworking of the midrashic motif can now be fully outlined. By means of circumcision one is opened up in such a way that God may be revealed: the physical opening engenders a space in which the theophany occurs. Indeed, only one who is circumcised can withstand the manifestation of God. In the *Zohar*, however, circumcision is not only a prerequisite for the vision of God, but the phallus itself is the locus of such a vision: one sees God from the circumcised flesh or from the semiological seal of the covenant imprinted on that flesh. In one passage the zoharic authorship interprets the same verse from Job, "This, after my skin will have been peeled off; but I would behold God from my flesh" (19:26), which was interpreted in an altogether different way in the section from *Genesis Rabbah*[57] that I discussed at the outset:

> He began another discourse and said, "But I would behold God from my flesh"(Job 19:26). Why [is it written] "from my flesh"? It should be rather "from myself"! It is, literally,

> "from my flesh." What is that [flesh]? As it is written, "The holy flesh will be removed from you" (Jer. 11:15), and it is written, "And my covenant will be in your flesh" (Gen. 17:13). It has been taught: he who is marked with the holy seal of that sign [of circumcision] sees the Holy One, blessed be He, from that very sign itself.[58]

The flesh from which one beholds God, according to the verse from Job, refers to the flesh of circumcision, the seal of the covenant. One is said to see the Holy One from the sign of the covenant inscribed in one's flesh, the letter *yod*. As we have seen, in the case of the *Zohar* the letter *yod* is not simply interpreted as a sign of the covenant between God and Israel, it is the sign of the Holy One himself. The double function of the word *ʾot* in Hebrew holds the key to unlocking the meaning of the kabbalistic doctrine: *ʾot* is both a sign and a letter. One sees God from the sign on one's body, but that sign is nothing other than the letter *yod*. Here we meet a convergence of anthropomorphic and letter symbolism: the physical organ in its essential character is interchangeable with the letter, and the letter with the physical organ. The rite of circumcision thus ushers the individual into a semiological—as well as ontological—relationship with God: the seal of the covenant itself is the divine letter (or sign) inscribed on the flesh. This is the mystical sense of the Jobian claim that from the flesh—that is, the phallus or the place of the covenant—one beholds God.

The dynamic of circumcision, the play of closure-openness, informs us about the nature of mystical hermeneutics as well: that which is hidden must be brought to light, and the medium of disclosure is the seal of the covenant. In various ways the zoharic authorship establishes a structural affinity between the act of disclosing esoteric truths and that of sexual ejaculation, or in other words between the phallus and the mouth, the covenant of the foreskin and the covenant of the tongue.[59] Thus, for example, the *Zohar* interprets Ecclesiastes 5:5, "Don't let your mouth cause your flesh to sin," as referring either to sins of a sexual nature[60] or to the sin of disclosing esoteric truths that one has not received from one's teacher.[61] The impropriety of illicit sexual behavior is parallel to the impropriety of revealing hidden truths that one has not properly received.[62] Indeed, in one place the zoharic authorship interprets the prohibition against idolatry in Exodus 20:4 as the sin of "lying in the name of God."[63] Yet there are two explanations offered for this: one who lies in God's name is either one who reveals secrets of Torah (for Torah equals the name of God)[64] or one who has sexual relations with a non-Jew (for phallus equals the name).[65] As

Yehuda Liebes has pointed out, the common denominator here can only be that both sorts of sin involve the phallus.[66] Liebes has further shown that, according to the *Zohar*, the mystic exegete below is the symbolic correlate of the *sefirah* of *Yesod* (the phallus) above. When the time is ripe, the exegete, that is, the *ṣaddiq* in the world, discloses what has been concealed: "It has been taught: In the days of R. Simeon people would say to one another, 'Open your mouth and illuminate your words.'[67] After R. Simeon died, they would say, 'Don't let your mouth cause your flesh to sin.'"[68]

The relation of the phallus and disclosure/concealment of mystical truth is made even clearer in the following remark:

> R. Simeon opened and said, "A base fellow reveals secrets, but a trustworthy soul conceals the matter" (Prov. 11:13). . . . Concerning he who is not settled in his spirit and who is not faithful, the word that he hears goes inside him like that which revolves in water[69] until it is cast outside. Why? Because his spirit is not a firm spirit (*ruḥa᾽ de-qiyyuma᾽*). But he whose spirit is a firm one, concerning him it is written, "a trustworthy soul conceals the matter." "A trustworthy soul" (*we-ne᾽eman ruaḥ*), one whose spirit is faithful (*qiyyuma᾽ de-ruḥa᾽*), as [it is written], "I will fix him as a peg (*yated*) in a firm place" (Isa. 22:23). The matter is dependent on the secret (*be-raza᾽ talya᾽ milta᾽*). It is written, "Don't let your mouth cause your flesh to sin." The world only exists through the secret.[70]

The one who keeps the secret is the "trustworthy soul," *ne᾽eman ruaḥ*, which is rendered by the *Zohar*, *qiyyuma᾽ de-ruḥa᾽*.[71] There can be no doubt that this is a reference to the *ṣaddiq*, the symbolic correlate below to *Yesod*, whose status as a righteous person is particularly related to the phallus.[72] Such a person is here called by the term *qiyyuma᾽ de-ruḥa᾽*, which may be translated as the "pillar of the spirit,"[73] for he is one who sustains the spirit, holds it in its place. The word *qiyyuma᾽* functions in the *Zohar*, *inter alia*, as a phallic symbol,[74] and may have that shade of meaning in this context as well. The faithfulness or steadfastness of one's spirit is therefore a condition especially connected to the phallus. This interpretation is further substantiated by the prooftext from Isaiah wherein the word *yated*, "peg," also must be seen as functioning as a phallic symbol. This symbolism, moreover, enables us to decipher the remark that the "matter is dependent on the secret," that is, on the phallus or its symbolic correlate, *Yesod*, which is appropriately called "secret" for it is the divine gradation that is hidden and concealed from the eye.[75] Hence, R. Simeon admonishes his comrades, "Don't let your mouth cause your flesh to sin," for the world exists only through the secret, sustained by means of that foundation or pillar (*Yesod*) that must be concealed. Just as the proper disclosure of esoteric truth is bound up with the flesh, the phallus or *Yesod*,[76] so too an improper disclosure is a sin bound up with this limb.

Textual interpretation, like circumcision, involves the dynamic of closure/openness: as the one who is circumcised stands in relation to the *Shekhinah*, so the exegete—through interpretation—enters into an intimate relation with the *Shekhinah*. The duplicity of the text as that which simultaneously conceals and reveals—indeed conceals as that which reveals and reveals as that which conceals—is a thoroughly appropriate metaphor to convey the erotic quality of the hermeneutical stance.[77] Inasmuch as there is this structural affinity between the interpretative task and the phallus—related to the dialectic of concealment and disclosure[78]—the exegete must be circumcised, for penetration into the text is itself an act of sexual unification. This dynamic doubtless underlies the zoharic prohibition of Torah study for the uncircumcised:

> R. Abba said: Praiseworthy is the portion of Israel, for the Holy One, blessed be He, desired them more than all the idolatrous nations. And on account of His love for them He gave them His laws of truth, planted the Tree of Life in their midst, and placed His *Shekhinah* amongst them. Why? For Israel are marked by the holy sign (*reshimaʾ qadishaʾ*) on their flesh, and it is known that they are His, from those who belong to His palace.[79] Therefore all those who are not marked with the holy sign on their flesh do not belong to Him; it is known that they all derive from the side of impurity.[80] It is therefore forbidden to join with them and to converse with them concerning words [or matters] of the Holy One, blessed be He. It is also forbidden to instruct them in words of Torah, for the entire Torah is the name of the Holy One, blessed be He, and each letter of the Torah is bound to the Holy Name. It is forbidden to instruct the person who is not marked by the holy sign on his flesh in the words of Torah. How much more so to be engaged in it![81]

One who is uncircumcised cannot study Torah, for the Torah is the name of God and study of it involves unification with the name. Only one who is circumcised can be united with the name, and hence only such a person can study Torah. The final remark, that it is forbidden to be engaged in the study of Torah with one who is uncircumcised, serves to emphasize that the esoteric dimension of the tradition cannot be divulged to anyone who does not have the holy sign inscribed on his flesh.[82] The aspect of hiddenness or secrecy is indicative of the very essence of the *sefirah* that corresponds to the phallus.[83] Indeed, the word *sod,* secret or mystery, is attributed specifically to the divine gradation of *Yesod.* Secrets of Torah, therefore, cannot be transmitted to one who is uncircumcised:

> R. Abba opened [his exposition] and said: "The secret of the Lord is with those who fear Him [to them He makes known His covenant]" (Ps. 25:14). "The secret of the Lord is with those who fear Him": the Holy One, blessed be He, has not given the upper secret of the Torah except to those who fear sin. To those who do fear sin the upper secret of Torah is disclosed. And what is the upper secret of the Torah? I would say, it is the sign of the holy covenant (*ʾot qayyamaʾ qadishaʾ*), which is called the secret of the Lord, the holy covenant.[84]

The secret of the Lord given to those who fear sin is the holy covenant of God, the *berit qodesh,* that is, the *sefirah* that corresponds to the phallus, *Yesod.* The secrecy and concealment of this particular emanation is emphasized by Moses de León in his Hebrew theosophic writings as well. Thus, for example, in *Sefer ha-Rimmon* he writes that *Yesod* is "called secret (*sod*) for its matter is secrecy, a hidden mystery of the Creator."[85] The process of circumcision, the removal of the foreskin and the uncovering of the corona, is a disclosure of the secret. In the disclosure of the phallus, through the double act of circumcision, the union of the masculine and the feminine aspects of God is assured. "When the holy sign [*Yesod*] is uncovered it overflows and the bride [*Shekhinah*] . . . then stands in completeness and her portion is illuminated."[86] Circumcision, therefore, is here viewed as a necessary precondition for studying Torah—exoteric and esoteric—just as in other contexts it is depicted as a necessary precondition for visionary experience or prophetic theophany. He who is closed—uncircumcised—cannot open the text just as he cannot behold the divine Presence. The relationship of exegete to text is like that of the visionary to the *Shekhinah.* Indeed, it may be said that, according to the *Zohar,* insofar as the Torah is the corporeal form of the divine, textual study itself is a mode of visionary experience.[87]

The opening of circumcision is thus not only the opening through which one may see God, but it is the opening through which one may study the holy text, the Torah. The particular relation between the covenant of circumcision and the activity of Torah study is further brought to light in the following passage:

> R. Yose asked R. Simeon: It is taught that words [such as] *we-ʾaggidah, wa-yagged,* and *wa-yaggidu,* all [point to] the secret of wisdom [*razaʾ de-ḥokhmataʾ*]. Why does this word [the root *ngd*] allude to the secret of wisdom? He [R. Simeon] said to him [R. Yose]: Because [in] this word the *gimmel* and *dalet* are found without any separation. This is the secret of wisdom, a word that comes in completeness in the secret of the letters. Thus it is when they [the letters] are in wisdom, but *dalet* without *gimmel* is not completion, and so *gimmel* without *dalet,* for the one is bound to the other without separation. The one who separates them causes death for himself; and this secret [the separation of *gimmel* and *dalet*] is the sin of Adam. Therefore this word [*ngd*] is the secret of wisdom. And even though at times there is a *yod* between the *gimmel* and *dalet,* there is no separation [in that case], for all is one bond.[88]

The word *higgid,* to "tell" or "speak," alludes to the secret of wisdom, for in the root of this word, *ngd,* the letters *gimmel* and *dalet* are contiguous. Symbolically, the *gimmel* corresponds to *Yesod* and the *dalet* to *Shekhinah,* for *Yesod* is that which "bestows upon" (*gomel*) the *Shekhinah* who is the "poor one" (*dal*).[89] The secret of wisdom, therefore, involves the unification of the ninth and tenth *sefirot,* the masculine *Yesod* and the feminine *Shekhinah.* It is this (sexual) unification, moreover, that constitutes the nature of discourse.[90] Speech is thus understood by the same structural dynamic that characterizes the play of divine sexuality and the dual nature of circumcision. In the act of coitus the *gimmel* is uncovered—thereby re-enacting the primal disclosure of circumcision—and consequently pours forth to the *dalet.* The *yod* that is between them is the sign of the covenant (the corona of the penis) that acts as a bridge uniting masculine and feminine. Indeed, the three consonants, *gimmel, yod, dalet,* spell the word *gid,* which in rabbinic literature is sometimes used as a euphemism for the phallus. The unification of the masculine *gimmel* and the feminine *dalet* through the *yod* results in the formation of the *gid,* that is, the penis that comprises both male and female. This, no doubt, is the underlying meaning of the concluding statement that, "even though at times there is a *yod* between the *gimmel* and *dalet,* there is no separation, for all is one bond." The penis (*gid*) is itself the locus of the androgynous aspect of God, the *gimmel* and *dalet, Yesod* and

Shekhinah. It is from this union, moreover, that discourse (*ᵓaggadah*) proceeds and the secret is disclosed.

I can now sum up the various steps that have been taken along the way in this analysis. Already in rabbinic midrash a clear nexus is established between circumcision and the visualization of God, or a godlike appearance. In the earlier midrashic passages it seems that this nexus is focused on a deontological conception well known from many rabbinic sources: through the doing of good deeds, that is, through fulfilling God's commandments, one is rewarded. In this particular case the good deed is circumcision, and the reward is the epiphany of God. In a later midrashic context the nexus is reasserted, this time however based on an ontological criterion that only one whose sexual organ is circumcised can stand in the presence of God's glory. This is because it is necessary for one to remove the unholy foreskin before one can withstand the manifestation of God. The author of the *Zohar* further develops this mesh of ideas in the framework of his theosophical conception. Visualization of God, as study of the Torah, involves the unification of man with the feminine potency of the divine; therefore, only one who is circumcised can be said to either see God or study the Torah. Moreover, just as the act of circumcision itself comprises two elements that correspond to the masculine and feminine dimensions of God, so too an act of seeing God—prophetically or textually—comprises these very elements. The opening of circumcision is an opening of the flesh that is, at the same time, an opening within the divine. When the foreskin is removed and the phallus uncovered, then the corresponding limb above, the divine phallus or *Yesod*, likewise is uncovered. In this uncovering the secret of God is disclosed. The hermeneutical process is a structural re-enactment of circumcision, involving as it does the movement from closure to openness.[91] The opening of the flesh eventuates in the opening of God, which is re-experienced as the opening of the text.

In conclusion, it may be said that the writing of the *Zohar* itself, a disclosure of hidden layers of meaning, may be understood in light of the various structures that I have sought to uncover. The particular relation established between the phallus (*Yesod*) and secret (*sod*) lends further support to the view that the very process of textual interpretation undertaken by the author of the *Zohar* was understood in terms of this dynamic of closure/openness. The bringing forth of that which was hidden, which is, after all, the raison d'être of this classic of Jewish mysticism, can only be comprehended in light of this dynamic. Yet, as we have seen, the transition from closure to openness is itself characteristic of divine revelation. It can be assumed, therefore, that the writing of this text proceeded from some such experience of divine immediacy—in a word, exposure to God. Students of Jewish mysticism are apt to lose sight of the deeply experiential character of this work. While it is true that the *Zohar* is nominally and structurally a midrash, that is, a commentary on Scripture, I have tried to show that in this text the hermeneutical mode is inseparably wedded to the visionary. This study has provided one vantage point through which this merging of epistemic modes can be understood. Both the visualization of God and the hermeneutical task are predicated upon a physiological opening that corresponds to an ontological opening within the divine. Disclosure of what has been concealed—through the opening of the flesh—is the basic structure common to visionary experience and mystical hermeneutics.

◆ 3 ◆

ERASING THE ERASURE/GENDER AND THE WRITING OF GOD'S BODY IN KABBALISTIC SYMBOLISM

He made his gods in a form that cannot be erased.

—Ancient Egyptian Tomb Inscription

Set your heart to know the glorious and tremendous name. Engrave it upon your heart never to be erased. For in this connection the rabbis say that the sacred names are not to be erased. Since they point to a picture of God, how then can that which depicts be erased since He who is depicted can never be erased?

—Abraham Abulafia, *Ḥayye ha-Nefesh,* MS Munich, Bayerische Staatsbibliothek 408, fol. 65a

If for the purpose of establishing harmony between a man and his wife the Torah said, Let My name that was written in sanctity be erased by the water, how much more so may it be done for the sake of establishing peace for all the world!

—B. Sukkah 53b

I

This chapter attempts to bring together several essential aspects of the theosophic kabbalistic tradition that hitherto have either never been discussed or have been treated separately in the scholarly literature. More specifically, I am concerned with the motif of divine writing as it relates to the attribution of body and gender to God.

The central role accorded language in the kabbalistic tradition, indeed in the more general history of Jewish mysticism,[1] has been well noted by scholars as has been the function played by sexual imagery.[2] Little attention, however, has been given to the interface of these two topics. The project of thinking through these themes should enhance not only our knowledge of the relevant symbolic structures operative in this cluster of intriguing religious images but should also engender a more general understanding of gender symbolism in theosophic kabbalah.

Although the issue of gender as a fundamental and somewhat distinctive feature of kabbalistic theosophy has long been recognized by scholars, the fact is that there is still much work to be done in terms of appreciating the subtle nuances of gender symbolism in this complex body of literature. The attribution of gender in the theological plane and its relationship to gender in the sphere of human society still needs to be worked out more fully by researchers in the field of kabbalah,[3] particularly in an area that comprises such issues as recommended intentions during conjugal relations.[4] It is widely presumed by contemporary scholars, influenced particularly by semiotics, that perspectives on the body and gender are cultural constructions rather than biological data.[5] Self-knowledge is invariably embodied knowledge, but knowledge of body (of which gender is an essential component) is permeated with signs that must be decoded in light of cultural-specific assumptions. Inasmuch as that is the case it is necessary to consider very carefully the use of gender in theosophical discourse, for the images of God necessarily reflect images of human beings that are constructed within specific cultural contexts. It is of vital significance, therefore, to assess this dimension of kabbalistic symbolism for the twofold purpose of relating kabbalah to other forms of spiritual expression in the rabbinic societies of the High Middle Ages as well as the wider sociocultural environment in which it took shape in its various forms. Are the views expressed by the theosophic kabbalists with respect to the divine body and gender typical or idiosyncratic? Are the more general cultural molds broken or reinforced? Such questions lie beneath the surface of this study. The analysis of the specific themes discussed here—divine language and textual embodiment—will elucidate not only a critical nexus of symbols but should also provide an avenue to explore the larger problems and issues regarding gender and symbol as they pertain to the Weltanschauung of the theosophic kabbalists.

II

The fascination with God's writing can be traced to the Bible itself. Thus, for example, the Tablets of the Covenant that Moses was said to have received on Sinai are described as "God's work, and the writing was God's writing, incised upon the tablets" (Exod. 32:16).[6] In several other verses God is described as the one who inscribes the tablets (Exod. 24:12, 31:18, 34:1; Deut. 4:13, 5:19, 9:10; 10:4). The act of God's writing is affirmed as well in the instruction to the Israelites, "You shall observe faithfully, all your days, the laws and practices; the Teaching and Instruction that He wrote down for you; do not worship other gods" (2 Kings 17:37),[7] and in the prophet's musing in the voice of God, "The many teachings that I wrote for him have been treated as something alien" (Hosea 8:12). A passing reference to God's book in Psalms 139:16 likely presupposes as well the mythic notion of divine writing. The motif of divine scripture also underlies the passage in Zechariah where the divine curse assumes the personification of a flying scroll; that is, the word of God is transformed into a literary artifact (Zech. 5:1–4).[8] The activity of God's writing or recording events is implied as well when in his attempt to gain divine forgiveness after the sin of the Golden Calf, Moses makes the following condition with God: "Now, if You would forgive their sin [well and good]; but if not, erase me from the record which You have written" (Exod. 32:32). God is not persuaded by Moses' request and simply responds: "He who has sinned against Me, him only will I erase from My record" (ibid., 33). The contextual sense indicates that the record referred to here is a kind of "book of life" in which are recorded the actions of the righteous.[9] God as worldly judge and heavenly king inscribes the deeds of humanity in a book in a way comparable to an earthly king (cf. Dan. 7:10; Esther 6:1). To be erased from God's book represents the ultimate perdition: the memory of one's being is completely obliterated. Thus in one context the Psalmist wishes the following punishment for his enemies: "May they be erased from the book of life, and not be inscribed with the righteous" (Ps. 69:29). In the ancient Near Eastern context of biblical religion, inscription serves as an aid to memory; in fact, the written record is a token of cultural remembrance (cf. Ps. 102:19); hence the expressions *ʾavnei zikkaron*—the stones of remembrance in the vestment of the high priest upon which were engraved the names of the sons of Israel—(Exod. 28:12, 39:7) and *sefer zikkaron*—the scroll of remembrance in which are recorded the names of those individuals who feared the Lord and esteemed His name (Mal. 3:16;

Dan. 12:1; cf. Esther 6:1). The connection of inscription and memorialization is in evidence as well in the prophetic statement regarding the eunuchs who keep the Sabbaths and the covenant of God: "I will give them, in My House, and within My walls, a monument and a name (*yad wa-shem*) better than sons or daughters; I will give them an everlasting name which shall not perish" (Isa. 56:5). To have one's name inscribed upon a monument within the Temple exceeds the promise of progeny as a guarantee of being memorialized. To be inscribed is to be committed to memory, which is a blessing of eternal life even better than having children; to be erased is to be wiped from memory, which is eternal damnation.[10] One other verse is worth citing in this context: "Then the Lord said to Moses, Inscribe this in a document as a reminder, and read it aloud to Joshua: I will utterly blot out the memory of Amalek from under the heaven" (Exod. 17:14). Eternally memorialized within Israelite culture (and, subsequently, ritualized in rabbinic Judaism as a specific mandate to be recalled through oral recitation[11]) is God's desire to erase the memory of Amalek. How paradoxical: the writing of God's desire to eradicate the memory of Amalek actually perpetuates that memory. Indeed, the Jew must recall what God wishes to forget.[12] For the purpose of this study the most important point is the essential link that is established between memory and writing.[13] Suffice it here to say that within the biblical corpus the prevalent motifs connected with divine writing are the inscription of the laws and the recording of events (or names) in a scroll of remembrance. The latter motif is transformed in apocalyptic literature into the heavenly book in which are inscribed the righteous and the sinful actions of human beings.[14] It is interesting that the two scriptural motifs are combined in a recently published fragment from Cave 4 of the Dead Sea Scrolls, which, in accord with other apocalyptic sources,[15] posits the existence of a heavenly book that contains all the mysteries of human history:

> For the law (*meḥoqeq*) is etched (*ḥarut*) by God for all [ ] sons of Seth. And the Book of Memory (*sefer zikkaron*) is inscribed before him (God) for those who observe his word. And it is the Vision of the Haguy (*ḥazon he-haguy*), as a Book of Memory. And he bequeathed it to Enosh with the people of the spirit. Because he created it as a sacred blueprint (*ke-tavnit qedoshim*). But Haguy had not as yet been entrusted to the spirit of flesh since it had as yet not known the distinction between good and evil.[16]

The biblical images briefly noted above engendered the two most important characterizations of God as writer that informed the aggadic imagination of the rabbis: the first concerns the linguistic creation of the world, and the second, the divine inscription of human deeds in a book.[17] For the purposes of this study it is the former motif that will be elaborated. At the outset it is necessary to distinguish two distinct lines of thinking regarding the linguistic creativity of the divine in the rabbinic imagination: on the one hand, there is (to borrow Derridean terminology) the logocentric view and, on the other, the grammatological. The former emphasizes that God created the world by fiat or divine utterance, a motif expressed in biblical literature[18] as well, reflecting various myths of divine speech as a creative force found in other ancient Near Eastern cosmologies of both Egyptian and Mesopotamian provenance.[19] This is epitomized, for instance, in the rabbinic statement that the world was created by means of ten logoi (*ma ͗amarot*), which clearly places the primary valence on God's speech rather than writing.[20] The emphasis on divine fiat as the vehicle for creation is also evident in a common expression used to refer to God in rabbinic sources, "the one who spoke and the world came into being," *mi-she-͗amar we-hayah ha-͑olam.*[21] In some aggạdic passages that express the notion of God creating the world by means of specific letters, such as the letter *bet,*[22] or those of the divine name (usually either *yod* or *he͗*),[23] it is the power of utterance that endows language with its special efficacy.[24] One example will suffice: according to the tradition attributed to R. Yoḥanan and transmitted by R. Abbahu, the biblical expression *be-hibar͗am* (Gen. 2:4) must be decoded as *be-he͗ bar͗am,* i.e., God created heaven and earth by means of the letter *he͗*, "for all the letters take hold of the tongue but the *he͗* does not take hold of the tongue. Thus, the Holy One, blessed be He, did not create His world through toil and effort, but rather 'by the word of God' (Ps. 33:6) and already 'the heavens were made' (ibid.)."[25] By contrast, the notion of God creating the world by sealing the abyss with the letters of his name found in apocryphal and esoteric literature does not involve verbal utterance of the name but rather its written inscription.[26] The magical background of this notion is attested by the aggadic tradition regarding David inscribing the Ineffable Name (*shem ha-meforash*) upon a sherd and casting it into the abyss (*tehom*) to control the raging floodwaters.[27] The abyss is suppressed by something akin to a magical bowl that is the seal of the divine name. Once the harmony has been broken it is possible for one to restore the original magical power of the written seal by pronouncing a magical formula that consists of precisely what was inscribed on the seal.[28] But the primary element that endows the sherd with its efficacy is that it is an artifact that contains the letters of the divine name. The implication of this tradition is fully developed by two later versions of the aggadah, the first in the midrashic collection, *Tanḥuma͗*; the second is found in the writings of the medieval German Pietists. According to the former, the name of God is replaced by the Torah; that is, God is portrayed as sealing the abyss with the Torah.[29] It is evident from this version that the principle power lay in the scripted form of the Hebrew letters and not in vocal expression. In the case of the latter, the tradition that is transmitted involves God creating a stone (*ṣeror*) upon which he engraved the name of forty-two letters and which he placed at the opening of the abyss to contain the waters.[30] Here there is an explicit attestation that the power to control cosmic forces (if not explicitly to create) is linked especially with the act of divine inscription.

Analogously, one finds some rabbinic sources that privilege the act of writing as the prime means of creation rather divine speech. This is especially evident in those passages that depict the Torah as God's tool in creation, echoing earlier speculation on divine Wisdom.[31] The Primordial Torah is to be understood primarily as a graphic/visual rather than an oral/aural reality.[32] This orientation is evident, for instance, in the aggadic traditions regarding the Primordial Torah being written as black fire upon white fire[33] or upon the forearm of God.[34] Mention should also be made here of the aggadic tradition regarding the list of ten things created at twilight on the first Sabbath that includes *ketav*, *mikhtav*, and *luḥot*.[35] There are various opinions suggested by different rabbinic commentators to explain the precise meaning of the *ketav* (writing) and *mikhtav* (script)[36] or, as it is vocalized by some authorities, *makhtev* (pen),[37] but all of these sources share the belief that with respect to the Decalogue the graphic aspect preceded the oral, for the tablets were inscribed from the time of creation.[38] Despite the explicit claim of Scripture that God first spoke the Ten Commandments to the congregation of Israel and then inscribed them on the two tablets of stone (cf. Deut. 5:19; see also Exod. 20:1, 19; Deut. 9:10), the rabbis, operating with a notion of tablets that were inscribed from the primeval days of creation, assumed that the Ten Commandments were read (either directly by God or through Moses) from the tablets that were already inscribed.[39] Even the eleventh-century northern French exegete, R. Solomon ben Isaac of Troyes (Rashi), who suggested that the Primordial Torah was originally oral, still maintained that it was committed to writing on the last day of creation prior to its being revealed, and that the Ten Commandments too were inscribed on the stone tablets before they were orally revealed to Israel at Sinai.[40] Just as God creates the world through the written text rather than the verbal utterance, so too the words of revelation are not first spoken by God but inscribed in a book.[41] Reversing the usual order, verbal discourse is the representation of writing. Orality is preceded by an archewriting.[42]

+ remember oral = fem.
written - masc.
So that this is an REVERSAL similar to other reversals

The chirographic orientation is applied in the most detailed manner in the work of ancient Jewish esotericism, the *Sefer Yeṣirah,* which specifies that the means of creation comprise the thirty-two paths of wondrous wisdom that include the ten *sefirot* and twenty-two letters of the Hebrew alphabet.[43] The most important predicate to express the process of divine creativity is, as is evident from the opening passage of the work, to engrave (*ḥaqaq*); indeed, God (who is designated by a litany of names) is said to have engraved the thirty-two paths of mysterious wisdom. The metaphor of divine writing is extended in the continuation of this passage where it is stated that God created the world by means of three books.[44] Priority is thus given to the written/graphic dimension of divine language (the basic constituents being the consonants of the Hebrew alphabet) over the aural/verbal: scripted forms rather than spoken words serve as the instruments of divine creativity.[45] In a subsequent passage, describing the second *sefirah* referred to as the "pneuma from the pneuma" (*ruaḥ me-ruaḥ*), the predicate *ḥaqaq* is paired with *ḥaṣav* (to hew); that is, the four directions of the world are said to be engraved and hewn in this *sefirah.*[46] These two predicates are paired in a number of subsequent passages as well.[47] It is evident from other passages in *Sefer Yeṣirah* that underlying these verbs, which connote the process of engraving and hewing in stone, is a graphic as opposed to an oral theory of cosmogony. The principal act of creation is writing rather than speaking, even though it is fairly obvious that the theory of language developed in this work is based largely on phonetic paradigms;[48] indeed, one of the basic divisions of the twenty-two letters employed in *Sefer Yeṣirah* is based on the fivefold phonetic classification: four gutturals, four palatals, five linguals, five dentals, and four labials.[49] The graphic dimension of divine creativity is amplified in the following passage from the second part of the work that deals more elaborately with alphabetic cosmogony: "Twenty-two letters[50]: He engraved, hewed, weighed, permutated, and combined them, and formed by their means the soul of every creature[51] and the soul of everything to be formed in the future."[52] From other descriptions of the process of divine creativity it is evident that the principal metaphor is that of writing. To take one example that is applied to the three matrix letters, the so-called *ʾimmot* (mothers), *ʾalef, mem,* and *shin*: God is said to have made these letters respectively kings over the elements of air, water, and fire, and to crown each one and to combine it with the other letters.[53] It is obvious that the image of tying a crown to these letters is intended to convey the notion of scribal activity on the part of God.[54] We may conclude from this case that the primal linguistic act of the divine is indeed writing. It should be recalled, moreover, that the second part of *Sefer*

Yeṣirah indicates clearly that the basic stuff of the material world is constituted by letters; a direct correspondence is thus established between letters and the different realities that make up the created cosmos. Here the mystical and magical elements converge: one who properly knows the inherent property of the Hebrew language can manipulate creation or can in effect become a creator.[55] Thus near the conclusion of the book the very qualities attributed to the Creator are applied to Abraham: "he looked and saw, investigated and comprehended, engraved and combined, hewed and contemplated,[56] and he was successful,[57] and the Master of everything appeared to him and He placed him in His bosom, and He kissed him on his head and called him[58] My beloved."[59]

To the two traditions mentioned already we can add a third that finds expression in several other esoteric writings, presumably from Late Antiquity, the *Shiʿur Qomah* texts. In some of the recensions of this work it appears that the letters are not merely the means by which God creates or the basic stuff of the reality created, but rather the nature of the material form of the divine. Some ancient Jewish mystics thought it possible to apprehend God in a human shape and assigned to the limbs of that shape Hebrew letters that make up the divine names.[60] To see the iconic form of God is to behold the letters engraved upon the limbs.[61]

III

The different traditions that I have briefly mentioned, and numerous other variations of these that cannot be discussed in this context,[62] all converged to give birth to the rich and complex systems of speculation on the Hebrew language in the various trends of Jewish mysticism in the High Middle Ages, known generically as kabbalah, the esoteric tradition of Judaism. Let me note very briefly that an especially important use of the older motifs concerning the linguistic nature of divine creativity, which had a decisive impact on the medieval mystics, can be found in the poetic and philosophic (or exegetical) writings of several figures from the Hispano-Jewish Golden Age.[63] The contextualization of the mythical images within some philosophical framework marks an important stage in the development of medieval Jewish intellectual history that in a fundamental way anticipates the approach of the kabbalists. One would do well, therefore, to avoid seeing the kabbalists' attempt to express profound myths in some kind of speculative discourse as something completely novel; this strategy informs religious philosophy and poetry in at least two centuries preceding the literary flourishing of theosophic kabbalah in Provence and northern Spain.[64]

Turning more specifically to kabbalistic literature, it should be noted that my remarks here are concerned with only one of the several dominant streams of mystical activity from this period, the kabbalah that placed its primary emphasis on the secret knowledge and visual experience of the ten divine attributes (*sefirot*) that collectively constitute the living and dynamic side of God.[65] It is within this literature that the motif of divine writing is pushed to its theological limit, yielding some of the most powerful myths and symbols in the history of Judaism, if not the history of religions more generally.[66] Building upon the earlier aggadic and mystical sources the kabbalists affirm that the letters are the instruments of creation as well as the substance of creation; basic to the kabbalistic tradition, therefore, in striking contrast to the philosophical position articulated by Maimonides, is the essentialist as opposed to the conventionalist theory of language: words, and in particular the Hebrew language, reflect the very nature of the entities that are named.[67] Moreover, following in the footsteps of *Sefer Yeṣirah,* the primary act of divine creativity for the theosophic kabbalists consists of God's inscribing or engraving,[68] although some kabbalists include the process of marking (*reshimah*) that precedes the acts of engraving (*ḥaqiqah*) and hewing (*ḥaṣivah*).[69] Moreover, in the kabbalistic literature it is, first and foremost, God's own being that is so inscribed. Thus, for example, one of the first known kabbalists of medieval Europe, Isaac the Blind, characterizes the ontological chain of the sefirotic entities in terms of linguistic metaphors: "each cause [i.e., *sefirah*] receives from the cause above it, for the attribute [or measure, *middah*] draws from the attribute that is hewn, and that which is hewn from the engraved, and that which is engraved from the inscribed, and that which is inscribed from that which is hidden."[70] The transition from that which is hidden and presumably without speech, the allusive Thought that extends into the Infinite, to that which is articulated in varying degrees (inscribed, engraved, and hewn) represents the movement from *deus absconditus* to *deus revelatus,* from erasure to inscription. It is critical that the emergence of divine speech is here depicted in images appropriate to the process of writing. Similarly, Isaac's disciple, Ezra ben Solomon of Gerona, describes the process of emanation of the primordial essences (*hawwayot*) from the divine Thought in terms of letter combination and permutation that reflect a graphic as opposed to a phonetic model:

> "Then He saw it" (Job 28:27), He looked in the Pure Thought like a person who imagines an action, initially it arose in

> His heart and afterwards He began to act and to be occupied with it. . . . According to the images that were in it He formed that principle that emanated from it. "And he gauged it" (*wa-yesapperah*), the three *sefarim* [i.e., the three occurrences of the word *sfr* in the beginning of *Sefer Yeṣirah*], *sefer, sefar,* and *sippur,* which are Wisdom (*Ḥokhmah*), Understanding (*Tevunah*), and Knowledge (*Daʿat*). "He measured it," i.e., the essences did not stand in accordance with the order of the properties of the edifice, and He, blessed be He, brought forth those essences and arranged them according to an order and produced a structure from them, after the combination (*ṣeruf*), weighing (*shiqqul*) and permutation (*hamarah*) of the twenty-two letters, each one bound to the other and one parallel to the other.[71]

Another telling image that underscores the primacy of the image of writing in kabbalistic ontology is found in Azriel of Gerona who describes divine Thought as the "book that comprises the signs of the Will."[72] Even more poignant is Jacob ben Sheshet's comment that the "scribe is the First Cause[73] of the letters inscribed in Wisdom,[74] for the scribe cannot write until he sees the letter inscribed in his heart."[75] From these examples, and many others that could have been cited, it can be concluded that in the early theosophic kabbalistic texts the grammatological has precedence over the logocentric: the scripted form proceeds the spoken word.[76] According to several of the earliest documents of theosophic kabbalah the ten *sefirot* are depicted as the inner essence of the twenty-two letters; hence both *sefirot* and letters (together comprising the thirty-two paths of wisdom specified in *Sefer Yeṣirah*) constitute the configuration of the divine, the former corresponding to the soul, and the latter to the body.[77] A particularly interesting formulation of this idea is found in a citation in the name of R. Nissim[78] contained in the *ʾAvne Zikkaron* of Abraham ben Solomon Adrutiel:

> Moreover, consider in your thought that the new reality (*ha-meṣiʾut ha-meḥudash*) is a mountain of darkness, and the darkness is the privation of light. This mountain is a symbol (*mashal*) for the letters, which are like the stones in the building of houses and the settlement of countries.[79] All the time that the stones are not hewn from the mountain there is no reality to the stones and they are only darkness. When the stones are carved, hewn, weighed and combined[80] they are clothed in light, and from that point they build

> houses. Thus it was with respect to the creation of heaven and earth, for all the letters were prior to everything, dark like the dark mountain or like the piece of wood that is matter without form. After it was in the supernal will and it arose in thought to create the world He clothed the letters in the effluence of His great, wondrous, bright and translucent light. By the power of this engraving, hewing, weighing, permuting, combination and enclothing the paths (*netivot*) were made, and these paths became the essences (*hawwayot*) and from them everything was made, for from the matter of the letters, which are twenty-two, together with the ten *sefirot,* which are the essence of divinity (*ʿeṣem ha-ʾelohut*), [shines] the effluence of Ein-Sof. When [the letters] are clothed in the essence of divinity they too become the essence of divinity and therefore everything is made from them.[81]

The relation of the letters to the *sefirot* is well summarized in the following comment of Menaḥem Recanaṭi, an Italian kabbalist who was active in the early part of the fourteenth century: "All the letters of the Torah—in their forms, in their conjunctions, and in their separations, and in inclined and twisted letters, in missing and superfluous, small and large, crowns of the letters, closed and open, and their order—are the alignment of the ten *sefirot.*"[82] The letters, therefore, comprise the visible form of God, and the Torah scroll itself is the "divine edifice hewn from the name of the Holy One, blessed be He."[83] The idea expressed by Recanaṭi is based on earlier sources, especially the kabbalists of Gerona, representing one of the foundational beliefs of theosophic kabbalah: the Torah is the name of God, which is visualized as an anthropos. Thus the scroll itself is characterized as the divine edifice or form.[84] Recanaṭi's particular formulation reflects similar claims made in the anonymous kabbalistic work *Sefer ha-Yiḥud,* where it is explicitly stated that the forms of the letters of Torah are the shape of God.[85] Hence, it is incumbent on every Jew to write a Torah scroll for himself for by so doing one makes God for oneself; anyone who changes any letter of the Torah alters the divine form.[86] Joseph of Hamadan, another kabbalist contemporary with the author of the aforementioned work, observes in a corresponding way:

> The Torah scroll alludes to a great matter for it is made in the pure and holy chain and it is His name, blessed be He. Therefore He commanded us that each person must make a Torah scroll for himself so that he will discern and know that He loves the Torah and it alludes to the unity and the fear of the pattern of the Creator, blessed be He. . . . Another

> [explanation] for why God, blessed be He, commanded each and every Jew to make a Torah scroll for himself is that this alludes to the fact that all of Israel are one form. . . . Since all Jews are one supernal pattern, and each and every Jew is a limb from the chariot, therefore each and every Jew must take a Torah scroll for himself so that he will attach the limb to the [corresponding] limb in the pure and holy chain. . . . Therefore God, blessed be He, commanded each and every one of us to make a Torah for himself.[87]

In another context Joseph of Hamadan asserts that by studying the Torah, or by even seeing the letters of the Torah scroll, one beholds the "pattern of the supernal form," that is, the divine image.[88] The point is epitomized as well in the following statement in the anonymous work *Sefer ha-Temunah*[89]:

> These twenty-two letters with which the Torah was written . . . are specified in a great and hidden secret, and it is without doubt the true image (*ha-temunah ha-ʾamitit*), as it is written, "he beholds the image of the Lord" (Num. 12:8), and this is the secret of the names of the Holy One, blessed be He, and the power of His actions. Permission has not been given to explain but some of them. They are the secret of the *sefirot* and the attributes (*middot*) and the secret of the angel and the secret of God. . . . The secret of the *sefirot* [is that they] are in the image and form of an anthropos.[90]

The Hebrew letters are the matrix from which the divine shape is formed and in whose image Adam was created.[91] God, therefore, is author and text simultaneously, or, to put the matter somewhat differently, God authors himself. Thus, the classic work of theosophic kabbalah from thirteenth-century Spain, the *Zohar*, begins its commentary on the first word of Scripture with the words: *be-reish hurmanutaʾ de-malkaʾ galif gelufe bi-ṭehiru ʿillaʾah boṣinaʾ de-qardinutaʾ*, "in the beginning of the will of the King the hardened spark began to engrave engravings in the supernal lustre."[92] The first stirrings of emanation within the infinite Godhead are depicited as the hardened spark,[93] the aspect of the divine that gives shape to the sefirotic forms,[94] making engravings in the supernal lustre, the ether of the Infinite in which the emanative processes occur.[95] It is evident from this text, as well as parallel passages in zoharic literature, that the spark functions as a kind of stylus[96] and the lustre[97] the tablet upon which are made the engravings,[98] the linguistic signs that disclose the

Obviously the "spark" was from an older myth— they "hardened" it, thus masculinizing it

inner, supernal forms of the sefirotic entities.[99] In a passage parallel to the one cited above we read: "In the beginning of the will of the King [he] engraved [in the lustre] nine engravings by the shining spheres and one that was hidden and unknown. He engraved engravings and struck (*baṭash*) within one spark."[100] The text continues with a lengthy description of the emergence of the letters *ʾalef* to *ṭet*, corresponding to the nine gradations, from *Ḥokhmah* to *Malkhut*, that first appeared as engravings (*gelifin*) or shining spheres (*gilgule ṭehirin*) within the lustre (*Keter*). In this particular context the subject, the hardened spark, is elliptical, although it is evident from parallel sources that one can assume it is precisely that spark that is the active agent engraving the engravings and striking against the first *sefirah* to bring forth the other *sefirot* from potentiality to actuality. The essentially linguistic nature of the spark is underscored in another passage, apparently belonging to the *Sitre Torah* stratum of zoharic literature,[101] that attempts to frame this theosophic doctrine in terms of a more normative notion of the Primordial Torah. The text mentions nine points or vowels (*niqqudin*) that emerge from the point, or *Ḥokhmah,* that came out of Ein-Sof and that rule over all the letters. Additionally, thirteen cantillation notes (*ṭaʿame de-ʾoraitaʾ*) emanate from these points, and together they total twenty-two, corresponding to the number of letters.

> These twenty-two points and notes are the secret of the hardened spark, the measure of everything (*boṣinaʾ de-qardinutaʾ li-meshaḥtaʾ de-kholaʾ*). In this mystery is every measure in length, width, depth and height. There is no measure that departs from this dimension, from the secret of the nine vowels (*niqqudin*) and thirteen notes (*ṭeʿamin*). Upon this secret the Torah exists in all its aspects, and all the secrets and deep mysteries of the Torah do not go out from this secret. By means of this secret the hardened spark produced a measure for all the measures. This secret was not given to reveal except to those who fear sin in whose hands is the secret of faith. They are allowed to reveal it.[102]

The primary act of the spark is thus engraving or inscription, a point well conveyed in the following account offered by the kabbalist Simeon Lavi, who describes the spark of darkness (*boṣiṣaʾ de-qadrinutaʾ*) as a mental point (*nequdah maḥshavit*) that emanates from the powerful light hidden by God:

> The [sages], blessed be their memory, said that in the beginning of the spreading forth of this spark in order to be disclosed and revealed it made a fixed mark (*roshem*

> *qavuʿa*) and this is the first point like a person who begins to write for he marks one point from which the letter will begin to extend, for it is not possible to write any letter without the beginning of a point. Similarly, this spark marks a marking and makes one point for the unveiling of the emanation (*gilluy ha-ʾaṣilut*), and this is the attribute of Wisdom concealed from the eyes of all the living and it is like the hidden point that has no space through which to enter it. That spark formed in that point all the forms of the will (*ṣiyyure ha-ḥefeṣ*) in a subtle, mental form (*ṣiyyur daq maḥshavi*) according to its image and likeness.[103]

The inscriptions made by the spark, therefore, contain the forms of all that which will emerge in the subsequent stages of emanation. In the uppermost aspect of the Godhead there are graphemes that represent the ideal forms of all existence. This motif underlies the cryptic remark at the beginning of the *Sitre ʾOtiyyot*, a section in *Zohar* that deals at length with the mysteries of language connected to cosmology: "By means of the inscribed letters engraved upon the concealment of existence the chariots rise in holy chariots."[104] Moreover, it is clear that the zoharic authorship, consistent with standard medieval views,[105] reflecting in turn ancient Greco-Roman as well as Near Eastern cultural assumptions,[106] identified the writing instrument (pen or chisel) with the phallus, on one hand, and the tablet or page with the female on the other.[107] It is evident from other zoharic passages that the act of engraving[108]—which signifies in its most elemental sense the process of forming or giving shape by digging out space from slabs of matter[109]—is understood in sexual terms as phallic penetration; hence in some contexts, an illustration of which we have already seen, a verb with an obvious phallic connotation, *baṭash*, "to knock against" or "to strike," is employed in place of "to engrave."[110] Thus, for example, in one passage the letters within the brain are said to be punctuated when the hardened spark strikes against the pure ether of the brain.[111] This text is significant, for it assumes that in the uppermost recesses of the Godhead, that which is anthropomorphically depicted as the brain, there are letters, and second that the vowel points emerge as a result of the activity of the spark striking in the brain. What is elsewhere described as the *ṭehiru*, the "lustre," that is inscribed by the hardened spark is here portrayed as the brain that is filled with pointed letters.

The thematic basis for the zoharic attempt to portray the activity of the hardened spark within the divine thought or will in erotic terms is the Galenic view, widespread in medieval literature, concerning the origin of the semen in the brain. This notion is expressed in the earliest

oy vey!

kabbalistic documents to appear in Provence and Gerona, the *Sefer ha-Bahir*[112] and the writings of Isaac the Blind and his disciples.[113] In the case of the latter it is evident that this view is set ontologically in terms of the homologous structure of the brain and the penis, such that both are depicted as the letter *yod.*[114] That is, there is a *yod* within the brain that corresponds to the penis that is also represented by the *yod,* a motif found in earlier aggadic sources.[115] It is not explicitly stated by Isaac or his disciples that the upper *yod* in the brain is a kind of phallus (or an aspect of the brain that corresponds to the phallus), but it does appear to function in precisely that way. It is likely that the more fully formulated images of the latter texts are already part of the earlier kabbalistic system but they simply were not committed to writing in all of their mythic detail.

In this connection it is significant to note a comment in one of the recensions of the *Sefer ha-ʿIyyun,* the so-called *Contemplation-Short,* the base text from a collection of literary sources that have been portrayed as stemming from a distinctive circle most likely active in Castile in the second half of the thirteenth century.[116] In the formative stage of the process of autogenesis God is said to have created from the Wondrous Light (*ʾor mufla ʾ*), the first of the powers (*koḥot*) that emanate from the Primordial Wisdom (*ḥokhmah ha-qedumah*), the *Ḥashmal* (electrum), the beginning of the upper beings, which is described further as a scale (*peles*) that "overflows (*mashpiʿa*) its powers to every side, from the middle to the top and from the top to the middle, from the middle to the left and from the left to the middle, from the right to the left and to every side."[117] The word *peles,* translated according to its conventional usage as scale,[118] may also have the connotation of phallus in this context.[119] That is, it is possible that the author of this text is using a word whose consonants (פלס) have a double signification, one word in Hebrew, and a different word in Latin. What suggests this semantic ploy to me is the fact that the image of spreading forth in every direction is not really appropriate for a scale understood in its usual sense, whereas this imagery is most certainly appropriate for the phallus, which is frequently characterized as a spring that overflows. However, the image of the scale may itself have phallic connotations, a motif that is drawn explicitly in Jewish esotericism[120] based perhaps on the rabbinic interpretation of the scales (*moʾznayim*) mentioned in Psalms 62:10 as the instrument that God uses in pairing male and female souls before their corporeal birth.[121] Utilizing this motif, the zoharic authorship portrays the harmonious union of masculine and feminine elements of the Godhead in terms of the image of the scale, or, more precisely, being balanced on the scale.[122] The image of the scale is also employed in zoharic literature to denote the primary tool of divine creativity insofar as the process of emanation is occasionally depicted as weighing or balancing.[123] In that respect it may be said that the scale is identical with the hardened spark (*boṣina᾽ de-qardinuta᾽*) or the line of measure (*qav ha-middah*),[124] the two alternative ways of designating that faculty of the Godhead. Indeed, the action of the *qav ha-middah*, and sometimes the *boṣina᾽ de-qardinuta᾽*, is portrayed as producing a measure (*meshiḥa᾽* or *meshaḥta᾽*), which has the double connotation of measuring either by extending a line (projecting)[125] or by balancing and weighing on a scale.[126] The appropriateness of these identifications, moreover, may lie in the fact that just as the spark and the line are phallic symbols[127] so too is the scale or, more specifically, the tongue of the scale. Hence, the weights of the scale are thought to correspond to the testicles and the tongue in the middle to the *membrum virile*.[128] This precise symbolism is utilized, for example, in a later Lurianic text to characterize the masculine and the feminine potencies of the Godhead:

> *Ze῾eir* and his *Nuqba᾽* are in the secret of male and female, that is, the scale mentioned in the *Sifra᾽ di-Ṣeni῾uta*, for just as in a scale there is a weight from one side and another weight from the other side and that which is set in the middle, He established [them] in the secret of "Male and female He created them and called their name Adam" (Gen. 5:2). And that which unites (*ha-ḥibbur*) is the tongue that is set in the middle.[129]

Perhaps already implicit in the Iyyun text mentioned above is some such understanding of the scale; hence the world *peles* connotes at the same time "scale" and "phallus." Support for my interpretation is found in the continuation of the text where the letter *yod* of the Tetragrammaton is said to correspond to the *Ḥashmal*, for it comprises ten powers.[130] Beyond the obvious application of the *yod* to the *Ḥashmal*, given the numerical equivalence of that letter as ten, it may be relevant that *yod* is the letter generally associated with the phallus insofar as it is the sign of the covenant of circumcision. That this was the intention of the original author of *Contemplation-Short* seems to be verified by a passage in a text that has been determined to have been one of the major sources for the Iyyun composition, the kabbalah of R. Meshullam the Zadokite from the city of Tréport in the kingdom of Brittany.[131] According to this text[132] the four letters of the Tetragrammaton correspond to four theosophic powers (*koḥot*)—*Ḥashmal* (electrum), *῾Arafel* (thick darkness), *Kisse᾽ ha-Nogah* (throne of light), and *᾽Ofan ha-Gedullah* (wheel of greatness)—that collectively make up the body of the Presence (*guf ha-Shekhinah*). For the purposes of this analysis the description of the first power is relevant:

> *Ḥashmal* is the great cherub (*ha-keruv ha-gadol*): sometimes it is transformed into a male and sometimes into a female.[133] Accordingly, you will find in Ezekiel's prophecy [both] *ḥashmal* and *ḥashmalah*, which is the feminine.[134] Concerning this matter[135] Moses said, "the cherubim and the flaming sword that revolved" (Gen. 3:24). Moreover, it refers to the secret of faith (*sod ha-ʾemunah*)[136]—for the *yod* from the Name indicates that he[137] created the universe. Therefore[138] an infant is called *ke-ravyah*, for the creature (*ha-beriyah*) arises from the *yod*.

It lies beyond the confines of this chapter to enter into all the complex details alluded to in the above passage. Suffice it here to say that Meshullam posits that the *Ḥashmal* is an androgynous being, comprising both male (*ḥashmal*) and female (*ḥashmalah*), and the union thereof constitutes the secret of faith. The attribution of this characteristic to the *Ḥashmal* is facilitated by its being identified as the great cherub, for, according to rabbinic tradition, the cherubim were both male and female.[139] The male aspect of the *Ḥashmal* is further represented by the *yod*, the first letter of the Tetragrammaton, which corresponds to this power. It is in virtue of this (masculine) character, represented by the *yod*, that the *Ḥashmal* is also described as the one that creates.[140] I suggest that the demiurgic power is linked to the *Ḥashmal* because the *Ḥashmal* corresponds to the *yod* and the *yod*, in addition to being the first letter of the Tetragrammaton, is the sign of the covenant inscribed on the penis, the organ of fecundity. That the demiurgic quality is associated with the *yod* is suggested as well in the last statement of the above passage: the infant (*tinoq*) is called "like a child," *ke-ravyah*, reflecting the talmudic etymology for the word *keruv* (cherub),[141] for it is the creature, *ha-beriyah* (the word *beriyah*, בריה, is comprised of the same letters as the word *ravyah*, רביה) that arises from the *yod*, the penis or aspect that corresponds to the penis in its productive capacity. That the *yod* has phallic connotations is made explicit in a subsequent section of this small and highly compact treatise: "'The river that goes from Eden' (Gen. 2:10), that is the *yod*, 'to water the Garden,' the beloved."[142]

It thus may be concluded from the textual evidence brought above that a central tenet in the theosophy developed by the Iyyun circle and some of its sources is the identification of the *Ḥashmal* as the androgynous male, the masculine element represented by the *yod* and the feminine by the Primordial Ether (*ʾalef*) that encompasses that *yod*. This power is also represented in some of the relevant sources as the scale (*peles*) that overflows to every side; this scale, the letter *yod* or the *Ḥashmal*, may be termed the "upper phallus" or an aspect in the supernal regions of the Godhead that corresponds to the penis. Further support for my interpretation may be derived from the reworking of the image of the *peles* in a later recension of this text, the so-called *Contemplation-Long*, where other obvious phallic symbols, such as the key that opens and closes (see further discussion below) and the vibrating light that emits a multiplicity of sparks, are applied to the scale.[143] In another Iyyun text, the *Sefer ha-Yiḥud ha-ʾAmiti*, the power of Memory (*koaḥ ha-zekher*), identified also as the Foundation of the World (*yesod ʿolam*), that is, the masculine gradation or the phallus, is said to be found in the Primordial Ether (*ha-ʾavir ha-qadmon*).[144] It is likely that the latter should be viewed as the feminine element that both encircles and contains the masculine[145] in a way comparable to the description of the ether (or supernal lustre) that surrounds the Infinite according to the zoharic passage discussed above.[146] This Memory, moreover, lodged in the center of the Ether, is said to be the essence of the divine being that causes the life-force to overflow (*mashpiʿa*) to all the godly powers that emanate from the Mystery of Unity of the Ether.[147] It is possible that this formulation reflects the view expressed in what may be considered (together with *Contemplation-Short*) to be a core document of the Circle, the *Maʿayan ha-Ḥokhmah*,[148] in which the fountain is identified as a *yod* that is encircled by the Primordial Ether, also identified as the Holy Spirit,[149] the circle that encompasses the *yod*.[150] That the *yod* is to be understood in decidedly phallic terms can be illustrated from the explicit description of it as the "gushing fountain" whose "waters spread out into twenty-four parts."[151] In what is perhaps even more suggestive language, one passage describes the *yod* in the following way: "Its roots are rooted and its streams are connected and the droplets based in the *tiqqun* of the circle."[152] Again it would seem that the circle represents the feminine receptacle that receives the drops from the *yod* or the overflowing stream.[153] Hence, we may conclude that in this text as well we have the phallic symbol of the *yod* combined with the Primordial Ether.

I would suggest that the conception expressed in the Iyyun material, together with the other kabbalistic sources regarding the form of the *yod* in the brain and the latter as the origin of semen, influenced the mythical image used in the *Zohar* to characterize the entity of the Godhead, the *boṣinaʾ de-qardinutaʾ*, which is the fount of letters and vowels as well as that which gives shape to the lights that emanate from the Primordial Darkness or Nothingness.[154] The zoharic authorship adopted the purportedly scientific view of Galen and related motifs expressed in the theosophic kabbalists and developed (or articulated) complicated mythical ideas that involve the inner workings of the highest recesses of God. One other text in particular is worth citing, for in significant ways it runs parallel to the passage from the beginning of the *Zohar* cited above:

> I have seen in the mysteries[155] of creation that says as follows: that concealed holy one engraved engravings in the womb of a lustre[156] in which the point is inserted. That engraving he engraved and hid in it like one who hides everything under a key, and that key hides everything in a palace. Even though everything is hidden in that palace the essence of everything is in that key. That key closes and opens. In that palace there are many hidden treasures.[157]

This passage relates in symbolic language the unfolding of the first three *sefirot* from the Infinite. The relationship of Ein-Sof to *Keter* is here depicted in terms of the former engraving in the latter; in relation to Ein-Sof, therefore, *Keter* is characterized as feminine, the womb in which the engravings are made. Within *Keter*, moreover, is the next emanation, *Ḥokhmah*, depicted as the point inserted in the womb. The point is further characterized as the key[158] that conceals everything that it contains in the palace, which corresponds to the third emanation, *Binah*. It is evident that in this text as well the engraving is a symbolic trope to describe the male principle acting upon, indeed inseminating, the female. The phallic nature of the key and the act of inscription is underscored in the continuation of the text that notes that within the forty-nine gates of *Binah*[159] there is "one lock and one subtle place so that the key may enter it, and it is not marked except by the marking of the key." The erotic significance of the inscribing of the hardened spark is expressed poignantly in the zoharic section that deals elaborately with the mystery of the *qav ha-middah:*

> The *ᶜayin* and *dalet* [of Deut. 6:4] are enlarged, [for they spell the word] *ᶜed* [witness] to attest to the secret of secrets, to bring forth a measure that measures the secret of faith. The one who knows this secret knows the secret of his Master and inherits the two worlds, this world and the world-to-come. This measure is called the line-of-measure, and this was given to the holy, supernal sages who know the secret of their Master and are occupied with His glory . . . and they are the true righteous ones in whom

> is the secret of the upper Faith. To them is given to know and to contemplate for they do not turn right or left. The line-of-measure: length and width. The line-of-measure: depth and height. The line of measure: circle and square. Thirteen gates exist to be known, and they are twenty-six on the two sides, when they are engraved in their engravings everything is one in this measure.[160] The line-of-measure goes up and down, it is engraved in its engravings on every side. The light that does not exist in a light engraves and emits a spark of all sparks, and strikes within the will of wills and is hidden in it, and is not known.[161]

It may be concluded from these and other passages that in zoharic literature engraving letters, or more generally the process of writing or inscription, is a decidedly erotic activity: the active agent of writing is the male principle; the written letters are the *semen virile*; and the tablet or page upon which the writing is accomplished is the female principle.[162] It is not insignificant that in one context the *Zohar* specifies that the semen that the masculine potency of the divine (symbolized as a point, *Ḥokhmah*) bestows upon the feminine (the palace, *Binah*, that receives and encloses the point) consists of the "inscribed letters, the secret of the Torah that comes out from that point."[163] The point is made in another passage commenting on the word *yishkav*, "he shall lie," in Genesis 20:15: "The word *shekhivah* [lying down] in every place connotes the alignment [or positioning] (*tiqquna*ʾ) of the female in relation to the male so that he might place in her the forms of all the letters, and that is [the meaning of] *yishkav* [whose letters may be read as] *yesh kaf-bet* [there are twenty-two], *yesh* is the supernal world, the secret of the Torah, the hidden point, that arouses in her the twenty-two (*kaf-bet*) letters, and that is [the meaning of] he will lie (*yishkav*)."[164] The mystical significance of cohabitation is thus related to the male, *Ḥokhmah* or the mystery of Torah, bestowing upon the feminine the twenty-two letters of the Hebrew alphabet. It is obvious, therefore, that the letters must be seen as the semen that the male imparts to the female. In still other zoharic contexts it is evident that writing (*ketivah*) symbolizes the flow of energy that streams forth from the masculine (in some cases referred to as the book from which the writing emerges) upon the feminine.[165] On the other hand, the *Zohar* also characterizes the seed implanted in the feminine as the three vowel-points: *ḥolam, shuruq*, and *ḥiriq*.[166] The description of the masculine potency (*Ḥokhmah*) impregnating the female (*Binah*) either by means of the letters or the vowels is a replication of the first act of divine creativity, which, as I have noted above, is depicted by means of the image of the hardened spark engraving the supernal lustre. I have suggested elsewhere that the hardened spark is the masculine element of the Infinite, and the supernal lustre the feminine.[167] According to zoharic theosophy, the hyphenated reality of the Infinite, comprising Ein-Sof and *Keter*, is androgynous, and the first act of divine creativity is the stimulation of the spark that corresponds to the penis.[168] The original moment of divine inscription, therefore, is mythologized as an act of sexual self-gratification.[169] The motif of autoeroticism underlying the creation myth of the *Zohar* is predicated on the bisexual character of the Infinite. The arousal of the divine will is a form of self-excitation that takes place as the spark strikes and engraves in the supernal lustre, also described as the ether of the Infinite, which functions as the uterus or the primeval waters of creation that receive the spark. To be sure, from one perspective it is inappropriate to speak of a differentiation along the lines of gender in this stage of the Godhead; that is, neither male nor female exists as a distinct entity or hypostasis within the Infinite. From another perspective, however, it can be said that this one entity contains both masculine and feminine characteristics. The primary arousal of which I have spoken in explicit sexual terms has to be seen against this ontological assumption pertaining to the nature of the Infinite. What I have tried to convey is that the mythic representation, involving a highly charged eroticism, reaches to the very top of the ontic chain, according to the zoharic authorship and some of the earlier sources. The play of sexuality is the most appropriate mythical expression to convey something of the nature of the infinite Godhead in the first phases of creativity. Hence the erotic myth indicates something of the basic texture of reality.

The intent of the zoharic mythos was well understood by later interpreters, particularly the disciples of Isaac Luria. Thus, for example, in an unpublished Lurianic text the first act of the Infinite, even prior to the self-withdrawal or constriction (*ṣimṣum*), is depicted in language that suggests sexual self-gratification: "Before all the emanation the Ein-Sof was alone delighting in Himself" (*qodem kol ha-ʾaṣilut hayah ha-ʾein-sof levado mishtaʿasheʿa be-ʿaṣmuto*).[170] It is evident from the continuation of the text, which describes the emergence of a *yod* from the light of Ein-Sof, that this passage is an elaboration or commentary on the zoharic passage *be-reish hurmanutaʾ de-malkaʾ*, "in the beginning of the will of the King."[171] Analogously, the opening text in the collection of Israel Sarug's teaching, *Limmude ʾAṣilut*, begins: "Before everything you must know that the Holy One, blessed be He, took delight in Himself, i.e., He was joyous and He took delight."[172] Paraphrasing this text Scholem wrote: "In the beginning

Ein-Sof took pleasure in its own autakric self-sufficiency, and this 'pleasure' produced a kind of 'shaking' (*niᶜanuᶜa*) which was the movement of *Ein-Sof* within itself."[173] Scholem does not explicitly note the obvious erotic undertones of this text: the self-pleasure is a form of sexual arousal.[174] While the employment of the motif of delight or play (*shaᶜashuᶜa*) with reference to God and the Torah prior to the creation of the world is found in much older sources of rabbinic provenance, based ultimately on the description of Wisdom in Proverbs 8:30 (cf. Ps. 119:77, 92, 143),[175] the Lurianic materials reflect its particular usage in the writings of Moses Cordovero where it connotes, *inter alia*, the activity of Ein-Sof before anything else existed.[176] In the Cordoverian texts the delight, when applied to this stage of the process, relates to the first stirrings of the divine thought,[177] the self-contemplation of the Infinite,[178] which represents the beginnings of the desire to emanate. The overtly erotic element evident in the Lurianic material, as well as in subsequent Sabbatian sources,[179] is latent in the relevant passages from the corpus of Cordovero.[180] That the delight (*shaᶜashuᶜa*) involves sexual play in the Sarugian text is further supported from the motif of shaking (*niᶜanuᶜa*),[181] which is said to produce the "primordial points" that were engraved in the power of judgment; from these "primordial points," to be understood as seminal drops, emerged the Torah, which is also called the garment (*malbush*). The linguistic nature of the primary shaking is also evident from the description of the self-amusement or gratification comprising ten shakings in the form of a *yod*, which corresponds to ten letters (I presume the reference is to the first ten letters of the Hebrew alphabet). God's self-pleasure produces the motion of shaking that, in turn, results in the construction of the Torah, the divine garb constituted by various letter combinations and permutations. Interestingly, this process is connected with the attribute of judgment, for as a result of this process the infinite light of Ein-Sof receives limit and boundary; indeed the very act of engraving is one of setting limits to produce determinate shapes of the letters that constitute the garment of God and is therefore associated with the judgmental aspect of the divine.[182] Here we confront an important dialectical element in the gender symbolism of theosophic kabbalah: although the instrument of engraving corresponds to the phallus and the letters engraved to the semen imparted to the female, the act of engraving itself, portrayed as sexual self-excitation, is an expression of divine judgment that is associated with the female.[183] The desire of the (male) Infinite to procreate by discharging seminal fluid is impelled by an impulse of the feminine attribute of limitation. In dialectical fashion typical of kabbalistic metaphysics, the drive of male projection is incited by the feminine quality of limitation and constriction. This urge manifests itself in God toying with himself, which eventuates in a gesture of shaking. What is essential for this analysis is the fact that the shaking that results from the self-pleasure is a decidedly linguistic act, indeed the graphic act of writing.[184] As Naftali Bachrach, reflecting the Sarugian teaching, in one place puts it: the engraving of the hardened spark referred to in *Zohar* 15a involves the "letters that stand in the world of delights (*ʿolam ha-shaʿashuʿim*) that surrounds the light of Ein-Sof."[185] The implications of Sarug's view are well drawn in a second passage from his *Limmude ʾAṣilut*:

> Know that Ein-Sof, blessed be He, took delight in Himself. . . . Know that Ein-Sof is the place for all the worlds, and when it arose in His simple Will to emanate the world of Ein-Sof and the worlds of Emanation, Creation, Formation, and Making, He took delight in Himself, as it were. . . . Ein-Sof, blessed be He, contemplated that the worlds that He thought of emanating needed judgment in order to bestow reward and punishment, and had He not taken delight [in Himself] there would have been no place for judgment, nor would there have been a place even for the engraving that He engraved in His essence, for that is judgment in relation to Ein-Sof. Therefore He took delight [in Himself] for He is like water or fire that shakes when the wind blows upon it, and it shines like lightning to the eyes, and glistens hither and thither. Thus Ein-Sof shook in Himself and He shone and sparkled from within Himself to Himself, and that shaking is called delight. From that self-delight[186] there arose the power of the estimation of the engraving, which is the Torah in potentiality. . . . The delight aroused the power of judgment and from that power there arose the measure of the engraving, as mentioned, which is the Torah in potentiality . . . the engraving is alluded to in the section of *Zohar* on Genesis: "In the beginning of the will of the King He began to engrave engravings in the supernal lustre" (*be-reish hurmanutaʾ de-malkaʾ galif gelufe bi-ṭehiru ʿillaʾah*). That is to say, in the beginning when the delight arose in His simple Will, as we said, which is the beginning of the imagining that He estimated in relation to Himself so that He would have dominion, and all dominion is from the aspect of judgment. . . . Know that from this delight there arose the engraving . . . and this engraving is the light, i.e., the Torah that is born from the delight as has been

> mentioned. Thus the estimation is in relation to Ein-Sof and the engraving is the Torah.[187]

While it is clearly the case that the Sarugian text and some of the other relevant sources embellish the zoharic myth, it is significant to stress that the fundamental notion of the primordial act of the Infinite involving sexual self-gratification that yields linguistic structures is found already in the *Zohar* and is not the innovation of later kabbalists. On the contrary, it would appear that the later complicated mythical structures are midrashic embellishments of the zoharic sources.

It may be concluded, therefore, that the zoharic authorship privileged writing over speaking as the primary act of God: inscription rather than speech is the first thing accomplished when the will to create is stirred within the uppermost recesses of the divine. It is of interest to consider in this connection one other text in which the activities of the spark are applied to the Sinaitic revelation, for in this case as well one discerns the precedence that the *Zohar* gives to the graphic over the phonetic: the Israelites saw the letters of the divine words before they heard them.[188] Commenting on the first word of the Decalogue, *ʾanokhi* (Exod. 20:2), the zoharic authorship reflects:

> Secret of secrets for those who know the wisdom. At the moment when these letters came forth in the secret that is comprised as one, the spark came forth to engrave. The measure extended ten cubits on this side, and out came seventy-one sparks within sparks, and the flames sparkled, rising and falling. Afterwards they were quieted and they rose higher and higher. It extended ten cubits on the other side, and again sparks came forth like the first time, and so it was on every side. The spark expanded, whirling round and round, and sparkling flashes rose higher and higher. The heavens blazed and all the supernal hosts blazed and sparkled as one. Then the spark turned from the side of the South, it extended and turned from there to the East, and from the East to the North, until it circled and returned to the South as in the beginning. Then the spark rotated and disappeared, sparks and flames were quieted. Then these engraved, fiery letters came forth, shining like gold when it glistens in the flames, like the smith when he purifies silver and gold, he takes them out from the burning fire, all is bright and pure. So too the letters that come out are pure and bright within the measure of the spark. Therefore it is written, "the word of the Lord is refined" (Ps. 18:21), like one who refines silver and gold. When these letters came

> out they all emerged pure, engraved, bright, sparkling and flashing, and all of Israel saw them flying through the air, going to every side, engraving themselves on the stone tablets.[189] Come and see: when these letters, in the secret that comprises male and female,[190] came forth, bright and engraved, one letter rose above them for it inscribed and engraved these letters and crowned them, and that letter went in the midst of all of them, from the secret of the spark it was engraved. That letter is the letter *waw* for it rose above all the other letters and engraved them upon everything.[191] The secret is: "All the people saw the voices and lightning and the blare of the horn" (Exod. 20:18). "The voices" (*ʾet ha-qolot*)—these are the other letters that came forth from these voices . . . and they were seen in the air by the eyes of everyone. It is written "the voices" (*ʾet ha-qolot*), and it is not written "All the people saw voices" (*we-khol ha-ʿam roʾim qolot*), but rather "the voices" (*ʾet ha-qolot*), these are the letters that come forth from them.[192] "And the blare of the horn" (*qol ha-shofar*)—this is the letter *waw* that rose above all the letters and engraved them . . . for the secret of the letter *waw* is called the "blare of the horn." Therefore it says "they saw" (*roʾim*). When they heard they heard only the voice of one word, as it is written, "You heard the sound of words (*qol devarim*)" (Deut. 4:12), that voice (*qol*) that is called words (*devarim*), for he said one word exclusively . . . *ʾAnokhi*: the secret of Remember (*zakhor*), the secret of the Male (*dekhuraʾ*) that strikes and illuminates the Speech (*dibbur*), and these letters came forth to be crowned, and they saw and heard these letters.[193]

In this passage, the event of revelation is treated as a form of emanation.[194] Just as the flashing and the protruding of the spark represents the dynamic of the emanative process, so too these activities mark the different phases of revelation. In both cases, moreover, the primary act of the spark is one of writing. More specifically, at Sinai, according to the zoharic interpretation, there were three stages: the inscription of the letters by the spark, the emergence of the voice that is identified as the letter *waw*, and the transformation of the voice into speech. The first two stages are visual, whereas the third is auditory. That is, the letters that emerged in the initial phase from the engraving spark or extending measure, as well as the letters that came forth in the second phase from the letter *waw*—also identified as the *qol ha-shofar*, the blare of the horn, or *Tifʾeret,* which is the voice that comes forth from *Binah*—were seen and not heard. Only in the last stage when the voice was transformed into speech were the letters heard as audible sounds; this occurred when the letters were concretized in the tenth of the emanations, the *Shekhinah*, which represents the logos or speech (*dibbur*) of God. The Israelites, therefore, saw the letters being engraved on the stone tablets before they heard the words of God.[195] It is significant that the spark is depicted in this passage in overtly phallic terms and its primary activity is the inscription or engraving of letters upon a material surface that assumes a feminine character.

IV

In sum, it may be concluded that underlying the theosophic symbolism, developed especially in zoharic literature, is a phallocentric understanding of writing. One would do well to recall here Derrida's critique of Lacan—and, indeed, of Western philosophy more generally—who places primary emphasis on speech (logos), which is the phallus or ultimate signifier. From the Derridean perspective there is a correlation in Western metaphysics between phallocentrism and logocentrism. If we apply these categories to theosophic kabbalah, then, we may say that primacy is given to writing over speech, but even the former is depicted in phallocentric terms. The turn to writing as the primary mode of linguistic expression of the divine over speech—God writes before he speaks—does not preclude a phallocentric orientation. The most powerful myth in zoharic kabbalah, textually placed in the beginning of the *Zohar*, which mirrors the ontic beginning of existence, involves the characterization of God begetting himself through the process of inscription that unfolds through the upper phallus etching the supernal tablet. Far from avoiding an anthropomorphic or mythical portrayal of the Infinite, the zoharic authorship boldly carries the mythos into the highest regions of the Godhead.

By extension, human writing too is endowed with sacred significance as a mode of *imitatio dei*; that is, the act of writing involves the unification of masculine and feminine achieved by the former striking against the latter. This function of writing is especially applied to the composition of kabbalistic texts that expound secret matters. The purpose of such writing is to unite the male and female aspects of the divine. The salient theurgical component here should not obscure the mystical dimension, for from the kabbalistic vantage point, writing of secrets is a decidedly phallic activity that ensues from an ecstatic state wherein the mystic is united with the feminine divine Presence. The performative nature of this theoretical issue is underscored in the following proscription extant in manuscript for the writing of a kabbalistic document dealing with the ten *sefirot*.[196] The scribe is instructed to immerse himself ritually on Friday and to don clean clothing. On the night of Sabbath he is to lie down in his bed, wearing the clean clothing and a prayer shawl, and after reciting the obligatory prayer of *Shema*ᶜ, he is to utter a special prayer directed to the first of the hypostatic emanations, *Keter*. The logic of this is made clear at the very beginning of this text where it is stated that *Keter* rules over the act of writing. It is emphasized again that the prayer must be uttered on Sabbath, for on that day the scribe is given the power and permission to write. While it is not stated explicitly, I assume that the text implies that the scribe should abstain from sexual intercourse on Friday evening, the time that is normally viewed as propitious for a man to fulfill his marital obligation. The scribe is to repeat the aforementioned ritual on Saturday evening, and then on Sunday he is to write the kabbalistic text (with an elaborate incantational introduction) on parchment prepared from deerskin and with a new writing quill. Moreover, the writing is to take place before the ark in the Synagogue prior to his having eaten. The scribe is instructed as well to cloak himself in a prayer shawl and to place the crown of the Torah scroll upon his head. The full mystical implication of this act is made clear from the verse that the scribe is instructed to recite as he places the crown upon his head: "You shall be a glorious crown in the hand of the Lord, and a royal diadem in the palm of your God" (Isa. 62:3). The coronation enacts the unification of the male scribe and the feminine Presence symbolized by the crown of the Torah scroll and alluded to in the biblical expressions "glorious crown," *ᶜaṭeret tifʾeret* (i.e., the *ᶜaṭarah* of *tifʾeret*) and "royal diadem," *ṣenif melukhah*. It is this union that empowers the scribe to write mystical secrets. Thus, after placing the crown on his head and uttering Isaiah 62:3, the scribe is instructed to recite another verse: "My heart is astir with gracious words; I speak my poem to a king; my tongue is the pen of an expert scribe" (Ps. 45:2). He then takes the writing quill in hand, utters one final supplication, and begins to write the explication of the ten *sefirot*. According to this extraordinary text, then, not only is it the case that writing kabbalistic secrets has the theurgical role of uniting the masculine and the feminine aspects of the Godhead, but rather the scribal activity itself is consequent to a unificatory experience. Having united with the Presence, depicted by the placing of the crown of the Torah scroll upon his head, the scribe can assume the position of the phallus to disclose the secrets of the divine.

As I have suggested at length elsewhere, circumcision especially expresses the phallic nature of writing, for through this ritual the letter/

sign of the covenant (*ʾot berit*) is inscribed on the flesh.[197] The incision on the penis of the infant boy is the first act of writing, which all other acts of writing emulate.[198] It is of interest to note in this context the following custom reported in the printed version of *Maḥzor Vitry*, an anthology of prayers and rituals compiled by Simḥah ben Samuel, a disciple of Rashi. The particular passage cited, however, reflects a later addition to the work:

> It is a custom that [some time] shortly after a circumcision ten [men] would gather and they would take a Pentateuch as the baby was in a crib, dressed beautifully like the day of the circumcision. They would put the book on him and say, "This one should fulfill what is written in this" . . . and they would place the inkstand and pen in his hand so that he would merit to become an excellent scribe in the Torah of the Lord.[199]

While this older custom does not have the specific gender implications that are typical of the theosophic kabbalistic sources that treat circumcision as the union of male and female, it is nevertheless of extraordinary relevance that the infant boy is given an inkstand and pen so that he may be blessed with a future career as scribe. I assume that underlying this practice was the belief that the pen corresponds to the penis. The kabbalistic authors set this parallelism within a larger ontological framework by assuming that the ritual of circumcision is itself an act of inscription upon the *membrum virile* that represents further the union of male and female elements in the divine pleroma. A later Hasidic authority, Ṣadoq ha-Kohen of Lublin, well captured the significance of the kabbalistic symbolism when he commented that "writing is in the foundation of the male, which is the pen that writes, and the foundation of the female is the paper that receives the writing."[200] R. Ṣadoq notes, moreover, that the scriptural commandment to write a Torah scroll and the extension of this mandate to commit to writing one's novel interpretations of Oral Torah constitute a rectification for sins pertaining to the penis (*tiqqun ha-yesod*). Insofar as the pen corresponds to the penis and the paper or parchment to the feminine, the act of writing is ritualized as a remedy for sexual improprieties. This is clearly an expansion of the motif expressed in earlier sources regarding the inscription of circumcision, that is, just as the rite of circumcision involves the writing of the letter of the divine name on the penis, so other acts of writing constitute a rectification for sexual sins (related principally to the penis), for they embrace the merging of male and female. Conversely, it can be said that from the kabbalistic perspective every act of sexual union is an inscription of the male upon the female—indeed in the theosophic kabbalistic tradition the seminal fluid is constituted by the Hebrew letters. Just as the corpus of the divine is made up of letters so too each human body. In its most elemental sense, therefore, the semen whence the human fetus is produced itself is made of letters. Hence, when the male inseminates the female, he is, in effect, inscribing the letters upon her.

We are now in the position to evaluate the questions raised at the outset regarding gender and kabbalistic symbolism. It should be fairly obvious that far from breaking the normal patterns of either traditional rabbinic culture or of the standard medieval society the theosophic kabbalists reinforce the general molds and relegate the feminine to a secondary role. In terms of the central motif studied here the feminine represents the material surface upon which the inscription is made. By assigning gender characteristics to the activity of writing, and by further affirming that act of writing as the primary action on the part of the Infinite, the zoharic authorship and those who follow in the path of this work (especially the sixteenth-century kabbalists) tacitly assume that the main and most basic act of God is phallocentric. This has far-reaching ramifications for the attitude that scholars should adopt with respect to the nature of the Infinite in some of the classical works of theosophic kabbalah. That is, the more rational or philosophical presentation (on occasion reflected in the kabbalistic literature itself) that would remove the issue of personality and gender from the characterization of the Ein-Sof must give way to a far more radically mythical portrait that posits an androgynous nature in the Godhead even prior to the unfolding of the multiplicity of sefirotic potencies.[201] The foundational myth of theosophic kabbalah, therefore, is predicated on the attribution of gender to the Infinite, with the masculine pole representing the most primitive of divine energies. The primal activity of the Godhead is depicted in zoharic kabbalah as the hardened spark striking, knocking, and engraving the supernal lustre or ether. In the last analysis, as I have argued in detail elsewhere,[202] for theosophic kabbalists the Godhead is a male androgyne, with the female representing an extension of the male. Despite the frequent attributions of masculine and feminine attributes to the divine, and a great emphasis placed on the holy union of the two, a careful scrutiny of the kabbalistic sources indicates that like many other medieval and renaissance thinkers, reflecting in turn philosophical and medical assumptions of Late Antiquity, the kabbalists assumed that there was a one-sex body and that that body was male.[203] To be sure, there is a fair amount of gender slippage in kabbalistic texts such that the male can become female and the female male. Yet this slippage must always be understood within a hierarchical relationship of the sexes: the weakened male is effeminized, and the strengthened female is masculinized. The kabbalistic myth of the divine androgyne therefore has to be set within an androcentric framework that informs theological, metaphysical, psychological, biological, and sociopolitical views: God is a masculine persona who comprises male and female. This conceptual assumption underlying the most basic myth of the divine androgyne is expressed in the zoharic image of the hardened spark engraving in the supernal lustre. With that originary inscription the erasure of the Infinite is erased, the nameless receives a name, and the forms of all being are etched by the (masculine) spark upon the (feminine) tablet. The full force of the myth of this process is articulated explicitly by the Lurianic kabbalists who depict the act of inscription as a moment of sexual self-arousal in the highest recess of the divine.

◆ 4 ◆

CROSSING GENDER BOUNDARIES IN KABBALISTIC RITUAL AND MYTH

Despite the acknowledged fact that the trend of medieval Jewish mysticism known as theosophic kabbalah is distinguished in the religious history of Judaism by the explicit and repeated use of gender symbolism to characterize the nature of the divine, the state of research in this area is still somewhat rudimentary. Indeed, the majority of previous studies on gender in the relevant kabbalistic literature have been marred by a conspicuous lack of sophistication. Most scholars who have written on issues relevant to this subject matter have taken for granted that the occurrence of gender images should be interpreted within a framework of what may be called a "naive biologism," i.e., the presumption that the differences between male and female are linked essentially and exclusively to biological functions. Needless to say, such an orientation fails to recognize that the latter in and of themselves are indicators of sexual but not gender differentiation. While there is obviously a correlation between biological sex and gender identity, the two are not equivalent as recent scholars in the fields of cultural anthropology and feminist psychology have emphasized. Gender identity is engendered by cultural assumptions concerning maleness and femaleness that interpret the body. In that respect we should speak of gender as a sociocultural construction that is a matter of semiology (reading cultural signs) rather than physiology (marking bodily organs). The body is a sign whose signification is determined by the ideological assumptions of a given society. There is no body without culture as there is no culture without body.[1]

In this chapter I will attempt to illuminate the role of gender in kabbalistic symbolism by exploring the phenomenon of crossing gender boundaries, the transformation of the feminine into the masculine and the masculine into the feminine. An examination of these phenomena will disclose that the theosophic myth that informed kabbalistic symbolism and ritual reflects the androcentric and patriarchical norms of medieval society in general and that of rabbinic culture more particularly. Even though the kabbalists consistently speak of the unity and perfection of God in terms of the union of masculine and feminine, the idea of ultimate wholeness or oneness is predicated on a reconstituted male androgyne.[2] The kabbalistic representation of androgyny, therefore, is that of the one male force who represents the ideal anthropos that comprises both masculine and feminine traits. Applying the mythic account of the creation of man and woman in the second chapter of Genesis to the divine, the kabbalists posit that the female is part of the male. Just as the Yahwist version of creation depicts woman, who comes from man, as secondary and derivative, so in the kabbalistic theosophic appropriation of that myth the feminine aspect of the Godhead is supplementary and ontically inferior to the masculine.[3] The privileging of the male will become evident in both forms of gender transformation discussed in this chapter.

I. On Being Male

Ontic Containment of the Feminine in the Masculine

The theoretical presumption underlying the possibility of the female becoming male is the notion that femaleness is in fact only an aspect of masculinity. The ontic inclusion of the feminine in the masculine is a recurring and fundamental motif in theosophic kabbalah from the incipient stage of its literary manifestation.[4] Consider, for example, the following description of the sefirotic pleroma:

> Therefore [the sixth emanation] is called the median line, and corresponding to it below is the Foundation (*Yesod*), which is the phallus (*berit*) and the end of the body (*sof ha-guf*). Endurance (*Neṣaḥ*) and Majesty (*Hod*) correspond to the thighs, Endurance is the right leg and Majesty the left leg. Thus you have the form of an anthropos fixed in the ten *sefirot*. . . . The Foundation is called the Righteous (*Ṣaddiq*) . . . and it corresponds to the phallus (*berit*) and it is the one that unites the secret of circumcision for it is joined to the Kingdom (*Malkhut*), which is the tenth that is the Crown (*ᶜAṭarah*). Therefore, the rabbis, blessed be their

> memory, said that the Community of Israel is the mate of Beauty (*Tif'eret*). The Crown is symbolized by the tongue, and she is this world, for she is [assigned] the governance of this world by means of the overflow that reaches her from the Foundation.[5]

The divine potencies (*sefirot*) are circumscribed within the shape of an anthropos. That the sex of that anthropos is male is obvious from the explicit reference to the penis. By contrast, no mention is made of a corresponding feminine form or even of the female genitals. The aspect of the divine that corresponds to the feminine, the tenth gradation, is linked anatomically either to the corona of the penis or to the tongue of the singular masculine form.[6]

The ontological dependence of the female on the male is expressed in a striking way in a kabbalistic commentary on the secret of illicit sexual relations (*sod ʿarayot*), which reflects the unique terminology and thought of the kabbalist Joseph of Hamadan, active in the late-thirteenth and early-fourteenth centuries:

> In the middle of a person are two orifices that separate him into two things . . . sometimes male and sometimes female. Similarly, his face and his back are two faces, the great face and the small face. Thus is God and His equanimous unity, His name and His essence are one thing, for there are two faces, the great face and the small face, *zeʿeir ʾanpin* and *rav ʾanpin*, the face that is illuminated and the face that is not illuminated, the speculum that shines and the speculum that does not shine. . . . This was the form of the cherubim, the form of male and female.[7]

It is evident from this text that the male and the female aspects of the divine, represented respectively by the technical terms "great face" and "small face," *rav ʾanpin* and *zeʿeir ʾanpin*,[8] are comprised within one anthropomorphic figure. The two faces are respectively the front and the back of that one form. Moreover, genital dimorphism is attributed not to a pair of independent organs, but rather to the two orifices found in one body.

In spite of the fact that Joseph of Hamadan's writings are replete with graphic and dramatic descriptions of the feminine persona who complements and receives the overflow from the masculine,[9] he too posited one divine form that is an androgynous male. Thus, for example, in one passage he writes:

> The secret of the letter *dalet* and [the letter] *gimmel* is one image of the body of the holy King, for the *gimmel* reveals

> the head, neck, right arm, and part of the body, [symbolized by the letter] *yod*, and the letter *dalet* the image of the whole body and the left arm. Thus the whole body is completed by these two letters. . . . The head, arms, and body are complete, but the holy legs are not revealed except in the letter *he*ʾ for it has two holy legs. And the *he*ʾ is called the Matrona.[10]

The complete body of the divine anthropos is represented by the vertical alignment of the contiguous letters *gimmel*, *dalet*, and *he*ʾ. Significantly, the feminine character, designated by the technical term *Matrona*, is located in the legs of this corporeal form. Although no mention is made of the male genitals, it is fairly obvious that the upper part of the anthropomorphic figure is masculine, referred to specifically as the "body of the holy King." The divine anthropos consists of the unity of the masculine and the feminine, but the latter is portrayed as an aspect of the former; that is, the two comprise the singular image of the body of the King.[11] The goal of the *hieros gamos* is to overcome the apparent sexual duality so that the female is reintegrated into the male.[12] Joseph of Hamadan conveys this notion in his artful interpretation of the verse, "Draw me after you, let us run! The king has brought me to his chambers. Let us delight and rejoice in your love, Savoring it more than wine—Like new wine they love you!" (Song of Songs 1:4):

> By way of kabbalah this alludes to the second cherub that corresponds to the Bride, the Community of Israel, who is perfect in all the perfections and comprises all beauty. She began to praise the bridegroom who is the King, Lord of the hosts, for everything is one, blessed be He. Concerning the one who separates these two attributes the verse says, "You shall not make for yourself a sculptured image, or any likeness" (Exod. 20:4). How is this so? Since God, blessed be He, is one, he creates a division within Him by making the attribute of Kingdom separate. It is like one who takes a stick and with his knife cuts it and makes from it two things. Therefore, the verse says, "You shall not make for yourself a sculptured image, or any likeness," [the word *pesel*, "sculptured image"] indicates that one should not cut (*yifsol*) in a place where it is not appropriate. Therefore, it is written, "You should not have other gods" (Exod. 20:3), for everything is one matter, blessed be He. . . . Thus, the Bride, the Community of Israel, says before the Bridegroom, "Draw me after you, let us

> run!"—i.e., [the meaning of] "draw me" (*mashkheni*) is spread your wings over me and cover me with skin, from the [Aramaic] word [for skin] *mashkha*ʾ, as I have alluded—"and pour forth your good anointing oil over me." "Let us delight" [the plural signifies] the Bridegroom and the Bride together. "The king has brought me to his chambers," the chambers of the nuptial canopy. "Let us delight in you," in the attribute of the *Ṣaddiq*. "Savoring it more than wine," for he pours forth the good oil.[13]

The myth of sexual coupling as it took shape within the monistic framework of kabbalistic speculation, combined with an androcentrism rooted both in classical Jewish sources and in medieval European society more generally, produced the idea well formulated by Joseph of Hamadan: the yearning of the feminine potency to receive the *semen virile* from the masculine translates theologically to the desire to avoid positing two divine powers. Idolatry, or the making of a sculptured image, is essentially the psychological tendency to reify the feminine as a distinct deity.[14] Ironically, the eroticized language of the verse from Song of Songs underscores the reintegration of the female in the male rather than affirming the ontic autonomy of the bride over and against the bridegroom.

The point is epitomized as well in the following comment in an anonymous kabbalistic text:

> These two cherubim are *Tifʾeret Yisraʾel* and his *Malkhut*, and they are two-faced (*du-parṣufim*). Concerning them it is said according to the hidden meaning (*nistar*), "Male and female He created them" (Gen. 1:27). This is the perfect human (*ha-ʾadam ha-shalem*), and the cherubim depicted in the Sanctuary were in their pattern. They were made of one hammered work[15] to indicate the perfect unity (*ha-yiḥud ha-shalem*). In their pattern Adam and Eve were created, and this is the secret of "Let us make Adam in our image and in our likeness" (Gen. 1:26). . . . You already know that these two countenances are the Written Torah and the Oral Torah, and they are one Torah for them.[16]

Just as the two cherubim of gold were made from one material substance, so too the corresponding *sefirot* above, as well as the man and woman below in the earthly sphere, derive from one ontic source, and that source is the masculine anthropos. Analogously, we can speak of a Written Torah and an Oral Torah, but in essence they are one. The union of the Written Torah and the Oral Torah is, in effect, the reintegration of the feminine in the masculine. As the anonymous author of *Sefer ha-Yiḥud* put it:

> I have already informed you that the Written Torah is the form of *Tif'eret*. . . . [W]hen a person reads the Written Torah alone and he does not merit to read the Oral Torah, concerning him it says "a querulous one alienates his friend," *we-nirggan mafrid 'alluf* (Prov. 16:28). This is like the situation of the bridegroom being in the nuptial chamber while the bride is still standing in her father's house. . . . He is like a person who has no God for he divides the one power into two powers. But the true unity is in *Tif'eret* to establish the Written Torah with the Oral Torah as one. When a person is involved with the two Torot and harmonizes them as one, then the two countenances that were turned back-to-back face one another face-to-face. . . . [T]hen all attributes of judgment disappear . . . and the white face, the face of mercy, is merciful, and the blessing is found in all the lower realities. . . . This is the true and perfect unity, and this unity depends on *Tif'eret*.[17]

The union of male and female is predicated ultimately on the absorption or containment of the left side (passive, judgmental, constraining female) in the right side (active, merciful, overflowing male).[18] Indeed, the negative valorization of the feminine in certain kabbalistic texts, especially the zoharic literature, is underscored by the fact that when the female potency is separated from the masculine the potential exists that she will evolve into a punitive or even demonic force.[19] Sexual coupling of male and female is indicative of an androgynous unity that has been fractured. In the ideal state, gender differentiation is neutralized and the female is absorbed back into the male. Reuven Ṣarfati expressed the matter as follows:

> The statement "they felt no shame" (Gen. 3:1) was before the sin because they were in the pattern of above for "in the image of God He created them,[20] male and female He created them" (Gen. 1:27). That is, as we have said, they were created in the pattern that is above. Before the fruit was separated from the tree they had no [sexual] desire at all . . . they experienced no arousal through the genitals. "Male and female He created them" in the pattern that is above. The allusion is to the androgyne (*du-parṣufim*). The moon was not yet diminished and there was none to give

> or receive for the chain was doubled in itself (*ha-shalshelet haytah kefulah be-ʿaṣmo*), that is, they were created as twins in the pattern that is above.[21]

Prior to the sin of Adam and Eve there was no sexual lust, because male and female were not separate entites. Adam and Eve were in the pattern of the androgyne above. In the ideal state there was no gender bifurcation, no distinction between that which gives and that which receives. The locus of masculinity and femininity was in the phallus, a point alluded to by the statement that the "chain was doubled in itself." The divine grade that corresponds to the male organ comprised both masculine and feminine. The task of *homo religiosus* is to restore the feminine to the masculine, to unite the two in a bond that overcomes gender differentiation by establishing the complete male who embodies masculine and feminine. Ontologically, there is only one gender in kabbalistic theosophy, for the female is part of the male. The reintegration of the feminine in the masculine facilitated by traditional religious observance mimics the ontological situation of the Godhead prior to the primordial cleft or fission of the male androgyne into a division of sexes.[22]

Androgynous Phallus and the Eclipse of the Feminine

The theological imagination of kabbalists has been completely dominated by phallocentricity. The point is epitomized in the following comment included in *collectanea* of kabbalistic exegesis, *Sḥibbolet shel Leqeṭ*, arranged by Moses Zacuto: "The essence of the Creator is *Yesod* for the *Nuqbaʾ* is only a receptacle that receives the semen that *Yesod* gives her, and she is the speculum that does not shine."[23] In no uncertain terms the author of this passage has stated that the divine nature is principally and essentially linked to *Yesod*; the feminine is but a vessel that receives the seminal drop from the phallus, and thus what is significant about her is judged exclusively from the vantage point of the phallus. The force of the phallocentric mentality on the part of the kabbalists goes even further, for according to the engendering myth of kabbalistic theosophy the locus of the feminine is the phallus. The aspect of the divine that is the ontic source of both masculinity and femininity corresponds to the male organ. The point is made quite simply in one of the first kabbalistic works to surface in twelfth-century Provence, *Sefer ha-Bahir*: in one passage we read that the letter *ṣaddi* (which stands for the *Ṣaddiq*, the righteous one who is in the position of the phallus in the divine anthropos) orthographically can be broken into a *yod* on top of a *nun*, the former symbolizing the male potency (the sign of the covenant of circumcision) and the latter the female (perhaps related to the word *neqevah*).[24] Contained within the one letter is the duality of male and female. One should speak, therefore, of an androgynous phallus. The symbolism of the bisexual phallus is operative in other bahiric passages as well, for example, in the description of both the final *nun* and the open *mem* comprising male and female.[25] One of the most interesting expressions of this motif is found in the following passage:

> Another explanation: "[I am awed, O Lord,] by Your deeds. Renew them in these years" (Hab. 3:2). To what may this be compared? To a king who has a precious stone, and it is the delight of his kingdom. In the time of his joy he embraces it and kisses it, places it upon his head and loves it. Habakuk said, even though the kings[26] are with you, that precious stone is a treasure in your world. Therefore [it says] "Renew them in these years." What is the meaning of the expression "years"? As it says, "God said, 'Let there be light' " (Gen. 1:3). There is no light but day, as it is written, "the greater light to dominate the day and the lesser light to dominate the night" (ibid., 16). The "years" are from the "days," as it is written, "Renew them in these years," in the midst of that very jewel that gives birth to the years. And it is written, "From the east I will bring forth your seed" (Isa. 43:5). The sun shines in the east. You said that the jewel is the day!? I only said, "And there was evening and there was morning, a first day" (Gen. 1:5), as it is written, "When the Lord God made earth and heaven" (ibid., 2:4).[27]

Gershom Scholem noted that in this passage, as well as in other bahiric texts, the image of the precious stone is a symbol for the *Shekhinah*, the feminine aspect of the divine. Historically, wrote Scholem, this symbolism could be explained "either as reflecting aggadic symbolism, where the Torah appears as a jewel in God's treasure and where the soul is compared to a pearl, or—equally well—as a reversion to the language of Gnosticism, where the Sophia or soul is likewise described as a gem or pearl."[28] While it is undoubtedly correct that the image of the jewel here and elsewhere serves as a symbol for the feminine potency, in this particular redactional context it is the androgynous nature of the jewel that is emphasized.[29] This is underscored by the end of the passage, which connects the image of the precious stone that gives birth to the motif of the seed coming forth from the east. From other contexts in the *Bahir* it is evident that the latter is a phallic image.[30] Hence, the introduction of this motif in this setting indicates that the masculine potency, the sun shining in the east, is paired with the feminine. Indeed, from the verses cited in the concluding part of the paragraph it is clear that all duality is removed, since the male and the female together constitute one entity that is the phallus, the precious stone that is the day comprising morning and night, a union symbolized as well by the two divine names, YHWH and Elohim. Time itself—in its double aspect of darkness and light— ensues from the androgynous phallus.[31]

The contextualization of the feminine in the phallus is considered by Joseph of Hamadan to be one of the mysteries of Torah. More specifically, this secret is linked by Joseph of Hamadan to the aggadic tradition that in the age of R. Joshua ben Levi the rainbow was not seen.[32] That is to say, in the generation of righteousness the masculine and the feminine aspects of the divine are so perfectly united that neither is seen in isolation from the other. In the final analysis, the feminine is itself part of the divine grade that corresponds to the male organ[33]: "When the supernal, holy, and pure phallus (*ha-gid ha-ᶜelyon ha-qadosh we-ha-ṭahor*) is seen in the attribute of mercy it is called the covenant (*berit*) and when it is seen in the attribute of judgment it is called the rainbow (*qeshet*)."[34] The one gradation appears either as a manifestation of the masculine mercy (the *berit*) or of the feminine judgment (the *qeshet*), but both are expressions of the divine phallus.

Many sources could be cited to illustrate the notion of the androgynous phallus in kabbalistic literature, but I would like to focus on two texts in particular for, in my view, they express succinctly the complex gender symbol that I contend is characteristic of a fundamental structure of theosophic kabbalah as it takes shape in its medieval European context. The first passage reads as follows: "The sword is the Foundation, and this is the saying of the rabbis, may their memory be for a blessing,[35] 'the fiery ever-turning sword' (Gen. 3:24), sometimes female and sometimes male."[36] The fiery sword placed at the east of Eden symbolizes the attribute of God that corresponds to the phallus, the ninth gradation, called *Yesod,* that comprises both male and female. Utilizing the rabbinic description of the fiery sword in the Garden of Eden as androgynous, the kabbalist expresses the fact that sexual duality is contextualized in the divine phallus.[37] The second citation is taken from Joseph of Hamadan reflecting on the verse, "Tell the Israelite people to bring Me gifts; you shall accept gifts for Me from every person whose heart so moves him" (Exod. 25:2):

> "To bring Me gifts," *wa-yiqḥu li terumah,* this alludes to the *Shekhinah* who is called offering (*terumah*). "From every," *me᾿et kol,* that is, the upper phallus (*berit ha-ᶜelyon*), which is the attribute of the *Ṣaddiq.* This is the attribute of

> the All (*middat ha-kol*) and it is called "man" (*ʾish*). From him "you shall accept gifts for Me," *mimenu tiqḥu ʾet terumati*, they took two attributes, *Ṣaddiq* and the attribute of *Malkhut*, the secret of the two cherubim. From him "you shall accept gifts for Me." Until here is the explanation of the verse in the way of kabbalah.[38]

Significantly, this passage follows a discourse on the verse, "Let him kiss me with the kisses of his mouth" (Song of Songs 1:2), which is interpreted as a depiction of the erotic yearning of the second cherub, the female *Malkhut*, to unite with the first cherub, the male *Yesod*. Immediately after giving expression to the rich drama of the bisexual myth, the kabbalist articulates the ontological principle that circumscribes this myth: the female is taken from the supernal phallus.

To put the matter in slightly different terms, the kabbalistic texts offer another example of a one-sex theory that is well documented in classical, medieval, and Renaissance sources: the feminine is but an extension of the masculine.[39] The practical religious implications of this ontology are perhaps felt nowhere more sharply than in kabbalistic accounts of the rite of circumcision, a theme that I have discussed before but to which my path keeps returning.[40] For example, according to an anonymous thirteenth-century kabbalistic text, circumcision "alludes to the perfect unity, and the matter of the androgyne (*du-parṣufim*) is explained in it; examine and discover with respect to the exposure of the corona."[41] The corona of the penis symbolically corresponds to the feminine *Shekhinah*, a correlation facilitated by the fact that the word *ʿaṭarah*, "crown," is the technical name of the corona as well as one of the designations of the *Shekhinah*.[42] Insofar as the male organ is the ontic source of both masculine and feminine, the religious significance of circumcision lies in the fact that by means of this ritual the androgynous unity of God is established.[43] Judged from the human vantage point, this rite affords one the opportunity to gain access to the two aspects of the divine. The matter is spelled out more clearly in the secret of circumcision by Joseph Gikatilla:

> The secret of the covenant is the corona (*ʿaṭarah*), in the mystery of the glorious crown (*ʿaṭeret tifʾeret*). When a person is circumcised and enters into the secret of the holy covenant (*berit ha-qodesh*), he enters the two gradations that are one unity (*ḥibbur ʾeḥad*), the Crown (*ʿaṭeret*) and the Eternally Living One (*ḥei ha-ʿolamim*), the secret of the All. Everything is one unity. Therefore the [foreskin] is cut and [the membrane] pulled back, for these two matters are one.[44]

Within the symbolic representation of theosophic kabbalah the feminine is localized in the male's reproductive organ. I am not saying that kabbalists are not cognizant of the obvious fact that men and women are biologically distinguished by their genitals. It is the case, moreover, that the divine feminine is described, albeit rarely, in terms of her own genitals in contradistinction to the penis. The physiological differentiation between the sexes below is thus applied to the divine hypostases above. The point I am making, however, concerns the gender valorization of the feminine over and against the masculine and not the issue of sexual differences linked to the body. The overwhelming evidence, in my opinion, indicates that from the perspective of gender the feminine is ontologically localized in the masculine. To illustrate my claim, let me mention one zoharic passage that says explicitly that the sign of the covenant (the penis) is that which distinguishes the male from the female.[45] Precisely in that context, however, the zoharic authorship makes the point that the female is taken from the male and hence must be restored to the masculine. The symbol of reconstituted masculinity is the *ᶜolah,* the burnt offering that is said "to rise from the feminine [*Shekhinah*] to the masculine [*Yesod*], and from that place and above everything is masculine, and from the feminine and below everything is feminine."[46] In this context the zoharic authorship clearly recognizes the distinction between the upper "world of the masculine" (*ᶜalma᾽ di-dekhura᾽, ᶜolam ha-zakhar*) from *Binah* to *Yesod* and the lower "world of the feminine" (*ᶜalma᾽ de-nuqba᾽, ᶜolam ha-neqevah*) that comprises the *Shekhinah* and her angelic forces.[47] Both worlds are configured in the shape of an anthropos, but in the case of the former, the head is feminine and the end of the body (*siyyuma᾽ de-gufa᾽*, i.e, the genitals) masculine, whereas with respect to the latter, the head and end are feminine. It is noteworthy that even in this passage, where the sexual differentiation between *Shekhinah* and the upper sefirotic potencies is clearly enunciated, the *Zohar* still describes the process by means of which the feminine is restored or elevated to the masculine. That the female is only a relative male is affirmed in the continuation of this passage where an explanation is offered for why Ephraim takes the place of Joseph in the enumeration of the twelve tribes. Since the tribes represent the adornments of the *Shekhinah,* which are feminine, it was necessary for Joseph, the male potency *par excellence,* to be removed. But in what sense is his substitute, Ephraim, more feminine than Joseph? Clearly not in a biological sense. It must be the case rather that Ephraim assumes a feminine character insofar as he symbolically represents the *Shekhinah.* This symbolic representation, I submit, implies the (relative) masculine status of the *Shekhinah* rather than the feminine status of the biblical figure.

Even in those passages that treat the female as something distinct from the male, the phallocentric orientation is evident, for the feminine is portrayed as a receptacle that conceals the penis[48] or receives the seed from the male.[49] From this vantage point the male is contained in the female. The nature of the containment, however, is fundamentally different in this case than in the containment of the feminine in the masculine. In the latter instance, the containment signifies the absorption of that which is contained (female) in that which contains (male), whereas in the former that which is contained (male) transforms the nature of that which contains (female). The female receptacle provides the space in which the male organ extends. Theosophically, the female containing the male is the secret of the spatial dwelling of the divine, the garment in which the glory is clothed. Space in general, and sacred space in particular, partakes of the symbolic nexus of building, dwelling, and presencing, a mystery boldly described by Joseph of Hamadan:

> The matter of the Tabernacle concerning which the Torah said, "On the first of the month, the Tabernacle was set up" (Exod. 40:17). This signifies that another Tabernacle was set up together with it.[50] This alludes to the image of the chariot, for it is precisely the image of the holy, pure, supernal chariot. Therefore, the Holy One, blessed be He, said to Moses, our master: "Tell the Israelite people to bring Me gifts" (Exod. 25:2), that is, to your God. Let them make a body and a soul and I will assume bodily form in it (*ʾetgashem bo*). "To bring Me," they took My Torah. They took the image of My chariot and I too "shall take," that is, I will be garbed in the Tabernacle.[51]

The Tabernacle below is in the pattern of the Tabernacle or chariot above, i.e., the feminine Presence. The religious purpose of the Tabernacle is to provide a dwelling in which the divine takes shape. In this kabbalistic version of incarnation, the phenomenon of sacred space is valorized as the female axis of divinity. The role assigned to the female is to house or clothe the masculine. The gender of femininity is valued as the clearing where the male organ is manifest.

It may be concluded, therefore, that the experience of genderedness imparted by the mythic symbols of kabbalistic theosophy is such that the feminine is judged exclusively from the vantage point of the phallus.[52] This is a far-reaching claim that has major implications for a proper understanding of the use of masculine and feminine images to characterize the divine in theosophical kabbalah. On the surface kabbalistic texts abound with male and female representations of

God, and one might be tempted to find in them the roots for religious and/or social egalitarianism. The task, however, is to penetrate beneath the surface so that one may appreciate the gender images in their proper historical and cultural light. When that is done it becomes fairly obvious that the gender imagery operative in kabbalistic thought is thoroughly androcentric.

Scholem's attempt to contrast the kabbalistic viewpoint with that of the encratist tendency of ancient Gnosticism on the grounds that the former involves the conjunction of male and female as opposed to the latter, which advocates the overcoming of sexual differentiation by re-establishing an original androgynous state, is ultimately flawed.[53] A more nuanced understanding of gender in the kabbalistic sources does not warrant such a distinction. On the contrary, the goal of gnosis expressed in the Gnostic source mentioned by Scholem, the *Gospel of Thomas*, to "make the female male,"[54] is indeed an entirely appropriate slogan for the kabbalists. The union of God is predicated on the unity of male and female, but that unity is determined further by reintegrating the female in the male such that the primary male androgyne is reconstituted. Gender imagery in the kabbalistic sources reflects the binary ideology of the general medieval culture, as well as the specific rabbinic society, that reinforced the division of the sexes along hierarchical lines, delegating to the female a subservient role. The male is valorized as the active, dominant, primary sex and the female the passive, dominated, and secondary one.[55] Gendered differences are transcended when the female divests herself of her essential femininity, when she becomes part of the male, since the latter embodies the generic anthropos and hence represents the most basic elemental force of the divine. The female is described as being contained in rather than containing the male. While it is certainly the case that the kabbalists emphasize time and again that the complete anthropos comprises masculine and feminine, and indeed the messianic era is understood precisely in terms of the erotic union of the male and the female aspects of the divine—the "secret of faith"[56] or the "perfection of everything"[57]—the nature of the feminine is such that this union entails the overcoming of the femaleness of the female. Redemption is a state wherein male and female are conjoined, but in that union the female is enfolded back into the male whence she derived.[58] The point is underscored in the following comment of the disciple of Isaac Luria, Moses Yonah, in his *Kanfe Yonah*:

> You already know the pearl in the mouth of the kabbalists concerning [the verse] "From my flesh I shall see God" (Job 19:26). And the rabbis, blessed be their memory, already

> said,[59] It is the way of he who has lost something to search and look for that which he has lost, and it is the way of the man to go after the woman. For this reason the essence of the union, that is, the essence of the arousal to have sexual union and to illustrate love is from the side of the male.[60]

The significant aspect of this kabbalistic appropriation of the talmudic dictum is the opening citation from Job. This suggests that the feminine is part of the phallus, and thus sexual copulation is a means to restore the unity of the male organ. Scholem's distinction between the conjunction of male and female and the re-establishment of a primordial androgyne cannot be upheld.

Coitus as the Masculinization of the Female

When the complex theosophic discourse is applied to the anthropological sphere, it is evident that here too it is the task of the female to become male, especially through sexual union.[61] It is no doubt true that the kabbalistic interpretation of human sexuality is based on the assumption that the relationship between male and female below mirrors the relationship of the masculine and the feminine potencies above.[62] As in the case of the kabbalistic understanding of rituals more generally, in the particular case of sexuality, this mirroring is not merely passive but is predicated rather on the notion that the acts below affect and have an impact on the corresponding realities in the divine realm. By means of carnal intercourse, therefore, the union of a man and his wife assists in the unification of the male and the female aspects of God, especially the sixth and the tenth emanations. A typical expression of this idea is found in the following zoharic text:

> The Holy One, blessed be He, praises the Community of Israel and the love of the Holy One, blessed be He, is [directed] towards her to join her. Therefore, the one who is married must praise the Holy One, blessed be He. It has been taught . . . when a man cleaves to his mate and his desire is to receive her, he worships before the holy King and arouses another union, for the desire of the Holy One, blessed be He, is to cleave to the Community of Israel. The Holy One, blessed be He, blesses the one who arouses this matter and the Community of Israel blesses him.[63]

Despite the overt affirmation of heterosexual intercourse between a man and his wife as a sacral *imitatio dei*, it can be shown from at least two vantage points that in the kabbalistic worldview carnal coupling must be judged from a purely androcentric perspective.[64] In the first instance, it is evident that the union of male and female is intended to augment the divine image in the world through procreation.[65] This divine image, however, corresponds to the phallus. Simply put, through conjugal intercourse the woman provides the vehicle by which man extends his phallus.[66] The point is made with particular poignancy in the following zoharic passage:

> On account of the holy soul in a person he must augment the image of the supernal King in this world.[67] This secret is that the waters of the river that flows and comes forth never stop. Therefore, the river and source of a person should never stop in this world. The river alludes to the holy covenant sealed in his flesh, which is in the pattern of that river, an allusion to the [masculine] *Ṣaddiq* who is joined to [the feminine] *Ṣedeq* as one above. Therefore, below a man should unite with his wife in holiness in order to be strengthened through her in this world. Whenever a man is not successful in this world, the Holy One, blessed be He, uproots him and plants him several times as before.[68]

The end of the passage provides the key to the text as a whole: the purpose of sexual union is to produce offspring, so that the man does not have to endure the punishment of transmigration of the soul.[69] The sexual act reflects the union above of the ninth and tenth emanations, *Ṣaddiq* and *Ṣedeq*, the man corresponding to the former and the woman to the latter. The ultimate goal of this union, however, is the extension and augmentation of the divine image in the world through reproduction.[70] As Moses de León plainly states in one of his Hebrew theosophic writings: "Therefore, he who fears his Creator should take a wife and have children from her, to extend his form so that he can enter the palace. You already know that regarding the one who does not have a child in this world, his image is cut off from the image of the All (*temunat ha-kol*)[71] and he does not enter the palace."[72]

From yet another perspective the kabbalistic understanding of sexual intercourse has to be seen as rooted in a cultural androcentrism: the carnal union of masculine and feminine obliterates the essential femaleness of the female insofar as the feminine left is contained in and transformed by the masculine right or, in terms of another metaphor used in the *Zohar*, the feminine judgment is sweetened by the masculine mercy as a result of sexual copulation.[73] I have already alluded to this facet of the kabbalistic understanding of sexuality, but it is necessary to explore it at this juncture in more detail. Let us consider the following zoharic text:

> The feminine extends in her side and cleaves to the sides of the male until she is separated from his sides and she comes to join with him face-to-face. When they are joined they appear as one actual body. From here we learn that a man alone appears as half a body, and he is entirely mercy, and similarly the woman.[74] When they are joined as one, everything appears as one actual body. Thus, when the male joins with the female, everything is one body, and all the worlds are in joy for they are all blessed from the complete body.[75]

The relationship of man and woman below reflects that of the male and female aspects of the sefirotic pleroma, respectively the sixth and tenth emanations. Just as the divine male and female together form one complete body, the male half representing the attribute of mercy and the female half the attribute of judgment, so too in the case of human beings. In the continuation of the above passage, the zoharic authorship emphatically affirms man's ontic status as comprising both male and female, the latter contained in the former. The ontically inferior and derivative status of the feminine is alluded to in the statement that "the beauty of the woman is entirely from the beauty of the male."[76] The overriding theological purpose of sexual intercourse is to ameliorate divine judgment by mercy, which translates in gender terms to the masculinization of the feminine. The transformation of the female into male, ensuing from sexual copulation, is affirmed explicitly in one text as follows: "R. Yose said, Thus have I heard from the holy lamp [i.e., R. Simeon bar Yoḥai]: When [the male and female forces] are united to show that the female is contained in him as one entity, the female is called by the name of the male, for then the blessings of the Matrona are found and there is no separation in her at all."[77] The matter is expressed in another zoharic passage as follows:

> R. Eleazar was standing before R. Simeon, his father. He said to him, It is written, "Enjoy happiness with a woman you love all the fleeting days of life" (Eccl. 9:9). He said to him, Come and see: "Enjoy happiness with a woman you love," this is a great secret, for a person must comprise life in this place,[78] the one without the other does not go, and a person must contain the attribute of the day in the night and the attribute of the night in the day.[79] This is [the meaning of] "Enjoy happiness with a woman you love." What is the reason? For this is your portion in life, for life does not dwell except upon this.[80]

Man's task in conjugal union is to combine the masculine and the feminine. Yet, a careful reading of the above passage, and others in which the same theme is addressed, indicates that the issue is the containment of the female in the male. Hence, in the continuation of the passage it is emphasized that the left is contained in the right[81] so that "everything that a person does should be contained in the right."[82] The point is reiterated in another passage: "Come and see: R. Eleazar said, every woman is characterized as judgment until she tastes the taste of mercy, as it has been taught: from the side of the man comes white and from the side of the woman comes red. When the woman tastes some of the white, the white dominates."[83] It is evident that in this context the image of tasting is a metaphorical expression for sexual intercourse.[84] The union of man and woman results in the transformation of the feminine into the masculine, the overpowering of the red of judgment by the white of mercy, the containment of the left in the right. The point is made explicitly by Joseph of Hamadan as well: "The pure and holy overflow and the good oil descends upon the attribute of the *Shekhinah* in the pure and holy chain (*shalshelet ha-qedoshah we-ha-ṭehorah*).[85] Therefore it is written, 'We will add wreaths of gold to your spangles of silver' (Song of Songs 1:11), so that the judgment [symbolized by the gold] will be mixed with mercy [the silver], and it is one thing like the flame bound to the coal that is unified in its colors. Everything becomes one."[86]

In the final analysis, the affirmation in theosophic kabbalistic sources of sexual mating sanctioned by marriage did not imply metaphysical or social equality between the sexes. The literary evidence proves just the opposite: the positive valorization of human sexuality must be interpreted within a social framework that is thoroughly androcentric.[87] The point is epitomized in the late-thirteenth-century treatise on marital relations, the ʾ*Iggeret ha-Qodesh* (The Holy Epistle).[88] According to this text, both man and woman are assigned specific intentions during coitus that help determine the character of the offspring: the task of the man is to be mentally bound to the upper realm so that he can draw down the efflux of divine light onto the *semen virile*, whereas the task of the woman is to synchronize her thoughts with her male partner. Although the language of this text does not explicitly affirm the transformation of the female into a male, it is evident that the role of the woman is to become integrated in the man, so that she gains indirect access to the divine realm. While the male directly contemplates the sefirotic entities and is thereby conjoined with them, the female can hope to form a mental image of her male partner and thereby assist in the shaping of the fetus. The intention (*kawwanah*) of the woman is entirely directed towards and subsumed under the male.[89] To be sure, the man and the woman are said to correspond respectively to the divine hypostases of *Ḥokhmah*, Wisdom, and *Binah*, Understanding (and the offspring they produce corresponds to *Da ͨat*, Knowledge, representing the union of the two). This symbolic correspondence, however, does not signify the attribution of an equal social role to the earthly man and woman.[90] On the contrary, primary emphasis is placed on the man, whose intentions and thoughts produce and determine the nature of the semen. The goal is for the man to harmonize his intention with that of his wife so that she produces the seed first and, following the rabbinic dictum,[91] gives birth to a male.[92] The logical implication is drawn explicitly by the anonymous author of this kabbalistic work, commenting on the statement in B. Berakhot 20a concerning R. Yoḥanan's sitting by the bathhouses so that the women exiting from ritual immersion could look at his face and be blessed with offspring as beautiful as he: "Thus with the key that we have placed in your hand you can understand the action of that pious one who would sit at the gates of the bathhouses so that the thought [of the women] would cleave to his form, and his form would cleave to the supernal entities."[93]

Expressed in slightly different terms, the androcentric perspective is evident as well in the following zoharic passage:

> When is a man called one? When there is male and female, and he is sanctified in the supernal holiness and he has the intention to be sanctified. Come and see: when a man is in the union of male and female, and he intends to be sanctified as is appropriate, then he is complete and he is called one without any blemish. Therefore, a man should gladden his wife at that time, to invite her to be of one will with him. The two of them together should have the same intention for that matter. When the two are found as one, then they are one in soul and body.[94]

The intent of the female must be synchronized with that of the male so that the male will be unified and completed by her participation and cooperation in the sexual act. As a result of the sexual union, the woman may be impregnated and hence empowered to procreate. Through the process of reproduction the femaleness of the woman is transformed into maleness since she becomes an active potency that gives birth.[95] The point is underscored in one zoharic passage that describes the *Shekhinah*, on the basis of Ecclesiastes 5:8, as the king who dwells upon a house inhabited by a man who unites with his wife in order to procreate. In her capacity as the active power that gives birth to the souls that are joined to the body produced by the union of a husband and wife, the feminine *Shekhinah* is masculinized.[96] One may assume that this gender transformation applies as well to the earthly female when she gives birth.

In support of my last claim, I cite a passage that conveys the idea that the transformation from femaleness to maleness represents the ideal movement for the earthly woman during intercourse, emulating thereby the progession in the divine realm. The text is an anonymous kabbalistic exposition on the commandment of levirate marriage, *sod ha-yibbum*, whose provenance, I surmise, is thirteenth-century Catalonia:

> It is written in *Sefer ha-Bahir*[97] that the Holy One, blessed be He, created seven holy forms, and the forms are divided into two hands, two legs, a head and the body. Thus there are six, and these six [are male]. [It is written] "male and female He created them" (Gen. 1:26) . . . the seventh form is the female. Thus the woman completes the seven forms. When the Holy One, blessed be He, created Adam, He combined all seven forms together, and afterward He separated the seventh so that the woman would be the seventh form of the man, and the man is not complete without her, as it is written, "it is not good for man to be alone,"[98] and it is written, "they will be as one flesh."[99] . . . Just as Sabbath is rest for the six days so too the woman is rest for the six forms, for without her a man is not stationary, he wanders to and fro. As the rabbis, blessed be their memory, said, "the one who dwells without a wife dwells without goodness."[100] And this is what the rabbis, blessed be their memory, said, "a person is not exempt from [the commandment] to procreate until he has a boy and a girl,"[101] so that what is born to him corresponds to the seven forms. This is also what they alluded to by the fact that a man and not a woman is commanded with respect to procreation, for most of the forms and their essence are in the male, and the woman is but the completion. This is [the intent of] what the rabbis, blessed be their memory, said, "a woman who produces seed first gives birth to a male," for the seed of the man, in which there are the six forms, annuls the seed of the woman which has but one form. The male comes by way of the male and the female by the power of the female.[102]

The feminine potency is here portrayed as the seventh form that completes or perfects the other six. That this completion involves the female being reintegrated into the male is obvious from the examples adduced in the realm of human relationships. The lack of autonomy of the feminine is underscored in the continuation of the text that elaborates on the biblical law that the male child and not the female inherits the property of the father. It is most significant that the woman is depicted as the vehicle that allows the man to produce offspring. While the talmudic opinion that a man fulfills his obligation of procreation by having a child of each sex is theosophically reinterpreted,[103] it is clear from the end of the passage that having male children is privileged for the female ontically is only the completion of the masculine. Indeed, conjugal intercourse replicates the structure above: the seminal fluid symbolizes the six male forms and the vaginal secretion the seventh female form. Following the rabbinic view, which in turn reflects the Hippocratic and Galenic standpoint,[104] conception requires the mixing of two seeds, but the desired situation involves the domination and the superiority of the male so that a male child is conceived. By secreting her fluids first the woman allows the sperm of the man to dominate, and thus the embryo that is conceived is male. Through the production of male progeny the woman's task to complete the male structure is accomplished.

Masculine Transvaluation of Motherhood: The Phallic Womb

By giving birth in general, and to male offspring in particular, the female assumes the role of the engendering male. Although pregnancy and childbirth are generally thought to be the exclusive burden (perhaps even curse) of the woman, following the explicit claim of Genesis 3:16, in kabbalistic literature they are valorized as positive, masculine traits. The biological woman assumes the male gender through these bodily functions. The point is alluded to in the following zoharic text: "R. Yose said: from the time a woman gets pregnant until the day she gives birth there is nothing in her mouth but that her child should be a male. Thus it says, 'When a woman brings forth seed and bears a male' (Lev. 12:2)."[105] The intention of the woman expressed verbally to bear a male child has the effect of masculinizing her so that she produces seed like a man and gives birth to a boy. According to the zoharic exegesis, the bringing forth of the male seed on the part of the woman is accomplished through the orifice of the mouth, which corresponds to the procreative organ of the male, a parallelism that is a foundational structure in Jewish esotericism. By uttering her desire to have a boy the woman takes the place of a male who procreates.

Still other zoharic sources indicate that the female who gives birth is depicted as male. In his discussion of the feminine element of divinity in kabbalistic symbolism, Scholem noted that one must distinguish between two aspects of femininity—corresponding to the upper and lower *Shekhinah*—the active energy and creative power, on the one hand, and the passive receptivity, on the other. The former is associated more specifically with the image of the "upper mother," the third gradation or *Binah,* and the latter with the "lower mother," the tenth gradation or *Malkhut.*[106] Scholem comes close to realizing the complex inversion of gender that this symbolism presupposes when he remarks that the "male symbol" of the Creator or Demiurge (applied to *Binah*) "represents that aspect of the feminine that is in principle denied to the lower *Shekhinah.*"[107] Analogously, Scholem remarks that "when the *Shekhinah* functions as a medium for the downward flow of life-giving energies, it is understood in male symbols."[108] In spite of these momentary insights, however, Scholem's analysis in general (as that of most other scholars who have written on the subject) suffers from a lack of attentiveness to the dynamic of gender metamorphosis. That is, he too readily describes the symbolic valence of motherhood as a feminine trait, assuming that the biological function reflects the meaning of the theosophic symbol. Thus, when describing the active forces of the *Shekhinah,* Scholem speaks of the "maternal, birth-giving, and creative element that comes about as a result of the very act of receiving." The dual role of giving and receiving is designated by Scholem as the "dialectics of femininity."[109] In my view, the idea of motherhood in kabbalistic symbolism is decidedly masculine, for the womb that gives birth is valorized as an erectile and elongated phallus.[110] One would do better, therefore, to refer to the creative and maternal element of the female as the transvaluation of the feminine into the masculine.[111]

In light of this gender transformation one can appreciate the active characterization of the divine gradation that corresponds to the upper mother. Indeed, as noted above, in zoharic literature and other texts influenced by it, *Binah,* the feminine counterpart to the second emanation, *Ḥokhmah,* is called the "world of the masculine" (*ʿalma ʾ di-dekhura ʾ*) as opposed to the lower *Shekhinah,* which is called the "world of the feminine" (*ʿalma ʾ de-nuqba ʾ*), for *Binah* is the womb from which the other emanations that constitute the divine anthropos derive. Many of the images and symbols that are employed in the *Zohar* and related sources to depict the ninth gradation, *Yesod,* which corresponds to the divine phallus, are used as well in relation to *Binah,* the gradation that is referred to as the mother or the womb that receives the seed from *Ḥokhmah,* the father. To be sure, the attribute of *Binah* is empowered to give birth by virtue of the semen that she receives from *Ḥokhmah,* but that reception transforms her phallically into a spring that overflows. As Moses de Léon in one of his writings expresses the matter: "She is called *Binah* when the concealed Thought emanates, and this is the source of life, for from there is the issue of life, for the secret of the Mother, the supernal well, hidden in her secret and her character, the hidden world, the concealment of his strength."[112] The archetype of the mother, *Binah,* is here portrayed as simultaneously concealing the masculine strength (i.e., the phallus) and revealing it in the overflow that issues forth from her. The dialectic of hiddenness and disclosure, passive receptivity (symbolized by the image of the well) and active creativity (symbolized by the image of the source of life), characterizes the lower feminine, *Malkhut,* as well in relation to *Yesod.* To cite again Moses de León, who succinctly conveys the point: "When the holy sign is revealed it overflows and the perfect bride, [of whom it is said] 'the glory of the princess that is inward' (Ps. 45:14), stands in her completeness and illuminates her portion."[113] The feminine can be productive only to the extent that she receives the overflow from the masculine and is thereby transformed from a passive receptacle to an active agent. The gender metamorphosis is epitomized in the mystical interpretation of Noah's entry into the ark: "When the Righteous joins the ark then all the beings issue forth to be established and the souls fly out from there. When everything comes forth from the ark . . . by means of the power of the Righteous, there is existence for all the beings that issue forth from the ark by the power of the covenant of the living Righteous."[114] The uterus that contains the fecundating phallus is transformed thereby into an instrument of the male principle.

The phallic nature of *Binah* is underscored in a striking way in the following comment of Isaac of Acre (active in the early part of the fourteenth century) on the passage in *Sefer Yeṣirah* that speaks of the covenant of unity set in the middle of the ten *sefirot* corresponding to the mouth or tongue that is set in the middle of the ten fingers and the penis that is set between the ten toes:

> All the functioning limbs are in pairs except for the mouth and the penis. . . . These two are single to inform you that even though you find opposites in the world you should not say that they could not derive from a simple thing, for you already see that the mouth is one and it comes from another, and similarly the penis is an opening to bring forth the semen but it is one. Corresponding to the penis in a man is the *sefirah* called *Yesod* for from there the souls emerge, and *Binah* corresponds to the mouth in a man for from it comes forth the issue of life. The two of them corre-

> spond to one another. The two of them are called *Shekhinah,* the upper one *Binah* and the lower one *Malkhut. Yesod* and *Malkhut* are bound together, and *Binah* is the tongue . . . *Yesod* is the penis and it is called *qeshet* for it throws with strength and vigor below. . . . He who sins with respect to these two is called one who "alienates his friend," *mafrid ʾalluf* (Prov. 16:28) or cuts the shoots, *meqaṣṣeṣ bi-neṭiʿot,*[115] for he separates (*mafrid*) *Yesod* from *Malkhut* or *Binah* who is the "mother of the children" (Ps. 113:9). *Binah* is called *yod-heʾ* and *Yesod* is *waw-heʾ*, and the one who creates a division in *Binah* is called *ʿeryah,* and the secret is "All bared and ready is your bow," *ʿeryah teʿor qashtekha* (Hab. 3:9), and the one who creates a division in *Yesod* is called *ʿervah.*[116] The *sefirah* of *Yesod* binds together the upper *Shekhinah* and the lower one, and similarly the tongue is the bond of love through speech between a man and his wife or between two lovers. Therefore lovers kiss one another through their mouths.[117]

The union of the Godhead, represented by the Tetragrammaton, depends upon the binding of *Binah* (signified by the first two letters of the name) and *Yesod* (signified by the last two letters), which correspond respectively to the orifice of the mouth above and the penis below. The structural and functional homology between the two is disrupted when they are separated, an act that is compared to the uncovering of the genitals. Moreover, just as *Yesod* is bound to *Binah,* so too is it bound to *Shekhinah,* upon which it overflows like the penis that discharges semen. Interestingly enough, however, the heterosexual imagery of the kiss used at the end of the citation depicts symbolically the union of *Binah* and *Malkhut* rather than *Yesod* and *Malkhut.* The bond of love between the upper and the lower *Shekhinah* is secured by the tongue of speech that corresponds to the phallic *Yesod.*

In the zoharic corpus too the very concept of motherhood is shaped by the parallelism set between the divine grades of *Binah* and *Yesod.* Thus, for instance, another designation of *Binah* in zoharic literature is the "concealed world" (*ʿalmaʾ de-itkkaseyaʾ*, corresponding to *ʿolam ha-nistar* in Moses de León's Hebrew writings), a term that relates specifically to the character of *Binah,* the divine mother, as that which encompasses and encloses her offspring.[118] The aspect of concealment, frequently associated with the phallic *Yesod,* is linked to the image of *Binah* as the mother who sits upon her children.[119] The masculine element is especially highlighted in those contexts where the image of the mother hovering over her children is combined with that of the mother nursing her babies.[120] Breast-feeding too is valorized as a phallic activity (the milk obviously taking the place of the semen) insofar as anything that sustains by overflowing is automatically treated as an aspect of the phallus.[121] The point is underscored in one zoharic passage that reflects on the word *ʾeḥad* in *shemaʿ yisraʾel yhwh ʾelohenu yhwh ʾeḥad,* "Hear, O Israel, the Lord is our God, the Lord is one" (Deut. 6:4). In line with earlier kabbalistic sources,[122] the zoharic authorship interprets the three letters of this word as a reference to the ten *sefirot;* the *ʾalef* corresponds to the first *sefirah, Keter,* the letter *ḥet* the eight *sefirot* from *Ḥokhmah* to *Yesod,* and the *dalet* the *Shekhinah,* who is the impoverished (*dal*) emanation. According to the masoretic orthography, however, this *dalet* is enlarged, which theosophically signifies that the *Shekhinah* cleaves to the upper gradations. In this state the *Shekhinah* is "augmented and all the world suckles from her, and the breasts 'were like towers, so I became in his eyes as one who finds favor' (Song of Songs 8:10)."[123] The *Zohar* contrasts the existential situation of the *Shekhinah* in exile and in a state of blessing and augmentation: the first instance is depicted by the verse, "We have a little sister, whose breasts are not yet formed" (Song of Songs 8:8), whereas the latter is conveyed in the aforecited verse, "My breasts are like towers, so I became in his eyes as one who finds favor" (ibid., 10). The maturation of the *Shekhinah* from a woman without breasts to one with full-grown breasts in effect symbolizes her gender transformation from a female to a male.[124] Thus the breasts are described in the obvious phallic image of a tower from which all beings are sustained.[125] The phallic function of the breasts is alluded to as well in the expression, "as one who finds favor," (*ke-moṣʾet shalom;* the term *shalom* serving in zoharic literature as in other kabbalistic compositions as one of the designations for the divine phallus).

The motherly quality of brooding over the offspring is also connected with the concept of *teshuvah,* "return." That is, the emanations are in stationary position in relation to their source.[126] This too is the theosophic symbolism of Yom Kippur, the Day of Atonement; on that day all things return to their ontic source to be sustained by the overflow of the primal concealment. Thus, on that day there is an aspect of disclosure, for the fifty gates of *Binah* open up to every side, but there is also an aspect of concealment, for the Mother remains covered and hidden. The latter motif is connected with the prohibition of uncovering the nakedness of the father and the mother (Lev. 18:7), the precise Torah portion that is read in the afternoon service of Yom Kippur.[127] In a profound inversion of symbolism, the concealment of the Mother enables her to sustain her offspring, and in that act of nourishing she is masculinized. Theosophically interpreted, the sin of disclosing the genitals of the mother creates a blemish above that separates the Mother from her children; repentance is, quite literally, causing the Mother to return to her place where she continues to assume the masculine role of feeding and sustaining the offspring in a manner that is concealed.[128] When the Mother and children are united, the genitals are covered, and the children nurse from her in a pattern that resembles the primary opening of the womb through the attribute of mercy. By contrast, when the Mother and children are separated, the genitals are uncovered and the attribute of judgment dominates.[129]

That the divine Mother is described in the same or proximate terms used to describe the phallus indicates that the female who gives birth is valorized as a male, for the act of birthing is treated as a form of expansion or ejaculation that is characteristically masculine.[130] The act of procreation is decidedly phallic. Hence, the tenth of the emanations, the *Shekhinah,* which is characterized as feminine vis-à-vis the upper emanations, is masculine in relation to what is beneath her, and indeed is referred to frequently as *Malkhut* on account of this procreative quality.[131] According to one text in the *Zohar,* interpreting the verse, "Drink water from your cistern, running water from your own well" (Prov. 5:15), when the *Shekhinah* receives the influx from the upper masculine divine potencies she is transformed from an empty cistern (*bor*) that has nothing of its own into a well (*be'er*) that is full and overflows to every side: the impoverished *dalet* becomes an open *he'*.[132] In the aspect of overflowing, the queen becomes king and the open womb symbolically assumes the role of a phallus; thus one of the most common and influential symbols of the feminine Presence is King David. The appropriateness of this symbol is not due to a feminization of David, but rather the masculinization of the *Shekhinah.*[133] It is in light of this masculine quality, moreover, that the *Shekhinah* too is called "mother," or to be more precise, the "lower mother" in relation to *Binah,* the archetypal image of the great mother. To cite one textual illustration: "From this Female are united all those that are below, they are sustained from her and to her they return, and she is called the mother of them all."[134] The concept of motherhood is predicated on the quality of overflowing and sustaining. In relation to the world, then, the *Shekhinah* assumes male characteristics and is thus depicted as a mother. "The upper world of the masculine is bound to the lower one, which is the world of the feminine, and the lower is bound to the upper, and the one is like the other. It is said that there are two worlds . . . and even though the two are feminine one is adorned as a male and the other as a female. . . . The one is a mother and the other is a mother. One is called the 'mother of the children' (Ps. 113:9) and the other is called the 'mother of Solomon.' "[135]

In this connection it is also of interest to note the interpretation of the verse, "On the third day, Esther put on royal apparel and stood in the inner court of the king's palace, facing the king's palace, while the king was sitting on his royal throne in the throne room facing the entrance of the palace" (Esther 5:1), in the following zoharic passage: " 'On the third day,' when the power of the body was weakened and she existed in spirit without a body, then 'Esther put on royal apparel' (*wa-tilbash ʾesther malkhut*). . . . She was adorned in the supernal, holy *Malkhut*, she most certainly was clothed in the Holy Spirit."[136] The text goes on to record that Esther was allowed to be clothed in the Holy Spirit as a reward for her reticence to disclose information about her upbringing to Ahasuerus (see Esther 2:20). The significant point for this analysis is that Esther takes on, or is united with, the aspect of God referred to as *Malkhut*, the tenth emanation that corresponds to the feminine *Shekhinah*, only when she overcomes her own physical status. To become the divine feminine involves a denial of biological womanhood. The underlying conceptual point here is identical to the issue raised before; namely, the engendering aspect of the *Shekhinah*, designated as *Malkhut*, is related to the masculine potency of God; hence, only when the distinctive bodily characteristics of the woman are subjugated by the spirit that is related to the masculine can she receive the overflow (or the Holy Spirit) from the divine realm. Ironically enough, according to the complex gender system of theosophic kabbalah, conception, pregnancy, giving birth and nursing are all seen as male traits. A perfect homology thus exists between the divine and the mundane spheres: just as the divine feminine can assume the qualities of the male, so too the earthly biological woman can be gendered as masculine. One may speak, therefore, of a kind of spiritual transvestism that is logically implied by kabbalistic myth: a woman actualizes her fullest potential *qua* human when she is adorned with the qualities of the male, realized principally through conception and procreation. The point is affirmed in the following zoharic text:

> The Mother [*Binah*] lends her garments to the Daughter [*Shekhinah*] and adorns her in her ornamentation. When does she adorn her in her ornamentation as is appropriate? When all the males appear before her, as it is written, "[Three times a year all your males shall appear] before the Sovereign, the Lord," *ʾel pene ha-ʾadon yhwh* (Exod. 23:17), and this [the *Shekhinah*] is called Sovereign (*ʾadon*), as it says, "the Ark of the Covenant of the Sovereign of all the earth," *hinneh ʾaron ha-berit ʾadon kol ha-ʾareṣ* (Josh. 3:11). Then the *heʾ* goes out and the *yod* enters, and she is adorned in

> the garments of the male corresponding to all the males in Israel.[137]

The gender transformation of the feminine *Shekhinah,* the Daughter, into a male is here depicted in terms of the reception of the garments and adornments of *Binah,* the Mother. This process ensues when the Israelite males appear before the *Shekhinah* during the three annual festivals. On those occasions the *Shekhinah* assumes the role of the Ark of the Covenant, for she is a receptacle that contains the phallus, like the ark that contains the tablets of the covenant. In this containment, however, the feminine is masculinized or becomes part of the phallus. This ontic transformation is characterized in terms of letter symbolism as well: the *heʾ*, symbolic of the feminine, departs, and the *yod,* symbolic of the masculine, enters. The masculine overtakes the feminine, and in the process the feminine is itself transformed. At this point the *Shekhinah* can properly be described as putting on the garments of *Binah,* which are referred to as the garments of the male. The visual participation of the lower males transforms the *Shekhinah* in such a way that she takes the position of *Binah* in relation to the lower realm.

The implications of the zoharic symbolism are succinctly expressed by the sixteenth-century master Isaac Luria in the following passage, commenting on the aforecited zoharic text:

> With the arousal of the lower beings and the appearance of all the males of Israel in the Temple,[138] which alludes to her, she turns into a male in actuality, adorned in the garment of a male, to disclose in her the holy covenant (*berit qodesh,* i.e., the phallus) in the image of *Binah,* for even though she is female she ends with the masculine. When she is clothed in the six extremities of the masculine whose end is *Yesod,* then she is called *Binah, ben yah,* and she is one with the All. Similarly, in the case of *Malkhut,* by means of the arousal of the lower beings . . . she becomes male and is called Lord (*ʾadon*), and this is [the import of the biblical idiom] the "face of the Lord," *pene ʾadon* (Exod. 23:17, 34:23). She becomes Elohim, "like mother, like daughter" (Ezek. 16:44).[139]

According to this Lurianic text, the *Shekhinah* is transformed into a male when the Israelite males enter the Temple, which is one of the symbolic representations of the *Shekhinah.* The males who appear before God in the Temple constitute the phallus that transforms the feminine *Shekhinah* into a male and thus endows her with the titles

"Lord" and "Elohim." The phallic transference, moreover, is alluded to in the biblical idiom, to "appear before the Sovereign," which should be rendered quite literally to "appear before the face of the Lord," that is, the phallus.[140] Through this gender transformation the *Shekhinah* emulates the attribute of *Binah,* which likewise is characterized as a female that becomes male. In the case of *Binah* this transformation occurs as a result of the production of the six emanations from *Ḥesed* to *Yesod* that collectively represent the male divine anthropos; hence the name *Binah* is decomposed into the form *ben yah,* for the Mother is named *Binah* on account of the male form that she produces, causing herself to be transmuted into the masculine. More specifically, it is on account of the last of those six emanations, *Yesod,* that *Binah* receives its phallic character. As it is expressed in another Lurianic text:

> Even though the point of the supernal Zion that is within *Binah* is not discernible, there is found in it the concealed potency of femininity and the revealed potency of masculinity, and through this aspect *Yesod* is called Zion. . . . These two aspects are Joseph and Benjamin, one is the female waters, and this is the spring of the well that is never separated from the well, and the other is the male waters in the secret of Joseph the Righteous, one is above and the other below, entering and exiting, entering to bring in the male waters and exiting to bring forth the female waters corresponding to the male waters.[141]

According to this text, the womb of the divine Mother, referred to by the technical expression "point of the supernal Zion,"[142] is depicted as a parallel to the phallus below. Even though that aspect of *Binah* is treated as bisexual—it comprises the potencies of masculinity and femininity—it is clearly the feminine that assumes the central position insofar as it is the male element that is disclosed. The male element of *Binah* is homologous to the phallic *Yesod.* Indeed, we are to distinguish two aspects of the phallus, the upper one named "Joseph" and the lower one named "Benjamin." These two aspects, moreover, correspond respectively to the seminal secretions of the male and the female waters, a motif discussed in the concluding section of this chapter. The important point to note in this context is the gender transformation implied in this text: the uterus of the divine Mother is depicted as the upper aspect of the phallus and is correlated with the male waters, whereas the penis of the divine Son is depicted as the lower aspect of the phallus and is correlated with the female waters.

Homoeroticism as a Mystical Ideal of Transvaluation

One of the obvious implications of my argument that the feminine is to be localized in the phallus is that the female images related to God must be transposed into a masculine key. That is to say, even when a given text overtly refers to God in feminine terms it is implicitly speaking about the male deity, and most specifically the corona of the penis.[143] Thus, in kabbalistic texts, especially evident in the zoharic corpus, the peak mystical experience of seeing the feminine Presence is transmuted into a visualization of the exposed corona.[144] In light of this gender metamorphosis and hermeneutical transformation, one must wonder if there is not a latent homoeroticism in the kabbalistic sources. What does it mean to say that the phallus is the ultimate object of the kabbalists' contemplative gaze and devotion?

There is no question here regarding the acceptance and ultimate affirmation of heterosexuality as the required sexual mores in Jewish society. Even if there were occasional instances of homosexual relations in kabbalistic circles, it would not challenge in any serious way the repeated emphasis on heterosexuality as the sole appropriate mode of sexual behavior inasmuch as human sexuality within any rabbinic framework is for the most part legitimated by procreation. The negative attitudes toward homosexuality notwithstanding, the issue that I am raising involves the symbolic valence accorded homoeroticism in the larger mythic framework of theosophic kabbalah. That is, if the female is ontically part of the male, and indeed anatomically part of the penis, attitudes toward the female would be absorbed in a phallocentrism that may theoretically—if not practically—embrace homoeroticism as the proper means to characterize the relationship of the different members of the mystical fraternity as well as the relationship between that fraternity and God.[145] The stated goal of the enlightened kabbalists (*maskilim*) is to join the *Shekhinah*, the feminine Presence. This communion should be viewed as both theurgical and mystical. On the one hand, it benefits the divine by enhancing the unity of the male and the female aspects of the Godhead, and, on the other, it is the basic datum of the religious experience of the individual mystics. *Prima facie*, it would seem that the kabbalists avoid the issue of homosexual union with God by identifying the *Shekhinah*, the feminine potency par excellence, as the object of their mystical communion. Erotic language could be appropriated to describe that communion inasmuch as God was imaged as female.[146] But if the feminine *Shekhinah* is in fact transmuted into the *ʿaṭeret berit*, the corona of the penis, what does that say about the sexual quality of the cleaving of the mystics to the *Shekhinah*? The phallocentrism of kabbalistic symbolism so overwhelms the perspective on gender that the female is reduced to an aspect of the male. Does not the logic of the mythos imply that the divine phallus is the ultimate object of the kabbalists' visual contemplation and mystical communion? Is there any need for the female as such when the feminine is ontically localized in the male organ?[147]

In a separate study I have argued that, according to the zoharic text, the mystical fellowship represents the constitution of the divine face. The gathering of the comrades and their master is valorized as a sexual union identified as a face-to-face encounter. In this encounter the comrades represent the feminine persona that stands facing the male, the master who embodies the cosmic foundation and divine phallus.[148] Just as I have argued at length above that the sexual union of male and female is, in truth, an ontological reconstitution of the male, a reintegration of the female into the male, so too male-to-male bonding can be understood in heterosexual terms. In either case the issue is the reconfiguration of the male, but in one instance that reconfiguration involves transmuting heterosexual language into homosexual images and in the other homosexual language into heterosexual symbols. In the present context I will cite Joseph of Hamadan, who provides an exemplary illustration of the gender transformation to which I have alluded.

According to one passage written by this kabbalist, the righteous (a cipher for the mystics) are said to "cleave to the Matrona like a son to his mother," and they are further described as suckling the splendor of the Matrona from her breasts.[149] In the continuation of this passage, the overtly feminine images of the breasts and the process of lactation are transformed into masculine traits.

> Moreover, that letter *he*ʾ [symbolic of the Matrona] is a half-moon, and it is a half-circle in the manner that the seventy members of the Sanhedrin sat, and the point in the middle is the head of the court (*ʾav bet din*), and from there judgment issues from the letter *he*ʾ, as it is written, "God stands in the divine assembly [among the divine beings He pronounces judgment]" (Ps. 82:1), and the *Shekhinah* is in the middle. . . . All the souls of the righteous are crowned by the holy letter, as the sages of old said, "This indicates that the Holy One, blessed be He, in the future shall be a crown on the head of all the righteous."[150] The righteous are crowned by this holy letter and they cleave to the splendor of the *Shekhinah*, the holy Matrona.[151]

That the feminine Presence to which the mystics cleave is valorized as masculine is signified by the image of the point in the middle of the half-moon or half-circle.[152] In her function as the midpoint that sustains the righteous, the *Shekhinah* is transformed into a male, symbolized by the technical expression of the head of the court, the *ʾav bet din*, a title that is appropriately applied to the *Shekhinah* inasmuch as that gradation is an expression of divine judgment.[153] To be sure, Joseph of Hamadan elsewhere affirms that both the masculine and the feminine personifications of the divine have breasts that are designated euphemistically as the holy apples.[154] Indeed, the breasts of women are said to be larger than those of men because they have the biological function of nursing.[155] The point I am making, however, involves the gender signification of this biological fact. When the physiological issue is viewed from the standpoint of gender it becomes clear that the lactation of the breasts functionally transforms the female into a male, as I have argued above with respect to the *Zohar*. In the moment that the *Shekhinah* feeds others through her breasts, she assumes the role of the phallus that sustains by means of its seminal overflow.[156]

It must be concluded, therefore, that the breast that gives milk is functionally equivalent to a penis that ejaculates. If that is the case, then the righteous described as suckling from the splendor of the breasts of the *Shekhinah* are, in fact, cleaving to and drawing from the corona of the divine phallus. This is made explicit in a second passage from Joseph of Hamadan:

> When a person departs from this world to his world, he is detained in the Garden of Eden below until his mate comes, and they ascend to the heavenly academy, and they are crowned round about in the crowns of the Holy One, blessed be He, within the body of the holy King. The Matrona sits in the middle and the righteous and pious ones are all around and they suckle from that point in the middle that is the *Shekhinah*. From that point they receive food, manna from the dew and the efflux of the supernal heaven. . . . They are nourished from the splendor of the Matrona, all of them encircled on the right and the left. Therefore the beginning of the word *ṭivu* [goodness] is the letter *ṭet* for from there the upper and lower entities derive benefit and from there everything is blessed and sustained, and everything is joyous when that holy letter that shines in several supernal holy beings in this world and the world-to-come is revealed.[157]

The source of sustenance is depicted in this passage as the corona of the penis (symbolized by the letter *ṭet*) rather than the breasts of the *Shekhinah*. From a phenomenological vantage point the corona of the penis easily interchanges with the breasts inasmuch as the function of the latter transforms the evidently female part of the anatomy into a male organ. In light of this transformation it again becomes obvious to what extent there may be a homoerotic underpinning to the kabbalistic representation of the *Shekhinah*. Ostensibly, the cleaving to the *Shekhinah* on the part of the mystics is portrayed as a union of masculine and feminine, but it may signify rather the joining of the males to the corona of the phallus, that which bears the sign of the holy covenant. The erotic bond with the *Shekhinah*, therefore, marks the reconstitution of the androgynous phallus, a restoration of the female back to its ontological source in the male.

II. On Becoming Female

Do we have evidence in kabbalistic literature for movement such that the male becomes female? Is it ever appropriate, according to the kabbalists, for the male to divest himself of his maleness and adopt the characteristics associated with femininity in relation to the masculine God? Given the hierarchical nature of the gender attribution in these sources one would not expect to find such a reciprocal process. Yet, there is precisely a dynamic of this sort that is fully articulated in the kabbalistic theosophy of Isaac Luria, as transmitted by his various disciples. The remainder of this chapter explores in some detail the theme of the male becoming female in the myth and ritual of Lurianic kabbalah. Obviously, many of the motifs in this corpus are exegetical elaborations of earlier sources, especially zoharic passages. I will only mention briefly some of the background ideas and images from the *Zohar* that are indispensable for a proper appreciation of the later material.

The motif that serves as the basis for my discussion is that of the upper and the lower waters, the former depicted as masculine and the latter as feminine. This motif, briefly alluded to above, is expressed in classical rabbinic sources,[158] perhaps reflecting some form of Gnostic speculation,[159] where the dual waters have an exclusively cosmological reference. In later kabbalistic literature, especially the *Zohar*, this motif is developed further and assumes as well a theosophic connotation.[160] The obvious gender symbolism associated with these waters, based on the model of orgasmic secretions, is drawn quite boldly in the following zoharic passage: "The upper waters are male and the lower female, and the lower are sustained by the male. The lower waters call out to the upper like a female who opens up for the male, and she spills water corresponding to the male water that produces semen. The female is nourished by the male."[161] Perhaps the most interesting development of this motif in zoharic literature involves the idea of the souls of the righteous entering into the *Shekhinah* where they are integrated into the lower female waters, the *mayyin nuqbin*, that arouse the upper male waters, *mayyin dukhrin*. To cite one representative text:

> The desire of the female for the male is not realized except when a spirit enters into her and she discharges fluid corresponding to the upper masculine waters. So too the Community of Israel [the *Shekhinah*] does not arouse the desire for the Holy One, blessed be He, except by means of the spirit of the righteous who enter into her. Then the fluids flow within her corresponding to the male fluids, and everything becomes one desire, one bundle, one bond. This is the will of everything, and the stroll that the Holy One, blessed be He, takes with the souls of the righteous.[162]

In an extraordinary reversal of gender symbolism, the penetration of the souls of the righteous into the feminine Presence results in their stimulating and becoming part of the fluids secreted by the female that, in turn, arouse the seminal fluids of the upper male potency of the divine. The ontic status of the righteous is determined precisely by this role: "Rachel gave birth to two righteous individuals, and this is appropriate for the sabbatical year is always situated in between two righteous individuals, as it is written, 'The righteous (*ṣaddiqim*, i.e., in the plural) shall inherit the land' (Ps. 37:29), the righteous above and the righteous below. The supernal waters flow from the righteous above and from the righteous below the female flows with water in relation to the male in complete desire."[163] It is clear from any number of passages that the zoharic authorship sees this task as the purpose of the nocturnal ascent of the righteous[164]: "When the soul rises it arouses the desire of the female toward the male, and then the fluids flow from below to above, and the pit becomes a well of flowing water . . . for this place is perfected by the soul of the righteous, and the love and desire is aroused above, and it becomes one."[165] The entry of the righteous soul into the *Shekhinah* entirely reverses the gender roles normally associated with each of the relevant agents in this drama, for the masculine soul becomes feminine as it is integrated as part of the feminine waters, and the feminine aspect of the Godhead becomes masculine insofar as the pit is transformed into a well of flowing waters. The feminization of the righteous accounts as well for the image of God taking a stroll with the souls of the righteous, an act that is a euphemism for sexual intercourse, based ultimately on the phallic understanding of the feet.[166] This image is entirely appropriate because the souls of the righteous are female partners in relation to the masculine deity. Again we must confront the possibility of an impicit homoeroticism that necessitates the feminization of the human male vis-à-vis the divine who is valorized as masculine.[167] If, however, there is a latent homoeroticism in the zoharic symbolism, it should be noted that it is still expressed within a purely heterosexual context; that is, the male righteous constitute the feminine waters that arouse the overflow of the masculine waters upon the divine feminine. The issue is rendered more complex by the fact that, as I have argued, the divine feminine is itself part of the male organ.

The ideas expressed in the zoharic corpus are elaborated in kabbalistic materials that derived from sixteenth-century Safed, especially those composed by members of the circle of Isaac Luria.[168] What is most important, in the Lurianic literature this motif is applied to specific rituals in which it is clear that the goal of the male adept is to become female. Thus, for example, in *Shaᶜar ha-Kawwanot,* Ḥayyim Vital offers the following explanation for the gesture of shutting the eyes[169] that is required when the *Shemaᶜ,* the traditional proclamation of divine unity, is recited:

> Before you say "Hear O Israel [the Lord, our God, the Lord is one]" (Deut. 6:4) you should close your two eyes with your right hand and concentrate on what is written in the [zoharic section] *Sabbaʾ de-Mishpaṭim* [regarding] the beautiful maiden that has no eyes.[170] We have explained in that context that the meaning [of this expression] is Rachel who ascends at this point [of the prayer] in the aspect of female waters in relation to the Father and Mother.[171]

To appreciate the complex symbolism underlying this comment, it is necessary to bear in mind that, according to the Lurianic interpretation of the liturgical order, the mystical significance of the *Shemaᶜ* is "to raise the female waters from the Male and Female to the Father and Mother so that the Father and Mother will be united and the [influx of the] consciousness (*moḥin*) will come down to the Male and Female."[172] The worshiper thus joins the feminine hypostasis so that he may rise with her in the aspect of the female waters to facilitate the union of the lower two masculine and feminine configurations (*parṣufim*) in the Godhead, *Zeᶜeir ʾAnpin* and *Nuqbaʾ di-Zeᶜeir,* which, in turn, stimulate the union of the upper masculine and feminine configurations, the Father (*ʾAbbaʾ*) and Mother (*ʾImmaʾ*).[173] The latter union results in the overflowing of the male waters (*mayyim dukhrin*) from *Zeʿeir ʾAnpin* to *Nuqbaʾ di-Zeʿeir* in the moment of coupling that is consummated during the *ʿAmidah*, the standing prayer of the eighteen benedictions. What is most significant for this discussion is that, according to the Lurianic interpretation, the male adept ritually covers his eyes to transform himself into the divine grade that is symbolized by the zoharic image of a beautiful maiden without eyes, the configuration (*parṣuf*) called *Nuqbaʾ di-Zeʿeir* that corresponds to the last of the ten *sefirot*, the *Shekhinah*. One can speak here of a process of effeminization of the worshiper, a motif that has not been sufficiently noted in discussions of Lurianic symbolism and ritual. The motif of the males becoming integrated into the female waters is part of this larger phenomenon of gender metamorphosis. To be sure, the union of the righteous souls with the *Shekhinah* is based on the fact that they correspond to the male aspect of the divine, the *membrum virile*. However, once these souls enter into the *Shekhinah* they become incorporated as part of her and constitute the female waters that further stimulate coitus in the higher grades of the divine realm.[174] Thus, in another context Luria describes the righteous in the following terms: "When they sacrifice their lives in sanctification of God through the verse, 'Hear O Israel,' they unite the Bridegroom and the Bride, and this is one sancitification (*qiddush*), for the Bridegroom betroths (*meqaddesh*) the Bride. When he sacrifices himself he is considered as one who has died and through his soul the union of the female waters is accomplished, and the Other Side is pleased with his body and thus does not enter to separate the Bridegroom and the Bride."[175] In accord with the zoharic precedent, Luria understands the liturgical recitation of Deuteronomy 6:4, as well as the supplication prayer to be discussed below, as an occasion to enact the spiritual death of the worshiper.[176] The erotic nature of that spiritual death is underscored by the fact that the worshiper penetrates the feminine *Shekhinah* where he is integrated as part of the female waters in an effort to assist the unification of the masculine and the feminine potencies of the divine.[177]

The assimilation of the male into the female is characterized as the male closing his eyes in emulation of the beautiful maiden without eyes. The ritual gains its mystical valence from the fact that the eyes function as a symbol for the male sexual organ while still remaining eyes, or, to put the matter somewhat differently, the eyes are the aspects in the head that function like the genitals in the lower region of the body. Hence, the female persona of the divine is depicted as the beautiful maiden without eyes.[178] The male worshiper must partake of the character of the feminine by emasculating himself, a procedure that is ritually fulfilled through the shutting of the eyes. The interpretation that I have offered is confirmed by a second passage in *Sha ᶜar ha-Kawwanot* that deals more generally with the closing of the eyes during prayer.[179] In this text Vital has imputed new theosophic meaning to a well-established prayer gesture that has as its purpose the augmentation of intention during worship[180]: by closing his eyes the male worshiper becomes the beautiful maiden without eyes. According to this passage, the mystical significance of prayer in general, enacted by means of this gesture, is connected to the fact that the male is assimilated into the female in order to arouse the unity of the masculine and the feminine above. The point is well made in the following passage supposedly written by Luria himself:

> The appropriate intention of a person's prayer is above in the supernal depth, in the secret of the point of Zion, and there is the concealment of the supernal holy phallus, whence there extends two kinds of overflow by means of the supernal union. . . . The union is complete when he is in the path that is not known above or below. . . . The matter is that there must be an arousal of the lower entities in the way of the lower union, to elevate the female waters. Therefore, one must intend one's prayers until there, and consequently that path will elevate the female waters to the male waters. This path is not known above or below, neither in the secret of the female waters nor in the secret of the male waters. . . . The union is not complete except by means of that path. When there is no arousal below, there is no union by means of that path, for there are no female waters.[181]

The mandate for the male worshiper, therefore, is not simply to act as a stimulus to arouse the secretions of the female but rather to be integrated into them.[182] It is evident, however, that the crossing of gender boundary implied here is not predicated on any ambiguity regarding or open challenge to the status accorded the respective genders in kabbalistic thought. On the contrary, the hierarchy of gender roles in classical kabbalah is only reinforced in the Lurianic material. That is, the male's becoming female is necessary so that the female may become male through the activation of the masculine principle of beneficence. Vital expresses this in the context of describing the supplication prayer (*nefillat ᵓappayim*) that succeeds the *ᶜAmidah* in the traditional morning liturgy on Monday and Thursday:

> Now is the time of the descent of the drop of male waters of grace into the female Rachel. One must first raise the

> female waters in order to receive afterwards the male waters, according to the secret, "When a woman brings forth seed and bears a male" (Lev. 12:2). And the rabbis, blessed be their memory, said,[183] "a woman who produces seed first gives birth to a male."[184]

Without entering further into the complicated symbolism articulated in the continuation of the above passage, related specifically to the descent of the righteous into the realm of the demonic shells to liberate the entrapped sparks,[185] suffice it to say that for Luria the male fulfills an essential religious task by becoming female, by being assimilated into the female waters that rise to stimulate the male waters, which in turn inseminate the female so that she gives birth to a male. To translate this web of symbols grammatologically: he becomes she so that she arouses he to turn she into he. This circular process of reconstituted masculinity is referred to in Lurianic kabbalah as the secret of impregnation (*ʿibbur*). To cite one textual witness: "Just as the souls of the righteous elevate the female waters each night during sleep to *Malkhut*, and she renews them, according to the secret, 'They are renewed every morning' (Lam. 3:23), and the explanation of this renewal is that she illuminates them in the aspect of expanded consciousness (*moḥin de-gadlut*) . . . so too when *Zeʿeir ʾAnpin* ascends in the secret of the female waters he is renewed by means of the Father and Mother."[186] The stimulation of the female waters has the sole purpose of assisting in the rebirth of the male through the masculinized feminine in a state of increased consciousness. In the final analysis, the androcentric and phallocentric orientation adopted by kabbalists is so pervasive that even the positive values normally associated with the feminine are assigned to the male. This is captured in the brief comment of Vital that "there are five aspects of grace (*ḥasadim*) of the Mother and five aspects of grace of the Father, and the aspects of grace of the Mother are the acts of strength of the Father."[187] As noted above, according to standard kabbalistic symbolism, grace is associated with the masculine and strength with the feminine. It follows, therefore, that the male attributes in the Mother must be transposed into female attributes of the Father.

In conclusion, it can be said that there is a psychodynamic model in the classical texts of theosophic kabbalah of the male becoming female just as there is one of the female becoming male. It is indeed appropriate, in fact mandatory, for the male to divest himself of his maleness and assume the posture of the feminine. For sixteenth-century kabbalists, especially the followers of Lurianic kabbalah, this gender transformation is the essential dynamic enacted in the structure of the liturgy. This movement, however, reifies the standard binary hierarchy of gender symbolism: the male becomes female only in order to add strength to the female to renew herself as male. The female must either be restored to the male or turned into a male by the male becoming female. From the vantage point of kabbalists this is the secret that establishes the covenant of unity.

The logical implications of this gender symbolism are explicitly drawn in the Lurianic corpus: the ultimate rectification of the break in the Godhead is attained when there is a reconstitution of the female as male, i.e., the ultimate purification of the demonic forces involves a restoration of judgmental forces to mercy. As Vital expresses the matter in one context:

> Thus there are two aspects to the female of *Ze^ceir ᵓAnpin*, one when she is contained initially in the male, and the second when she is separated from him, and he gives her the crown of strength. . . . And thus you can understand why the aspect of the female is always judgments for her root is the aspect of the kings that died. They are called kings (*melakhim*) from the word kingship (*malkhut*). When she separates from him and becomes an autonomous aspect, then the two of them are in the secret of a husband and his wife, the male alone and the female alone.[188]

At the core of the zoharic myth of the Edomite kings, who symbolize the forces of impurity within the Godhead, is the ontological problem of the feminine. The death of the kings thus represents the purification of the feminine. Again to quote Vital: " 'These are the kings who ruled in the land of Edom' (Gen. 36:31), for when they emerged the aspect of these kings immediately began to be purified to produce the aspect of the feminine for Him."[189] The purpose of the divine catharsis is to purify the feminine aspect of the divine, but the ultimate purification is attained only when the feminine is restored to the male, when the other is obliterated in the identity of sameness. The messianic era is thus described as the final obliteration of the evil force (related exegetically to Isaiah 25:8), which entails a restitution of the world to a primeval state of chaos. In that stage the feminine is completely integrated in the masculine, a point represented symbolically by the overcoming of the divine name that numerically equals fifty-two (the force of the feminine operating independently of the male) by the names that equal sixty-three and seventy-two, which correspond respectively to the feminine and the masculine.[190] The reconstitution of the female as male is represented as well by the image of the female being the crown of her husband[191] or the eschatological teaching of the rabbis

(B. Berakhot 17a) that in the future the righteous sit with their crowns on their heads.[192] The eschaton signifies the reintegration of the feminine as part of the masculine, an ontic unity that was rendered asunder in the beginning of creation. The mythical element of the Lurianic cosmogony is predicated on the notion that fission of the Godhead is a cathartic process by means of which the (feminine) "other" is discarded so that it may be purified and ultimately restored to its ontological source in the male androgyne. Both the image of the woman being the crown of her husband and that of the righteous sitting with their crowns on their heads signifies the ultimate unification that involves the recontextualization of the feminine as part of the phallus, a mystery related by Vital to the eighth of the Edomite kings who survived, Hadar, who corresponds to "*Yesod* that comprises male and female, which is the crown that is in him."[193]

The full force of this mythic conception will be appreciated if we bear in mind that in other contexts Vital tries to preserve the relatively autonomous aspect of the feminine by distinguishing between the feminine as the corona of the phallus and the feminine as a separate configuration. Thus, for example, in *Shaʿar ha-Kawwanot*, he writes:

> This is [the intent of] what is written, "under His feet there was the likeness of a pavement of sapphire" (Exod. 24:10), for *Yesod*, which is called the pavement of sapphire (*livnat ha-sappir*), is underneath His feet, which are *Neṣaḥ* and *Hod*. . . . *Yesod* is the aspect that is appropriate to hide and to conceal, and on account of His glory, blessed be He, they did not publicize it but only explained its place, which is beneath His feet. *Yesod* itself is composed of male and female in the secret of the phallus (*yesod*) and the corona (*ʿaṭarah*) that is in him, as I have already informed you that the corona (*ʿaṭarah*) is not the secret of *Malkhut* in itself but rather the containment of the masculine in all ten *sefirot*, and this [*ʿaṭarah*] is the aspect of *Malkhut* in him [*Yesod*]. But the essential *Malkhut* is Rachel, *Nuqbaʾ di-Zeʿeir ʾAnpin*, and this is simple for [it is written] "But I would behold God from my flesh" (Job 19:26), the corona (*ʿaṭarah*) is one matter and the female (*neqevah*) is another independent matter.[194]

We find a similar approach in the following passage in *ʿEṣ Ḥayyim*:

> The aspect of *Malkhut* in each and every configuration (*parṣuf*) of these five configurations is in this manner: *Malkhut*, which is in the masculine configuration, such as

> *ʾAbbaʾ* and *Zeʿeir ʾAnpin,* is in the aspect of the corona (*ʿaṭarah*) that is on the *ṣaddiq* who is called *Yesod,* in the secret of "Blessings light upon the head of the righteous," *berakhot le-roʾsh ṣaddiq* (Prov. 10:6). . . . *Malkhut* in the feminine configuration, such as *ʾImmaʾ* and *Nuqbaʾ di-Zeʿeir ʾAnpin,* is also in the aspect of the corona of the phallus (*ʿaṭeret yesod*) that is in her, for the phallus (*yesod*) in her is the womb and the corona in her is the aspect of the pulp of the apple (*besar ha-tapuaḥ*) that is over her, which is called in the language of the sages, blessed be their memory, *shippule meʿayyim* [the lower part of the abdomen], in matters pertaining to the signs of barren women, as is known.[195] However, the comprehensive *sefirah* of *Malkhut,* the final configuration of the five configurations, which is called *Nuqbaʾ di-Zeʿeir ʾAnpin,* is a complete configuration like the other configurations.[196]

Here again Vital tries to preserve some ontological autonomy of the feminine. The aspect of *Malkhut* in the male configurations (*ʾAbbaʾ* and *Zeʿeir ʾAnpin*) is the corona of the penis, and in the upper female configuration (*ʾImmaʾ*) the aspect of *Malkhut* is the part of the womb that corresponds to the phallus. Only in the case of the final configuration (*Nuqbaʾ di-Zeʿeir ʾAnpin*) can one speak of a fully formed feminine that compliments the male.

These examples, and others that could have been cited, do not challenge my presumption that the female in an originary and ultimate sense is part of the male organ. Indeed, the aforecited passages in which Vital describes the autonomous character of the feminine relate to the ontic situation of *Malkhut* before the final *tiqqun,* a process, as I have argued, that is predicated on the restoration of the female to the male, principally in the image of the corona of the phallus. The ontological containment of the female in the male is expressed in another context by Vital in which he relates the four species of plants used on Tabernacles (citron, palm branch, myrtle, and willow) to the letters of the Tetragrammaton:

> *Yod* [alludes to] *Ḥesed, Gevurah,* and *Tifʾeret,* and they are the three myrtle branches (*hadassim*); *heʾ* [alludes to] *Neṣaḥ* and *Hod,* and they are the two willows of the brook (*ʿarve naḥal*); *waw* [alludes to] *Yesod,* and this is the palm branch (*lulav*); the final *heʾ* is the citron (*ʾetrog*), and this is the [aspect of] *Malkhut* that is in him, which is the corona of the phallus (*ʿaṭarah she-ba-yesod*) called the head of the righteous one (*roʾsh ṣaddiq*), but it does not refer to *Nuqbaʾ*

> *di-Ze*ʿ*eir* ʾ*Anpin*, as many have thought. This is a well-known mistake for *Malkhut* of *Ze*ʿ*eir* ʾ*Anpin* himself, which is united with him, is symbolized by the union of the secret of the final *he*ʾ of the Tetragrammaton. However, the feminine has its own complete name, which is Elohim or Adonai, as is known. Therefore [the citron] is called the "fruit of the tree of splendor," *peri* ʿ*eṣ hadar* (Lev. 23:40), that is to say, the fruit of the phallus (*peri shel ha-yesod*), which is called ʿ*eṣ hadar*. The fruit that is in him is the corona (ʿ*aṭarah*). The phallus (*yesod*) is also called *hadar* according to the mystery of "show deference to the elderly," *hadarta pene zaqen* (Lev. 19:32). . . . [The citron] is the [aspect of] *Malkhut* in the phallus of *Ze*ʿ*eir* ʾ*Anpin*, and this is the reason for the prohibition of separating the citron from the palm branch when it is lifted up. One must unite them together for the palm branch is the phallus and the citron is the corona that is conjoined to it without separation.[197]

As an autonomous entity the feminine has her own name, either Elohim or Adonai, but as part of the male she is the final *he*ʾ of the Tetragrammaton. The independent position attributed to *Malkhut* signifies a subsidiary state that is overcome by the unification of male and female and the consequent restoration of the female to the male. When the feminine is evaluated from the vantage point of the unique divine name, which represents the essential and elemental force of God's being, she is the completion of that name rather than a distinct potency. The Tetragrammaton represents the male androgyne, the perfect male who comprehends within himself both masculine and feminine characteristics. The mythic structure is instantiated by the ritual of lifting up the palm branch in the right hand and the citron in the left. To separate the two is to create a division between the masculine and feminine. When the two are joined together the female is reintegrated into the male in the form of the corona of the phallus.

That this was the ontic situation of Ein-Sof prior to the process of emanation is stated explicitly by Menaḥem Azariah of Fano:

> The head that is no head is in relation to them [the head that is nothing and the head of ʾ*Arikh* ʾ*Anpin*] in the secret of Ein-Sof on account of His great concealment. . . . Here He is called in truth the head that does not know and that is not known for He does not know the root of His essence from a higher place just as a man does not know the essence of his soul. He is not known at all to anyone outside

> Him . . . He is the world of the masculine, and *Malkhut* is not discernible in Him except in the secret of the crown that is included in *Yesod*.[198]

The Infinite is entirely masculine, for the feminine aspect is located ontically in the corona of the penis. From the vantage point of the kabbalists history is moving toward a state where the feminine will be restored to the masculine so that the androgynous quality of the Godhead will be reconstituted in the manner that it was before the independent force of the feminine was operative in the concatenation of worlds. The ultimate purpose of religious ritual is to serve as a catalyst to transform the feminine into the masculine, but to attain that goal it is necessary for the male to become female. The dialectics of gender transformation are succinctly expressed by Pineḥas of Korets:

> The one that bestows is garbed in the garment of the one that receives and by means of this the one that receives becomes equal to the one that bestows. By this means the aspect of *Malkhut*, which is the aspect of the one that receives, becomes equal in her stature to the one that bestows as it was prior to the indictment of the moon. This is the aspect of the righteous sitting with their crowns upon their heads. That is, the aspect of *Malkhut* becomes the aspect of the crown . . . surrounding the head, for she ascends to the aspect of the head since the one who bestows receives pleasure from the one that receives. . . . Thus it is written "Mordecai left the king's presence in royal robes" (Esther 8:15), that is, Mordecai is the aspect of the one that bestows who is garbed in the garment of the one who receives, that is, *Malkhut*, which is the aspect of the one who receives. By means of this the two of them are of equal stature, for from the one who receives is made the aspect of the one who bestows and from the *shoshanah*, which is the aspect of the feminine, the aspect of *Malkhut*, is made the aspect of *shushan*, the aspect of the masculine. And this is [the meaning of the continuation of the verse] "And the city of Shushan rang with joyous cries."[199]

The secret of redemption consists of the female becoming the corona of the male organ, but that can be achieved only when the male puts on the garment of the female. Despite the reference in the above passage to the attainment of an equal stature on the part of the male and the female, the fact of the matter is that the gender hierarchy is not fully overcome. The female is rendered equal to the male when she rises from the status of the one who receives to the one who bestows, a process that is facilitated by the descent of the one who bestows to the status of the one who receives. In the redemptive moment the female is transformed into an aspect of the male and the original androgynous state is reconstituted.

◆ Notes ◆

1. Female Imaging of the Torah: From Literary Metaphor to Religious Symbol

This study was published in *From Ancient Israel to Modern Judaism Intellect in Quest of Understanding: Essays in Honor of Marvin Fox,* ed. J. Neusner, E. S. Frerichs, and N. M. Sarna (Atlanta, 1989), 2:271–307, and is here reprinted with permission of Scholars Press.

1. The point was made earlier by A. Green, "Bride, Spouse, Daughter: Images of the Feminine in Classical Jewish Sources," in *On Being a Jewish Feminist,* ed. S. Heschel (New York, 1983), p. 253. The scholarly literature on the Jewish conception of Wisdom is vast. I will mention here only several studies that emphasize the view that the figure of Wisdom in Israel is derived from or represents a revision of an authentic mythic goddess. See U. Wilckens, *Weisheit und Torheit* (Tübingen, 1959), pp. 193–95; H. Conzelmann, "The Mother of Wisdom," in *The Future of Our Religious Past,* ed. J. M. Robinson (New York, 1971), pp. 230–43; B. L. Mack, *Logos und Sophia* (Göttingen, 1977), pp. 34–62; E. S. Fiorenza, "Wisdom Mythology and Christological Hymns," in *Aspects of Wisdom in Judaism and Early Christianity,* ed. R. Wilkens (Notre Dame, 1975), pp. 29–33; B. Lang, *Wisdom and the Book of Proverbs: An Israelite Goddess Redefined* (New York, 1986), pp. 126–36; and M. Hengel, *Judaism and Hellenism: Studies in Their Encounter in Palestine During the Early Hellenistic Period,* trans. J. Bowden (Philadelphia, 1974), 1:154–55. For the feminine characterization of Sophia in Philo of Alexandria, especially as the "daughter of God," see H. A. Wolfson, *Philo, Foundations of Religious Philosophy in Judaism, Christianity and Islam* (Cambridge, Mass., 1947), 1:256, and J. Laporte, "Philo in the Tradition of Biblical Wisdom Literature," in *Aspects of Wisdom in Judaism and Early Christianity,* pp. 116–18. In the case of Philo there is some evidence for an interchange between the feminine figure of Wisdom and the masculine Logos; see Mack, *Logos und Sophia,* pp. 153–58,

and Hengel, *Judaism and Hellenism,* 2:111 n. 418. Such a process is clear as well in the case of early Christian doctrine where the Jewish conception of the incarnation of Wisdom in the Torah served as the basis for the eventual Christological identification of Jesus with Sophia, as expressed, for instance, in Matthew 11:28–30. See J. M. Robinson, "Jesus as Sophos and Sophia," in *Aspects of Wisdom in Judaism and Early Christianity,* pp. 1–16, and V. R. Mollenkott, *The Divine Feminine* (New York, 1983), pp. 100–1. On the possible influence of Jewish-Wisdom speculation on the Gnostic conception of Sophia, see the review of the problem by G. MacRae, "The Jewish Background of the Gnostic Sophia Myth," *Novum Testamentum* 12 (1970): 86–101.

2. See Hengel, *Judaism and Hellenism,* 1:161.

3. See H. A. Fischel, "The Transformation of Wisdom in the World of Midrash," in *Aspects of Wisdom in Judaism and Early Christianity,* pp. 70–71, 82, and J. Neusner, *Torah: From Scroll to Symbol in Formative Judaism* (Philadelphia, 1985), pp. 118–19.

4. This theme has been discussed by many scholars. See Hengel, *Judaism and Hellenism,* 1:171, and other sources cited in 2:111–12 n. 420. On the anthropomorphization of the Torah scroll in Jewish texts and rituals, see also the evidence adduced by H. E. Goldberg, "Torah and Children: Some Symbolic Aspects of the Reproduction of Jews and Judaism," in *Judaism Viewed from Within and from Without: Anthropological Studies,* ed. H. E. Goldberg (Albany, 1987), pp. 111–18. Goldberg (pp. 113–14) entertains the possibility that the Torah scroll is metaphorically linked either to a male (most likely, the royal personage of the king) or to a female. Additional support for his claims can be gathered from the sources that I discuss in this study, although I think the weight of the evidence suggests that the female personification is more prevalent and that many of the ritualistic behaviors associated with the Torah are rooted in this conceptual ground. An interesting and highly mythical personification of the Torah scroll as the masculine king appears in Kaleb Afendopolo, *Patshegen Ketav ha-Dat,* MS New York, Columbia University X893 Af2, fol. 16b.

5. B. Shabbat 89a. See ibid., 88b, where in a different aggadic tradition the same expression is used to describe the Primordial Torah.

6. See my discussion in Chapter 3, "Erasing the Erasure," p. 190 n. 175. In response to the original version of this chapter David Aaron (in a letter dated July 1, 1991) suggested that it might be more prudent to distinguish at least two different approaches in the rabbinic materials, one inclined toward a metaphorical understanding of the feminine Torah, and the other inclined toward a hypostatic conception. Aaron also drew my attention to a passage in the poem *ʾatah khonanta ʿolam be-rov ḥesed,* by Yosse ben Yosse, cited in E. Fleischer, *Hebrew Liturgical Poetry in the Middle Ages* (Jerusalem, 1975), p. 85 (in Hebrew), which parallels *Genesis Rabbah* 1:1, ed. J. Theodor and Ch. Albeck (Jerusalem, 1965), pp. 1–2 and 8:1, p. 57. The description of God delighting in the light of the law, *be-ʾor dat shiʿashaʿta,* does seem to

suggest a hypostatic conception rather than a merely metaphorical one. That the *sha*ʿ*ashu*ʿ*a* here has an erotic connotation is suggested further by the description of the Torah as frolicking before God, *we-*ʾ*eṣlekha siḥaqah*. Cf. the reading in *Piyyuṭe Yosse ben Yosse*, ed. A. Mirsky, 2nd ed. (Jerusalem, 1991), p. 178: *we-raglekha siḥeqah*. As the editor notes ad locum, in this context the word *raglekha* means *lefanekha*, "before you." It is likely that for Yosse ben Yosse the term *sha*ʿ*ashu*ʿ*a* also has the connotation of a mental process. Thus, in another passage from the same poem (*Piyyuṭe Yosse ben Yosse*, p. 189) the expression *sha*ʿ*ashu*ʿ*a midrash*, which parallels *hege*ʾ *kitve qodesh*, has the connotation of midrashic exegesis that complements the recitation of Scripture. Cf. the description of God and the Primordial Torah in the poem ʾ*azkir gevurot* ʾ*eloha* in *Piyyuṭe Yosse ben Yosse*, p. 128: ʾ*amon saḥaqo dat sha*ʿ*ashu*ʿ*av hi*ʾ *hegyono* ʿ*ad* ʿ*amod segullah*. From this context it is clear that *sha*ʿ*ashu*ʿ*a* involves mental contemplation or meditation (*higgayon*).

7. P. Megillah 4:1, ed. Venice, 74d.

8. The phrase "son of the Torah" is a common designation in the rabbinic corpus for one who studies Torah. See the examples adduced by Neusner, *Torah: From Scroll to Symbol in Formative Judaism*, p. 143.

9. B. Qiddushin 33b.

10. R. Meyer, *Tradition und Neuschöpfung im antiken Judentum* (Tübingen, 1965), p. 84. See Hengel, *Judaism and Hellenism*, 1: 170–71.

11. In treating the genesis and emergence of the feminine conception of Torah in kabbalistic sources as primarily an internal literary development rather than a transformation of ancient terms and ideas by means of an external, essentially non-Jewish system of belief, my approach differs fundamentally from that of Scholem who generally saw this development as a "gnostic transfiguration" of aggadic modes of discourse. See, in particular, G. Scholem, *Origins of the Kabbalah*, trans. A. Arkush and ed. R. J. Zwi Werblowsky (Princeton, 1987), pp. 92–93, 96, 234. However, at times Scholem expressed himself differently and assumed the existence of an ancient "theosophic aggadah" that may have yielded through exegetical reflection subsequent kabbalistic motifs. See G. Scholem, *On the Mystical Shape of the Godhead*, trans. J. Neugroschel and ed. J. Chipman (New York, 1991), pp. 158, 170–71.

12. Cf. *Exodus Rabbah*, 30:6, where the father is identified as the Holy One, blessed be He, and the mother with the Torah. The passage there seems to be based on B. Berakhot 35b, where the father is likewise identified with the Holy One, blessed be He, but the mother with the Community of Israel (*kenesset yisra*ʾ*el*).

13. See, e.g., *Pesiqta*ʾ *Rabbati*, ed. M. Friedmann (Tel Aviv, 1963), 20, 95a, where the Torah is parabolically characterized as the king's daughter and a bride. In that context, however, no mention is made of the identity of the

groom, though one may reasonably conjecture that it is Israel. See ibid., 96b. Cf. *Leviticus Rabbah* 20:10; *Numbers Rabbah* 12:4; *Deuteronomy Rabbah* 8:7; and *Song of Songs Rabbah* 8:13.

14. Cf. B. Sanhedrin 101a, and *Exodus Rabbah* 33:1.

15. See B. Berakhot 57a, and Pesaḥim 59b. Cf. references in the following notes.

16. *Sifre on Deuteronomy*, ed. L. Finkelstein (New York, 1969), 345, p. 402. Cf. parallel in *Midrasch Tannaïm zum Deuteronomium*, ed. D. Hoffmann (Berlin, 1909), p. 212.

17. B. Sanhedrin 59a. Cf. Judah Loew of Prague, *Ḥiddushe ᵓAggadot* (Jerusalem, 1972), on Tractate Sanhedrin, p. 163; idem, *Tifᵓeret Yisraᵓel*, ed. H. Pardes (Jerusalem, 1979), ch. 68, p. 533; idem, *Gur ᵓAryeh* (Jerusalem, 1972), 1:57.

18. B. Pesaḥim 49b.

19. Cf. *Exodus Rabbah* 33:6. D. Boyarin, *Carnal Israel: Reading Sex in Talmudic Culture* (Berkely, Los Angeles, and Oxford, 1993), pp. 134–96, has shown that the female image of Torah in rabbinic societies gave rise to an erotic attachment to the Torah expressed in the male homosocial community of study.

20. According to some midrashic sources, God's coming to Sinai to give the Torah to Israel is described parabolically as a bridegroom coming to meet his bride. In such cases Israel, and not the Torah, is the bride. Cf. *Mekhiltaᵓ de-Rabbi Ishmael*, ed. H. S. Horovitz and I. A. Rabin (Jerusalem, 1970), Baḥodesh, 3, p. 214; *Mekhiltaᵓ de-Rabbi Simeon bar Yoḥai*, ed. J. N. Epstein and E. Z. Melamed (Jerusalem, 1955), pp. 142–43; *Tanḥumaᵓ*, Qedoshim, 2; *Deuteronomy Rabbah* 3:12 (God is compared to the groom, Israel to the bride, the Torah to the marriage contract, and Moses to the scribe who writes that contract); cf. *Yalquṭ Shimᶜoni*, pt. 1, § 279. The passage is cited in the name of *Bereᵓshit Rabbah* in Judah ben Yaqar, *Perush ha-Tefillot we-ha-Berakhot*, ed. S. Yerushalmi (Jerusalem, 1979), pt. 1, p. 90; cf., however, p. 104, where another part of the same source is correctly given as *Devarim Rabbah*. For an alternative use of the same theme, see ibid., pt. 2, p. 37: "There are some who explain that [in the second of the seven wedding blessings] the canopy (*ḥupah*) is mentioned and afterward the marriage (*qiddushin*) to allude to the fact that before God gave the Torah to Israel He placed them under a canopy, that is, the clouds of glory [see below nn. 43 and 44], and afterward gave them the Torah, which is like a [document of] marriage, for His name was sanctified upon His people, Israel." See ibid., p. 38, where Judah ben Yaqar repeats this explanation, but adds at the end: "Therefore the blessing of *ᵓerusin* is made first because the giving of the Torah and the commandments is the essence." See also commentary of Rashi to Exod. 19:17 and Deut. 33:2, and M. Taᶜanit 4:8 and parallel in *Numbers Rabbah* 12:8. Cf. *Pirqe Rabbi ᵓEliᶜezer*, ch. 41, where the image of Moses as the best man is added to that of God as the groom and Israel as the bride.

The kabbalistic transformation of this aggadic motif provides yet a third way to construe this relationship: the event at Sinai is the wedding of the Holy One, blessed be He, the masculine potency of the divine that corresponds to the Written Torah, and the *Shekhinah*, the feminine potency that corresponds to the Oral Torah. Cf. *Zohar* 1:8a; 3:98a–b.

21. *Pesiqta᾿ de-Rav Kahana᾿*, ed. B. Mandelbaum (New York, 1962), 12, pp. 210–11.

22. See above, n. 20.

23. *Midrash ha-Gadol on Exodus*, ed. M. Margulies (Jerusalem, 1983), p. 384.

24. Similarly, there was a widely accepted midrashic tradition—attributed in some sources to R. Joshua of Sikhnin in the name of R. Levi—to read the words *kallot moshe* in Num. 7:1, "On the day that Moses finished setting up the Tabernacle," as *kallat moshe*, "the bride of Moses." Cf. *Pesiqta᾿ Rabbati* 5, 18a; *Pesiqta᾿ de-Rav Kahana᾿* 1, p. 9; *Tanḥuma᾿*, Naso, 20; *Tanḥuma᾿*, ed. Buber, Naso, 28; *Numbers Rabbah* 12:8; *Midrash ᾿Aggadah*, ed. S. Buber (Vienna, 1894), p. 89; commentary of Rashi to Num. 7:1; *Midrash ha-Gadol on Numbers*, ed. Z. M. Rabinowitz (Jerusalem, 1983), p. 104; *Zohar* 1:236b; 2:5b, 140b; 3:4b, 148a, 226b (*Ra῾aya᾿ Mehemna᾿*). It must be pointed out, however, that in the case of Num. 7:1, unlike Exod. 31:18, the spelling of the word *kallot* according to the masoretic text is in the plene form and not the defective; hence the rabbinic exegesis creatively changes the accepted orthography. This was already noted by the author of the *Ra῾aya᾿ Mehemna᾿*; see *Zohar* 3:254a. Cf. also the commentary of *Minḥat Shai* to Num. 7:1; Judah Loew of Prague, *Gur ᾿Aryeh* (Jerusalem, 1972), 4:28a–b; and Buber's note to his edition of *Pesiqta᾿ de-Rav Kahana᾿*, 6a n. 104.

25. Cf. *Exodus Rabbah* 41:5 and parallels in *Tanḥuma᾿*, Ki Tissa᾿, 16 and *Tanḥuma᾿*, ed. Buber, Ki Tissa᾿, 11, 56a–b, and *Bereshit Rabbati*, ed. Ch. Albeck (Jerusalem, 1940), p. 111.

26. On the possibility that Moses de León authored this text, see G. Scholem, "Meqorotav shel ma῾aseh R. Gadi᾿el ha-Tinoq be-Sifrut ha-Qabbalah," in *Le-᾿Agnon Shai*, ed. D. Sadan and E. E. Urbach (Jerusalem, 1959), pp. 294–95; idem, *Major Trends in Jewish Mysticism* (New York, 1954), pp. 183, 200; and idem, *Kabbalah* (Jerusalem, 1974), p. 432. Other scholars, however, beginning with Menaḥem ben Judah de Lonzano (1550–c. 1624), attribute the work to Eliezer ben Isaac of Worms, also known as Eliezer ha-Gadol, an eleventh-century German talmudist. Cf. I. Abrahams, *Hebrew Ethical Wills* (Philadelphia, 1926), 1:31–49, and J. Dan, *Hebrew Ethical and Homiletical Literature* (Jerusalem, 1975), pp. 93–94 (in Hebrew).

27. *᾿Orḥot Ḥayyim*, § 25.

28. B. Berakhot 6a.

29. *Deuteronomy Rabbah* 8:7, ed. S. Lieberman (Jerusalem, 1964), p. 121.

30. *Numbers Rabbah* 12:4.

31. This fact has been pointed out by several scholars. See M. Idel, "The Concept of Torah in the Hekhalot and Its Metamorphosis in the Kabbalah," *Jerusalem Studies in Jewish Thought* 1 (1981): 40 (in Hebrew) and references to other scholarly literature given in n. 49 ad locum.

32. See, however, the reading established in E. E. Urbach, "Perush le-silluq ha-qalliri le-farashat sheqalim ʾaz raʾita we-safarta," *Sefer Ḥayyim Shirman*, ed. S. Abramson and A. Mirsky (Jerusalem, 1970), p. 20: "the measure of the king (*middat melekh*) is superior in all."

33. I have utilized the text printed in I. Baer, *Seder ʿAvodat Yisraʾel* (Berlin, 1937), p. 57. See L. Zunz, *Literaturgeschichte der synagogalen Poesie* (Berlin, 1865), p. 43, and L. Landshuth, *ʿAmude ha-ʿAvodah Reshimat Roshe ha-Payyṭanim u-Meʿaṭ mi-Toldotehem ʿal Seder ʾAlfaʾ Betaʾ ʿim Mispar Piyyuṭehem ha-Nimṣaʾim be-Sifre Tefillot* (Berlin, 1857), p. 27.

34. The Hebrew *she-yikanes ʿal* has the negative connotation of entering against someone. See, however, Scholem, *Origins*, p. 170, who translates: "Whoever enters my daughter's presence is as one who enters my presence," and cf. the translation in F. Talmage, "Apples of Gold: The Inner Meaning of Sacred Texts in Medieval Judaism," in *Jewish Spirituality from the Bible through the Middle Ages*, ed. A. Green (New York, 1986), p. 347 n. 21: "If any one reaches my daughter, it is as if he reaches me." The rather neutral translation exemplified by these two scholars misses the point of the midrashic parable. Support for my rendering may be gathered from the continuation of the text where the word *bizah*, "to desecrate," is used in place of *nikhnas ʿal*, "to enter upon."

35. *Tanḥumaʾ*, Pequde, 4.

36. See the anonymous commentary on the seventy names of God from the circle of the German Pietists quoted by Idel, "Concept of the Torah," p. 42 n. 53: "The Torah [is] the glory of the Holy One, blessed be He." I have elaborated on the ontic identification of the Torah and the glory in German Pietistic texts and some of their sources in "The Mystical Significance of Torah Study in German Pietism," *Jewish Quarterly Review* 84 (1993): 43–78, esp. 62–77.

37. Cf. the view attributed to R. Joshua ben Levi in *Song of Songs Rabbah* 8:13: "In every place that the Holy One, blessed be He, placed His Torah, He placed His *Shekhinah*." This view opposes the previous one, attributed to the "rabbis" generally, which maintained that God calmed the angels by assuring them that while He would give His daughter, i.e., the Torah, to the people of Israel who inhabit the earth, He would not place His *Shekhinah* below.

38. *Batte Midrashot* (Jerusalem, 1980), 2:419.

39. See D. F. Sawyer, *Midrash Aleph Bet* (Atlanta,1993), pp. 22–23.

40. See, however, the description in Sawyer, *Midrash Aleph Bet*, p. 23: "Midrash Aleph Beth is not an esoteric or magical text, and this observation

marks it out not only from Sefer Yeṣirah, but also from the Alphabet of R. Akiba and the rest of the corpus of Jewish mystical texts." On the presumed "anti-esoteric stance" of this midrashic collection, see ibid., p. 32. The evidence adduced by Sawyer does not seem to me compelling inasmuch as the text does indeed abound in images of the celestial realm, the throne of glory, and various groups of angels, which are obviously related to Jewish mystical speculation. I thus have not changed my original assessment that this text is an important link in the chain of Jewish esotericism.

41. See *Batte Midrashot,* 2:445, where the Holy One, blessed be He, is said to be answered "from within the chamber [or sanctuary] of His glory (*ḥupat kevodo*)." For this use of the word *ḥupah,* cf., e.g., P. Megillah 1:14, 72c–d. As is well known, the image of the bridal chamber (symbolizing the divine Pleroma) is a central motif in certain Gnostic writings, including the wedding hymn in the *Acts of Thomas* and in other Valentinian texts such as the *Gospel of Philip* (Nag Hammadi II.3:65, 10–12; 67, 15, 30; 69, 1ff.; 70, 17–22, passim) and the *Exegesis on the Soul* (Nag Hammadi II.6:132, 13, 25). Cf. also Irenaeus, *Against Heresies* 1.7.1. cited in B. Layton, *The Gnostic Scriptures* (New York, 1987), pp. 294–95. See R. M. Grant, "The Mystery of Marriage in the Gospel of Philip," *Vigiliae Christianae* 15 (1961): 129–40, and M. Marcovich, "The Wedding Hymn of Acta Thomae," *Illinois Classical Studies* 6 (1981): 367–85, reprinted in *Studies in Graeco-Roman Religions and Gnosticism* (Leiden, 1988), pp. 156–73. The striking correspondence of the bahiric description of the lower Sophia with the "daughter of light" in the gnostic bridal hymn in the *Acts of Thomas* has already been noted by Scholem, *Origins,* pp. 94–95.

42. *Batte Midrashot,* 2:424. See now the analysis of this passage in Sawyer, *Midrash Aleph Bet,* pp. 105–6. Sawyer adequately describes the erotic relationship of the Torah to God, based in her opinion on Song of Songs 2:14, but she is quick to point out that there is no presumption here of a union between God and Torah. She notes as well that this midrashic text deliberately distinguishes the feminine concept of Torah from God. Placing the Torah within the created world and describing her as the consort of Moses suggests the author's "reactionary" orientation in relation to esoteric motifs. While I agree with the assessment that the feminine Torah here is clearly demarcated from the divine, I am not fully convinced of the argument that there is no mythical conception of Torah embracing her erotic relationship to God. The fact that in a subsequent passage from this midrashic text the Torah is described as being betrothed to Moses does not mitigate against the autonomous tradition concerning the relationship of the Torah to God. There are two distinct tradition complexes, ultimately exegetical in nature, that are preserved in this one text.

43. Cf. *Re᾿uyot Yeḥezqel,* ed. I. Gruenwald, in *Temirin,* ed. I. Weinstock (Jerusalem, 1972), 1:131. The relationship between this text and that of *Midrash ᾿Alfa᾿ Betot* was noted by Gruenwald in his comment to line 82 ad locum. It is of interest to note that in several other contexts in the *Hekhalot* literature God's sitting on the throne is compared to a groom entering the bridal

chamber; the throne, also referred to as the "beautiful vessel," is thus given a definite feminine quality. Cf. *Synopse zur Hekhalot-Literatur*, ed. P. Schäfer, et al. (Tübingen, 1981), §§ 94, 154, 687; *Geniza-Fragmente zur Hekhalot-Literatur* ed. P. Schäfer (Tübingen, 1984), p. 185. See also *Geniza-Fragmente*, p. 105, where it says of the angel MYHShGH that he "beautifies the Ḥashmal, adorns TRPZWHYW the king, and all the attributes of His throne like a bride for her bridal chamber (*we-khol middot kiss'o ke-khallah le-ḥupatah*)." In the last passage it is again clear that the throne is considered to be feminine in nature. Such a tradition is also found in other *merkavah* texts and had an important impact on the medieval mystical theosophies of the German Pietists and Spanish kabbalists. See A. Farber, "The Concept of the Merkabah in Thirteenth-Century Jewish Esotericism—'Sod ha-'Egoz' and Its Development" (Ph.D. dissertation, Hebrew University, 1986), pp. 116–17, 571–74, 617–27 (in Hebrew); M. Idel, "Métaphores et pratiques sexueles dans la cabale," in Ch. Mopsik, *Lettre sur la sainteté: le secret de la relation entre l'homme et la femme dans la cabale* (Paris, 1986), p. 340 n. 35; and E. Wolfson, "Circumcision and the Divine Name: A Study in the Transmission of Esoteric Doctrine," *Jewish Quarterly Review* 78 (1987): 95 n. 53. For a later use of this theme, see the text on Meṭaṭron discussed by M. Idel, "Additional Fragments from the Writings of R. Joseph of Hamadan," *Da'at* 21 (1988): 49 n. 16 (in Hebrew).

44. P. Ta'anit 2:1, 65a. Cf. the reading in *Yalquṭ Shim'oni*, pt. 2, § 535: " 'Let the bridegroom come out of his chamber' refers to the ark, 'the bride from her canopy' refers to the Torah scroll."

45. See *Batte Midrashot*, 2:423, 427, 445.

46. Ibid., p. 447.

47. The linkage of sexuality and dance is a well-attested phenomenon in various religious cultures. For a representative study, see J. L. Hanna, *Dance, Sex and Gender: Signs of Identity, Dominance, Defiance, and Desire* (Chicago and London, 1988). See J. Miller, *Measures of Wisdom: The Cosmic Dance in Classical and Christian Antiquity* (Toronto, 1986), pp. 136, 321, 399, 408, 447. See also the comments of S. Freud, *The Complete Introductory Lectures on Psychoanalysis*, trans. and ed. J. Strachey (New York, 1966), p. 157.

48. Cf. *Synopse*, § 189, where the holy beasts are described as singing with their mouths, clapping with their hands, and dancing with their feet, as they encircle the enthroned glory; and cf. § 411 where the *nogah* is said to have danced before the divine king (cf. §§ 34 and 870). The motif of angelic beings dancing before God is found as well in *Seder Rabbah di-Bereshit*; see ibid., §§ 850 and 852. See the discussion of the latter passages in E. K. Ginsburg, *The Sabbath in the Classical Kabbalah* (Albany, 1989), pp. 103–4. Ginsburg perceptively associates the angelic dancing (*meraqqedin*) with the talmudic phrase, "how does one dance before the bride," *keiṣad meraqqedin lifne ha-kallah* (B. Ketuvot 16a). The image of the Torah as the adorned bride dancing before the divine Presence may reflect an existent practice in which the Torah scroll was dressed up as a bride on her wedding day. Indeed, one is reminded by this

image of the Simḥat Torah celebration in which dancing with the Torah figures as a prominent feature. Interestingly enough, both the custom to dance with the Torah and that of crowning the Torah (to be sure, already in M. ᵓAvot 4:13 one finds the expression *keter Torah,* the crown of Torah, but in that context this image has a purely figurative connotation without any objective correlate)—a practice that eventually became the normative course of action for all year round and not specifically on this one festival—originated apparently in the Babylonian academies during the Geonic period in connection with Simḥat Torah. See A. Yaari, *Toledot Ḥag Simḥat Torah* (Jerusalem, 1964), pp. 24–25. Underlying both these ritualisitc performances, but especially the former, is the aggadic image of the Torah as the bride. On the day when the cycle of Torah reading is completed, the scroll is crowned like a bride, thus recalling the day of revelation at Sinai, which itself was likened to a wedding celebration. That the crown placed on the Torah is to bring to mind the bridal crown is obvious from the fact that in the original Geonic responsum the halakhic question to be examined is whether or not a groom could place on his head during his own wedding the crown that was used to crown the Torah during the festival. The wedding motif is even stronger in a later version of this responsum in the fourteenth-century halakhic compedium *ᵓOrḥot Ḥayyim,* by Aaron ha-Kohen of Lunel, where a noticeable change in language is easily detected: "The Gaon wrote: It is forbidden to place the crown that has been placed on the Torah scroll on the head of the one who completes [the reading] on the day of Simḥat Torah." That is, the original prohibition of placing the crown on the head of a groom has been understood as the specific prohibition of placing the crown on the head of the last one called up to the Torah. This reflects the institution of the *ḥatan Torah,* i.e., the groom of the Torah, a particular name applied already in the school of Solomon ben Isaac of Troyes in the eleventh century to the one who was called up to the Torah for the concluding section of Deuteronomy. The name *ḥatan Torah,* as Yaari has shown, represents a subtle change from what appears to have been the original title, *ḥatam Torah,* i.e., the one who seals or concludes the Torah (cf. M. Megillah 4:1). *Ḥatan Torah,* by contrast, means the "groom of the Torah," thus complementing the feminine image of the Torah as the bride. In the version of the Geonic responsa of R. Aaron it is assumed that the one reading the Torah is the groom of the wedding celebration and the Torah is the bride. Indeed, in the course of the generations from medieval times through modernity many customs have arisen in connection with the Torah and *ḥatan Torah* that are reminiscent of things done at actual weddings. See Goldberg, "Torah and Children," p. 118.

49. The notion that the souls of the righteous are hidden beneath the throne of the glory is a much older motif in Jewish sources. Cf. B. Shabbat 152b and parallels.

50. On Moses' posture as the official translator of the Bible according to this text, see *Batte Midrashot,* 2:447.

51. Ibid., p. 424. The passage from this relatively late text draws on much earlier ideas regarding the pre-existence of the Torah and other elements,

including the throne and the souls of Israel, to the creation of the world. Cf. *Genesis Rabbah* 1:4, p. 6, and *Pirqe R. ʾEliʿezer*, ch. 3.

52. Judah ben Barzillai, *Perush Sefer Yeṣirah*, ed. S. J. Halberstam (Berlin, 1885), p. 268. See Scholem, *Origins*, p. 92.

53. In the printed editions of the *Bahir* the reading is *mukhlelet*, which I have rendered as "comprised." G. Scholem, *Das Buch Bahir* (Leipzig, 1923), p. 151, similarly translates the word *mukhlelet* as "enthalten." Cf. parallel, in slightly different imagery, in *Sefer ha-Bahir*, ed. R. Margaliot (Jerusalem, 1978), § 190, where it says that God took one-thousandth from the splendor of the hidden light and "built from it a beautiful and adorned precious stone (*ʾeven yeqarah naʾah u-mequsheṭet*) and comprised within it all the commandments (*we-khillel bah kol ha-miṣwot*)." It is not impossible that there is a play on words in § 196 between *mukhlelet* and *mekhullelet*, "to be comprised" and "to be crowned." If the latter is implied, then it would fit nicely with the two verbs that precede it, viz., *mequsheṭet* and *meʿuṭeret*, conjuring further the image of the bride arrayed on her wedding day. Cf. § 91 where the crown (i.e., the *Shekhinah*) is identified as the precious stone that is *mekhullelet u-meʿuṭeret*. Cf. the manuscript reading used by Scholem, *Das Buch Bahir*, p. 62 n. 9, *meʿuṭeret we-mukhlelet*, which he translated as "der gekrönte Edelstein, in dem [Alles] zusammengefaßt ist" (p. 61). Cf. also *Bahir*, § 146, where the sixth of the ten logoi is described as the *kisseʾ ha-kavod ha-meʿuṭar ha-mukhlal*, rendered by Scholem, *Das Buch Bahir*, p. 104, as "Der Thron der Herrlichkeit, der gekrönt ist, eingefaßt." For a similar use of the root *kll* in an eleventh-century *piyyuṭ* from southern Italy, see *The Poems of Elya bar Schemaya*, ed. Y. David (Jerusalem, 1977), p. 128 (in Hebrew), where *hukhlelah* is used synonymously with *hukhtarah*. Tracing the particular usage of such key words as this may prove helpful in determining the literary provenance of parts of the *Bahir*. On the merging of the images of the crown and the throne, cf. the following passage describing the bride (Sophia) in the wedding hymn in the *Acts of Thomas*: "On the crown of her head sits the king" (translated in Marcovich, "Wedding Hymn," p. 160).

54. *Sefer ha-Bahir*, § 196. See Scholem, *Origins*, p. 174.

55. The theurgical dimension of Torah study is repeated in *Sefer ha-Bahir*, § 185, where it is stated that "whoever studies Torah bestows love (*gommel ḥesed*) upon his Creator, as it is written, '[O Jeshurun, there is none like God], riding the heavens with your help' (Deut. 33:26), that is to say, when you study Torah for its own sake (*torah lishmah*) then you help Me [i.e., God], and I ride the heavens."

56. The connection between *ʾoṣar* and Torah is based on earlier midrashic sources. Cf. *Midrash Tehillim*, ed. S. Buber (Vilna, 1891), 119:9, p. 493: "*ʾOṣarot* refers to the Torah, as it is written, 'A precious treasure (*ʾoṣar nehmad*) etc.' (Prov. 21:20)." And cf. *Midrash ʾOtiyyot de-R. ʿAqivaʾ*, ed. S. Wertheimer, *Batte Midrashot*, 2:348: "*ʾOṣar* is the Torah, as it is said, 'The fear of the Lord is his treasure (*ʾoṣaro*)' (Isa. 33:6), and Torah is fear, as it is said, 'And all the

peoples of the earth shall see that the Lord's name is proclaimed over you, and they stand in fear of you' (Deut. 28:10)." Besides the nexus established between fear and Torah (repeated in *Sefer ha-Bahir*; see reference in n. 58), from the last citation it is clear that in this text Torah is already identified with the name of God, a theme more fully exploited in medieval kabbalah.

57. In the standard printed edition of the *Bahir* the reading is "and *Binah*, which is the attribute of judgment." This reading, also attested in MS Munich, Bayerische Staatsbibliothek 209, fol. 36a, is obviously corrupt as *Binah* was already mentioned in the enumeration of divine potencies between *Ḥokhmah* and *ᶜEṣah* (i.e., *Ḥesed*). See the more accurate reading preserved in Menaḥem Recanaṭi, *Perush ᶜal ha-Torah* (Jerusalem, 1961), 39d: "In the *Sefer ha-Bahir* [it is written]: counsel (*ᶜEṣah*) is the bestowing of kindness (*gemilut ḥasadim*), strength (*Gevurah*) is the attribute of judgment." This reading is reflected as well in Scholem's translation, *Das Buch Bahir*, § 129, p. 140: 'Rat'—das sei das Wohltun, 'Starke'—das sei Prinzip der Strenge."

58. *Sefer ha-Bahir*, § 186.

59. Cf. the commentary of *ʾOr ha-Ganuz*, ad locum. For a different explanation, cf. *Maᶜarekhet ha-ʾElohut* (Jerusalem, 1963), 66a, where the bahiric symbolism is interpreted as a reference to the ninth *sefirah* or *Yesod*. Scholem, *Das Buch Bahir*, p. 141 n. 2, suggests that the "fear of God" in the *Bahir* has a double meaning: it can refer either to *Binah* or to the *Shekhinah*. See, however, *Origins*, p. 136, where Scholem unequivocally states that in the *Bahir* the "fear of God" refers symbolically to the third *sefirah* or *Binah*. This interpretation indeed fits several other passages in the *Bahir*, most notably §§ 103 (Scholem, § 72) and 190 (§ 131). In the latter case, however, it is clear that an intrinsic connection is established between the primordial light, which is identified as the "fear of God," and the *Shekhinah*.

60. The use of the expression *bat melekh* to refer to the *Shekhinah*—also identified as "prayer," the "tenth kingdom," and the "angel of the Lord,"—is found in the pseudo-Hai passage incorporated in Eleazar of Worms, *Sefer ha-Ḥokhmah*; cf. MS Oxford, Bodleian Library 1812, fols. 60b–61a. Concerning this passage, see Scholem, *Origins*, pp. 184–86; J. Dan, *The Esoteric Theology of German Pietism* (Jerusalem, 1968), pp. 118–29 (in Hebrew); Farber, "Concept of the Merkabah," pp. 231–44; and M. Idel, *Kabbalah: New Perspectives* (New Haven and London, 1988), p. 195. It is not clear from the passage in question if one is justified to go further and identify the *bat melekh* with the Torah as in the bahiric material. Farber, "Concept of the Merkabah," p. 242 n. 40, correctly notes that in another section of *Sefer ha-Ḥokhmah* the Torah is identified as *malkhut*, *bat*, and *Shekhinah*. See also Wolfson, "Mystical Significance of Torah Study," pp. 76–77. Given the explicit identification of the Torah and the *Shekhinah* in this passage, it is reasonable to assume that in the first passage as well such an identification is operative. Cf. Eleazar's *Sefer ha-Shem*, MS London, British Museum 737, fols. 320a–b: "The *yod* is placed at the beginning of the name [YHWH] for the *Shekhinah* is [found] in ten. It is

written, 'I will be sanctified in the midst of the Israelite people' (Lev. 23:32), for [the expression] 'Israelite people,' *bene yisraʾel,* [numerically equals] 603, and if you add ten [represented by the letter *yod*] to them there is [a sum of] 613. The ten are called the Israelite people for then there are 613. Therefore, the Torah is only read in a group of ten." In this passage there seems to be an implicit identification of Torah, *Shekhinah,* and the community of Israel. The feminine quality of the hypostasized Torah also seems to be implied in another passage in *Sefer ha-Shem,* MS London, British Museum 737, fol. 308b. In that context Eleazar describes the Primordial Torah as the "flying scroll" (cf. Zech. 5:1) in the throne of glory. Cf. *Sefer ha-Roqeaḥ* (Jerusalem, 1967), p. 109, and other sources noted by Idel, "Concept of Torah," p. 42 n. 53.

61. The sequence of images in the *Bahir* is close to that which is found in Judah ben Barzillai's *Perush Sefer Yeṣirah,* p. 57. See Scholem, *Origins,* p. 93.

62. Cf. *Sefer ha-Bahir,* § 77, where this wisdom is identified as the *Shekhinah.*

63. The image of the king's daughter also appears in *Sefer ha-Bahir,* §§ 54, 63, 93.

64. Ibid., § 2. Cf. § 65, and Scholem, *Origins,* pp. 92–93.

65. Ibid., § 54.

66. Ibid., § 55. The scriptural reference is to Proverbs 24:3. For discussion of the bahiric text, see Scholem, *On the Mystical Shape,* pp. 164–65.

67. This has already been recognized by Scholem; see *Das Buch Bahir,* p. 40 n. 2, and *Origins,* p. 170. See also in the Margaliot edition of *Sefer ha-Bahir,* § 54 n. 3.

68. *Exodus Rabbah* 33:1.

69. *Sefer ha-Bahir,* § 136.

70. See Scholem, *Origins,* p. 132.

71. *Sefer ha-Bahir,* § 137. See Scholem, *Origins,* pp. 144–45.

72. *Sefer ha-Bahir,* § 138.

73. Ibid., § 143. See Scholem, *Origins,* pp. 134, 145, 175. The language of the *Bahir* is appropriated, without the source being named, by Asher ben David, *Perush Shem ha-Meforash,* ed. M. Ḥasidah, *Ha-Segullah* 1 (Jerusalem, 1934), p. 6, reprinted in J. Dan, *Qabbalat R. ʾAsher ben David* (Jerusalem, 1980), p. 18. For another example of the influence of the *Bahir* on this kabbalist, see Scholem, *Das Buch Bahir,* p. 145.

74. Cf. B. Ḥagigah 12a.

75. *Sefer ha-Bahir,* § 147.

76. Cf. Maimonides' introduction to the *Mishneh Torah*: " 'And I will give you tablets of stone and the Torah and the commandments' (Exod. 24:12). 'Torah' refers to the Written Torah, 'and the commandments' refers to that which is called the Oral Torah." The Oral Torah is identified as commandment in B. Berakhot 5a. Cf. *Zohar* 2:166b; 3:40b.

77. *Sefer ha-Bahir*, § 149.

78. See, e.g., *Commentary on Talmudic Aggadoth by Rabbi Azriel of Gerona*, ed. I. Tishby (Jerusalem, 1945), pp. 3, 49, 53 (in Hebrew), and Ṭodros Abulafia, *Sha ʿar ha-Razim*, ed. M. Kushnir-Oron (Jerusalem, 1989), p. 73.

79. This is to be distinguished from another idea expressed in thirteenth-century kabbalah concerning the revelation of the Written Torah, the masculine potency, through the mediation of the Oral Torah, the feminine potency. See, e.g., Ezra of Gerona, *Perush le-Shir ha-Shirim*, in *Kitve Ramban*, ed. by C. D. Chavel (Jerusalem, 1978), 2:487. See also the text cited and discussed by G. Scholem, *On the Kabbalah and Its Symbolism*, trans. R. Manheim (New York, 1969), pp. 49–50. According to the author of that text, the Written Torah that we have on this earth has already passed through the medium of the Oral Torah; the Written Torah in and of itself is a purely mystical construct. Scholem assumed that the aforementioned text was written by Isaac the Blind. See, by contrast, M. Idel, "Kabbalistic Materials from the School of R. David ben Yehudah he-Ḥasid," *Jerusalem Studies in Jewish Thought* 2 (1982/83):170 n. 9 (in Hebrew).

80. See Ginsburg, *Sabbath in the Classical Kabbalah*, pp. 175–76 n. 231. On some other aspects of Judah ben Yaqar's mystical treatment of the Sabbath, see ibid., pp. 108–9.

81. In this context, however, ben Yaqar cites the source as part of *Genesis Rabbah*; see n. 20, above.

82. This characterization was originally used to describe the status of the Primordial Torah, or the Torah in a state before the world existed. Cf. P. Sheqalim 6:1; *Tanḥuma ʾ*, Bereshit, 1. The usage in this context is clearly secondary.

83. *Perush ha-Tefillot we-ha-Berakhot*, pt. 1, p. 90.

84. Ibid., p. 104.

85. Indeed, the crown for ben Yaqar, as for other kabbalists, is a symbol for sexual unification.

86. See *Perush ha-Tefillot we-ha-Berakhot*, "Addenda," p. 27.

87. I have followed the explanation of this difficult passage offered by several of the standard commentaries on Naḥmanides' commentary. Cf. Shem Ṭov ibn Gaon, *Keter Shem Ṭov*, in *Ma ʾor wa-Shemesh*, ed. J. Koriat (Livorno, 1839), 27a.

88. Cf. *Perush ha-Ramban ʿal ha-Torah,* ed. C. D. Chavel (Jerusalem, 1969), 1:133, ad Gen. 24:1.

89. I have rendered the biblical expression literally, which accords with the kabbalistic interpretation proferred by Naḥmanides.

90. Cf. B. Yevamot 49b.

91. *Perush ha-Ramban ʿal ha-Torah* 1:11, ad Gen. 1:1.

92. Ibid. 1:454, ad Exod. 25:3.

93. See, e.g., ibid. 1:39, 64–65, ad Gen. 2:20 and 9:12.

94. Ibid. 2:491, ad Deut. 33:1.

95. *Rabbenu Baḥya ʿal ha-Torah,* ed. C. D. Chavel (Jerusalem, 1981), 3:478, ad Deut. 33:4. The zoharic influence on this passage has been noted by E. Gottlieb, *The Kabbalah in the Writings of R. Baḥya ben Asher ibn Halawa* (Jerusalem, 1970), p. 20 (in Hebrew).

96. *Zohar* 3:35b–36a.

97. See Y. Liebes, *Studies in the Zohar,* trans. A. Schwartz, S. Nakache, and P. Peli (Albany, 1993), pp. 68–69.

98. *Zohar* 2:99a–b. This parable has been the focus of much scholarly discussion of which I will here mention only a few relevant examples. See Scholem, *On the Kabbalah,* pp. 55–56; I. Tishby, *The Wisdom of the Zohar,* trans. D. Goldstein (Oxford, 1989), pp. 1084–85; Idel, *Kabbalah: New Perspectives,* pp. 227–28; and E. R. Wolfson, "Beautiful Maiden without Eyes: *Peshaṭ* and *Sod* in Zoharic Hermeneutics," in *The Midrashic Imagination,* ed. M. Fishbane (Albany, 1993), pp. 155–203, esp. 169–70, 185–87. See also reference to my study cited in n. 101, below.

99. For the Aramaic equivalent to this expression, cf. *Zohar* 1:242b.

100. Cf. *Zohar* 1:21b, 236b, 239a.

101. See E. R. Wolfson, "The Hermeneutics of Visionary Experience: Revelation and Interpretation in the *Zohar,*" *Religion* 18 (1988): 321–24. A greatly expanded version of this study appears as the seventh chapter of my monograph *Through a Speculum That Shines: Vision and Imagination in Medieval Jewish Mysticism* (Princeton, 1994).

102. It is worthwhile comparing the zoharic imagery to the description in Joseph Gikatilla of the king stripping naked before the queen. In the case of Gikatilla, the king represents the Tetragrammaton, which stands symbolically for the sixth emanation, that discards all the other names and appellations. See *Shaʿare ʾOrah,* ed. J. Ben-Shlomo (Jerusalem, 1981), 1:196. Cf. ibid., p. 206, where the image of the king removing his garments and uniting with his wife is used to describe more specifically the process by which the Tetragrammaton removes its appellations and garments and unites with the spiritual elite of

Israel. Cf. ibid., p. 218, and see discussion of Gikatilla's imagery in Ch. Mopsik, *Lettre sur la sainteté: le secret de la relation entre l'homme et la femme dans la cabale* (Paris, 1986), pp. 98–99. The Torah is not mentioned explicitly in any of these passages, but in other contexts (ibid., pp. 48, 248) Gikatilla does equate the Torah and the Tetragrammaton, and it is therefore plausible to suggest that underlying his metaphor is a conception similiar to that of the *Zohar,* with the important distinction being that in the case of Gikatilla the Torah is portrayed as a masculine figure and in the *Zohar* it is feminine.

103. MS Berlin, Staatsbibliothek Or. Quat. 833, fol. 1b. For a discussion of this text and its conceptual background, see D. Cohen-Alloro, *The Secret of the Garment in the Zohar* (Jerusalem, 1987), p. 43 (in Hebrew).

104. Cf. *Zohar* 1:9a, 135b, 164a, 245a; 2:94b, 134b (*Ra ͑aya ͗ Mehemna ͗*), 149a, 155b, 188b, 209a; 3:22a, 35a, 58b, 60b, 61a, 213a, 268a–b, 298a; and *Zohar Ḥadash,* 28b, 29a, 95a (*Midrash ha-Ne ͑elam*).

105. M. ͗Avot 3:2, 3:6; B. Berakhot 6a; Sanhedrin 39b; Targum to Ps. 82:1; *Midrash Tehillim,* 105:1, p. 448; *Deuteronomy Rabbah* 7:2. See E. E. Urbach, *The Sages: Their Concepts and Beliefs* (Jerusalem, 1978), p. 33 (in Hebrew).

106. *Zohar* 3:36a.

107. *Zohar* 2:200a.

108. See commentary of *Niṣoṣe ͗Orot* to *Zohar* 2:200a.

109. Based on a standard rabbinic eschatological image; see, e.g., B. Berakhot 17a.

110. M. ͗Avot 1:13, 4:5.

111. *Tiqqune Zohar,* ed. R. Margaliot (Jerusalem, 1978), 11b.

112. Elsewhere in *Tiqqune Zohar* the aspect of *halakhah* is identified with the left side of *Shekhinah* and that of *qabbalah* with the right side. Alternatively expressed, *Shekhinah* is called *halakhah* when she goes to receive from her husband, and *qabbalah* after she has already recevied. For references see Tishby, *Wisdom of the Zohar,* p. 1117 n. 128.

113. See, e.g., *Tiqqune Zohar* 10, 25b; 21, 61b; 30, 73a; 36, 78a.

114. See, in particular, the following comment of Isaac the Blind reported by Jacob ben Sheshet in *Sefer ha-͗Emunah we-ha-Biṭṭaḥon,* in *Kitve Ramban,* 2:401: "And strength alludes to the Oral Torah, which is the strength and the crown (*͑aṭarah*) of the Torah."

115. See, e.g., *Tiqqune Zohar* 30, 73a; 36, 78a.

116. *Zohar* 3:256b. Yaari, *Toledot Ḥag Simḥat Torah,* p. 30, cites this passage in the name of the *Zohar,* without qualifying that it belongs to a later stratum, not authored by the same hand that composed the bulk of the *Zohar.*

117. The phallic interpretation of the Torah scroll is found, for instance, in the writings of Joseph of Hamadan. See M. Meier, "A Critical Edition of the *Sefer Ṭaʿamey ha-Miẓwoth* ("Book of Reasons of the Commandments") Attributed to Isaac ibn Farhi/Section I—Positive Commandments/With Introduction and Notes." (Ph.D. dissertation, Brandeis University, 1974), pp. 58, 78–80, and J. Zwelling, "Joseph of Hamadan's *Sefer Tashak*: Critical Text Edition with Introduction" (Ph.D. dissertation, Brandeis University, 1975), pp. 13, 93.

118. The correlation of the Oral Torah and the *Shekhinah* resulted in the personfication of the Mishnah in the maggidic revelations of Joseph Karo. See R. J. Zwi Werblowsky, *Joseph Karo: Lawyer and Mystic* (Philadelphia, 1977), pp. 108–11, 268–69.

119. *Tefillah le-Moshe* (Prezmysl, 1932), 134b–135a. Cf. the comments of R. Meir Poppers, in his commentary *ʾOr ha-Yashar*, ad locum: "The reason for [reading] the Torah during the prayer [service] is to unify the prayer, *Malkhut*, with the Torah, *Tifʾeret*. . . . Know that the secret of *Tifʾeret* is above, concealed within *Binah*, i.e., the Torah scroll is in the supernal Ark, and we take it out from there. We carry the Torah scroll to the table, which is [symbolically] *Malkhut*. The cantor, who represents *Yesod*, carries *Tifʾeret* [i.e., the scroll] below to *Malkhut*, which is the table." Cf. Isaiah Horowitz, *Siddur Shaʿar ha-Shamayim* (Jerusalem, n.d.), p. 231.

120. This symbolism is repeated on many occasions in Cordovero's writings of which I here mention a very modest sampling. Cf. *Pardes Rimmonim* (Jerusalem, 1962), 8:17, 48a; 23:22, 44a–b, s.v., *torah*; *Zohar ʿim Perush ʾOr Yaqar*, vol. 15 (Jerusalem, 1987), p. 88; and *Shiʿur Qomah* (Jerusalem, 1966), sec. 13, 13b–c.

121. *Shaʿar ha-Kawwanot* (Jerusalem, 1963), 109b. Cf. *ʿEṣ Ḥayyim* (Jerusalem, 1930), 8:6, 39c, and *Mavoʾ Sheʿarim* (Jerusalem, 1978), p. 49. In the latter context Vital also mentions another tradition according to which the Torah scroll alludes to (or symbolizes) *Zeʿeir ʾAnpin*, the Written Torah. Concerning this latter symbolism, see also *ʿEṣ Ḥayyim*, 20:3, 96d. Cf. *Shaʿar ha-Miṣwot* (Jerusalem, 1978), p. 79, where Vital identifies the Torah as the "Foundation of the Father," *Yesod de-ʾAbbaʾ*, which is within *Zeʿeir ʾAnpin*. See also *Shaʿar Maʾamere RaZa"L* (Jerusalem, 1898), 6d. There is no contradiction between these two symbolic correspondences for Torah insofar as, according to the Lurianic system transmitted by Vital, *Yesod de-ʾAbbaʾ* is revealed or clothed within the mind (literally, knowledge, *daʿat*) or *Tifʾeret* of *Zeʿeir ʾAnpin*; cf. *ʿEṣ Ḥayyim*, 37:3, 59a.

122. *Shaʿar ha-Kawwanot*, 48d.

123. Ibid. Cf. *Peri ʿEṣ Ḥayyim*, ed. Meir Poppers (Jerusalem, 1980), p. 302: "The secret of the Torah is the secret of *Yesod de-ʾAbbaʾ*, which is within *Zeʿeir ʾAnpin*. The unification that we perform is that the *Yesod de-ʾImmaʾ* is opened, and the lights of mercy and judgment go out from there. . . . The *Yesod* [of] *ʾImmaʾ* opens and the consciousness (*moḥin*) within it shines upon Jacob and Rachel [i.e., the lower two countenances, *Zeʿeir ʾAnpin* and *Nuqbaʾ*]."

124. Cf. *Shaʿar ha-Kawwanot*, 43c, where Vital describes the following custom of Luria after the Torah scroll was taken out of the ark and placed on the pulpit: "Then he would actually look at the letters of the Torah scroll, and he would say that by means of one's looking from close so that one could read the letters well the great light is drawn to a person." The connection between the letters of Torah and light is a motif developed in much older kabbalistic sources. For references, see Wolfson, "Hermeneutics of Visionary Experience," p. 337 n. 61.

125. Cf. *Shaʿar ha-Miṣwot*, p. 79; *Shaʿar Maʾamere RaZa"L*, 6d; and *Peri ʿEṣ Ḥayyim*, p. 352. In subsequent Hasidic thought the kabbalistic interpretation of *torah lishmah* as *torah le-shem heʾ* took on an entirely different connotation; see the study of Weiss referred to in the following note.

126. For a study of this pivotal idea in Beshtian Hasidism, see J. Weiss, *Studies in Eastern European Jewish Mysticism*, ed. D. Goldstein (Oxford, 1985), pp. 56–68. On the potential conflict between the mystical ideal of *devequt* and normative Torah study, see R. Schatz Uffenheimer, *Hasidism as Mysticism: Quietistic Elements in Eighteenth-Century Hasidic Thought*, trans. J. Chipman (Princeton, 1993), pp. 310–25.

127. Job 24:7, 10.

128. *Toledot Yaʿaqov Yosef* (Korets, 1780; reprint Jerusalem, 1966), 131b.

129. See Scholem, *On the Kabbalah*, pp. 43–44; Idel, "Concept of Torah," pp. 23–84; and *Kabbalah: New Perspectives*, pp. 244–46. The ontic identity of God and the Torah is often stressed in the teaching of Dov Baer of Miedzyrzecz, frequently expressed in the locution of the *Zohar*. Cf. *Maggid Devarav le-Yaʿaqov*, ed. R. Schatz Uffenheimer (Jerusalem, 1976), pp. 26, 40, 83, 149–50, 160–61, 171, 201–2, 227–28, 272. Cf. Menaḥem Naḥum of Chernobyl, *Meʾor ʿEinayim* (Brooklyn, 1984), 37a: "When one cleaves to the letters of the Torah, to behold the splendor of the life-force (*laḥazot be-noʿam ziw ha-ḥiyyut*) of the Infinite, blessed be He, which spreads forth in the letters of the Torah, he cleaves to God, blessed be He." On Torah as a means to cleave to the Infinite, see ibid., 13d, 94a.

130. See Weiss, *Studies*, pp. 58–59.

131. Elsewhere Jacob Joseph depicts the mystic's cleaving to the Torah in opposite terms, i.e., the mystic is the female lover, and the Torah is the male beloved. Thus he interprets the verse "I am my beloved's and my beloved is mine" (Song of Songs 6:3) as referring to "one who cleaves to the Torah, which is called my beloved (*dodi*), and then the Torah is [in a state of] 'my beloved is mine' " (*Ketonet Passim*, ed. G. Nigal [Jerusalem, 1985], pp. 175–76).

132. *Tifʾeret ʿUziʾel* (Jerusalem, 1986), p. 125. Cf. ibid., p. 61: "This is the reason why it says in every place 'Torah for her sake' (*torah lishmah*) and it does not say 'Torah for his sake' (*torah lishemo*) for in truth [God], blessed be He, desires the delight of the Torah (*shaʿashuʿa shel torah*) so that it will be palatable and sweet for those who study it as the love of a bridegroom for

the bride. Thus it is called betrothed. The Torah and the Holy One, blessed He, are one."

133. On the background of this teaching, see I. Tishby, " 'The Holy One, Blessed be He, the Torah, and Israel Are One': The Source of a Saying in the Commentary of Ramḥal on the Idra Rabba," *Kiryat Sefer* 50 (1975): 480–92, 668–74 (in Hebrew); B. Zak, " 'More on the Evolution of the Saying, 'The Holy One, Blessed be He, the Torah, and Israel Are One,' " *Kiryat Sefer* 57 (1982): 179–84 (in Hebrew). On Moses Ḥayyim Ephraim of Sudlikov's particular use of this expression, see Tishby, op. cit., pp. 482–84.

134. *Degel Maḥaneh ᵓEfrayim*, 52a. For a discussion of this passage with a slightly different emphasis, see Idel, *Kabbalah: New Perspectives*, p. 245.

135. *Meᵓor ᶜEinayim*, 40d.

136. See above, n. 48.

137. I have utilized the translation of Isaac Frank published in *S. Y. Agnon, Twenty-One Stories*, ed. N. N Glatzer (New York, 1970), p. 22.

138. Ibid., pp. 23–24.

139. Ibid., pp. 24–25.

140. Ibid., p. 25.

2. Circumcision, Vision of God, and Textual Interpretation: From Midrashic Trope to Mystical Symbol

This study originally appeared in *History of Religions* 27 (1987): 189–215, and it is here reprinted with permission of The University of Chicago Press.

1. The most comprehensive treatments of the *Zohar* in English are G. Scholem, *Major Trends in Jewish Mysticism* (New York, 1961), chs. 4 and 5; D. Matt, *Zohar: The Book of Enlightenment* (New York, 1983), pp. 3–39; and I. Tishby, *The Wisdom of the Zohar*, trans. by D. Goldstein (Oxford, 1989), pp. 1–126.

2. Conversely, according to the *Zohar*, the Jew who has sexual relations with a non-Jew is guilty of idolatry, i.e., worshiping other gods, which, in zoharic theosophy, means the forces of impurity. Cf. *Zohar Ḥadash*, ed. R. Margaliot (Jerusalem, 1978) 21a (*Midrash ha-Neᶜelam*); *Zohar* 1:131b; 2:3b, 87b; 3:84a, 142a (*ᵓIdraᵓ Rabbaᵓ*); and Tishby, *Wisdom of the Zohar*, p. 1365. On the connection between idolatry and adultery in earlier rabbinic sources, see S. Schechter, *Aspects of Rabbinic Theology* (New York, 1961), p. 250. Related to this nexus of motifs is the zoharic claim that sexual offenses result in the denial of visionary experiences of the face of the *Shekhinah*. Cf., e.g., *Zohar* 1:57a, and 2:214b.

3. Cf. *Zohar* 3:72b–73a, and ibid., 91b: "The holy name, which is the Torah, is not made known to one who is not circumcised and who has not entered (the) covenant." Cf. also *Zohar* 1:236b where it is said that Simeon and Levi circumcised the inhabitants of Shechem in order to teach them the secrets of Torah. In several contexts the zoharic authorship further restricts Torah study to males; cf. *Zohar* 1:126b; 2:166a. This is no doubt related to the link established between study of Torah and possessing the seal of circumcision. On the correlation of circumcision and Torah study in select zoharic passages, see E. R. Wolfson, "Circumcision and the Divine Name: A Study in the Transmission of Esoteric Doctrine," *Jewish Quarterly Review* 78 (1987): 77–112, esp. 103–6. In light of this nexus of circumcision and Torah it is of interest to recall the custom in some western Ashkenazi communities of using the liner cloth that was placed under the male child on the day of his circumcision as the binder for the Torah scroll. See B. Kirshenblatt-Gimblett, "The Cut That Binds: The Western Ashkenazic Torah Binder as Nexus between Circumcision and Torah," in *Celebration: Studies in Festivity and Ritual,* ed. V. Turner (Washington, D.C., 1982), pp. 136–46, and H. E. Goldberg, "Torah and Children: Some Symbolic Aspects of the Reproduction of Jews and Judaism," in *Judaism Viewed from Within and from Without: Anthropological Studies,* ed. H. E. Goldberg (Albany, 1987), p. 112. The restriction of Torah study to Jews is talmudic in origin; see the statement of R. Yoḥanan in B. Sanhedrin 59a, and that of R. Ami, a disciple of R. Yoḥanan, in B. Ḥagigah 13a. The talmudic restriction is not ostensibly connected with the issue of circumcision, but in other rabbinic sources an explicit connection along these lines is made. Cf. *Tanḥuma*ʾ, Mishpaṭim, 5, and *Exodus Rabbah* 30:12. Consider as well the remark of the Roman satirist, Juvenal (60–130 C.E.), in his *Saturae* 14, lines 96–104, cited and translated in M. Stern, *Greek and Latin Authors on Jews and Judaism* (Jerusalem, 1980), 2:102–3, concerning Moses' refusal to disclose the truths of Torah to any but the circumcised. The similarity between the view of Juvenal and that of the *Zohar* was noted by Y. Liebes, "The Messiah of the Zohar," in *The Messianic Idea in Jewish Thought: A Study Conference in Honour of the Eightieth Birthday of Gershom Scholem* (Jerusalem, 1982), p. 140 n. 205 (in Hebrew).

4. Concerning the assumption that Moses ben Shem Ṭov de León (c. 1240–1305) is the author of the *Zohar,* see references cited in n. 1. For a different approach, see Y. Liebes, *Studies in the Zohar,* trans. A. Schwartz, S. Nakache, and P. Peli (Albany, 1993), pp. 85–138.

5. The biblical injunction for circumcision (cf. Gen. 17:10–14, Lev. 12:3; cf. Exod. 12:48), and the normative practice derived from it, is clearly and unambiguously directed to the male child. There is documentary evidence in the writings of Strabo of Amaseia (first century B.C.E. to first century C.E.) that some Jews not only practiced circumcision on male children but excision on female children as well. See M. Stern, *Greek and Latin Authors on Jews and Judaism* (Jerusalem, 1976), 1:300, 315. See, however, L. H. Schiffman, *Who Was a Jew? Rabbinic and Halakhic Perspectives on the Jewish-Christian Schism* (Hoboken, N.J., 1985), p. 84 n. 35.

6. This is based in part on the fact that circumcision is referred to in the Bible (cf. Gen. 17:11) as an *ʾot*, i.e., a sign. The rabbis thus spoke of a "letter" (a secondary meaning of the word *ʾot*) that served as the "seal" of the covenant of circumcision, viz., the letter *yod*. Cf. *Tanḥumaʾ*, Ṣav, 14; Shemini, 8.

7. On the seal as a designation for circumcision, see G. W. E. Nickelsburg, "Stories of Biblical and Early Post-Biblical Times," in *Jewish Writings of the Second Temple Period*, ed. M. E. Stone (Philadelphia, 1984), p. 73, and references in n. 218.

8. See D. M. Levin, *The Body's Recollection of Being: Phenomenological Psychology and the Deconstruction of Nihilism* (London, 1985), pp. 202–3; J. Derrida, "Shibboleth," in *Midrash and Literature*, ed. G. Hartman and S. Budick (New Haven, 1986), pp. 307–47.

9. See Liebes, *Studies in the Zohar*, pp. 26–30.

10. See J. Neusner, *Midrash in Context* (Philadelphia, 1984), p. 83.

11. *Genesis Rabbah*, ed. J. Theodor and Ch. Albeck (Jerusalem, 1965), 48:1, p. 479; and cf. ibid. 48:9, p. 485. Philo, *Quaestiones et Solutiones in Genesin* (Loeb Classical Library) 3:49, writes that circumcision is the sign of election for "Israel, that is seeing God." It is difficult to ascertain if Philo had in mind some midrashic tradition akin to what we have found in the Palestinian *Genesis Rabbah*. On the Philonic etymology of Israel as "one who sees God," see P. Borgen, *Bread from Heaven* (Leiden, 1965), pp. 115–18, and other references given there, p. 115 n. 3, and G. Delling, "The 'One Who Sees God' in Philo," in *Nourished with Peace: Studies in Hellenistic Judaism in Memory of Samuel Sandmel*, ed. F. Greenspahn, E. Hilgert, and B. Mack (Chico, Calif., 1984), pp. 27–49. For Philo's views on circumcision, see R. Hecht, "The Exegetical Contexts of Philo's Interpretation of Circumcision," in *Nourished with Peace*, pp. 51–79.

12. The whole problem is presumably eliminated by the form-critical method of exegesis that ascribes different authorship to the two literary strata: Gen. 17:23–27 is a Priestly document that supposedly follows Gen. 17:1–14, which is P's instruction for circumcision, whereas Gen. 18:1–6 is a narrative complex derived from J (ending in Gen. 19:38). See Gerhard von Rad, *Genesis* (Philadelphia, 1972), pp. 202–4. Yet, one could argue that the crucial question is not that of disparate textual units but rather the literary whole achieved by a process of redaction. From this latter perspective, the conjunction of these passages raises the hermeneutical problem addressed by the ancient Jewish exegetes.

13. This is in keeping with what James Kugel has called the "verse-centeredness" of midrash; see his "Two Interpretations of Midrash," in *Midrash and Literature*, pp. 94–95.

14. A classic study of this rabbinic conception is A. Marmorstein, *The Doctrine of Merits in Old Rabbinical Literature* (New York reprint, 1968).

15. See Marmorstein, op. cit., s.v. circumcision; and see J. Neusner, *Genesis Rabbah: The Judaic Commentary to the Book of Genesis* (Atlanta, 1985), 2:178–79.

16. The foreskin is referred to several times in the Bible itself as the "flesh of the foreskin"; see Gen. 17:11, 14, 23, 24–25, and Lev. 12:3. On the use of the word flesh, *basar*, to designate the penis, see also Ezek. 16:26, 23:20. Needless to say, this semantic usage continues in rabbinic literature from the classical period well into the Middle Ages.

17. For a discussion on circumcision as the taxonomy for Judaism in antiquity, see J. Z. Smith, "Fences and Neighbors," in *Approaches to Ancient Judaism*, ed. W. S. Green, vol. 2 (Chico, Calif., 1980), pp. 9–15, and Schiffman, *Who Was a Jew?*, pp. 23–24.

18. Cf. *Bereshit Rabbati*, ed. Ch. Albeck (Jerusalem, 1940), p. 79. Cf. also the commentary of Naḥmanides on Gen. 18:1 (ed. C. Chavel [Jerusalem, 1960], 1:106–7): "The disclosure of the *Shekhinah* . . . is a reward for a precept that has already been fulfilled." According to another line of rabbinic interpretation, the nexus between Abraham's circumcision in Gen. 17 and the theophany at the beginning of chap. 18 is meant to teach us about the virtue of visiting the sick, for God himself in this case serves as the role model insofar as He comes to visit Abraham immediately after his circumcision. See, e.g., B. Baba Meṣiᶜa 86b; Soṭah 14a; *Genesis Rabbah* 8:13, p. 67.

19. See the comment of D. Freedman in *Midrash Rabbah* (London, 1939), 1:406 n. 4: "Deriving *niqqefu* from *hiqqif* [the expression used in Job 19:26], to surround, i.e. proselytes flocked, surrounding him, as it were."

20. See, e.g., Targum Pseudo-Jonathan on Gen. 12:5 (ed. E. G. Clarke with collaboration by W. E. Aufrecht, J. C. Hurd, and F. Spitzer [New York, 1984], p. 13); Targum Onkelos ad locum (*The Bible in Aramaic*, ed. A. Sperber [Leiden, 1959], 1:17); *The Fragment-Targums of the Pentateuch*, ed. M. L. Klein (Rome, 1980), 1:49, 132; 2:11, and *Genesis Rabbah* 39:14, pp. 378–79. For other relevant aggadic sources, see L. Ginzberg, *The Legends of the Jews* (Philadephia, 1968), 1:195–217, and M. Kasher, *Torah Shelemah* (New York, 1949), 3:555 n. 95.

21. Cf. Rom. 2:25–29, 4:9–12; 1 Cor. 7:18; Eph. 2:8–13; Gal. 5:2–6; Col. 2:11; and Phil. 3:3. On baptism, or the circumcision of the spirit, as a substitute for circumcision of the flesh, see Col. 2:12–13; Gal. 6:13–14; Origen, *Contra Celsum*, 5:48 (ed. H. Chadwick [Cambridge, 1953] p. 302); P. Borgen, "Paul Preaches Circumcision and Pleases Men," in *Paul and Paulinism: Essays in Honour of C. K. Barrett*, ed. M. D. Hooker and S. G. Wilson (London, 1982), pp. 37–46. It should be noted that some church fathers had trouble explaining the abolishment of circumcision in light of the fact that Jesus himself was circumcised; see Epiphanius, *Adversus Haereses Panarium* 28.5.2 (cited in M. Werner, *The Formation of Christian Dogma* [Boston, 1965], p. 90). There is ample Patristic evidence, moreover, that certain Jewish-Christian sects, such

as the Ebionites and Nazoraeans, still practiced circumcision and kept the Sabbath; see A. F. J. Klijn and G. J. Reinink, *Patristic Evidence for Jewish-Christian Sects* (Leiden, 1973), pp. 20, 23–24, 29, 35, 37, 39, 42, 44, 51.

22. See Schiffman, *Who Was a Jew?*, pp. 23–25, and Ginzberg, *Legends*, 5:263–69 n. 318.

23. Cf. *Tanḥuma*ʾ, ed. S. Buber (New York, 1946), Vayera 4: "R. Isaac Nafḥa." The same reading is found in *Tanḥuma*ʾ, Vayera 2, and *Aggadat Bereshit*, 19.

24. *Genesis Rabbah* 48:4–5, p. 480.

25. Cf. *Genesis Rabbah* 63:13, p. 698, where it is reported that R. Levi transmitted the following opinon in the name of R. Ḥama bar Ḥanina: Esau's rejection of his birthrite was tied to his hatred of the blood of circumcision. In this context it is clear that Esau functions as a symbol for the Christian Church; see I. Aminoff, "The Figures of Esau and the Kingdom of Edom in Palestinian Midrashic-Talmudic Literature in the Tannaitic and Amoraic Periods" (Ph.D. dissertation, Melbourne University, 1981), pp. 131–33. On this midrashic typology, see also Ginzberg, *Legends* 5:272 n. 19; G. D. Cohen, "Esau As a Symbol in Early Medieval Thought," in *Jewish Medieval and Renaissance Studies*, ed. A. Altmann (Cambridge, Mass., 1967), pp. 27–30, and references given on p. 27 n. 31. Cf. also *Genesis Rabbah* 65:9, pp. 726–27, where R. Levi and R. Isaac are involved in anti-Christian polemics as well; see Aminoff, op. cit., p. 136 n. 18, and pp. 217–20. On R. Isaac and R. Levi, and other third-century aggadists, as defenders of Judaism against the attacks of the church found in the Syriac Didascalia, see A. Marmorstein, "Judaism and Christianity in the Middle of the Third Century," *Hebrew Union College Annual* 10 (1935): 236 nn. 75–76, 243 nn. 111–12.

26. The point is underscored even more strongly in the reading preserved in *Tanḥuma*ʾ, Vayera 2, where in place of the expression *she-mal ʿaṣmo*, "who has circumcised himself," one finds *she-zavaḥ ʾet ʿaṣmo*, "he sacrificed himself." (In the original version of this chapter I mistakenly recorded this reading as that of *Genesis Rabbah*.) On the connection between circumcision and sacrifices, see G. Vermes, "Circumcision and Exodus IV 24–26," in *Scripture and Tradition in Judaism* (Leiden, 1983), pp. 178–92. Some scholars have even suggested that infantile circumcision in ancient Israel on the eighth day must be seen as a replacement for child sacrifice (cf. Ex. 22:29, Lev. 22:27); see W. Eichrodt, *Theology of the Old Testament* (Philadelphia, 1961), 1:138 n. 3. This point was noted by various medieval biblical exegetes as well. Cf., e.g., *Rabbenu Baḥya ʿal ha-Torah*, ed. C. D. Chavel (Jerusalem, 1981), 1:160–61, ad Gen. 17:13.

27. This interpretation can be traced to earlier sources; cf. Targum Pseudo-Jonathan on Gen. 17:3 (ed. E. G. Clarke et al., p.17); *Genesis Rabbah* 46:6, pp. 463–64, 47:3, pp. 472–73; *Tanḥuma*ʾ, Lekh Lekha 20; and *Pirqe R. ʾEliʿezer*, ch. 29.

28. The same analogy or parable appears in the lost *Midrash Avkir* as cited in the midrashic anthology *Yalquṭ Shim ͑oni,* pt. 1, § 82.

29. *Numbers Rabbah* 12:8; see M. Saperstein, *Decoding the Rabbis: A Thirteenth-Century Commentary on the Aggadah* (Cambridge, Mass., 1980), pp. 97–102.

30. Such an interpretation is found in an earlier midrashic source, which doubtless served as the basis for this passage; cf. *Song of Songs Rabbah* 3:20. The connection of this verse to the rite of circumcision was probably also suggested to the midrashist by the words "wearing a crown," the latter being a reference to the corona of the phallus disclosed by the act of circumcision (see n. 55 below).

31. The equation of uncleanliness or impurity with uncircumcision is biblical in origin; cf. Isa. 52:1 and Ezek. 44:7. In rabbinic literature one of the names of the evil inclination is "uncircumcised" or the "foreskin"; see Schechter, *Aspects of Rabbinic Theology,* p. 243.

32. On the cutting of the foreskin as a symbol for the excision of sensual desires in the writings of Philo, see Hecht, "Philo's Interpretation of Circumcision," pp. 51–79. The connection between circumcision and the weakening of sexual desire was affirmed as well by medieval Jewish philosophers; see, e.g., Judah ha-Levi, *Sefer ha-Kuzari* 1:115; Maimonides, *Guide of the Perplexed* 3:49.

33. I have treated the homology of the eye and the penis in several other studies. Here I mention two striking textual examples not noted elsewhere. In his *Siddur Mal ͗ah ha- ͗Areṣ De ͑ah* (Thiengen, 1560), in the section on the Hallel prayer, Naftali Herz Treves connects the verse, "They have eyes but cannot see" (Ps. 115:5) with the description of Balaam, "the word of the man whose eye is open" (Num. 24:3) and comments that "he who is not circumcised has no eye." The correlation of the eye and the penis is underscored in a profound way in the following reflection of Meshullam Shraga Feibush Heilperin, *Sefat ͗Emet* (Lemberg, 1879), 51d–52d:

> The beginning and cause of the sin of Adam was in the eyes, as was stated above. However, the essence of his sin was in the aspect of the covenant [i.e., the penis], the secret of Joseph the Righteous, the Foundation of the World, as [the rabbis] blessed be their memory said, Adam stretched his prepuce [cf. B. Sanhedrin 38b] and in the 130 years that he separated from his wife he produced spirits and demons by means of the semen of nocturnal emissions. The rectification of the aforementioned sin is still pending, and every Jew is obligated to rectify his sin in the aspect of his soul. The righteous who guards the covenant is the one who rectifies this sin and together with that the aspect of the vision is also rectified, for the eyes are the two *yods,* and the one is dependent on the other [i.e., the eyes and the penis]. . . . The sin of Adam

> concerned the fact that through the secret of the covenant [i.e., the penis] the vision of the eyes was blemished, for [the eyes] are the two *yods* of the form of the face that is the image of God. The rectification for this is extended to all the branches until the end of all the exiles. Joseph the Righteous guarded the covenant and rectified the aspect of the eyes.

This Hasidic master has captured in a succinct way the nexus of ideas that has had a profound impact on the orientation of the kabbalists in the world. In particular, one sees from this quote the extent to which the kabbalistic tradition yields a psychosexual understanding of history itself. That is, the historical process is marked by the gradual rectification of the sexual offense of spilling semen in vain committed by Adam. This sin created a blemish in the faculty of sight—based on the correlation of the eye and the penis—that is only rectified in the fullest sense by the righteous one in the messianic era. Needless to say, countless other texts could have been cited in support of my claim but the two examples that I have brought suffice to make the point. The structural parallelism in the Jewish sources between the eye and the male organ should, of course, be placed within a larger intellectual framework that has informed Western thought, most acutely expressed in the French feminist critique of the linkage of ocularcentrism and phallocentrism. See recent discussion in M. Jay, *Downcast Eyes: The Denigration of Vision in Twentieth-Century French Thought* (Berkeley, Los Angeles, and London, 1993), pp. 493–542. By contrast, according to Freud (*The Interpretation of Dreams,* trans. and ed. J. Strachey [New York, 1965], pp. 234–35, 394), the eye can symbolically represent the female genital orifice. Following this line of interpretation, David J. Halpern ("A Sexual Image in Hekhalot Rabbati and Its Implications," *Jerusalem Studies in Jewish Thought* 6:1–2 [1987]: 117–32; idem, *The Faces of the Chariot: Early Jewish Responses to Ezekiel's Vision* [Tübingen, 1988], pp. 393–96) explains the reference in *Hekhalot Rabbati* (*Synopse zur Hekhalot-Literatur,* §§ 246–47) to the five hundred and twelve eyes of the celestial beasts who bear the throne as a symbolic representation of the vagina. The terrifying nature of these eyes is related to the anxiety of a child confronted with adult sexuality. In *Through a Speculum That Shines: Vision and Imagination in Medieval Jewish Mysticism* (Princeton, 1994), p. 93, I have argued that in other passages in *Hekhalot Rabbati* (*Synopse,* §§ 102, 105, and 152) the eye functions as a phallic symbol. In that context I neglected to mention the passages discussed by Halperin, but I would contend that in that case as well the eyes symbolize the phallus and not the vagina. Interestingly, Halpern ("A Sexual Image," p. 129 n. 25) does note that the word for "eye," *ᶜayin,* can also mean "spring," but he does not deduce the obvious phallic significance from that connotation. On the representation of the male organ by objects from which water flows, see S. Freud, *The Complete Introductory Lectures on Psychoanalysis,* trans. and ed. J. Strachey (New York, 1966), pp. 154–55.

34. *Zohar* 1:98b. The nexus of circumcision and cleaving to the *Shekhinah* is alluded to as well in the zoharic claim that before entering the land of Israel (a symbol for *Shekhinah*) Joshua had to circumcise the people; see 1:93b. On

the connection between the land of Israel and circumcision, see commentary of Rashi to B. Berakhot 48b, s.v., *ṣarikh she-yizkor bah berit*; commentary of Naḥmanides to Gen. 15:18; Jacob ben Sheshet, *Sefer ha-ʾEmunah we-ha-Biṭṭaḥon*, in *Kitve Ramban*, ed. C. D. Chavel (Jerusalem, 1968), 2:378; and Menaḥem Recanaṭi, *Perush ʿal ha-Torah* (Jerusalem, 1961), 84d.

35. *Zohar ʿim Perush ʾOr Yaqar* (Jerusalem, 1970), 5:4.

36. *Zohar* 1:97b.

37. Ibid., 88b–89a.

38. Ibid., 91a–b.

39. See, e.g., Simeon Lavi, *Ketem Paz* (Jerusalem, 1981), 1:224: "Before Abraham was circumcised his prophecy was in that lower vision, the image of an image. However, after he was circumcised his prophecy was in the higher vision, as it says, 'And the Lord appeared to Abram.' " The "lower vision" is identified by Lavi as the realm of celestial palaces below the world of emanation, whereas the "higher vision" is the *Shekhinah*, the last emanation that reflects all the upper ones. In addition to difficulties that one may have fitting this interpretation into the text, Lavi contradicts himself, for prior to this passage he wrote: "All the prophecies of the prophets were from the palaces that are below the hidden emanation, below *ʿAṭeret* [i.e., *Shekhinah*] except for Moses . . . [whose prophecy] was in *ʿAṭeret* itself." An alternative explanation is offered by Moses Cordovero in his commentary *ʾOr Yaqar* (Jerusalem, 1967), 4:181. According to him, the change in the visionary status of *Shekhinah* had nothing to do with the divine potency itself but, rather, with the level of comprehension of Abraham. Cordovero's explanation undermines the theurgical dimension of circumcision stressed by the author of the *Zohar* himself, especially in 1:97a.

40. Cf. Moses de León, *Sheqel ha-Qodesh*, ed. A. W. Greenup (London, 1911), p. 67: "And contemplate that the secret of the covenant (*sod ha-berit*) is universal faith (*derekh kelal ʾemunah*). When the foreskin is removed from the phallus—this is the secret of faith. Yet the removal of the foreskin to enter into the secret of the faith [is not complete] until one pulls down [the membrane] and the corona is revealed. When one reaches the corona one enters into the mystery of the way of faith and is bound to faith." See below, nn. 46 and 55.

41. See *Zohar* 1:32a, 47b, 69a, 71b, 72b, 117a; 3:14a, 115b, and G. Scholem, "Colours and Their Symbolism in Jewish Tradition and Mysticism," *Diogenes* 109 (1980): 69.

42. Cf. *Zohar* 1:93a, 96b, 98b (*Sitre Torah*); 2:57b; 3:14a. See Tishby, *Wisdom of the Zohar*, pp. 1176–78, 1364–65. Kabbalists explained the androgynous nature of circumcision in terms of the two procedures required in the circumcision ritual by rabbinic law (B. Shabbat 137b): *milah* (incision of the foreskin) and *periʿah* (uncovering of the corona), which correspond symbolically to the two divine emanations, *Yesod* and *Shekhinah*. Cf. *Zohar* 1:13a,

32a–b; 2:40a, 60b, 125b; 3: 91b, 163a. In my later work I have utilized an expression of Eliade to refer to the kabbalistic understanding of circumcision as a rite of symbolic androgynization. The ontological presumption underlying this mythic interpretation of the circumcision ritual is that the feminine element is itself contextualized as part of the phallus.

43. On the connection between the divine name and circumcision, cf. *Zohar* 1:95a, 96b; 2:3b, 32a, 59b, 87b; 3:13b, 91a; *Tiqqune Zohar*, ed. R. Margaliot (Jerusalem, 1978), 24, 70a; 22, 65b; 61, 94b; and Tishby, *Wisdom of the Zohar*, p. 1364. On the correlation between circumcision and the Tetragrammaton in thirteenth-century German Pietistic and Spanish kabbalistic sources, see my study referred to above in n. 3.

44. *Zohar* 1:89a.

45. Cf. ibid 2:61a, 86a, 216a; 3:73a–b.

46. Ibid., 1:98a. The connection between circumcision, visionary experience, and theurgy is brought out clearly in a comment of de León in his *Sefer ha-Mishqal*. Cf. "*Sefer ha-Mishkal:* Text and Study," ed. J. Wijnhoven (Ph.D. dissertation, Brandeis University, 1964), p. 133: "The foreskin is the shell standing on the outside and the phallus is the core on the inside. . . . This is the secret of the proper matter when a person enters the secret of faith. Concerning this secret it says, 'All your males shall appear before the Lord your God' (Deut. 16:16). For one must cleave [to God] and show that place [the phallus] in its Source, the branch in its Root, to unite everything in the bond of the secret of His unity, with one bond and in one secret, so that 'the Lord will be one and His name will be one' (Zech. 14:9)." The implicit homoerotic element of this passage is evident, for the mystics are bound to God exclusively through the male organ. The ultimate object of the visionary encounter is not the feminine personification of the divine but the corona of the *membrum virile*. Cf. *Zohar* 2:38a, 124a, 183a; 3:165b, 168a.

47. Cf. *Zohar* 1:36a, 145b, and 2:25b. In terms of my more recent work on gender imagery in kabbalistic symbolism, I would refer to this phenomenon as the restoration of the feminine to the masculine or the reconstitution of the male androgyne.

48. *Zohar* 1:91b. On Abraham's flirtation with the demonic in the *Zohar*, see E. R. Wolfson, "Left Contained in the Right: A Study in Zoharic Hermeneutics," *AJS Review* 11 (1986): 34 n. 34.

49. Cf. *Zohar* 1:103b (and the parallel in de León's *Sefer ha-Mishqal*, pp. 131–32): "Come and see: before Abraham was circumcised his seed was not holy for it emerged from the foreskin and clove to the foreskin below. After he was circumcised the seed emerged from holiness and clove to the holiness above." On the separating of the foreskin from the phallus as an enactment of the separation of the holy and the demonic, cf. *Zohar* 1:13a, 95a–b; 2:255b; 3:72b–73a; *The Book of the Pomegranate: Moses de León's Sefer ha-Rimmon*, ed. E. R. Wolfson (Atlanta, 1988) pp. 226–29; *Sheqel ha-Qodesh*, p. 67 (cited

above, n. 40); *Tiqqune Zohar*, Haqdamah, 11a; 37, 78a; Tishby, *Wisdom of the Zohar*, p. 1364; and J. Wijnhoven, "The Zohar and the Proselyte," in *Texts and Responses: Studies Presented to Nahum N. Glatzer on the Occasion of His Seventieth Birthday*, ed. M. Fishbane and P. Flohr (Leiden, 1975), pp. 124–25.

50. *Zohar* 2:36a.

51. On the *Shekhinah* as "the opening," *ha-petaḥ*, or "the gate," *ha-sha*ᶜ*ar*, cf. *Zohar* 1:7b, 11b, 37a, 47b, 54b, 97b, 103a–b; 2:36a, 158a, 237b; and 3:14a, 71b, 256b.

52. Ibid. 1:97b (*Sitre Torah*); see also ibid., 21a, 103a–b (translated by Matt, *Zohar*, pp. 65–68).

53. *Zohar* 2:36a.

54. See n. 6 above.

55. Cf. *Zohar* 1:13a, 56a, 95a; 2:36a; 3:142a (*ʾIdraʾ Rabbaʾ*), 215b, 220a; *Book of the Pomegranate*, p. 227; and *Sheqel ha-Qodesh*, p. 63. In some zoharic contexts the letter *yod* refers to the *Shekhinah*, which is said to correspond to the corona of the phallus. (The later symbolism is based on the fact that the word for the corona, *ᶜaṭarah*, literally "crown," is a technical name for *Shekhinah*.) Cf. *Zohar* 1:93b, 266a (*Ra*ᶜ*ayaʾ Mehemnaʾ*); 2:258a (*Ra*ᶜ*ayaʾ Mehemnaʾ*); 3:256a (*Ra*ᶜ*ayaʾ Mehemnaʾ*), 257a (*Ra*ᶜ*ayaʾ Mehemnaʾ*), 263a; *Tiqqune Zohar*, 13, 29a; 18, 31b; 19, 39b; 21, 62b; 30, 73b; 47, 85a; 70, 120a; and Isaac of Acre, *Sefer Meʾirat* ᶜ*Einayim*, ed. A. Goldreich (Jerusalem, 1982), p. 113.

56. Cf. *Zohar* 3:142a (*ʾIdraʾ Rabbaʾ*): "Everything is dependent upon the opening of the phallus, which is called *yod*. And when the *yod* is revealed, the opening of the phallus, the upper *Ḥesed* [Mercy] is revealed . . . and this [gradation] is not called *Ḥesed* until the *yod* is revealed. . . . Come and see: Abraham was not called complete with respect to this *Ḥesed* until the *yod* of the phallus was revealed. And when it was revealed, he was called complete, as it is written, 'Walk before Me and be complete.' "

57. The connection of this zoharic passage to that of *Genesis Rabbah* was noted by Lavi in his *Ketem Paz*, 230b.

58. *Zohar* 1:94a. Cf. *Tiqqune Zohar* 19, 41b, and Tishby, *Wisdom of the Zohar*, p. 1364.

59. The correspondence between a "covenant of the foreskin" and a "covenant of the tongue" was first articulated in the Jewish mystical and cosmological text *Sefer Yeṣirah* 1:3. Cf. the reading established by I. Gruenwald, "A Preliminary Critical Edition of Sefer Yeẓira," *Israel Oriental Studies* 1 (1971): 141, and the English rendering in idem, "Some Critical Notes on the First Part of Sefer Yeẓira," *Revue des études juives* 132 (1973): 486: "Ten *sefirot belimah*: ten corresponding to the number of the ten fingers, five against five, and the covenant of the oneness is constituted in the centre [as expressed] in the

circumcision of the tongue and the mouth and in the circumcision of the foreskin." Cf. further *Sefer Yeṣirah* 6:4, where it is said that God made a covenant with Abraham "between the ten toes of his feet and it is the covenant of circumcision" and a covenant "between the ten fingers of his hands which is the tongue." Some scholars assume that the covenant of the tongue or the mouth refers to a vow of secrecy, mentioned explicitly in *Sefer Yeṣirah* 1:8, not to disclose mystical truths in public; see Gruenwald, "Some Critical Notes," pp. 487, 490–91. See below, n. 81. On the proposed structural parallel in rabbinic thought between recitation of a blessing and male intercourse, based on the link between oral transmission and phallic emission, see Goldberg, "Torah and Children," pp. 115–16.

60. Cf. *Zohar* 1:8a.

61. Ibid. 2:87a. Cf. ibid. 3:79a, 105b, 106b, 128a (*ʾIdraʾ Rabbaʾ*). In 3:159a the verse is used to support the view that one must not inquire about certain things that are hidden from finite minds and are known only by God. The last usage may reflect the fact that this verse is applied to the apostate Elisha ben Abuyah in the famous rabbinic legend of the "four who entered Pardes"; cf. B. Ḥagigah 15b and parallels. The emphasis on the need to keep truths hidden and the impropriety of revealing a truth that has not been received directly from a teacher stands in marked contrast to the general impression that one gets from reading de León's writings in which the mystical imagination seems to have had an almost unbounded reign over disclosing esoteric matters. On this "innovative" approach of de León, in contrast to the more "conservative" approach of other mystics, such as Naḥmanides, see M. Idel, "We Have No Kabbalistic Tradition on This," in *Rabbi Moses Naḥmanides: Explorations in His Religious and Literary Virtuosity*, ed. I. Twersky (Cambridge, Mass., 1983), pp. 51–73. On the zoharic passages that emphasize secrecy and the esoteric quality of mystical truths, see Liebes, *Studies in the Zohar*, pp. 26–34. Cf. also the passage from Moses de León's *Mishkan ha-Edut*, cited by Scholem in *Major Trends*, pp. 201–2, and my extended analysis of the same passage (with a fresh translation) in my "Sefer ha-Rimmon: Critical Edition and Introductory Study" (Ph.D. dissertation, Brandeis University, 1986), 1:18–27.

62. It is impossible to make sense out of this unless one assumes that there is some basic kinship between the phallus and the mouth and that emission through one is like that of the other. Such a relation was in fact exploited by the kabbalists; cf., e.g., Joseph Gikatilla, *Ginnat Egoz* (Hanau, 1614), 25b: "Just as a person has the covenant of the mouth between the ten fingers of his hands, so you will find he has the covenant of the foreskin between the ten toes [literally, fingers] of his feet. . . . Contemplate that *peh* [mouth] corresponds [numerically] to *milah* [circumcision]." Gikatilla thus interprets the famous passage from *Sefer Yeṣirah* (see n. 59) in light of a numerical equivalence between the word for mouth, *peh*, and the word for circumcision, *milah*, insofar as both equal eighty-five. See the theosophic reworking of this numerical equivalence in *Tiqqune Zohar* 18, 32b: "The Oral Law [*torah she-beʿal peh*] is where the lower *Shekhinah* is. She is

called mouth [*peh*] from the side of the *Ṣaddiq* [*Yesod*], for the numerical value of *peh* equals that of *milah*." On this numerical equivalence, see also the text of the thirteenth-century Castilian kabbalist Jacob ben Jacob ha-Kohen, published by Scholem in *Madda*ᶜ*e ha-Yahadut* 2 (1927): 217. See also the commentary on *Sefer Yeṣirah* by Barukh Togarmi in G. Scholem, *The Kabbalah of Sefer Temunah and R. Abraham Abulafiah*, ed. J. Ben-Shlomo (Jerusalem, 1987), p. 232 (in Hebrew). The numerology was also employed by authors influenced by Ashkenazi traditions. Cf. *Perush Rabbenu* ᵓ*Efrayim* ᶜ*al ha-Torah*, ed. E. Korach and Z. Leitner, with consultation of Ch. Konyevsky (Jerusalem, 1992), p. 64, ad Gen. 18:1: "The numerical value of *milah* is *peh*, for there is no one who can offer an excuse (*pitḥon peh*) before the Holy One, blessed be He, except those who are circumcised"; cf. also Isaac bar Judah ha-Levi, *Pa*ᶜ*neaḥ Raza*ᵓ (Warsaw, 1860), 21a, who comments that the first letters of the expression *petaḥ ha-*ᵓ*ohel* spell *peh*, "mouth," which is numerically equivalent to the word *milah*, "to indicate that the one who is circumcised has a mouth with which to overcome the attribute of judgment."

63. *Zohar* 2:87a–b.

64. See G. Scholem, *On the Kabbalah and Its Symbolism*, trans. R. Manheim (New York, 1978), pp. 37–44, and references to the *Zohar* given on p. 39 n. 3; Tishby, *Wisdom of the Zohar*, pp. 1080–82, 1086; and M. Idel, "The Concept of the Torah in the Hekhalot and Its Metamorphosis in the Kabbalah," *Jerusalem Studies in Jewish Thought* 1 (1981): 49–58 (in Hebrew).

65. Cf. *Zohar* 2:87b, and above n. 43. On sexual relations between Jew and non-Jew in the period of the *Zohar*, see the remarks of Y. Baer, *A History of Jews in Christian Spain*, trans. L. Schoffmann (Philadelphia, 1978), 1:246–63.

66. Liebes, *Studies in the Zohar*, pp. 24–25.

67. B. Berakhot 22a.

68. *Zohar* 3:79a, 105b. Cf. *Zohar Ḥadash*, 94b (*Tiqqunim*): "The one who reveals secrets of Torah [to the wicked] causes the spring to be removed from the *Ṣaddiq*, who is the foundation of whom it is said, 'The secret of the Lord is with those who fear him' (Ps. 25:14), and from the *Shekhinah*, as it is written, 'The waters of the sea fail, and the river dries up and is parched' (Job 14:11). At that time the righteous (*ṣaddiqim*) below are impoverished from everything, impoverished from secrets of Torah and impoverished in the body. Whoever reveals secrets to the righteous causes the *Ṣaddiq* to shine with secrets of Torah."

69. Aramaic: *ḥizra*ᵓ *be-mayya*ᵓ. Cf. B. Baba Meṣiᶜa 60b: *mayya*ᵓ *de-ḥizra*ᵓ.

70. *Zohar* 3:128a (ᵓ*Idra*ᵓ *Rabba*ᵓ).

71. See Y. Liebes, *Sections of the Zohar Lexicon* (Jerusalem, 1976), pp. 377 n. 88, 381 n. 96 (in Hebrew).

72. The correlation of the righteous person, *ṣaddiq*, and sexual purity, is found in earlier rabbinic sources, but it is fully exploited in the kabbalistic texts, especially zoharic and related literature, insofar as the *ṣaddiq* is the earthly correlate to *Yesod*, the divine gradation that is in the position of the phallus. Cf. *Zohar* 1:59b; *Book of the Pomegranate*, p. 228; *Sheqel ha-Qodesh*, p. 62; *Sefer ha-Mishqal*, p. 74; and Tishby, *Wisdom of the Zohar*, pp. 1413–14.

73. On the meaning of *qiyyuma*ʾ in the *Zohar* as pillar, see Liebes, *Sections of the Zohar Lexicon*, p. 360 n. 20, and idem, *Studies in the Zohar*, pp. 26 and 173 n. 82.

74. See Liebes, *Sections of the Zohar Lexicon*, pp. 358 n. 13, 361 nn. 23–24, 371–73 n. 68.

75. The theosophic connection between the word "secret," the Aramaic *raza*ʾ, which is a translation of the Hebrew *sod*, and circumcision is based ultimately on Ps. 25:14, "The secret (*sod*) of the Lord is with those who fear Him, and to them He makes His covenant (*berito*) known." Cf. *Zohar* 1:2b, 236b; 3:43b (*Piqqudin*); *Book of the Pomegranate*, p. 226; and *Sheqel ha-Qodesh*, pp. 60–61. See Liebes, *Studies in the Zohar*, pp. 26–28. Finally, it should be mentioned that already in classical midrashic sources, e.g. *Genesis Rabbah* 49:2, pp. 488–89, Ps. 25:14 is interpreted to mean that circumcision is the "mystery" of God given to Abraham. See the kabbalistic interpretation of this rabbinic view in Ezra's commentary on the talmudic aggadot, MSS Vatican, Biblioteca Apostolica ebr. 294, fol. 42b and Vatican, Biblioteca Apostolica ebr. 441, fol. 30a.

76. In this regard it is of interest to note that in one of his Hebrew theosophic works, *Sefer ha-Nefesh ha-Ḥakhamah* (Basel, 1608) sec. 12, de León refers to the proliferation of kabbalistic lore as the flowing or spreading forth of the "spring of mystery," *ma*ʿ*ayan ha-sod*. The text is cited by Scholem, *Major Trends*, p. 396 n. 150, and an English translation appears on p. 201. Scholem interprets this passage as a "veiled reference" to the dissemination of the *Zohar*. See my criticism in "Sefer ha-Rimmon: Critical Edition and Introductory Study," 1:15–17. The "spring" is an obvious phallic symbol, which would thus be appropriately applied to *Yesod*. It follows, therefore, that even in this passage de León links the disclosure of esoteric truth with a phallic symbol, namely, the pouring forth of the fountain or spring.

77. Cf. the parable of the Princess (the Torah) and her lover (the mystic exegete) in *Zohar* 2:99a–b, where the hermeneutical relationship is depicted in terms of an erotic game of hide-and-seek. See Scholem, *On the Kabbalah*, pp. 55–56, and Tishby, *Wisdom of the Zohar*, pp. 1084–85. (Since the original publication of this study several scholars have discussed the parable in terms of the more general hermeneutical stance of the *Zohar*. See M. Idel, *Kabbalah: New Perspectives* [New Haven and London, 1988], pp. 227–29; E. R. Wolfson, "The Hermeneutics of Visionary Experience: Revelation and Interpretation in the *Zohar*," *Religion* 18 [1988]: 311–45, esp. 323–24 (a revised version of this study appears as the seventh chapter of my monograph, *Through a Speculum That Shines: Vision and Imagination in Medieval Jewish Mysticism* [Princeton,

1994]); and idem, "Beautiful Maiden without Eyes: *Peshaṭ* and *Sod* in Zoharic Hermeneutics," in *The Midrashic Imagination*, ed. M. Fishbane [Albany, 1993], pp. 155–203.) On the erotic quality of reading as a dialectic of concealment and disclosure, see R. Barthes, *The Pleasure of the Text*, trans. R. Miller (New York, 1975), pp. 9–10, 14.

78. See Liebes, *Studies in the Zohar*, pp. 26–30. The dialectic of concealment and disclosure related to *Yesod* is explicitly embraced in *Zohar* 2:186b. See also the formulation of Isaac ben Jacob ha-Kohen in Scholem, *Madda*ᶜ*e ha-Yahadut* 2 (1927): 268: "*Yesod* is compared to a door . . . sometimes it is closed and sometimes it is opened."

79. Cf. the parable in *Zohar* 1:245b, and its parallel in *Book of the Pomegranate*, p. 299.

80. The ontological distinction between Jew and non-Jew, the soul of the former deriving from the right, holy side and that of the latter from the left, demonic side, is one of the basic assumptions of zoharic anthropology. Cf. *Zohar Ḥadash* 78d (*Midrash ha-Ne*ᶜ*elam* on Ruth); *Zohar* 1:20b, 131a, 220a; 2:86a; *Book of the Pomegranate*, pp. 211–12; and E. R. Wolfson, "Mystical Rationalization of the Commandments in *Sefer ha-Rimmon*," *Hebrew Union College Annual* 59 (1988): 242–44.

81. *Zohar* 3:72b–73a. Cf. Joseph Gikatilla, *Sha*ᶜ*are* ᵓ*Orah*, ed. J. Ben-Shlomo (Jerusalem, 1978), 1:114–16:

> The covenant of *Binah* is the covenant of the mouth, the covenant of the tongue, and the covenant of the lips. . . . The covenant of the living God [i.e., *Yesod*] is called the covenant of peace . . . the covenant of Sabbath, the covenant of the rainbow . . . the covenant of circumcision. The covenant of Adonai [i.e., *Shekhinah*] corresponds to the covenant of the Torah. . . . And this is the secret: the covenant of the tongue and the covenant of the foreskin. . . . If Israel had not received the covenant of the flesh [circumcision] they would never have merited the Torah, which is the covenant of the tongue. . . . Therefore the Torah is only given to one who has received the covenant of the flesh, and from the covenant of the flesh one enters into the covenant of the tongue, which is the reading of the Torah.

Gikatilla's remarks are a theosophic exposition of *Sefer Yeṣirah* 1:3; see nn. 59 and 62 above. See also the formulation of Abraham Abulafia, ᵓ*Oṣar* ᶜ*Eden Ganuz*, MS Oxford, Bodleian Library 1580, fol. 5a: "If not for the covenant of circumcision it would not be possible to establish the covenant of the tongue, and if not for the covenant of the tongue there would be no basis for the covenant of circumcision."

82. Cf. the comment of Naḥmanides in his sermon *Torat ha-Shem Temimah*, in *Kitve Ramban*, 1:155, to the effect that the rabbinic teaching (see n. 3 above) that one who is not circumcised cannot study Torah "is true for

there are in it secrets of the account of creation as Onkelos mentioned, the secret of the account of the chariot, and many other secrets that were said orally and these are not transmitted except to the pious one in Israel."

83. See nn. 75 and 78, above. On the inherent hiddenness of the divine grade called the Supernal Righteous (*ṣaddiq ᶜelyon*), cf. *Sefer ha-Bahir*, ed. R. Margaliot (Jerusalem, 1978), § 193.

84. *Zohar* 1:236b.

85. *Book of the Pomegranate*, p. 228. Cf. *Sheqel ha-Qodesh*, p. 61, and *Zohar* 2:214a.

86. *Book of the Pomegranate*, p. 229.

87. I have treated this topic at length in "Hermeneutics of Visionary Experience" (see n. 77 above). Cf. *Zohar* 1:9a, 72a, 92b, 94b, 115b; 2:163b, 200a.

88. *Zohar* 1:234b.

89. The letter symbolism is derived from B. Shabbat 104b; see *Zohar* 1:3a, 244b; *Book of the Pomegranate*, p. 229, the fragment of Moses de León in MS Munich, Bayerische Staatsbibliothek 47, fol. 369b.

90. Various thirteenth-century writers intentionally confused the Hebrew word *higgid* with the Aramaic root *negad*, to "flow," "draw," or "pull." See, e.g., Jacob ben Sheshet, *Sefer ha-ᵓEmunah we-ha-Biṭṭaḥon*, in *Kitve Ramban* 2:368; Abraham Abulafia, *Shevaᶜ Netivot ha-Torah*, published by A. Jellinek, *Philosophie und Kabbala* (Leipzig, 1854), p. 3. It is evident that the zoharic interpretation of the various words related to the verb *higgid* reflects this etymology as well; i.e., the sexual understanding of speech is buttressed by the belief that the word *higgid* has the connotation of extending or overflowing, qualities associated with the phallus.

91. It is of interest to consider *Zohar* 1:93a, in which the discussion on the mystical significance of circumcision culminates with an actual visionary experience. After the comrades complete their discussion on circumcision, the man in whose house the discussion ensued says to them: "The completion of what you have said tonight will take place tomorrow. He said to them: Tomorrow you will see the face of the 'master of circumcision' [i.e., the prophet Elijah] . . . for he will come to circumcise my son. . . . R. Abba said: This is a request to [fulfill] a commandment and we shall sit in order to see the face of the *Shekhinah*." In my opinion, the face of the *Shekhinah* here, as in other zoharic passages, refers to the corona of the penis exposed as part of the rite of circumcision. Underlying the kabbalistic symbology is the displacement of the penis by the face or the head, a phenomenon well-attested in psychoanalytic dream-interpretation. See Freud, *Interpretation of Dreams*, p. 422; *Complete Introductory Lectures on Psychoanalysis*, pp. 191 and 268. (On a comparative note it would be of interest to discuss the kabbalistic understanding of the *ṣaddiq* as the face of the *Shekhinah* and the Shiite view of the *imām* as the supreme cosmic pole (*quṭb*) who is also the face of God in the mundane

sphere. See H. Corbin, *Face de Dieu, face de l'homme: Herméneutique et soufisme* [Paris, 1983], pp. 237–59. See also P. Fenton, "La Hierarchie des saints dans la mystique juive et dans la mystique islamique," in *ᶜAlei Shefer: Studies in the Literature of Jewish Thought Presented to Rabbi Dr. Alexandre Safran,* ed. M. Ḥallamish [Bar-Ilan, 1990], pp. 49–73.) In other contexts in the *Zohar* the seeing of the *Shekhinah* is connected particularly with the study of Torah in accord with kabbalistic principles; see n. 87 above.

3. Erasing the Erasure/Gender and the Writing of God's Body in Kabbalistic Symbolism

An abbreviated version of this chapter will appear in French translation in *Tranmission et passages en monde juif,* ed. E. Benbassa (Paris, 1995).

1. See G. Scholem, "The Name of God and the Linguistic Theory of the Kabbala," *Diogenes* 79 (1972): 59–80; *Diogenes* 80 (1972): 164–94; and E. Lipiner, *The Metaphysics of the Hebrew Alphabet* (Jerusalem, 1989; in Hebrew). For discussion on the function of language in theosophic and ecstatic kabbalah as well as Hasidism, see M. Idel, "Reification of Language in Jewish Mysticism," in *Mysticism and Language,* ed. S. T. Katz (Oxford and New York, 1992), pp. 42–79. For a more comprehensive discussion on the role of language in the ecstatic kabbalistic tradition, see M. Idel, *Language, Torah, and Hermeneutics in Abraham Abulafia* (Albany, 1989). For more specialized studies regarding letter symbolism in zoharic literature, see E. R. Wolfson, "Anthropomorphic Imagery and Letter Symbolism in the *Zohar,*" *Jerusalem Studies in Jewish Thought* 8 (1989): 85–111 (in Hebrew); and idem, "Letter Symbolism and Merkavah Imagery in the *Zohar,*" in *ᶜAlei Shefer: Studies in the Literature of Jewish Thought Presented to Rabbi Dr. Alexandre Safran,* ed. M. Ḥallamish (Bar-Ilan, 1990): 195–236. These studies examine some of the motifs discussed in this chapter as well as specific passages. I have returned to these texts on account of a sustained fascination with letter symbolism in Jewish mysticism and a belief that rethinking these issues from a new and more mature vantage point is a worthwhile undertaking. Like Edmund Husserl and countless other phenomenologists who have followed his path, it is my working assumption that on the pathways of thought one must constantly begin at the beginning.

2. See Ch. Mopsik, *Lettre sur la sainteté: le secret de la relation entre l'homme et la femme dans la cabale* (Paris, 1986), pp. 45–212, and in the same volume the appendix by M. Idel, "Métaphores et pratiques sexuelles dans la cabale," pp. 329–58 (English version in *The Jewish Family: Metaphor and Memory,* ed. D. Kraemer [New York and Oxford, 1989], pp. 197–224). See also A. E. Waite, *The Holy Kabbalah,* with introduction by K. Rexroth (Secaucus, N. J., 1975), pp. 377–405; G. Langer, *Die Erotik der Kabbala,* with preface by P. Orban (Munich, 1989); G. Scholem, *On the Mystical Shape of the Godhead: Basic Concepts in the Kabbalah,* trans. J. Neugroschel and ed. J. Chipman (New York, 1991), pp. 140–96; and E. R. Wolfson, "Woman—The Feminine as

Other in Theosophic Kabbalah: Some Philosophical Observations on the Divine Androgyne," in *The Other in Jewish Thought and History: Constructions of Jewish Identity and Culture,* ed. L. Silberstein and R. Cohn (New York, 1994) pp. 166–204.

3. See T. Fishman, "A Kabbalistic Perspective on Gender-Specific Commandments: On the Interplay of Symbols and Society," *AJS Review* 17 (1992): 199–245.

4. This remains a relatively neglected area of study. For preliminary treatments of this very complex issue, cf. the studies of Idel and Mopsik referred to in n. 2, and J. Cohen, *"Be Fertile and Increase, Fill the Earth and Master It": The Ancient and Medieval Career of a Biblical Text* (Ithaca and London, 1989), pp. 196–220; and idem, "Rationales for Conjugal Sex in RaABaD's *Baᶜalei ha-nefesh,*" *Jewish History* 6 (1992): 65–78. Although Abraham ben David of Posquières does assign the third of four intentions (*kawwanot*) required in sexual intercourse to the woman, his comments reflect an androcentric perspective; i.e., the woman must yearn for her husband and adorn herself before him in an attempt to please him. See my remarks in "Woman—The Feminine as Other in Theosophic Kabbalah," p. 201 n. 66, regarding the intention during coitus required of the woman according to the late-thirteenth-century kabbalistic work, *ʾIggeret ha-Qodesh.* See also K. Guberman, "The Language of Love in Spanish Kabbalah: An Examination of the *ʾIggeret ha-Kodesh,*" in *Approaches to Judaism in Medieval Times,* ed. D. R. Blumenthal, vol. 1 (Chico, Calif., 1984), pp. 53–95, esp. 69–70, 74–75, 83–89.

5. See, e.g., T. Laqueur, *Making Sex: Body and Gender from the Greeks to Freud* (Cambridge, Mass., 1990); J. Cadden, *Meaning of Sex Difference in the Middle Ages: Medicine, Science, and Culture* (Cambridge and New York, 1993); and N. F. Partner, "No Sex, No Gender," in *Studying Medieval Women: Sex, Gender, Feminism,* ed. N. F. Partner (Cambridge, Mass., 1993), pp. 117–41.

6. The biblical idea may be related to the motif of the Tablets of Destiny in Mesopotamian mythology that functioned as a kind of talisman conferring power upon its possessor. See S. G. F. Brandon, *Creation Legends of the Ancient Near East* (London, 1963), pp. 97, 114. For further discussion on the motif of celestial books or tablets, see R. Eppel, "Les tables da la Loi et les tables célestes," *Revue d'Histoire et de Philosophie Religieuse* 17 (1937): 401–12; R. Eppel and H. Bietenhard, *Die himmlische Welt im Urchristentum und Spät judentum* (Tübingen, 1951), pp. 231–54; G. Widengren, *The Ascension of the Apostle and the Heavenly Book* (Upsala, 1950); L. Koep, *Das himmlische Buch in Antike und Christentum* (Bonn, 1952); J. Daniélou, *Théologie du Judéo-Christianisme,* 2nd ed. (Paris, 1991), pp. 186–99. On the idea of a heavenly book in the ancient Near Eastern and Mediterranean world and its relationship to the concept of a holy scripture, see W. A. Graham, *Beyond the Written Word: Oral Aspects of Scripture in the History of Religion* (Cambridge and New York, 1987), pp. 50–51. A later reflex of this ancient semitic notion of the celestial *urschrift* can be seen in the Islamic conceptions (expressed in the Qurʾan) of *umm al-kitāb,* literally, the "mother of Scripture," and *al-lawḥ al-*

maḥfuz, the "preserved tablet," which is the *aṣl al-kitāb*, the "root of Scripture." See Graham, op. cit., pp. 84, 89, 206–7 n. 15. In general it may be said that the graphic orientation in Jewish sources shares a basic orientation with Islam, which may be contrasted with the logocentric approach prevalent in Christianity.

7. Cf., by contrast, Exod. 34:27–28, where Moses is described as the one who wrote down the ten commandments on the tablets. Cf. also Deut. 31:9, 19–24, where Moses is depicted as the one who wrote down the Teaching and gave it to the priests. In Deut. 27:3–8 the command to inscribe the Teaching upon the stones is given to the Israelites in general.

8. Cf. Odes of Solomon 23:21–22 where the letter, previously characterized as the thought of God that descended from the supernal realm (23:5), is said to have become "a large volume, which was entirely written by the finger of God. And the name of the Father was upon it; and of the Son and of the Holy Spirit, to rule forever and ever."

9. So the expression was understood by various medieval biblical exegetes in their respective commentaries to Exod. 32:32; cf., e.g., Samuel ben Meir, *Perush ha-Torah*, ed. D. Rosen (Breslau, 1882), p. 138; *Perush ha-Ramban ᶜal ha-Torah*, ed. C. D. Chavel (Jerusalem, 1984), 1:514–15; and *Perush ha-Ḥizquni ᶜal ha-Torah*, ed. C. D. Chavel (Jerusalem, 1988), p. 316. Cf., by contrast, *Perushe Rashi ᶜal ha-Torah*, ed. C. D. Chavel (Jerusalem, 1983), p. 307. Rashi interprets the reference to God's book as the Torah in its entirety. On Abraham ibn Ezra's interpretation of God's book as the heavens, see below, n. 63.

10. Cf. 1 Enoch 108:3. On the burning of testimonial books as a sign of punishment, see also pseudo-Philo 26:1–6.

11. Cf. B. Megillah 18a, and *Sifre on Deuteronomy*, ed. L. Finkelstein (New York, 1969), 296, p. 314, and numerous other references cited in n. 8 ad locum.

12. In Deut. 25:17–19 the paradox takes on a different dimension, for according to that text it is incumbent upon the Israelites not to forget to wipe out the memory of Amalek.

13. This link from a different vantage point is affirmed as well by Plato in *Phaedrus* 275 in the legend regarding the Egyptian god, Theuth (Thoth), who taught several arts, including writing, to the king Thammuz (also called Ammon). Theuth argues that the virtue of writing is "a recipe for memory and wisdom." The king objects, however, saying that this discovery would actually have the opposite effect; i.e., writing would foster forgetfulness rather than memory inasmuch as people would rely on external marks rather than on their own inner memories to recall something. Writing, therefore, serves not as a recipe for memory but only as a reminder. See R. Harris, *The Origin of Writing* (La Salle, 1986), p. 24. For the revival of this Platonic idea in Augustine, see G. Harpham, *The Ascetic Imperative in Culture and Criticism* (Chicago and London, 1987), pp. 114–15. On the connection between memory and

writting in other ancient and medieval figures, both in terms of the depiction of memory as a tablet upon which images are inscribed and the use of written texts as an aid or stimulus to memory, see M. J. Carruthers, *The Book of Memory: A Study of Memory in Medieval Culture* (Cambridge and New York, 1990), pp. 8–9, 16–32, 111, 246–47, 322 n. 32. On the role of memory as reconstructing the icons typographically impressed upon the soul like markings that are inscribed upon slabs of wax or tablets, see D. F. Krell, *Of Memory, Reminiscence, and Writing: On the Verge* (Bloomington and Indianapolis, 1990). For a contemporary assessment that echoes the Platonic critique, linking memory to oral culture and literacy or documentation to written culture, see Graham, *Beyond the Written Word*, pp. 14–15, and W. Parks, "The Textualization of Orality in Literary Criticism," in *Vox intexta: Orality and Textuality in the Middle Ages*, ed. A. N. Doane and C. B. Pasternack (Madison, 1991), pp. 46–61, esp. 57–58. Plato's discussion no doubt reflects a living debate concerning which medium, oral or written discourse, is the proper one for the transmission of philosophical knowledge. Concerning this issue see the essays collected in *Language and Thought in Early Greek Philosophy*, ed. K. Robb (La Salle, 1983).

14. Cf. the description of such a book in Testament of Abraham 12:7–18. It should be noted, however, that according to that apocalyptic source not God but rather two angels, one to the right and one to the left of the book, are the ones who record righteous deeds and sins. See also 1 Enoch 47:3; 2 Enoch 52:15; and Revelation 5:1ff.

15. Cf. 1 Enoch 81:1–2, 106:19–107:1; J. T. Millik, *The Books of Enoch: Aramaic Fragments of Qumrân Cave 4* (Oxford and New York, 1976), p. 334; and J. C. Reeves, *Jewish Lore in Manichaean Cosmogony: Studies in the Book of Giants Traditions* (Cincinnati, 1992), p. 154 n. 306.

16. 4Q417 f2i:15–18, published in *A Preliminary Edition of the Unpublished Dead Sea Scrolls: The Hebrew and Aramaic Texts from Cave Four, Fascicle Two*, ed. B. Z. Wacholder and M. G. Abegg (Washington, D.C., 1992), p. 66; English translation appears on p. xiii.

17. Cf. M. ʾAvot 2:1, 3:16; *Sifre Deuteronomy*, 307, p. 345; B. Rosh ha-Shanah 16b, 32b; Nedarim 22a; and *Tanḥuma*ʾ, Ṣav, 8. See L. Ginzberg, *The Legends of the Jews* (Philadelphia, 1968), 5:128 n. 141. According to other rabbinic sources, the book of judgment containing one's deeds is written by the person and produced by God; see sources mentioned by Ginzberg, op. cit., 5:76–77 n. 20. Needless to say, this image dominates the liturgical poetry composed over the generations for the High Holy days. Indeed, the central myth informing the liturgy of Rosh ha-Shanah and Yom Kippur is that of divine inscription and sealing the book of life. Interesting in this regard is the comment of Andrew of Victor, cited in B. Smalley, *The Study of the Bible in the Middle Ages* (Notre Dame, 1964), p. 148: "[A]ccording to a Jewish tradition, the sins of all men are preserved in writing on a shining white substance, that they appear more readily to the Judge's eye. Hence, the *books were opened* and read before the Ancient of Days, seated on his throne [Dan. 7:9–

10]. . . . Grievous sins are written in red and the other colours which adhere more faithfully to the parchment and strike the reader's eye more readily. . . . When sins are said to be written in books, what else does it mean but that God remembers as though they were written?"

18. Such an orientation is evident in the creation account in the first chapter of Genesis. See also Ps. 33:6, 9; Wisdom of Solomon 9:1; Ecclesiasticus 42:15; and 4 Esdras 6:38.

19. See R. T. R. Clark, *Myth and Symbol in Ancient Egypt* (London, 1959), pp. 44, 53 (see, however, text referred to below, n. 169); Brandon, *Creation Legends of the Ancient Near East*, pp. 32–37, 41, 86–87, 98, 149–50.

20. Cf. M. ᵓAvot 5:1.

21. This usage is widespread in standard rabbinic texts. See E. E. Urbach, *The Sages: Their Concepts and Beliefs* (Jerusalem, 1978), pp. 161–89 (in Hebrew).

22. Cf. *Genesis Rabbah*, ed. J. Theodor and Ch. Albeck (Jerusalem, 1965), 1:10, p. 8; P. Hagigah 2:1, 77c; and *Pesiqtaᵓ Rabbati*, ed. M. Friedmann (Vienna, 1880), 21:9, 109b.

23. Cf. *Genesis Rabbah* 12:9, pp. 108–9; P. Ḥagigah 2:1, 77c; B. Menaḥot 29b; *Pesiqtaᵓ Rabbati* 21:9, 109b; *Synopse zur Hekhalot-Literatur*, ed. P. Schäfer et al. (Tübingen, 1981), § 833 (*Seder Rabbah di-Bereshit*); *Masekhet Hekhalot*, ch. 7, in *Bet ha-Midrash*, ed. A. Jellinek (Jerusalem, 1967), p. 46; and *ᵓOtiyyot de-R. ᶜAqivaᵓ*, in *Batte Midrashot*, ed. S. Wertheimer (Jerusalem, 1980), 2:363. The creation of the world by means of the letters of the divine name is also implied in the oft-cited statement attributed to Rav to the effect that Bezalel, the builder of the Tabernacle, knew how to combine the letters by means of which heaven and earth were created; cf. B. Berkahot 55a; L. Blau, *Das Altjüdische Zauberwesen* (Budapest, 1898), p. 122 n. 7; Scholem, "Name of God," p. 71; and idem, *On the Kabbalah and Its Symbolism*, trans. R. Manheim (New York, 1969), pp. 166–67. See, by contrast, the interpretation of Urbach, *Sages*, p. 174, and Idel, "Reification of Language," p. 46. Cf. the tradition of the ancients (*divre qadmonenu*) reported by Abraham ibn Ezra, *Sefer ha-Shem* (Fürth, 1834), 19a, to the effect that the upper world (*ᶜolam ha-ᶜelyon*) was created by means of half the Tetragrammaton and the lower world (*ᶜolam ha-shafel*) by the other half. (Ibn Ezra cites in this context the view expressed in *Sefer Yeṣirah* to the effect that the six extremities of the cosmos are sealed by six permutations of the letters YHW, the divine name.) Cf. *The Religious Poems of Abraham Ibn Ezra*, ed. I. Levin (Jerusalem, 1975), 1:137 (poem no. 74). Ibn Ezra's comment is cited in slight variation by Jacob ben Sheshet, *Sefer ha-ᵓEmunah we-ha-Biṭṭaḥon*, ch. 4, in *Kitve Ramban*, ed. C. D. Chavel (Jerusalem, 1964), 2:363. In the same context Jacob ben Sheshet also relates another tradition to the effect that both the world-to-come and this world were created by *yod-heᵓ*, i.e., half the Tetragrammaton, which when spelled out equals twenty-six, the numerical value of the four letters that make up the name. See the cryptic allusion to this secret found in the series of traditions attributed to

the anonymous elder (*zaqen*), in MS Oxford, Bodleian Library 2396, fol. 4a. Ibn Ezra's remark influenced other notable Jewish mystics in the thirteenth and fourteenth centuries such as Abraham Abulafia and Isaac of Acre; see M. Idel, *Studies in Ecstatic Kabbalah* (Albany, 1988), pp. 58–59 n. 29. The influence of ibn Ezra is also discernible in the following comment in the collection of Jacob ben Jacob ha-Kohen's teachings, *Sefer ha-ʾOrah*, MS Milan, Biblioteca Ambrosiana 62, fol. 99b:

> This covenant [circumcision] is the seal (*ḥotamo*) of the Holy One, blessed be He, with which He sealed the heavens, as it is written in *Sefer Yeṣirah*, He sealed the heights (*rom*) with *yod-heʾ* [the first two letters of the Tetragrammaton] and the lower regions (*ha-taḥtonim*) He sealed with *waw-heʾ* [the final two letters]. And this is [alluded to in the verse] 'Let the heavens rejoice and the earth exult' [*yismeḥu ha-shamayim we-tagel ha-ʾareṣ*] (Ps. 96:11)—with half the name [*yod-heʾ*] He sealed the upper realities [alluded to in the words *yismeḥu ha-shamayim*, 'let the heavens rejoice'] and with half the name [*waw-heʾ*] He sealed the lower realities [*we-tagel ha-ʾareṣ*, "and the earth exult"].

It is of interest that Jacob ha-Kohen combines this cosmological teaching with the motif of circumcision as the inscription of the divine name as a seal on the flesh, which also functions in an apotropaic manner. Concerning the nexus of these different themes in select aggadic, German Pietistic, and kabbalistic sources, see E. R. Wolfson, "Circumcision and the Divine Name: A Study in the Transmission of Esoteric Doctrine," *Jewish Quarterly Review* 78 (1987): 77–112. According to another medieval tradition (attested in Hai Gaon, Rashi, Tosafot, Ḥaside Ashkenaz, and many kabbalists) the forty-two-letter name (mentioned in the name of Rav in B. Qiddushin 71a but not specified) is connected with creation. For some of the relevant sources, see Wolfson, "Letter Symbolism and Merkavah Imagery," pp. 217–218 n. 77; see also Blau, *Das Altjüdische Zauberwesen*, pp. 125, 132. There was also an Ashkenazi tradition that by means of the forty-two-letter name the world would be destroyed in the eschatological future. Cf. MS Oxford, Bodleian Library 1943, fol. 94b.

24. See J. E. Fossum, *The Name of God and the Angel of the Lord* (Tübingen, 1985), pp. 253–56, and N. Janowitz, *The Poetics of Ascent: Theories of Language in a Rabbinic Ascent Text* (Albany, 1989), pp. 25–27.

25. *Genesis Rabbah* 12:9, pp. 108–9.

26. Scholem, "Name of God," p. 69, cites two apocryphal writings (*Prayer of Menasseh* and *Book of Jubilees*) that express the notion of God creating the world or sealing the abyss by means of his name. Cf. Odes of Solomon 24:5; *Sefer Yeṣirah* 1:15 (cf. *Masekhet Hekhalot*, ch. 7, p. 47); *Synopse*, §§ 833, 840–41; Fossum, *Name of God*, pp. 245–53; D. Sperber, "On Sealing the Abysses," *Journal of Semitic Studies* 11 (1966): 168–74; and P. Hayman, "Was God a Magician? Sefer Yesira and Jewish Magic," *Journal of Jewish Studies* 40 (1989): 225–37, esp. 229–30. Cf. the echo of this motif in the aggadic tradition cited in

following note. Cf. *Synopse*, §§ 389 and 396, where the demiurgical characterizations are applied to Meṭaṭron. See also the comment in 3 Enoch (*Synopse* § 16) to the effect that God wrote with his finger, by means of a pen of fire, the letters through which heaven and earth were created on the diadem of Meṭaṭron. On this whole question, see my recent study, "Meṭaṭron and Shiᶜur Qomah in the Writings of Ḥaside Ashkenaz," to be published in the proceedings of the conference Mystik, Magie und Kabbala im Aschkenasischen Judentum, December 9–11, 1991, ed. K. E. Grözinger, esp. near n. 85. See also the passage in *Synopse*, § 318, where mention is made of the *ḥotam* (i.e., the magical seal/name) by which heaven and earth were sealed.

27. B. Sukkah 53a–b; cf. P. Sanhedrin 17:2, 29a.

28. See A. Altmann, "Gnostic Themes in Rabbinic Cosmology," in *Essays in Honour of the Very Rev. Dr. J. H. Hertz, Chief Rabbi . . . On the Occasion of His Seventieth Birthday*, ed. I. Epstein, E. Levine, and C. Roth (London, n.d.), p. 25; and Sperber, "On Sealing the Abysses," pp. 171–73. On different traditions of mystical and magical writing, see as well H. Glück, *Schrift und Schriftlichkeit: Eine sprach-und Kulturwissenschaftiche Studie* (Stuttgart, 1987), pp. 210–29.

29. See Sperber, "On Sealing the Abysses," p. 173.

30. See E. Slomovic, "Patterns of Midrashic Impact on the Rabbinic Midrashic Tale," *Journal for the Study of Judaism* 19 (1988): 76–83 (my thanks to Jeffrey Rubenstein for drawing my attention to this article).

31. Cf. *Genesis Rabbah* 1:1, p. 2; 18:4, p. 164; 31:8, p. 281; E. E. Urbach, "Fragments of the Tanḥuma Yelammedenu," *Qoveṣ ᶜal Yad* 14 (1966): 20 (in Hebrew). For discussion of these and other relevant aggadic sources, and their transformation in zoharic literature, see M. Oron, "The Narrative of the Letters and Its Source: A Study of a Zoharic Midrash on the Letters of the Alphabet," in *Studies in Jewish Mysticism, Philosophy and Ethical Literature Presented to Isaiah Tishby on His Seventy-Fifth Birthday*, ed. J. Dan and J. Hacker (Jerusalem, 1986), pp. 97–109 (in Hebrew).

32. On the Primordial Torah see also *Genesis Rabbah* 1:4, p. 6, and other parallel sources cited there in n. 4. For a different explanation regarding the relation of the verbal and visual aspects of the Primordial Torah, see Janowitz, *Poetics of Ascent*, pp. 102–3. Janowitz emphasizes the "shift from an ideology of divine language as spoken . . . to an ideology of the power of the written text. . . . Long after the deity spoke, the words are still available on earth, but now in the form of their written encapsulation in the text. The text is a receptacle of that divine speech." While there is clearly some justification for this view, it must be borne in mind that the classical sources of rabbinic Judaism develop an alternative orientation along the lines discussed in the body of this paper; viz., the graphic precedes the oral. Hence, the power of divine speech itself derives from the fact that God has recited that which is already encoded in written form in the Primordial Torah. On the question of

the primacy of the graphic or phonic, writing or speech, in Jewish sources, see also C. Sirat, "Par l'oreille et par l'œil: La Bible hébraïque et les livres qui la portent," in *The Frank Talmage Memorial Volume,* ed. B. Walfish (Haifa, 1993), 1:233–49. Sirat suggests a shift in signification from the verbal to the visual based on the multiplication of written books due to the spread of the Hebrew square alphabet. Hence, in the context of discussing the bibilical period, especially the time of Ezra, Sirat adopts a position similar to that of Janowitz: "cette Loi est éternellement fixée, mais les lettres qui la fixaient n'avaient de valeur que par la parole vivante; c'est par la parole qu'elles participaient de la divinité. L'écriture était l'outil du discours; elle était conventionnelle et c'est pourquoi elle a pu être changée" (p. 238). In the continuation of her study (pp. 240ff.) Sirat acknowledges that in rabbinic sources, both midrashic and mystical, a conception of divine scripture evolved that privileged the visual/graphic dimension over the aural/verbal. Thus consider her sweeping remark on p. 244: "Pour les Juifs rabbanites, la Loi est bien ce qui est écrit et non pas ce qui est entendu." The visual orientation to sacred scripture has prevailed through the ages, and the graphic dimension of the written letters has assumed symbolic signification. See also idem, *La lettre hébraïque et sa signification,* avec L. Avrin (Paris and Jerusalem, 1981), pp. 17–37. For a different view regarding the primacy of the written text in ancient Israelite culture, see comment of S. C. Reif, "Aspects of Medieval Jewish Literacy," in *The Uses of Literacy in Early Mediaeval Europe,* ed. R. McKitterick (Cambridge and New York, 1990), p. 135: "Both internal and external evidence demonstrates a substantial use of the written word in ancient Israel for archives, inscriptions and the establishment of religious authority. To that latter end a significant element in codification appears to have been textualization, which was regarded as a means of ensuring the permanence of knowledge, guidance and edification for the faithful." On the privileging of the oral to the visual in the cultural development of language, see the pioneering studies of W. J. Ong, *The Presence of the Word: Some Prolegomena for Cultural and Religious History* (Minneapolis, 1967) and *Orality and Literacy: The Technologizing of the Word* (London, 1982). See also the study of Graham cited above in n. 6 and W. H. Kelber, *The Oral and the Written Gospel: The Hermeneutics of Speaking and Writing in the Synoptic Tradition, Mark, Paul, and Q* (Philadelphia, 1983). On the primacy of orality and the treatment of writing as a representation of oral speech, see Harris, *Origin of Writing,* pp. 26–27, 76–121; and idem, "Quelques réflexions sur la tyrannie de l'alphabet," in *L'écriture: le cerveau, l'œil et la main,* ed. C. Sirat, J. Irigoin, E. Poulle (Brepols, Turnhout, 1990), pp. 195–99. See also H.-J. Martin, *Histoire et pouvoirs de l'écrit,* avec la collaboration de B. Delmas, préface de Pierre Chauni de l'Institut (Paris, 1988), pp. 20–24, 84–120. On the shift from the written to the oral in medieval European culture, see B. Stock, *The Implications of Literacy: Written Language and Models of Interpretation in the Eleventh and Twelfth Centuries* (Princeton, 1983), pp. 12–87, and idem, *Listening for the Text: On the Uses of the Past* (Baltimore and London, 1990), pp. 1–15. See also P. Zumthor, *La Lettre et la voix. De la 'Littérature' médiévale* (Paris, 1987); H. Keller, "Pragmatische Schriftlichkeit im Mittelalter. Erscheinungsformen und

Entwicklungsstufen. Einführung zum Kooquium in Münster, 17–19, Mai 1989," in *Pragmatische Schriftlichkeit im Mittelalter: Erscheinungsformen und Entwicklungsstufen*, ed. H. Keller, K. Grubmüller, and N. Staubach (Munich, 1992); and in the same volume, G. Dilcher, "Oralität, Verschriftlichung und Wandlungen der Normstruktur in den Stadtrechten des 12. und 13. Jahrhunderts," pp. 9–19. It is highly questionable if the anthropological approach to medieval Christian culture is valid for the study of medieval rabbinic culture. See study of Reif cited above.

33. Cf. P. Sheqalim 6:1; Soṭah 8:3; *Tanḥuma*ʾ, introduction; and *Midrash Konen*, in *Bet ha-Midrash*, 2:23. Cf. *Deuteronomy Rabbah* 3:12, where this characterization is used to describe the status of the Torah given to Moses on Mt. Sinai (parchment of white fire and written in black fire) from which he made a copy himself (interpreting Deut. 31:9, "Moses wrote down this Torah and gave it to the priests," as referring to the whole Torah which he purportedly copied on Mt. Sinai). Cf. *Song of Songs Rabbah* 5:9.

34. Cf. *Midrash ʿEser ha-Dibberot*, in *Bet ha-Midrash*, 1:62.

35. Cf. M. ʾAvot 5:6, and B. Pesaḥim 54a. See Ginzberg, *Legends*, 5:34 n. 99 and 52 n. 161.

36. Here I will offer a representative sampling of the different exegetical traditions. Cf. the interpretation of Sherira Gaon cited in *Teshuvot ha-Geʾonim*, ed. A. Harkavy (Berlin, 1887), pp. 11–12 (cf. *Otzar ha-Geonim*, ed. B. M. Lewin [Jerusalem, 1984], vol. 3, pt. 2: Tractate Pesaḥim, pp. 73–74), according to which the *ketav* signifies Adam's general linguistic capacity to write, i.e., to affix (*letaqqen*) signs and letters to his words, whereas *mikhtav* signifies specifically the holy script (*ketav ha-qodesh*), i.e., Hebrew, the language with which the Torah is written. See I. Goldziher, "Mélanges Judéo-Arabes," *Revue des études juives* 50 (1905): 188–90. According to another view transmitted in the name of Yehudai Gaon, the *ketav* refers to the twenty-two Hebrew letters and the *mikhtav* to the writing that was inscribed on the tablets. Cf. Nathan ben Yeḥiel of Rome, *Aruch Completum*, ed. A. Kohut, 4:357. s.v., *ketav*. According to the view of Hai Gaon, the *ketav* refers to speech (*dibbur*) and the *mikhtav* to writing (*ketivah*). See, by contrast, Ḥananel ben Ḥushiel, who explains in his commentary to B. Pesaḥim 54a that *ketav* refers to the form of the letters (*ṣurat ha-ʾotiyyot*), and *mikhtav* to the combination of letters (*ṣeruf ha-ʾotiyyot*) to form words that are spoken. Judah ben Barzillai, *Perush Sefer Yeṣirah*, ed. S. J. Halberstam (Berlin, 1885), p. 139, alludes to some of these Geonic interpretations. It is also of interest to note in this context Maimonides' commentary to M. ʾAvot 5:5, in *Mishnah ʿim Perush ha-Rambam*, ed. J. Kafiḥ (Jerusalem, 1965), Nashim and Neziqim, p. 298: "The *ketav* is the Torah that was written before Him, may He be elevated, as it is said, but we do not know how it was . . . and the *mikhtav* is the writing on the tablets." Typically, Maimonides avoids any reference to the aggadic motif of the Primordial Torah being written with black fire on white fire, not to mention the even more radical claim that it was written upon God's forearm (see n. 33). This constitutes another example of Maimonides' deliberate disregard for esoteric

traditions in the classical rabbinic sources. See Maimonides' introduction to the tenth chapter of Sanhedrin, *pereq ḥeleq*, principle 8, in Kafih, op. cit., p. 143. There Moses is described as a "scribe before whom they read and he wrote down everything, its dates, stories and commandments." In this context as well Maimonides avoids embracing the aggadic motif regarding the Primordial Torah in order to explain Moses' scribal activity. See, by contrast, *Perush ha-Ramban ʿal ha-Torah*, pp. 2, 7, where Naḥmanides explicitly utilizes this aggadic tradition to which he even refers as a *qabbalah*. While Naḥmanides asserts that Moses was like a scribe who copied the Primordial Torah written with black fire upon white fire, he also insists that the entire Torah reached the ear of Moses from the mouth of God; there is thus both a graphic and an aural aspect to Moses' reception of the Torah on Mt. Sinai; the oral aspect also comprises the esoteric way of reading the text. Cf. the commentary of R. Jonah Gerondi to M. ʾAvot 5:6: "The *ketav* refers to the Torah that was written before the Holy One, blessed be He, from the six days of creation in black fire upon white fire. *Mikhtav* refers to the form of the letters engraved on the tablets." Cf. the explanation of Rashi cited in the following note. For a convenient review of some of the relevant rabbinic interpreters, see M. M. Kasher, *Torah Shelemah*, vol. 29 ["The Script of the Torah and Its Characters"] (Jerusalem, 1978), pp. 28–31. See also Sirat, *La lettre hébraïque*, p. 19. Finally, it would be of interest to compare the Jewish tradition regarding the *makhtev* that precedes the world and the Islamic notion of the *qalam* (derived from the Quʾran) as the instrument by means of which heavenly matters are inscribed. See T. Izutsu, *God and Man in the Koran: Semantics of the Koranic Weltanschauung* (Tokyo, 1964), p. 160, and A. Schimmel, *Mystical Dimensions of Islam* (Chapel Hill, N.C., 1975), pp. 414–16. See below, n. 107.

37. This reading is attested in the writings of Rashi and those who followed his teachings. Cf. Rashi's commentary to M. ʾAvot 5:6: "The *ketav* refers to the fact that the material letters (*guf ha-ʾotiyyot*) were created from the six days of creation, and even though the Torah preceded the world by two thousand years, it did not have material letters, but rather it existed orally. The *makhtev* is the pen of the scribe, *grafie* in a foreign language [i.e., old medieval French; Rashi uses this word to explain *makhtev* in several places in his talmudic commentaries; cf. B. Qiddushin 21b; Shavuʿot 4b; and ʿAvodah Zarah 22b; cf. also Rashi's commentary to Ezek. 17:22], by means of which He engraved the ten commandments on the tablets that were given to Moses; that pen was created from before." Cf. Rashi's commentary to B. Pesaḥim 54a: "*Ketav* is the recitation of the name of the letters. *Mikhtav* is their being engraved and their form. Thus I have heard, but it seems to me that this *ketav* is the engraving of their form and the *makhtev* is the pen and stylus by means of which were written the engraving on the tablets." Cf. the formulation by the disciple of Rashi, Simḥah ben Samuel, *Maḥzor Vitry*, ed. S. Hurvitz (Nurnberg, 1923), p. 541: "The *ketav* refers to the order of writing (*tiqqun ha-ketav*) just as a letter revolves in its rotation . . . and the *mikhtav* is the pen through which the tablets were engraved, which is called *grafie*; I have received [that the correct vocalization is] *we-ha-makhtev*."

38. On the centrality of Scripture as holy writ in the Jewish and Christian tradition, see Graham, *Beyond the Written Word,* pp. 49–57. The emphasis on the written/graphic nature of the Torah has ramifications in the realm of ritual as well. For example, it is necessary for one who reads the Torah scroll liturgically to read from a scroll rather than to recite from memory in order to fulfill the requirement to read the Written Torah. Cf. B. Giṭṭin 60b; *Tanḥuma*ʾ, Ki Tissaʾ 35; and Maimonides, *Mishneh Torah,* Hilkhot Tefillah 12:8. The issue of the Oral Torah in Judaism and its relationship to verbal and written modes of discourse is a very important and germane topic that cannot be entered into in this context. See following note. For a recent discussion of this topic, see M. S. Jaffee, "How Much 'Orality' in Oral Torah? New Perspectives on the Composition and Transmission of Early Rabbinic Tradition," *Shofar* 10 (1992): 53–72. Regarding the issue of oral versus written as it relates more generally to sacred Scripture in a comparative framework of Hinduism and Judaism, see B. A. Holdrege, *Veda and Torah: Transcending the Textuality of Scripture* (Albany, 1995).

39. This is not to say that the oral dimension of the Sinaitic revelation was never stressed in rabbinic literature. Cf., e.g., the view of Ḥananel ben Ḥushiel cited in *Rabbenu Baḥya ʿal ha-Torah,* ed. C. D. Chavel (Jerusalem, 1981), 1:176, ad Gen. 18:19: "The Ten Commandments were heard from the mouth of God and were written by the prophet, peace be upon him, and the rest of the Torah was written by the prophet. And just as there is no difference between the commadments that were heard and those that are written, so there is no difference between the commandments that were written and those that are a tradition; all are equal." Yet, the bulk of the evidence points to the fact that Moses himself would have been copying from a prepared script, i.e., the Torah already existed in written form.

40. See Rashi's commentary to M. ʾAvot 5:6 quoted in n. 37.

41. Perhaps one of the most striking expressions of this belief is found in the statement of the nineteenth-century Hasidic master Ṣadoq ha-Kohen of Lublin, *Maḥshevot Haruṣ* (Piotrkow, 1912), 44b: "Thus I have received that the world in its entirety is a book that God, blessed be He, made, and the Torah is the commentary that He composed on that book." This statement implies, in a quintessentially Jewish manner, that God's initial book, the world, requires a commentary, Scripture, and that commentary engenders other commentaries that not God but human beings create in a seemingly endless effort to reveal the hidden depths concealed in the original traces of God's writing that make up the universe. R. Ṣadoq's comment, while perhaps not consciously intended in this manner, subverts any hermeneutical theory that would posit a final truth, a foundation that ends all play of meaning. In perfectly good Derridean fashion we may say that the way back leads not to an original truth, but rather to an origin that is a text that needs to be interpreted by another text. The materiality of the world is reduced to traces of textuality that summon interpretation. The originary interpretation is itself a text whose boundaries are fluid insofar as it too must be interpreted. The necessity of

commentary thus constitutes the very texture of existence from the vantage point of the Jew. There is nothing that is not inscribed within the book and therefore not open to interpretation, not even God's being. See J. Derrida, *Writing and Difference*, trans. A. Bass (Chicago and London, 1978), p. 67; idem, *Of Grammatology*, trans. G. Chakravorty Spivak (Baltimore and London, 1976), pp. 93, 158; and V. B. Leitch, *Deconstructive Criticism: An Advanced Introduction* (New York, 1983), pp. 24–39. On the textuality of God, see also E. Jabés, *The Book of Questions*, trans. R. Waldrop (Middletown, 1973), pp. 31–32, 122. It is interesting that in one passage in *Glas* (Paris, 1974), 268b–69b, Derrida does speak of the Torah, which comes out from "behind the curtain" (*derrière les rideaux*), as the "origin of literature," which he mimes. See S. Handelman, *The Slayers of Moses: The Emergence of Rabbinic Interpretation in Modern Literary Theory* (Albany, 1982), pp. 165–66. On the comparison of current literary theory of thinkers like Barthes and Derrida (tellingly referred to as a Jewish heretic hermeneutic) to rabbinic modes of interpretation, see Handelman, op. cit., pp. 79–81, 163–78. For the development of these motifs in the kabbalistic writings of Elijah ben Solomon, the Gaon of Vilna, see E. R. Wolfson, "From Sealed Book to Open Text: Time, Memory, and Narrativity in Kabbalistic Hermeneutics," in *Critical Jewish Hermeneutics*, ed. S. Kepnes (New York, 1995).

42. My formulation here is indebted to the description of Derrida's grammatology in Parks, "Textualization of Orality," p. 48.

43. The literarture on *Sefer Yeṣirah* is quite sizeable, and here I mention only some studies that deal more specifically with the linguistic mysticism of the work. See P. Mordell, *The Origin of Letters and Numerals according to the Sefer Yezirah* (Philadelphia, 1914); Scholem, "Name of God," pp. 72–76; Lipiner, *Metaphysics of the Hebrew Alphabet*, pp. 112–66; and most recently S. Wasserstrom, "Sefer Yeṣira and Early Islam: A Reappraisal," *Journal of Jewish Thought and Philosophy* 3 (1993): 1–30. Wasserstrom has revived the view of P. Kraus and L. Massignon that the received text of *Sefer Yeṣirah* reflects an Islamic milieu for its redactional setting.

44. See especially the reading established by I. Gruenwald, "A Preliminary Critical Edition of *Sefer Yeẓira*," *Israel Oriental Studies* 1 (1971): 140 (all subsequent references follow this edition), and translated by idem, "Some Critical Notes on the First Part of Sefer Yeẓira," *Revue des études juives* 132 (1973): 479: "He created His world in three books (*sheloshah sefarim*): in a book (*sefer*), a book (*sefer*), and a book (*sefer*)." While there are several *variae lectiones* of the last three words, it would appear that in the earliest texts, as is attested by a later authority, the kabbalist Isaac of Acre, the three occurrences of the word *sfr* should be vocalized as *sefer*, "book." See Gruenwald, "Some Critical Notes," p. 483, and op. cit., p. 480, where he suggests that the three books refer to the three divisions of letters mentioned in paragraph 9 of the first part of the work and operative in the second part. Cf. the reference to the three books known by Noah in the Qumran fragment (4Q534–36) published by R. Eisenman and M. Wise, *The Dead Sea Scrolls Uncovered* (Shaftesbury, 1992), p. 35.

45. In *Sefer Yeṣirah,* par. 15, another predicate is used to denote God's linguistic creativity, viz., *ḥatam,* to seal by means of a magical name. See above, n. 23. To be sure, the aural dimension of the letters is affirmed in *Sefer Yeṣirah,* par. 10, where it is stated that the first *sefirah,* the pneuma of the living God (*ruaḥ ʾelohim ḥayyim*) or the holy pneuma (*ruaḥ ha-qodesh*) comprises the voice (*qol*), breath (*ruaḥ*), and speech (*dibbur*). The possibility that this text points to some form of Logos speculation has been duly noted by Gruenwald, "Some Critical Notes," p. 500. See below n. 48.

46. *Sefer Yeṣirah,* par. 12.

47. Cf. ibid., pars. 13, 14.

48. By contrast, Gruenwald, "Some Critical Notes," pp. 501–4, suggests that the verbs *ḥaqaq* and *ḥaṣav* in *Sefer Yeṣirah* are "of a spiritual nature," which he connects to a more general theory of the Logos. The passage in *Sefer Yeṣirah,* par. 17, that Gruenwald cites, is significant, for according to that text the twenty-two elemental letters are said to be "engraved (*ḥaquqot*) in the voice, hewn (*ḥaṣuvot*) in the spirit, and set (*qevuʿot*) in the mouth in five places." This clearly would suggest that at least in this context the verbs *ḥaqaq* and *ḥaṣav* should not be understood in terms of writing but rather as metaphors for processes of speech. Yet, the midrashic sources noted by Gruenwald all seem to suggest that we are talking about the grammatological aspect of the divine Word; i.e., the rabbis mythicize the process by means of which the words of God at Sinai are inscribed upon the tablets of stone. This, it seems to me, ascribes priority to the written over the verbal, or, at the very least, treats the two as simultaneous occurrences: when the words are spoken, they immediately are concretized as graphemes upon the material surface. It is plausible that in the case of *Sefer Yeṣirah,* par. 17, something similiar is intended for the voice and spirit. Such an interpretation is implied in Isaac the Blind's commentary on this text; see G. Scholem, *The Kabbalah in Provence,* ed. R. Schatz (Jerusalem, 1970), appendix, p. 6 (in Hebrew). See also Judah ben Barzillai, *Perush Sefer Yeṣirah,* p. 227, where it is emphasized that one "cannot understand any voice (*qol*) without speech (*dibbur*) and one cannot see the speech without the engraving of the letters (*ḥaqiqat ha-ʾotiyyot*)." From this comment it would appear that the emergence of the letters is a twofold process that takes place concurrently; i.e., the aural and the visual occur simultaneously. See, however, "The Commentary of Isaac of Acre to the First Chapter of *Sefer Yeṣirah,*" ed. G. Scholem, *Kiryat Sefer* 31 (1955–56): 386 (in Hebrew). The textual reference to the covenant of the tongue (*berit ha-lashon*) is explained in terms of the "articulation and engraving of the letters (*keritat we-ḥaqiqat ha-ʾotiyyot*) by means of the tongue on the lips." It would appear from this context that Isaac understood the term *ḥaqaq* as enunciating in speech rather than engraving in writing. See ibid., p. 393, where the word *ḥaqiqah* is explicitly characterized as the "marking of the letters in the calling of the name" (*reshimat ha-ʾotiyyot bi-qeriʾat ha-shem*). See, however, p. 381, where both *ḥaqaq* and *ḥaṣav* seem to imply engraving and carving something material.

49. *Sefer Yeṣirah*, par. 17. For discussion of this fivefold division and its impact on later kabbalistic authors, see the material collected in A. Kaplan, *Sefer Yetzirah: The Book of Creation in Theory and Practice* (York Beach, Maine, 1990), pp. 102–8.

50. Some texts read here "elemental letters" (*ʾotiyyot yesod*).

51. The Hebrew reads here *kol ha-yeṣur,* which may denote all of creation, i.e, every created entity. See Scholem, *On the Kabbalah,* p. 168. M. Idel, *Golem: Jewish Magical and Mystical Traditions on the Artificial Anthropoid* (Albany, 1990), pp. 12–13, suggests that *yeṣur* in this context may denote specifically the human being.

52. *Sefer Yeṣirah*, par. 19.

53. Cf. *Sefer Yeṣirah*, pars. 32–34.

54. Cf. the oft-cited aggadah about God tying crownlets to the letters in B. Menaḥot 29b.

55. See Scholem, "Name of God," p. 76; idem, *On the Kabbalah,* pp. 166–70; and Idel, *Golem*, pp. 9–26. See also Hayman, "Was God a Magician?" pp. 233–37.

56. Some versions add here the word *ṣar* or *wa-yiṣṣer,* from the root *ṣur,* "to form." Although many of the predicates used to describe Abraham are clearly meant to convey the notion of linguistic creativity, in my view this particular expression, "to form," is not necessarily related to such activity as has been argued in the scholarly literature (see, e.g., Scholem, *On the Kabbalah,* p. 169 n. 3). On the contrary, as I have argued in detail elsewhere, it seems that this verb in *Sefer Yeṣirah* connotes visual imagining, involving therefore some sort of meditative technique. See E. R. Wolfson, *Through a Speculum That Shines: Vision and Imagination in Medieval Jewish Mysticism* (Princeton, 1994), p. 71 n. 67. See also Gruenwald, "Some Critical Notes," pp. 488–89.

57. Literally, "it arose in his hand." The standard printed edition reads here: "He was successful in creation (*beriʾah*), as it says, 'And the souls they made in Haran' (Gen. 12:5)." This appears to be a later gloss that adds midrashic support to the claim that Abraham, the purported recipient of the gnosis transmitted in *Sefer Yeṣirah,* mastered the technique of linguistic creation.

58. Cf. Isa. 41:8.

59. *Sefer Yeṣirah*, par. 61.

60. See M. Idel, "The Concept of Torah in the Hekhalot Literature and Its Metamorphosis in the Kabbalah," *Jerusalem Studies in Jewish Thought* 1 (1981): 43–45 (in Hebrew); K. E. Grözinger, "The Names of God and Their Celestial Powers: Their Function and Meaning in Hekhalot Literature," *Jerusalem Studies in Jewish Thought* 6:1–2 (1987): 53–69 (English section).

61. See Wolfson, "Anthropomorphic Imagery," pp. 147–48, and other references cited in n. 3.

62. See, for instance, the discussion of the linguistic process of combining letters and rotation of words as the primary act of divine creativity in E. R. Wolfson, "The Theosophy of Shabbetai Donnolo, with Special Emphasis on the Doctrine of *Sefirot* in His *Sefer Ḥakhmoni*," *Jewish History* 6 (1992): 296–97. Cf. *Shirat ha-Roke᾿aḥ: The Poems of Rabbi Eleazar ben Yehudah of Worms*, ed. I. Meiseles (Jerusalem, 1993), poem no. 7, p. 38 (in Hebrew), where the primary activity of the Torah in the beginning of creation is described in terms of rotating (i.e., combining) letters, *gilgel ᾿otiyyot*. Cf. Eleazar's *Sefer ha-Shem*, MS London, British Museum 737, fol. 292b, where the primal act of divine creativity is depicted as a vocalization of different combinations of letters.

63. See Y. Liebes, "Rabbi Solomon Ibn Gabirol's Use of Sefer Yeṣira and a Commentary on the Poem 'I Love Thee,'" *Jerusalem Studies in Jewish Thought* 6:3–4 (1987): 73–124 (in Hebrew). Abraham ibn Ezra metaphorically depicts the heavens as the book or books (see already Isa. 34:4 where the heavens are described as a scroll that is rolled up) in which God's actions are inscribed. See, e.g., *The Religious Poems of Abraham Ibn Ezra* 1:62 (poem no. 35), 72–74 (poem 41), 110 (poem 61), 120 (poem 66); 2:329 (poem no. 371); commentary on Exod. 32:32; Ps. 19:4–5, 69:29. On this image see also the interesting discussion of Simeon Lavi, *Ketem Paz* (Jerusalem, 1981), 1:262a–b. Cf. the views of Solomon ibn Gabirol and Moses ibn Ezra mentioned below, n. 162. In one very fundamental way, however, some medieval Jewish philosophers, who were heirs to the Aristotelian heritage, differed with their mystical counterparts by giving preference to the spoken over the written word, i.e., writing represents the oral word, a view in Western philosophy that Derrida has aptly called logocentrism. See R. Jospe, "The Superiority of Oral Over Written Communication: Judah Ha-Levi's *Kuzari* and Modern Jewish Thought," in *From Ancient Israel to Modern Judaism Intellect in Quest of Understanding: Essays in Honor of Marvin Fox*, ed. J. Neusner, E. S. Frerichs, and N. M. Sarna (Atlanta, 1989), 3:127–55, esp. 129–34, and Sirat, "Par l'oreille et par l'œil," p. 239.

64. See Liebes, "Ibn Gabirol's Use of Sefer Yeṣira," pp. 73–74; E. R. Wolfson, "Merkavah Traditions in Philosophical Garb: Judah Halevi Reconsidered," *Proceedings of the American Academy of Jewish Research* 57 (1989): 179–242, esp. 203ff.

65. I will not discuss here the linguistic elements found in other mystical sources from the thirteenth century, e.g., Abraham Abulafia, Joseph Gikatilla, the early writings of Moses de León, the compositions of Jacob ben Jacob ha-Kohen, especially his commentary on the letters, and so on. While this material is, of course, very relevant to the theme of this chapter, I have necessarily limited my discussion to theosophic kabbalah proper. For discussion of language in the case of Abulafia, see references to Idel's work cited above, n. 1. On the nontheosophic linguistic mysticism in the early writings of de León (or

other members of his circle) and Gikatilla, see A. Farber, "On the Sources of Rabbi Moses de León's Early Kabbalistic System," in *Studies in Jewish Mysticism, Philosophy and Ethical Literature*, pp. 67–96 (in Hebrew), and my study, "Letter Symbolism and Merkavah Imagery," cited in full in n. 1.

66. Even though some kabbalistic texts accord priority to the act of speaking when discussing the linguistic nature of creation or revelation (see below, n. 68), I am of the opinion that the vast majority privilege writing over speech. The centrality of writing was recognized by Scholem who tried to collapse the distinction between the two modes of linguistic discourse from the kabbalistic vantage point. See "Name of God," p. 67: "For the Kabbalists, linguistic mysticism is at the same time a mysticism of writing. Every act of speaking . . . is at once an act of writing and every writing is potential speech." See idem, *Origins of the Kabbalah*, trans. A. Arkush and ed. R. J. Zwi Werblowsky (Princeton, 1987), p. 277 (referred to below, n. 76). See D. Biale, *Gershom Scholem Kabbalah and Counter-History* (Cambridge, Mass., and London, 1979), pp. 99–100.

67. See Scholem, "Name of God," pp. 60–61, 176–77 (citing a key text from Jacob ben Jacob ha-Kohen); and cf. the opening passage in the treatise *Koaḥ YHWH*, printed in *Liqquṭe ha-Sha"S me-ha-ʾAri z"l* (Bene-Beraq, 1972), 37b–38a, where reference is made to Gikatilla's criticism of Maimonides on this score. Lavi, *Ketem Paz*, 262a–b, emphasizes that the forms of the Hebrew letters are not conventional or accidental but rather essential. The secret of the letters thus instructs one about the secret of creation. Cf. the kabbalistic fragment on the letters extant in MS Oxford, Bodleian Library 1958, fol. 368a, which begins with similiar language. Cf. the language used in an anonymous text extant in MS Oxford, Bodleian Library 1961, fols. 13a–b: "These former letters, natural and divine, are the cause of every matter and the foundation of every matter. Before He brought the world into existence they existed, before He created everything they were created. He searched them, engraved them, hewed them, and sealed them in His seal, His high and exalted name." Cf. the commentary on the alphabet in MS New York, Jewish Theological Seminary of America Mic. 1887, fols. 39b–43b, and especially the description of the fourth path of interpreting the alphabet, called the "hidden way" (*derekh ha-nistar*) on fol. 42a. According to this text the letters are divided into three groups that are correlated with the different ontic spheres in reality, the intelligible (or angelic), the heavenly, and the terrestrial. The underlying principle here is that the Hebrew letters are indicative of the very nature of reality. It seems that Scholem personally adopted such a view regarding the intrinsic power of language in general and Hebrew in particular as may be shown from a letter he wrote in 1926 to Franz Rosenzweig. The text is published in Hebrew translation in G. Scholem, *Explications and Implications: Writings on Jewish Heritage and Renaissance*, ed. A. Shapira (Tel-Aviv, 1989), 2:59–60 (in Hebrew), and see discussion in R. Alter, *Necessary Angels: Tradition and Modernity in Kafka, Benjamin, and Scholem* (Cambridge, Mass., 1991), pp. 36–37, 88–89.

68. Some mystical sources in fact emphasize the oral over the graphic as the primary mode of divine creativity. This is the case, e.g., in the thought of Shabbetai Donnolo who depicts the activity of letter combination in terms of consonants and vowels, implying thereby that the process involves recitation of the letters as they are permutated. See Idel, *Golem*, p. 75 n. 35, and Wolfson, "Theosophy of Shabbetai Donnolo," pp. 296–97. Priority to oral recitation is also evident in the cosmological theory espoused in one of the major and oldest documents from the Iyyun circle, the *Maᶜayan ha-Ḥokhmah*. Regarding this circle, see Scholem, *Origins*, pp. 309–54; M. Verman, *The Books of Contemplation: Medieval Jewish Mystical Sources* (Albany, 1992); and idem, "Classifying the Ḥug ha-Iyyun," in the *Proceedings of the Tenth World Congress of Jerusalem Studies*, Division C, Volume 1: Jewish Thought and Literature (1990): 57–64. On the centrality of this particular work within the corpus of the circle, see G. Scholem, *Reshit ha-Qabbalah* (Tel-Aviv, 1948), pp. 255–56 n. 2; idem, *Origins*, pp. 321, 331–37; Verman, *Books of Contemplation*, p. 146; and "Classifying the Ḥug ha-Iyyun," p. 60. See also M. Kallus, "Two Mid-Thirteenth Century Texts from the ᶜIyyun Circle" (M.A. thesis, Hebrew University, 1992), pp. 19–20. The aforementioned text begins with a description of the cosmological process that entails five stages of linguistic activity connected with the explicit divine name (*shem ha-meforash*): *tiqqun* (on the use of the word *tiqqen* in the sense of linguistic activity, perhaps letter combination, see already Judah ben Barzillai, *Perush Sefer Yeṣirah*, p. 227; and cf. the statements of Sherira Gaon and *Maḥzor Vitry* cited above, nn. 36–37; cf. the reference to *tiqqun ha-ᵓotiyyot* in the commentary on the seventy-two-letter name from the circle of *Sefer ha-Temunah* in MSS New York, Jewish Theological Seminary of America Mic. 8115, fol. 79b, Cambridge, University Library Add. 671, fol. 88b [on the provenance of this text, which is extant in many manuscripts and published in *Sefer Raziᵓel*, see G. Scholem, "The Secret of the Tree of Emanation by R. Isaac: A Treatise from the Kabbalistic Tradition of *Sefer ha-Temunah*," *Qoveṣ ᶜal Yad* 5 [1951]: 67 n. 2 (in Hebrew)]; on *tiqqun* as the technical term for writing the letters of a Torah scroll, see Maimonides, *Mishneh Torah*, Hilkhot Sefer Torah 7:9), *ṣeruf*, *maᵓamar*, *mikhlal*, and *ḥeshbon*. It is evident that these processes involve the phonetic dimension of linguistic creativity. Thus we read near the beginning of the text: "How is the *tiqqun* [accomplished]? To bring forth the word (*davar*) in the utterance (*maᵓamar*) and the utterance in the word, the *tiqqun* in the permutation (*ṣeruf*), the permutation in the *tiqqun*, the combination (*mikhlal*) in the computation (*ḥeshbon*) and the computation in the combination, until all the words are placed in the font of the flame (*maᶜayan ha-shalhevet*)." Cf. MSS Vatican, Biblioteca Apostolica ebr. 236, fols. 24a–b; Cambridge, University Library Add. Heb. 643, fol. 19a; Munich, Bayerische Staatsbibliothek 56, fol. 129b; and New York, Jewish Theological Seminary of America 1822, fol. 1a (a version of the text was published in *Otzar Midrashim*, ed. J. D. Eisenstein [New York, 1956], 2:307). For an English translation see Verman, *Books of Contemplation*, pp. 50–64, and cf. his analysis on pp. 146–63, esp. 160ff. Cf. the utilization of this material in *Contemplation-Standard* in Verman, pp. 90–91 and English

rendering on p. 100. See Scholem, *Origins*, p. 313, and p. 332: "Here it seems that the idea of the spoken word becoming inscribed in the air, issuing from the mouth of the person uttering it, was applied to the primordial processes of the creative divine speech." The phonetic aspect is underscored in a second passage from this text, cited in Verman, *Books of Contemplation*, p. 53: "The circle surrounds that which encompasses, thereby encircling that which stands, causing it to stand, thence to inquire, to be still, and finally to shout. As the shout issues forth, it gives birth, springs forth and expands." See also the beginning of a later Iyyun text (Scholem, *Reshit ha-Qabbalah*, p. 256 n. 3; Verman, *Books of Contemplation*, pp. 211–15), *Midrash R. Shimᶜon ha-Ṣaddiq*, MS Munich, Bayerische Staatsbibliothek 54, fol. 292a (a printed version of the text can be found in the commentary of Moses Boṭarel in the standard edition of *Sefer Yeṣirah* 2:3 [Jerusalem, 1961], 39a) that mentions these five processes and interprets *tiqqun* as arranging a divine name in its proper order such as the seventy-two-letter name derived from Exod. 14:19–21. It is also of interest to note the following interpretation of this text in a later source, the *Kelale Qiṣṣur Sefer ha-Peliʾah*, by David ibn Zimra, ed. S. Mussajof (Jerusalem, 1929), 5a: "God is only comprehended in five things: *tiqqun, ṣeruf, maʾamar, mikhlal*, and *ḥeshbon*. *Tiqqun* is to know the name as it is written. *Ṣeruf* is to combine it in the alphabet. *Maʾamar* is to produce a word from each and every combination, and afterward to include (*likhlol*) everything together, and consequently to know the computation (*ḥeshbon*) so that one will not err with respect to the computation of the letters." (My thanks to Daniel Abrams for providing me with a xerox copy of this text.) Finally, mention should be made of the fact that the phonetic as opposed to the graphic aspect of the technique of letter combination (applied as a mystical praxis for human beings) is emphasized in the literature of the Ḥaside Ashkenaz and Abraham Abulafia. See M. Idel, *The Mystical Experience in Abraham Abulafia* (Albany, 1988), pp. 14–24. The oral dimension of the technique of letter combination in conjunction with the utterance of divine names is implied in an ancient Aramaic poem included in *Hekhalot Zuṭarti*; see *Synopse* §§ 349, 361; see also reading preserved in T.-S. K21.95.B printed in *Geniza Fragmente zur Hekhalot-Literatur*, ed. P. Schäfer (Tübingen, 1984), p. 88. See G. Scholem, *Jewish Gnosticism, Merkabah Mysticism and Talmudic Tradition* (New York, 1965), p. 78.

69. See *Commentary on Talmudic Aggadoth by Rabbi Azriel of Gerona*, ed. I. Tishby (Jerusalem, 1945), p. 99 n. 9 (in Hebrew).

70. Scholem, *The Kabbalah in Provence*, appendix, p. 5. See also p. 8, where *reshimah* is clearly distinguished from *ketivah*, the letters only taking form in the latter stage.

71. *Perush le-Shir ha-Shirim* in *Kitve Ramban*, ed. C. D. Chavel (Jerusalem, 1964), 2: 483–84.

72. *Commentary on Talmudic Aggadoth by Rabbi Azriel of Gerona*, p. 116.

73. Given the identification of the First Cause as the Will, it follows that in this text, as in Solomon ibn Gabirol, *Meqor Ḥayyim* 5:38, the scribe is the

Will. The relation of Jacob ben Sheshet's text and that of ibn Gabirol was noted by Tishby, *Commentary on Talmudic Aggadoth by Rabbi Azriel of Gerona*, p. 116 n. 10. See below n. 162.

74. Cf. *Sefer ha-ʾEmunah we-ha-Biṭṭaḥon*, ch. 28, in *Kitve Ramban* 2:412, where the three grades of Torah are delineated in the following ascending order, from the lowest to the highest: the Oral Torah, the Written Torah, and the letters whence the Written Torah is written. Given the standard theosophic symbolism employed by Jacob ben Sheshet, it may be surmised that the Oral Torah corresponds to *Malkhut*, the Written Torah to *Tifʾeret*, and the letters to *Ḥokhmah*.

75. *Sefer ha-ʾEmunah we-ha-Biṭṭaḥon*, ch. 24, in *Kitve Ramban* 2:442. Cf. the formulation in the commentary on the four-letter-name AHW"Y from the Iyyun circle (see Scholem, *Reshit ha-Qabbalah*, p. 257 n. 7; idem, *Origins*, p. 315 n. 239; Verman, *Books of Contemplation*, p. 102 n. 202), extant in MS Munich, Bayerische Staatsbibliothek 408, fol. 125a: "This is the secret of 'I am the first and I am the last' (Isa. 44:6), He is the one engraved (*ḥaquq*), He is the first cause of everything and He is hidden from everything. The primary engraving (*ha-ḥaqiqah ha-qedumah*) was in the image of a perforation (*neqivah*) from the inner subtleness (*ha-daqah penimit*) . . . and from that engraving were made five heads, and it is the inner head of them all." According to this text, then, the divine creativity is depicted as a process of engraving, and the first engraving is characterized as a perforation. It is plausible that this image is meant to conjure the feminine aspect of that primary engraving, the word *neqivah*, "perforation," obviously related to *neqevah*, "female."

76. For a slightly different approach with regard to the relation between the verbal and the graphic aspects of language mysticism in the Provençal kabbalah, see Scholem, *Origins*, p. 277. In a dialectical fashion Scholem emphasizes that, for the kabbalist, every act of speech is at the same time an act of writing and vice-versa. (See idem, "Name of God," p. 67, quoted above, n. 66.) Scholem does, however, note in passing that the script for the kabbalist, unlike for the philologist, is the "true repository" of the secrets of language.

77. See, e.g., *Commentary on Talmudic Aggadoth by Rabbi Azriel of Gerona*, pp. 14–15, and other references to Isaac the Blind and Naḥmanides given on p. 14 nn. 13–14. See Scholem, "Name of God," pp. 165–69.

78. See commentary of Moses Boṭarel to *Sefer Yeṣirah*, 1:13, 35b and 39a.

79. The comparison of letters to stones that build houses when combined is based on *Sefer Yeṣirah*, par. 40.

80. All these verbs reflect the language of *Sefer Yeṣirah* with respect to the letters; see, e.g., par. 19.

81. MS New York, Jewish Theological Seminary of America Mic. 1746, fol. 5b, corrected in part by MS New York, Jewish Theological Seminary of America Mic. 1659, fols. 9a–b.

82. Menaḥem Recanaṭi, *Perush ʿal ha-Torah* (Jerusalem, 1961), 23b. See ibid., 25d. Recanaṭi's words were appropriated by Pico della Mirandola in the thirty-third of his kabbalistic theses as noted by Ch. Wirszubski, *Pico della Mirandola's Encounter with Jewish Mysticism* (Cambridge, Mass., and London, 1989), p. 45.

83. Recanaṭi, *Perush ʿal ha-Torah*, 23c.

84. See Scholem, *On the Kabbalah*, pp. 39–44.

85. MS New York, Jewish Theological Seminary of America Mic. 1737, fol. 20d. See M. Idel, "Infinities of Torah in Kabbalah," in *Midrash and Literature*, ed. G. Hartman and S. Budick (New Haven and London, 1986), p. 145.

86. See discussion in M. Idel, *Kabbalah: New Perspectives* (New Haven and London, 1988), p. 188.

87. "A Critical Edition of the *Sefer Ṭaʿamey ha-Miẓwoth* ("Book of Reasons of the Commandments") Attributed to Isaac ibn Farhi/Section I—Positive Commandments/With Introduction and Notes," ed. M. Meier (Ph.D., Brandeis University, 1974), pp. 79–80.

88. "Critical Edition of the *Sefer Ṭaʿamey ha-Miẓwoth*, p. 58. See Idel, "Concept of Torah," pp. 64–65.

89. Concerning this work, see Scholem, *Origins*, pp. 460–75.

90. *Sefer ha-Temunah* (Lemberg, 1892), 6a–b. Cf. the collection of teachings from the circle of *Sefer ha-Temunah* extant in MS Vatican, Biblioteca Apostolica ebr. 194, fol. 2b:

> I will explain to you the tradition concerning the explanation of the glorious and awesome explicit name according to its secrets and mysterious and hidden powers of which the ancient sages, blessed be their memory, made [theurgic] use. And the secret of the numerical value of the letters, their power and forms, and the action [that results] from them, and everything is at an appointed and set time. If you are pure and straight you will contemplate my words with wisdom and you will see with your eyes and will write them on the tablet of your clean heart and in your pure intellect for the "glory of God is to conceal the matter" (Prov. 25:2).

91. See Wolfson, "Anthropomorphic Imagery" (cited in full above, n. 1).

92. *Zohar* 1:15a. On the first act of divine creativity as engraving, cf. *Zohar* 3:128a (*ʾIdraʾ Rabbaʾ*), where the Ancient of Ancients is said to have engraved the primordial kings upon a curtain. See ibid., 135a.

93. Some have translated this neologism as the "dark flame" or "lamp of darkness" (see references in following note). In fact, the reading that would support such a translation is *boṣinaʾ de-qadrinutaʾ*, but as I have argued

elsewhere (see reference in n. 2), the correct rendering should be *boṣina᾿ de-qardinuta᾿*, which signifies the hard spark (some commentators have thus associated this idiom with the talmudic expression in B. Pesaḥim 7a *ḥiṭṭe qurdanaita᾿*, which Rashi explains as wheat that was very hard and inedible), the spark that is both extended and overflows, i.e., an aspect of the Infinite that corresponds to the phallus. The phallic nature of the hardened spark is expressed in a succinct fashion in a kabbalistic diagram that I examined in the manuscript collection of the Jewish Theological Seminary of America, Scroll #246. At the very top of the diagram are the words *᾿ein sof barukh hu᾿*, "the Infinite, blessed be He," and beneath them is the phrase *ʿaṭarah be-ro᾿sh ha-qadosh barukh hu᾿ reish hurmanuta᾿ de-malka᾿*, "the diadem on the head of the Holy One, blessed be He, the beginning of the will of the King." Based on the two meanings of the word *ro᾿sh* and its Aramaic equivalent *reish*, "head" and "beginning," the expression *reish hurmanuta᾿ de-malka᾿*, "the beginning of the will of the King," is associated with the head of God, *ro᾿sh ha-qadosh barukh hu᾿*. Moreover, it is obvious that *reish hurmanuta᾿ de-malka᾿* is an elliptical allusion to the passage in *Zohar* 1:15a, *be-reish hurmanuta᾿ de-malka᾿ galif gelufe bi-ṭehiru ʿilla᾿ah boṣina᾿ de-qardinuta᾿*. I suggest, therefore, that implicit in this kabbalistic scroll is the identification of the hardened spark as the diadem on the head of God, which is in fact a symbolic reference to the corona of the phallus. Concerning the attribution of a phallus to Ein-Sof, see further my discussion in "Crossing Gender Boundaries."

94. See I. Tishby, *The Wisdom of the Zohar*, trans. D. Goldstein (Oxford, 1989), pp. 276–77; Y. Liebes, *Sections of a Zohar Lexicon* (Jerusalem, 1976), pp. 145–51, 161–64 (in Hebrew); Scholem, *Origins*, p. 336 n. 278; and D. Matt, *Zohar: The Book of Enlightenment* (New York, 1983), pp. 207–8.

95. On the term *ṭehiru*, especially in the *Matnitin* and *Tosefta* sections of zoharic literature, see E. Gottlieb, *Studies in the Kabbala Literature*, ed. J. Hacker (Tel-Aviv, 1976), p. 174 (in Hebrew). Cf. *Zohar* 1:38a, where God is said to "engrave the engravings of the secret of faith within the radiances (*ṭehirin*) of the supernal mysteries." See parallel in *Zohar* 2:126b.

96. On the primordiality of a writing instrument see the aggadic tradition referred to above, n. 36. It is also of interest to note the magical tradition regarding the pen (*qolmos*) of God that one finds in practical kabbalistic texts. Cf., e.g., MS Oxford, Bodleian Library 1964, fol. 1a. On the magical tradition of angelic pens, see G. Scholem, *Kabbalah* (Jerusalem, 1974), p. 186.

97. In the fragment of the *Matnitin* section preserved in *Zohar* 1:251a the *ṭehiru setimu*, the concealed lustre, is described in both active and passive, masculine and feminine, terms. It appears, moreover, that in that text the activity of the *ṭehiru* resembles the *boṣina᾿ de-qardinuta᾿* according to other texts; i.e., it is not only the active principle of the first gradation, the will of the White Head (cf. *Zohar* 1:107b; 2:74a; 3:135a, 137b, 270b; Gottlieb, *Studies in the Kabbala Literature*, pp. 174–75), but it is also the active principle of all the gradations that form the sefirotic pleroma. The connection of the concealed

lustre mentioned in this text and the *boṣina*ʾ *de-qardinuta*ʾ is highlighted by a comparison of the text under discussion and a passage in *Zohar* 3:135b (ʾ*Idra*ʾ *Rabba*ʾ) as well as a *Matnitin* passage extant in MS Vatican, Biblioteca Apostolica ebr. 206, fol. 330a. Both texts are noted by Gottlieb, op. cit., pp. 175–76.

98. Cf. Lavi, *Ketem Paz*, 263c, who employs the expression *luaḥ ha-reshamim*, the "tablet of inscriptions," to refer to the entity mentioned at the beginning of the *Sitre* ʾ*Otiyyot*, the *serata*ʾ *de-qiyyuma*ʾ (I have followed Lavi's own vocalization), also identified as *Keter*, the first *sefirah* or divine Thought. See extended discussion and other scholarly references cited in Wolfson, "Letter Symbolism and Merkavah Imagery," p. 225 n. 100.

99. For the use of the term *galaf* to connote the inner reality or spirit, cf. *Zohar* 2:11a.

100. *Zohar Ḥadash*, ed. R. Margaliot (Jerusalem, 1978), 121d (*Matnitin*), printed in the Cremona edition of the *Zohar*, 18d. Cf. *Zohar* 1:65a.

101. See Liebes, *Sections of the Zohar Lexicon*, p. 50 n. 51.

102. *Zohar Ḥadash*, 105a.

103. *Ketem Paz*, 262b–c. See ibid., 43b–c, where the spark, described as the "hidden point" that emerges from the pressure of the splitting or sundering, strikes against Wisdom and punctuates it with a point, the beginning of the emanative process. See B. Huss, "The Doctrine of *Sefirot* in the *Ketem Paz* of Simeon Lavi," *Pe*ʿ*amim* 43 (1990): 73–74 (in Hebrew).

104. *Zohar Ḥadash*, 1b. For discussion of this text and related passages, see Wolfson, "Letter Symbolism and Merkavah Imagery," pp. 225–30.

105. See A. Leupin, *Barbarolexis Medieval Writing and Sexuality*, trans. K. M. Cooper (Cambridge, Mass., and London, 1989). On the correlation of sexuality and textuality, the body and the book, and the contrast between conventional forms of writing by men and various forms of labor performed by women, cf. the essays in *Equally in God's Image: Women in the Middle Ages*, ed. J. B. Holloway, C. S. Wright, and J. Bechtold (New York, 1990). On the phallic depiction of the pen and the act of poetic composition see, e.g., *The Poems of Joseph ibn Zaddik*, ed. Y. David (New York, 1982), p. 22 (poem no. 1). On writing instruments as male sexual symbols, see Freud, *Complete Introductory Lectures on Psychoanalysis*, p. 155.

106. See P. Dubois, *Sowing the Body: Psychoanalysis and Ancient Representations of Women* (Chicago and London, 1988), pp. 130–66.

107. For a similiar sexual interpretation of writing in Abraham Abulafia, see Wolfson, "Anthropomorphic Imagery," pp. 157–58. It is of interest to note here the view of the thirteenth-century Sufi Muhyiddin ibn ʿArabī that the second angelic hypostasis, the pen (*qalam*) or scribe (*katib*), writes upon a sacrosanct tablet (*lawḥ*), which is in relation to the former as Eve to Adam. That is, the pen or scribe is the active male (identified further as the Intelli-

gence) and the tablet the passive female. See Schimmel, *Mystical Dimensions of Islam*, p. 224; H. Corbin, "The Science of the Balance and the Correspondences between Worlds in Islamic Gnosis," in *Temple and Contemplation*, trans. P. Sherrard with the assistance of L. Sherrard (London, 1986), p. 74. For discussion of this theme in modern literary and psychoanalytic sources, see R. Scholes, "Uncoding Mama: The Female Body as Text," in *Semiotics and Interpretation* (New Haven and London, 1982), pp. 127–41; S. R. Suleiman, "(Re)Writing the Body: The Politics and Poetics of Female Eroticism," in *The Female Body in Western Culture: Contemporary Perspectives*, ed. S. R. Suleiman (Cambridge, Mass., and London, 1985), pp. 7–29. See also A. Bozarth-Campbell, *The Word's Body: An Incarnational Aesthetic of Interpretation* (University, Alabama, 1979).

108. It should be noted that the verb *galif* in zoharic literature can also connote writing rather than the technical sense of engraving. Cf., e.g., *Zohar* 1:3b; 2:139b; 3:78a–b, 264b.

109. In the process of engraving one removes material or makes a space by hollowing out the surface upon which the letters or shapes are engraved. The process of engraving can be seen as an act of clearing, for one creates spaces. In some respect, therefore, it is not unrelated to the kabbalistic doctrine of *ṣimṣum*, the primordial act of withdrawal or constriction, which is also depicted as a production of empty space. (My comments here reflect a conversation I had with Pinchas Giller on this very issue.) Kaplan, *Sefer Yetzirah*, pp. 13–14, interprets the passage from *Zohar* 15a regarding the act of engraving on the part of Ein-Sof in precisely this fashion. While it may be somewhat anachronistic to read this idea of *ṣimṣum* into the zoharic text, it is certainly evident that later kabbalists, especially in sixteenth-century Safed, interpreted the passage in precisely this way. See, e.g., the commentary attributed to Isaac Luria on *Zohar* 1:15a published in G. Scholem, "The Authentic Writings of the Ari in Kabbalah," *Kiryat Sefer* 19 (1942): 197 (in Hebrew). It is also significant that the act of engraving (*ḥaqiqah*) was viewed, as *ṣimṣum* itself, as an expression of *middat ha-din* or the setting of boundary and limit. See below, n. 168. In two of the earliest occurrences of the idea of *ṣimṣum* in kabbalistic literature, Naḥmanides' commentary on *Sefer Yeṣirah* and the preface to the commentary on the thirty-two paths of wisdom from the Iyyun circle, the carving of letters occurs within the darkness formed as a result of the primary withdrawal of the light. Especially in the latter text it appears that the "cutting of boulders and hewing of rocks" that occurs within the darkness is a form of further constricting the light. See Scholem, *Origins*, p. 450 n. 202; idem, *Kabbalah*, p. 129; and, most recently, M. Idel, "On the Concept *Ẓimẓum* in Kabbalah and its Research," *Jerusalem Studies in Jewish Thought* 10 (1992): 69–72 (in Hebrew). As Idel notes, in *Sefer ha-Bahir*, ed. R. Margaliot (Jerusalem, 1978), § 5, the same imagery is employed in a parable that explains the process of emanation: a king who wants to build a palace cuts the boulders and hews the rocks, and a fountain of water comes gushing out. It would appear that already in this case the cutting and hewing of the stones is a form of creating a clearing that allows the fount of life to gush forth. It is also

interesting to note that Simeon Lavi, *Ketem Paz*, 262b, mentions the aggadic motif of God hiding the primordial light in conjunction with the activity of the spark of darkness (the Aramaic *boṣina᾿ de-qardinuta᾿* is rendered by him as *sheviv ha-qadrut*; cf. *Ketem Paz*, 42c). This may be related to the motif of *ṣimṣum* as suggested briefly by Huss, "Doctrine of *Sefirot*," p. 73 n. 117, and elaborated further in his "*Genizat Ha-Or* in Simeon Lavi's *Ketem Paz* and the Lurianic Doctrine of *Ẓimẓum*," *Jerusalem Studies in Jewish Thought* 10 (1992): 341–62 (in Hebrew). For another possible connection between the doctrine of *ṣimṣum* and the zoharic hardened spark (or flame of darkness), see Idel, "On the Concept *Ẓimẓum*," p. 60 n. 7.

110. See sources discussed in Wolfson, "Letter Symbolism and Merkavah Imagery," pp. 232–33, and the relevant notes. To those one might add *Zohar* 1:65a; 2:74a (*Matnitin*), 254b; 3:292b (*᾿Idra᾿ Zuṭa᾿*). It also should be noted that a likely source for the zoharic terminology is the statement in the Iyyun text, *Maᶜayan ha-Ḥokhmah*, utilizing the image of an artisan striking with a hammer (*makkeh be-fatish*) in order to describe the dispersion of sparks from the Primordial Ether, also identified as the Holy Spirit; cf. MSS New York, Jewish Theological Seminary of America Mic. 1822, fol. 26a; Cambridge, University Library Heb. Add. 643, fol. 20b; Munich, Bayerische Staatsbibliothek 56, fol. 132a; and Vatican, Biblioteca Apostolica ebr. 236, fol. 26b. The same image is employed in an anonymous text extant in MS New York, Jewish Theological Seminary of America Mic. 8558, fol. 6a, which appears to be of Geronese provenance. The zoharic equivalence of *gelif*, "engrave," and *baṭash*, "strike," underlies the interesting comment of Judah Ḥayyat in his commentary, *Minḥat Yehudah*, to the anonymous work *Maᶜarekhet ha-᾿Elohut* (Jerusalem, 1963), 35b:

> All these parasangs (*parsa᾿ot*) in the *Shiᶜur Qomah* are letters, for each one is called a *parsah* for they are cut from dough [playing therefore on the words *parsah*, "parasang," and *perusah*, a slice or piece of bread] like stones hewn from mountains. . . . The large number of parasangs mentioned here alludes to the sparks that explode from the striking of the smith's hammer and they are the name produced from the combination of letters and the permutations made from the alphabets of *Sefer Yeṣirah* for by means of them were things created.

Ḥayyat is obviously drawing on another central nerve in Jewish esoteric literature based on the convergence of anthropomorphism and letter symbolism. See above, n. 61.

111. *Zohar Ḥadash* 73b; see reference to my study in the beginning of the previous note.

112. Cf. *Sefer ha-Bahir*, § 55.

113. Cf. the commentary of Ezra of Gerona to the talmudic aggadot, MS Vatican, Biblioteca Apostolica ebr. 441, fol. 53a; *Liqquṭe Shikheḥah u-Fe᾿ah* (Ferrara, 1556), 2a, 14a–b.

114. Cf. commentary of Isaac the Blind in Scholem, *The Kabbalah in Provence*, p. 2 (Appendix), and Ezra's commentary on the aggadot, MS Vatican, Biblioteca Apostolica ebr. 441, fol. 53a (both texts are cited in Wolfson, "Anthropomorphic Imagery," p. 151 n. 15). It is interesting to note in this connection the following text in Jacob ben Jacob ha-Kohen's *Sefer ha-ʾOrah*, commenting on the verse, "The Lord God had formed Adam from the dust of the earth; He blew into his nostrils the breath of life" (Gen. 2:7): "'He blew into his nostrils the breath of life,' this comes to teach you that this corresponds to the [expression] 'the Lord God' (YHWH Elohim), for the creation of Adam comes from the small *yod*, and the small *yod* from the large *yod*; therefore [the Torah] placed a sign in the [word] *wayyiṣer* (He formed)." Cf. MS Milan, Biblioteca Ambrosiana 62, fol. 110b. On the relation of this source to Jacob ha-Kohen, see Farber, "On the Sources," p. 94 n. 61. It would seem that in this context the small *yod* symbolizes Meṭaṭron, in whose image Adam is created, and the large *yod* symbolizes the divine essence represented by the *yod* of the Tetragrammaton. For a theosophic reworking of this text, cf. *Tiqqune Zohar*, ed. R. Margaliot (Jerusalem, 1978), 69, 116a. In that context the two *yods* correspond respectively to the upper and lower *Ḥokhmah*, the second and tenth of the gradations. Cf. J. Zwelling, "Joseph of Hamadan's *Sefer Tashak:* Critical Text Edition with Introduction" (Ph.D. dissertation, Brandeis University, 1975), p. 131: "Thus the Holy One, blessed be He, began His name with the letter *yod* for it is the holy mystery. There is a hidden head that is the secret of the supernal mystery, and the letter *yod* is sealed in the head of the holy phallus." According to this passage, the upper *yod*, which is associated anatomically with the head, refers to the first gradation, *Keter*, and the lower *yod*, which is the head of the phallus, refers to *Yesod*. Cf. ibid., p. 140: "Moreover, you find two *yods* in [the shape of the letter] *ʾalef*, the one that is above is the image of the head of the Holy One, blessed be He, and the one that is below is the image of the corona of the holy phallus, and its wings are spread over the Matrona." Cf. ibid., pp. 178–84, where the phallic nature of the upper *yod*, identified especially as the "core" (*moḥa*) of the "holy nut" (*ʾemgguzaʾ qaddishaʾ*) [cf. pp. 202, 228], is emphasized. On the association of three *yods* and three brains (*moḥin*), cf. *Tiqqune Zohar* 70, 122b. In that passage the three brains, symbolized by the *yods*, are said to be garbed by three ethers (*ʾavirin*), which are each represented by an *ʾalef*. One may discern in this text the influence of the Iyyun text, *Maʿayan ha-Ḥokhmah*; see above, n. 68.

115. See Wolfson, "Circumcision and the Divine Name," pp. 78–87.

116. See references to the works of Scholem and Verman cited above, n. 68.

117. Hebrew text in Verman, *Books of Contemplation*, p. 35, and a different English rendering on pp. 43–44: "and is like a scale whose powers have an effect on every direction."

118. This is precisely how Verman translates the Hebrew following conventional usage (see previous note); it seems to me, however, that his

rendering underplays (if not totally obscures) the dynamic image of overflowing related to the Hebrew word that is used in this context, viz., *mashpiʿa.*

119. Precisely such a connotation of the word *peles* is found in Abraham Abulafia, *ʾImre Shefer,* MS Munich, Bayerische Staatsbibliothek 40, fol. 250a.

120. It is worth considering if such sexual symbolism is implied in *Sefer Yeṣirah,* par. 23. On the concept of the balance in *Sefer Yeṣirah* see Wasserstrom, "Sefer Yeṣira and Early Islam," p. 12 n. 38. Wasserstrom suggests viewing the idea of balance in *Sefer Yeṣirah* in a comparative framework in terms of the idea of balance (*mīzān*) in Jabirian alchemy. On this motif see Corbin's study (noted by Wasserstrom) "The Science of the Balance and the Correspondences between Worlds in Islamic Gnosis," in *Temple and Contemplation,* pp. 55–131, and P. Lorry, *Alchemie et mystique en terre d'Islam* (Paris, 1989), pp. 124–41.

121. Cf. P. Taʿanit 1:8, 64d; Beṣah 5:2, 63a; *Leviticus Rabbah* 29:8; *Pirqe Rabbi ʾEliʿezer,* ch. 16 (Warsaw, 1852), 37b; *Bereshit Rabbati,* ed. Ch. Albeck (Jerusalem, 1940), p. 95; and *Zohar* 2:255a. The same symbolic meaning of scales as a matchmaking instrument underlies *Genesis Rabbah* 59:9, p. 637 (interpreting Hosea 12:8). Most of these sources were cited by Liebes; for reference see following note.

122. Cf. *Zohar* 2:176b (*Sifraʾ di-Ṣeniʿutaʾ*); 3:290a (*ʾIdraʾ Zuṭaʾ*); Liebes, *Sections of the Zohar Lexicon,* pp. 329–30; and idem, *Studies in the Zohar,* trans. A. Schwartz, S. Nakache, and P. Peli (Albany, 1993), p. 70. This usage seems to have been operative in Isaac the Blind's *Perush Sefer Yeṣirah,* pp. 8–9, as Liebes also noted. Cf. the commentary of Isaac Luria to *Sifraʾ di-Ṣeniʿutaʾ* in Ḥayyim Vital, *Shaʿar Maʾamere Rashbi* (Jerusalem, 1898), 22a: "male and female are called the scale." Cf. *Zohar ha-Raqiʿa* (Jerusalem, 1984), 119a; MS Oxford, Bodleian Library 1958, fol. 89b.

123. See, e.g., *Zohar Ḥadash* 2b (*Sitre ʾOtiyyot*): "everything exists in the scale, the balance that will order everything."

124. Cf. Jer. 31:39, and Liebes, *Sections of a Zohar Lexicon,* p. 146. The association of the scale and the hardened spark (or spark of darkness) and the line of measure was noted already by Liebes, op. cit., pp. 146, 329. See idem, *Studies in the Zohar,* pp. 68–69. Naftali Bachrach, *Gan ha-Melekh,* MS Oxford, Bodleian Library 1586, fol. 2b, associates the term *boṣinaʾ de-qardinutaʾ* with measuring (*medidah*) "like the line of a measure (*ḥut ha-mishqal*) of a craftsman who hangs it from above to below to see if the building is in a straight line." On the connection between writing a book and the word *qav,* cf. Abraham ibn Ezra's commentary on Ps. 19:5. According to the sixteenth-century kabbalist David ibn Zimra, *Meṣudat David* (Zolkiew, 1862), fol. 14b, the Torah scroll, which corresponds symbolically to the sixth emanation, the masculine *Tifʾeret,* is called *qav ha-shaveh,* a term used in earlier medieval sources to designate the equator. Cf. sources cited in Eliezer ben Yehuda, *A Complete Dictionary of Ancient and Modern Hebrew* (New York and London, 1960), 6: 5817–18, s.v., *qav* (in Hebrew). In earlier kabbalistic texts this term was used to denote the sixth emanation, which is the median line; see, e.g., *ʾAvne Zikkaron,* MS

New York, Jewish Theological Seminary of America Mic. 1764, fol. 36a. According to some zoharic passages (especially in *Tiqqune Zohar*) the hardened spark (or the line of measure) is connected with the sixth emanation and the letter *waw*; see Wolfson, "Letter Symbolism and Merkavah Imagery," pp. 231 n. 131, 234–35 nn. 144–45. This motif may be related to the Arabic concept of *khaṭṭ al-mustaqīm*, the straight line connecting the uppermost and lowest points in the cosmos. In the kabbalistic context this *qav ha-mishor* or *qav ha-yosher*, represented by the linear letter *waw*, is not only the line that connects the sefirotic emanations, but that which gives shape and boundary to the divine light, a usage attested to already in the Gerona kabbalists Jacob ben Sheshet, *Sefer Meshiv Devarim Nekhoḥim*, ed. G. Vajda (Jerusalem, 1968), p. 113, and Azriel of Gerona, *Commentary on Talmudic Aggadoth*, p. 89. See A. Altmann, "The Ladder of Ascension," in *Studies in Religious Philosophy and Mysticism* (Ithaca, 1969), pp. 41–72, esp. 67–69. It is evident that the references to such a line have much in common with the *qav ha-middah* of the zoharic tradition, as has been noted with respect to Azriel by Liebes, *Studies in the Zohar*, p. 189 n. 191. Cf. the interpretation of Gen. 1:9 in *Zohar* 1:18a–b. The relation of the term *qav ha-shaveh* to the *qav ha-middah* of the zoharic tradition needs to be explored in more detail.

125. See, e.g., *Zohar* 1:18b, where the word *yiqqavu* (Gen. 1:9) is rendered "the measure of the line and the measurement" (*medidu de-qav u-meshaḥtaʾ*). The extension of the hardened spark, referred to as the measure of the Creator (*shiʿuraʾ de-yoṣer ʿalmin*), specified further as the Tetragrammaton written in one particular permutation (יו"ד ה"א וא"ו ה"א), is linked exegetically with Isa. 40:12 as well as with Gen. 1:9. Cf. *Zohar* 3:164a, where reference is made to those who know the "measure of the extension of the explicit name that is engraved" (*medidu di-meshaḥtaʾ bi-shemaʾ gelifaʾ meforash*)." The connection of the *qav ha-middah* and the Tetragrammaton is explicated further by Ḥayyim Vital in his commentary to *Zohar* 1:15a; cf. *Shaʿar Maʾamere Rashbi*, 13a.

126. Cf. *Zohar Ḥadash*, 1b (*Sitre ʾOtiyyot*), 58c–d, 105a; *Tiqqune Zohar* 5, 19a. It is of interest to consider in this connection the rendering of the Hebrew *moʾznayim* (scales) in Targum to Prov. 20:23 as *mishḥataʾ*. See also Targum to Prov. 11:1 and 16:11 where the same word is rendered as *mesaḥaʾ*. In addition to "measure," the word *meshaḥtaʾ* in the *Zohar* has the connotation of "oil." This is significant, for it suggests that the measure is something fluid. Matt (*Zohar*, p. 249) aptly coins the expression "flowing measure." This twofold connotation clearly indicates a phallic reference as the *membrum virile* is obviously a measure in both senses; i.e., it is extended and overflows, indeed it overflows as it is extended and extends as it overflows.

127. It is of interest to note in this connection that in Moses de León's commentary on Ezekiel's chariot vision, MS New York, Jewish Theological Seminary of America Mic. 1805, fol. 20b, the *qav ha-middah* is portrayed as the masculine potency, *Yesod*, that is united with the feminine *Shekhinah*. For further discussion of this text, see Wolfson, "Woman—The Feminine as Other,"

pp. 199–200 n. 61. This symbolism is reflected as well in Moses ben Jacob of Kiev, *Shoshan Sodot* (Korets, 1784), 10a: "You have made a line-of-measure (*qav ha-middah*) called All (*kol*) and it is the Foundation (*yesod*), for you draw everything to this line, the Righteous, Foundation of the World (*ṣaddiq yesod ʿolam*), and from it to the Diadem (*ʿaṭarah*)."

128. Cf. *Zohar* 1:33b: "R. Yose said: the tongue of the scale (*tifsa ʾ de-shiqla ʾ*) exists in the middle, and a sign of this is [in the verse] 'measures of length (*ba-middah*), weight (*ba-mishqal*) etc.' (Lev. 19:35). *Mishqal* is the tongue that exists in the middle, and this is the secret of what is written *sheqel ha-qodesh*. And scales (*moʾznayim*) exist with it and they are balanced. What are the *moʾznayim*? As it is written, 'an honest balance' (*moʾzne ṣedeq*) (Lev. 19:36), and all of them exist in the balance, in the holy weight." It is evident from this passage that the tongue of the scale correponds to *Yesod*, or the middle line, and the weights to *Neṣaḥ* and *Hod*, which also represent the testicles. (It is likely that underlying the phallic symbolism of the scales is the sexual connotation of the number three, associated more particularly with the male genitals. Concerning the latter, see S. Freud, *The Interpretation of Dreams*, trans. and ed. J. Strachey [New York, 1965], p. 393; idem, *The Complete Introductory Lectures on Psychoanalysis*, trans. and ed. J. Strachey [New York, 1966], pp. 154, 163–64, 193.) The kabbalistic symbolism of the scales underlies the following comment in *Gan Hammeshalim we-HaHidoth, Diwan of Don Ṭodros Son of Yehuda Abu-L-ʿAfiah*, ed. D. Yellin (Jerusalem, 1932), 1:137 (in Hebrew): "This righteous one, the foundation of the world, balances all of them in the holy weight," *we-ṣaddiq zeh yesod ʿolam hikhriʿa ʾet kullam be-sheqel ha-qodesh*. Finally, in this connection one should consider the title of one of Moses de León's Hebrew works, *Sefer ha-Mishqal*, the "Book of Balance," composed in 1290. Cf. J. Wijnhoven, *"Sefer ha-Mishkal:* Text and Study" (Ph.D. dissertation, Brandeis University, 1964), p. 34. Consider also the title of another one of de León's works, *Sheqel ha-Qodesh*, composed in 1293 and published by A. W. Greenup (London, 1911). However, the term *sheqel ha-qodesh* can also function as a symbol for the feminine *Shekhinah* as is the case in *The Book of the Pomegranate: Moses de León's Sefer ha-Rimmon*, ed. E. R. Wolfson (Atlanta, 1988), p. 14 (Hebrew text), and see p. 19 n. 40 of English introduction.

129. MS Oxford, Bodleian Library 2296, fol. 5b. Cf. the commentary on *Sifraʾ di-Ṣeniʿutaʾ* printed in *Zohar ha-Raqiʿa*, 120b: "The *ʾalef* is the secret of the scale (*matqelaʾ*): a *yod* from one side, a *yod* from the other side, and the *waw* in the middle." On the phallic nature of the *matqelaʾ*, see also Naftali Bachrach, *ʿEmeq ha-Melekh* (Amsterdam, 1648), 8:3, 45b: "The scale was hidden in *Yesod* of [the lower] half of the supernal garment (*malbush ha-ʿelyon*) in which was hidden the light from which emerged the thread of Ein-Sof to sustain this [Primordial] Adam and bestow upon him the power of the scale." Cf. commentary on *Sifraʾ di-Ṣeniʿutaʾ* printed in *Limmude ʾAṣilut* (Munkács, 1897), 36d–37a (which should be compared to the commentary on *Sifraʾ di-Ṣeniʿutaʾ* attributed to the disciple of Luria and printed in *Zohar ha-Raqiʿa*, 119c). It is evident from the text of Bachrach, and its parallel in the aforementioned sources, that the *matqelaʾ* does not only designate an ontic state of balance, but refers rather to an actual grade that corresponds to the phallus.

Hence, the book of concealment that is weighed on the scale is identified as the garment (*malbush*) that comes to be from *Yesod*, the repository of all hidden matters. The garment, therefore, is depicted as the circular scroll that corresponds to the phallus. See also "Commentary on *ʾIdraʾ Rabbaʾ* of R. Joseph ibn Tabul," ed. I. Weinstock, in *Temirin* 2 (Jerusalem, 1982), p. 132 (in Hebrew).

130. The letter *yod* is connected with the *Ḥashmal* in other Iyyun texts; e.g., the *Perush Shem Mem-Bet ʾOtiyyot* published in G. Scholem, *Kitve Yad ba-Qabbalah* (Jerusalem, 1930), p. 214, and *Midrash R. Shimʿon ha-Ṣaddiq*, MS Munich, Bayerische Staatsbibliothek 54, fol. 294a (Moses Boṭarel's commentary on *Sefer Yeṣirah* 2:3, 39b). See Kallus, "Two Mid-Thirteenth Century Texts," pp. 17–18 n. 10.

131. See Verman, *Books of Comtemplation*, p. 204. See also Farber, "On the Sources," p. 95 n. 61, and idem, "The Concept of the Merkabah in Thirteenth-Century Jewish Esotericism: 'Sod ha-ʾEgoz' and Its Development" (Ph.D. dissertation, Hebrew University, 1986), pp. 119, 632–38 (in Hebrew).

132. The text is extant in MS Milan, Biblioteca Ambrosiana 62, fols. 109b–110a and is partially transcribed and translated in Verman, *Books of Contemplation*, pp. 207–10. I have noted below the instances where I have not followed Verman's translation on account of errors in transcription.

133. See the extensive note in Farber, "Concept of the Merkabah," pp. 633–38.

134. On the distinction between *ḥashmal* and *ḥashmalah* in the German Pietistic writings in terms of gender attribution related to the chariot realm, see Farber, "Concept of the Merkabah," pp. 112–15. A distinction between *ḥashmal* and *ḥashmalah rabbah* is drawn explicitly in one Genizah fragment of a Merkavah text. See *Geniza-Fragmente zur Hekhalot-Literatur*, ed. P. Schäfer (Tübingen, 1984), p. 156; and cf. ibid., p. 142.

135. The mansucript reads *ha-middah*, which I have rendered as "matter." Verman translated "word," probably reading the Hebrew as *ha-milah*.

136. Interestingly enough, this very expression, *sod ha-ʾemunah*, and its Aramaic equivalent, *razaʾ di-mehemanutaʾ*, were used by the Spanish kabbalists of the zoharic circle to designate the sefirotic pleroma, but especially in terms of the union of male and female. See Liebes, *Sections of the Zohar Lexicon*, p. 393, and *Book of the Pomegranate*, p. 68 n. 300. The expression "secret of faith" has precisely that connotation in the text transmitting Meshullam's kabbalah, presumably reflecting Ashkenazi provenance.

137. I have here departed from Verman's rendering, for he capitalized the pronoun "he," reflecting his assumption that the reference is to the Godhead. I have placed this in lowercase to convey the idea that the *Ḥashmal*, which corresponds to the *yod*, is the demiurgical force. That is to say, the creator in this text is a secondary divine power and not the Infinite.

138. The manuscript reads: *we-ʿal ken niqraʾin tinoq ke-ravyyah she-ha-beriyah qam me-ha-yod*. Verman's translation (p. 208) reads: "Therefore, they are

called 'you shall ascend like youths,' since created beings emanated from the yod." From his transcription (p. 207) it is evident that Verman read *tinoq* as *tesaq* (the Aramaic for "ascend"), mistaking the *nun* and *waw* of *tinoq* for a *samekh*.

139. Cf. B. Yoma 54a. On the bisexuality of the cherub in various thirteenth-century sources, see comments of Farber, "Concept of the Merkabah," p. 560.

140. On traditions concerning the demiurgical cherub, see E. R. Wolfson, "God, the Demiurge and the Intellect: On the Usage of the Word *Kol* in Abraham ibn Ezra," *Revue des études juives* 149 (1990): 92–93 n. 61, and other references cited there.

141. Cf. B. Sukkah 5b, and Ḥagigah 13b.

142. MS Milan, Biblioteca Ambrosiana 62, fol. 110a.

143. Verman, *Books of Contemplation*, p. 68 and English rendering on p. 78. On the phallic quality of the letter *yod* as that which extends or overflows, see also *Perush Shem Mem-Bet ᵓOtiyyot*, in Scholem, *Kitve Yad ba-Qabbalah*, p. 217: "the *yod* is the glory that spreads forth in the upper and lower beings."

144. For a wide-ranging discussion of the varied applications of this concept in the Iyyun material, see Scholem, *Origins*, pp. 331–47. See also Verman, *Books of Contemplation*, pp. 153–56.

145. The feminine quality of the Primordial Ether is made explicit in a text extant in MS New York, Jewish Theological Seminary of America Mic. 1884, fol. 20b, transcribed and translated by Verman, *Books of Contemplation*, pp. 202–3 (I have used this translation with some slight modifications): "A lion was crouched on top of the altar [attached] by a red chord. Its name was *ᵓaRᵓaRYetᵓa*. This [alludes to] 'for the Lord created something new in the land; a woman shall encircle a man' (Jer. 31:21). This is the Primal Ether (*ᵓavir ha-qadmon*). She is ascribed by the sages to be the final point (*nequdah ᵓaḥronit*)—sometimes she is emanated and sometimes she emanates; sometimes she receives and sometimes she overflows. She is two-faced: the tree of life and the tree of knowledge." The Primordial Ether is thus characterized as the female that surrounds the male, although she herself exhibits androgynous traits, sometimes active and other times passive. At the end of this text (see Verman, pp. 203–4) a kabbalistic tradition is reported in the name of Naḥmanides that underscores the feminine character of the Primordial Ether by identifying it with *Binah*, the third emanation, also symbolized by Leah.

146. See *Origins*, p. 333 n. 274, where Scholem remarks that the description of the Primordial Ether in the Iyyun compositions, particularly the *Maᶜayan ha-Ḥokhmah*, was the source for the image of the zoharic text. See also ibid., p. 336. Scholem did not, however, discuss the gender symbolism underlying these texts. The zoharic image of the Infinite breaking through its own ether has a striking parallel in another Iyyun text, the *Commentary on the Name*

(*Perush ha-Shem*), extant in MS New York, Jewish Theological Seminary of America Mic. 1805, fol. 59b: "As the sages of the chariot (*ḥakhme ha-merkavah*) alluded: before the Holy One, blessed be He, created the world His power was not recognized. When it arose in His mind to bring forth His actions, He broke through the Ether and then His splendor was seen, and it was called the glory of God, blessed be He." For discussion of this motif and citation of other relevant sources, see Scholem, *Origins*, pp. 341–42.

147. See Kallus, "Two Mid-Thirteenth Century Texts," pp. 7–8.

148. See above, n. 68.

149. MSS Vatican, Biblioteca Apostolica ebr. 236, fol. 26b; Cambridge, University Library Heb. Add. 643, fol. 20b; Munich, Bayerische Staatsbibliothek 56, fol. 132a; and *Otzar ha-Midrashim*, p. 309. Cf. Verman, *Books of Contemplation*, p. 56. See, however, MS New York, Jewish Theological Seminary of America Mic. 1822, fol. 2b, where the reading is "primordial light" (*ʾor qadmon*).

150. MSS Vatican, Biblioteca Apostolica ebr. 236, fol. 25b; Cambridge, University Library Heb. Add. 643, fol. 19b; New York, Jewish Theological Seminary of America Mic. 1822, fol. 1b; Munich 56, fol. 130b; *Otzar ha-Midrashim*, p. 308; English translation in Verman, op. cit., p. 53. This image had a profound impact not only on zoharic kabbalah but on Lurianic material as well, which is certainly indebted to many of the Iyyun texts. See, e.g., *Limmude ʾAṣilut*, 10c.

151. MSS Vatican, Biblioteca Apostolica ebr. 236, fol. 25a; Cambridge, University Library Heb. Add. 643, fol. 19a; New York, Jewish Theological Seminary of America Mic. 1822, fol. 1b; Munich, Bayerische Staatsbibliothek 56, fol. 130a; *Otzar ha-Midrashim*, p. 308; English translation in Verman, op. cit., p. 52. Scholem, *Origins*, p. 332, mentions the image of the *yod* as the *maʿayan ha-mitgabber,* but again does not note any phallic quality to it.

152. See references in n. 150. The image of casting drops is utilized in a second passage from this work where it again has obvious phallic connotations. Cf. MSS Vatican, Biblioteca Apostolica ebr. 236, fol. 27a; Cambridge, University Library Heb. Add. 643, fol. 20b; New York, Jewish Theological Seminary of America Mic. 1822, fol. 3a; Munich, Bayerische Staatsbibliothek 56, fol. 132b; and *Otzar Midrashim*, p. 309.

153. The correlation of gender and geometric shape—the circle and femininity, on one hand, and the line and masculinity, on the other—is more fully developed in later kabbalistic writings. See, e.g., M. Pachter, "Circles and Straightness: A History of an Idea," *Daʿat* 18 (1987): 59–90 (in Hebrew), and, more recently, R. Elior, "The Metaphorical Relation between God and Man and the Significance of the Visionary Reality in Lurianic Kabbalah," *Jerusalem Studies in Jewish Thought* 10 (1992): 54–55 (in Hebrew). On the use of the image of the circle to depict the divine nature in Jewish authors from the Renaissance, see S. Gershenzon, "The Circle Metaphor in Leone Ebreo's

Dialoghi D'Amore," *Daᶜat* 29 (1992): v–xvii (English section), and M. Idel, "Judah Moscato: A Late Renaissance Jewish Preacher," in *Preachers of the Italian Ghetto,* ed. D. B. Ruderman (Berkeley, 1992), pp. 52–56. While the image of the spring or fountain, the *maᶜayan,* is a rather obvious phallic symbol, one text in particular is noteworthy in this context because of its possible connection to Meshullam the Zadoqite whose influence on the Iyyun circle has been noted (see above, n. 131). I refer to a brief passage reporting the mystical rationale for illicit sexual behavior (*sod ᶜarayot*) in the name of R. Meshullam extant in MS Vatican, Biblioteca Apostolica ebr. 211, fol. 116a (see Verman, *Books of Contemplation,* p. 205). In that text the word *maᶜayan* functions symbolically as a designation of the phallus.

154. My suggestion thus presents an alternative to the view of Scholem, *Origins,* p. 336 n. 278, to the effect that the zoharic idea is based on the image of the "light of the source," which is the "light too dark to shine," in the *Maᶜayan ha-Ḥokhmah.* While I have also looked to the Iyyun material as a source for the zoharic idea of *boṣinaᵓ de-qardinutaᵓ*, I have traced it to another cluster of images in this corpus. For an entirely different explanation, see Y. Liebes, *Studies in Jewish Myth and Jewish Messianism,* trans. B. Stein (Albany, 1992), pp. 81–82.

155. The printed versions of *Zohar* read here *siṭre,* "sides" or "aspects," but an alternative reading (recorded, e.g., in the marginal notes of Ḥayyim Vital, *Derekh ᵓEmet*) is *sitre,* i.e., "mysteries." The latter version, *sitre bereshit,* the "mysteries of creation," should be understood as a textual reference. This reading is also attested in Lavi, *Ketem Paz,* 9d, and Abraham Azulai, *ᵓOr ha-Levanah* (Przemysl, 1899), 1c.

156. The printed text reads here *ṭemiru,* "that which is concealed," but I have followed the textual emendation suggested by Scholem and have translated the expression as *ṭehiru,* "lustre," the precise word used in the passage in *Zohar* 15a. See *Gershom Scholem's Annotated Zohar* (Jerusalem, 1992), p. 20, and the extended marginal note on p. 21.

157. *Zohar* 1:3b.

158. On the nexus between the image of keys and letters inscribed upon them, cf. *Zohar* 2:133b. Cf. *Zohar* 3:171b where Meṭaṭron is described as the "servant in whose hands are the keys of his Master." Meṭaṭron's possession of (magical) keys is expressed in older sources, e.g., 3 Enoch. Cf. *Synopse,* § 72. On the phallic nature of the key, cf. *Zohar* 1:37b, 56b (the forty-five keys given to Enoch when he ascended to the heavens are described as the "inscribed secrets of which the supernal angels make theurgic use"). Cf. *Zohar Ḥadash* 39d–40a, where "twelve supernal keys in the mystery of the holy name" are said to have been given to Meṭaṭron. The twelve keys, moreover, are comprised in four keys which are described as lights. See also *Tiqqune Zohar,* 18, 61a; 70, 137b. It is evident that underlying the zoharic usage is a magical connotation of the word *mafteaḥ* attested in earlier sources. See evidence adduced in L. H. Schiffman and M. D. Swartz, *Hebrew and Aramaic Incantation Texts from the Cairo Genizah* (Sheffield,

1992), pp. 24, 158–59 n. 85–88. For other relevant references cf. *Theological Dictionary of New Testament*, ed. G. Kittel and trans. G. W. Bromiley (Grand Rapids, 1965), 3:744–53, s. v. κλεὶς This connotation is implied, of course, in the well-known medieval Hebrew magical text strongly influenced by Christian magic, *Clavicula Salomonis*; cf. H. Gollancz, *Sepher Maphteah Shelomo (Book of the Key of Solomon): An Exact Facsimile of an Original Book of Magic in Hebrew* (Oxford, 1914). It is also possible that the association of *Ḥokhmah* and the image of the key is related to the motif of the intellectual key, *mafteaḥ ha-ra*ʿ*ayon*, used, e.g., by Abraham Abulafia in the sense of insight or vision that helps one comprehend deep matters. See M. Idel, "Maimonides and Kabbalah," in *Studies in Maimonides*, ed. I. Twersky (Cambridge, Mass., and London, 1991), pp. 65 n. 116, 67 n. 125. It is likely that the zoharic authorship combined the intellectualist and the magical connotations in a similiar way.

159. Based on the rabbinic tradition regarding the fifty gates of understanding, only forty-nine of which were revealed to human beings. Cf. B. Rosh ha-Shanah 21b.

160. Twenty-six is the numerical value of the four consonants that make up the Tetragrammaton.

161. *Zohar Ḥadash*, 57a.

162. Cf. Solomon ibn Gabirol, *Meqor Ḥayyim*, 5:38, where the divine will is compared to a scribe (see above, n. 73), the form to the writing, and the matter to a tablet or page. Similarly, in a fragment of Moses ibn Ezra's ʿ*Arugat ha-Bosem*, MS Oxford, Bodleian Library 1267, fol. 50a, the will is depicted as the one who writes (*kotev*), the form as the script (*mikhtav*), and the matter as the sheet or tablet that receives the scripted letters. The identification of the seminal fluid with the Hebrew letters also had an impact on kabbalistic anthropology and psychology; i.e., from the vantage point of theosophic kabbalah the human being as the divine anthropos is constituted by the twenty-two letters of the Hebrew alphabet. In some basic sense, therefore, the semen out of which the human fetus develops is itself constituted by these letters. See Wolfson, "Anthropomorphic Imagery," pp. 165–68; Ḥayyim Vital, ʿ*Eṣ Ḥayyim* (Jerusalem, 1910), 8:6, 39b and idem, *Sha*ʿ*ar Ruaḥ ha-Qodesh* (Jerusalem, 1874), 3d, cited by Lipiner, *Metaphysics of the Hebrew Alphabet*, p. 187.

163. *Zohar* 1:15b.

164. *Zohar* 1:156b (*Sitre Torah*). An interesting formulation of this idea is found in one of Moses de León's kabbalistic secrets, *sod ha-musaf*, the secret of the additional service in the Sabbath liturgy, extant in MSS Vatican, Biblioteca Apostolica ebr. 428, fol. 39a, Jerusalem, Schocken Library 14, fol. 87b, and Oxford, Bodleian Library 2295, fol. 3a:

> Indeed, he is the one who gathers all the letters at first and receives them. He begins with ʾ*alef* and ends with *taw*, and when he gives over to her he begins with *taw* and ends with ʾ*alef*. He begins from the place where he stopped and ends with the place

where he started, for he takes off his garment near his bride and with respect to the one who takes off his garment the first one that he puts on is the last one he takes off and the last one that he takes off is the first one that he puts on.

Underlying this passage is the notion that the seminal efflux of the divine—both in its upper and in its lower manifestation—is constituted by letters.

165. Cf. *Zohar* 1:37b; 2:200a; 3:40b.

166. *Zohar* 1:15b.

167. See reference to my article at end of n. 2. In this connection it is also interesting to note another motif in the Lurianic kabbalah concerning the thirteen hairs and white matter (*lavnunit*) of the skull of the *ʾArikh ʾAnpin,* the first manifestation after the *tiqqun* to rectify the shattering of the vessels in the *ʾAdam Qadmon.* Cf. Vital, *ʿEṣ Ḥayyim,* 13:5, 62d: "The hairs are themselves the aspect of the form of the letters that are written and the white matter is the aspect of the paper and white parchment upon which the letters are written." From the continuation of the discussion it is clear that the letters correspond to the masculine (hence they are in the shape of the linear *waw*), and the paper or parchment is the blank space, which corresponds to the feminine. Cf. *Shaʿar Maʾamere Rashbi,* 53b, and see Wolfson, "Anthropomorphic Imagery," p. 173 n. 113.

168. This interpretation is confirmed in the Cordoverian and Lurianic commentaries on the *Zohar* where one finds a phallic interpretation of the hardened spark as the *yod* or the semen that comes forth from the Ein-Sof. See R. Meroz, "Redemption in the Lurianic Teaching" (Ph.D. dissertation, Hebrew University, 1988), pp. 112–13 (in Hebrew). Cf. MS Oxford, Bodleian Library 1822, fol. 147a. See also MS Oxford, Bodleian Library 1856, fol. 54b (utilizing the image of the *yod* within the final *mem*).

169. The motif of masturbation as the originary event is found in ancient Near Eastern mythologies. See, e.g., the Pyramid Utterance 527 regarding the production of Shu and Tefnut, male and female, as a result of the masturbation of Atum the creator god or Re the sun god, cited and discussed in Clark, *Myth and Symbol in Ancient Egypt,* pp. 42–43. Particularly interesting is the Pyramid Text, par. 1146, where the serpent is described as the creator of multiplicity and the scribe of the divine book. It is evident, moreover, in a hymn from the Coffin texts, that the serpent performs creation by masturbation. The utterance from the mouth of the creator-serpent is connected with copulation or seminal emission. See Clark, op. cit., pp. 50–51, 91–92. See also Brandon, *Creation Legends of the Ancient Near East,* pp. 33–35. The mythic depiction of creation through masturbation is the patriarchal equivalent of the matriarchal myth of parthenogenesis. See M. Weigle, *Creation and Procreation: Feminist Reflections on Mythologies of Cosmogony and Parturition* (Philadelphia, 1989), pp. 72–74. The parallelism between the mouth (or tongue) and the phallus is also a foundational element in Jewish esotericism,

often related to *Sefer Yeṣirah*, par. 3, which speaks of the covenant of unity (*berit yiḥud*) set in the middle of the anthropomorphic shape corresponding to the covenant of the tongue and the mouth (*milat lashon u-feh*) and the covenant of the foreskin (*milat maʿor*). See also par. 61.

170. MSS Oxford, Bodleian Library 1783, fol. 48a and 1784, fol. 58a: For a list of other manuscript witnesses of this text, see Meroz, "Redemption in the Lurianic Teaching," p. 93. According to Meroz, this anonymous text belongs to the first of five stages in the development of Lurianic theosophy. See, in particular, the reading in MS Oxford-Bodleian 1741, fol. 128a: "When it arose in the will of the Emanator to produce the letters, at first He was alone, delighting in Himself." The text is now published on the basis of MS New York, Columbia University X893 M6862 in R. Meroz, "Early Lurianic Compositions," in *Massuʾot: Studies in Kabbalistic Literature and Jewish Philosophy in Memory of Prof. Ephraim Gottlieb*, ed. M. Oron and A. Goldreich (Jerusalem, 1994), pp. 327–30 (in Hebrew). The relevant passage appears on p. 327.

171. See Meroz, "Redemption in the Lurianic Teaching," pp. 111–12.

172. *Limmude ʾAṣilut*, 3a; cf. 21d–22a. A version of this text is printed in Joseph Solomon Delmedigo, *Maṣref la-Ḥokhmah* (Basle, 1629), 77b. Cf. the formulation in MS Oxford, Bodleian Library 2296, fol. 10b: "In the beginning of everything the Holy One, blessed be He, took pleasure in Himself (*mishtaʿasheʿa be-ʿaṣmo*), He was happy and delighted. And just as when a person is happy he shakes (*mitnoʿeʿa*) so God, blessed be He, as it were, shook, and from the shaking (*niʿanuʿa*) the Torah was created." On the image of shaking see below, nn. 181 and 184. The relationship of Israel Sarug and Isaac Luria has been re-examined by R. Meroz, "R. Yisrael Sarug—Luria's Disciple: A Research Controversy Reconsidered," *Daʿat* 28 (1992): 41–50 (in Hebrew).

173. *Kabbalah*, p. 132. See also Scholem, "Name of God," p. 181. In that context as well Scholem describes the *shaʿashuʿa* of Sarugian kabbalah as "joy, a sense of delight or self rapture . . . which evoked a movement in the *En-Sof.* This movement is the original source of all linguistic movement." Again, Scholem ignores the overtly sexual aspect of the divine play.

174. See Y. Liebes, "Tsaddiq Yesod Olam—A Sabbatian Myth," *Daʿat* 1 (1978): 105 n. 167 (in Hebrew). In that context Liebes concludes that the *shaʿashuʿa* in the Sarugian kabbalah is not described in explicit sexual language even though the divine thought has an erotic quality that is actualized in the emanative process. On the sexual connotation of the word *shaʿashuʿa* when applied to God in Lurianic texts, cf. *Shaʿar Maʾamere Rashbi*, 29b: "This delight is for the sake of the union to bring forth the male waters from above to below. Just as there is delight in the souls of the righteous below for the female waters so too must there be delight to have pleasure in order to produce the male waters." It is obvious that here "delight" (*shaʿashuʿa*) refers to sexual foreplay that above arouses the male waters and below the female waters. Cf. *Shaʿar Maʾamere Rashbi*, 8c, where *Binah* is described as taking delight in the letters in the likeness of the female waters. Both of these sources

have been noted by Meroz, "Early Lurianic Compositions," p. 315 n. 22. Meroz perceptively poses the question whether the expression *mishtaʿasheʿa* suggests the androgynous image of the Ein-Sof. This approach concurs with my own analysis and the conclusions I have reached independently. However, I have placed greater emphasis on the masculine aspect of this act of sexual self-gratification.

175. *Genesis Rabbah* 1:1, pp. 1–2, 8:1, p. 57; B. Shabbat 89a. In the latter instance the Torah is described as the "hidden delight" (*ḥemdah* [or, according to printed text, *ḥamudah*] *genuzah*; cf. B. Zevaḥim 116a) in which God "takes pleasure each day" (*mishtaʿasheʿa bah be-khol yom*). It is likely that here the word *mishtaʿasheʿa* already has overt sexual connotations. Cf. anonymous text extant in MS New York, Jewish Theological Seminary of America Mic. 1890, fol. 90a. For the development of the erotic connotation of God's relationship to Torah prior to creation, see the poems discussed in E. R. Wolfson, "Images of God's Feet: Some Observations on the Divine Body in Judaism," in *People of the Body: Jews and Judaism from an Embodied Perspective*, ed. H. Eilberg-Schwartz (Albany, 1992), pp. 153–54. On the motif of the female Torah in select aggadic, kabbalistic, and Hasidic sources, see E. R. Wolfson, "Female Imaging of Torah: From Literary Metaphor to Religious Symbol," in *From Ancient Israel to Modern Judaism Intellect in Quest of Understanding: Essays in Honor of Marvin Fox*, ed. J. Neusner, E. Frerichs, and N. Sarna (Atlanta, 1989), 2: 271–307, reprinted in a slightly revised form in this volume. On the sexual implication of the word *mishtaʿasheʿa*, cf. *Zohar* 1:156b (*Sitre Torah*); 2:202a; 3:61b, 267a. See also Naḥmanides' paraphrase of Abraham ibn Ezra in his commentary to Gen. 21:9. Finally, it must be noted that in the *Zohar* mention is frequently made of God taking delight in the righteous in the Garden of Eden. See, e.g., *Zohar* 1:178b, 245b; 2:173b, 217b; 3:193a. Is there a sexual element underlying this usage as well? See esp. *Zohar* 2:255a: "In each day every time that the lips are joined then it is the time that the Holy One, blessed be He, takes delight in the souls of the righteous. What is the delight (*shaʿashuʿa*)? Those lips are aroused and they precede that pleasure."

176. See J. Ben-Shlomo, *The Mystical Theology of Moses Cordovero* (Jerusalem, 1965), pp. 60–61 (in Hebrew), and B. Zak, "The Doctrine of *Ṣimṣum* of R. Moses Cordovero," *Tarbiz* 58 (1989): 226–27 (in Hebrew).

177. It should be noted that the verb *mishtaʿasheʿa* is connected with the mental processes of God in much earlier sources. See, e.g., the poems that I mentioned in "Theosophy of Shabbetai Donnolo," p. 315 n. 164, and the poem of Yosse ben Yosse discussed in "Female Imaging," end of n. 6. Cf. commentary of Rashi ad Exod. 32:16: *kol shaʿashuʿav shel ha-qadosh barukh huʾ ba-torah*. Cf. the kabbalistic interpretation of *Sefer ha-Bahir*, § 5 extant in MS New York, Jewish Theological Seminary of America Mic. 1777, fol. 5a: "The [meaning] of *shaʿashuʿim* is [derived] from the expression, 'I take delight in Your laws,' *be-ḥuqqotekha ʾeshtaʿashaʿ* (Ps. 119:16). The one who contemplates (*mistakkel*) something that is given from him is called one who takes

delight (*mishtaʿasheʿa*), from the expression, 'He paid no heed,' *loʾ shaʿah* (Gen. 4:5), in order to draw down the influx of Wisdom incessantly from the beginning until the end."

178. Cf. Moses Cordovero, *Zohar ʿim Perush ʾOr Yaqar* (Jerusalem, 1962), 1:12: "Before all that which was emanated came into being the Ein-Sof was alone, and delighted in the comprehension of His essence (*we-hayah mishtaʿasheʿa be-hassagat ʿaṣmuto*)." Similar language is used by Cordovero in *Shiʿur Qomah* (Jerusalem, 1966), sec. 47, 53a: "In the Ein-Sof it is not correct [to speak of] action (*ʿasiyyah*), formation (*yeṣirah*), creation (*beriʾah*) or speech (*ʾamirah*). . . . In His primordiality to all things the Ein Sof comprehends Himself [with a] perfect comprehension. He and His will are one and there is nothing outside of Him. He delights in His essence and the comprehension of His existence (*hishtaʿasheʿa be-ʿaṣmuto we-hassagat meṣiʾuto*) and there is nothing distinct from Him." This passage underscores the link between the sexual play of *shaʿashuʿa* and the process of self-contemplation (a point called to my attention by Pinchas Giller after he read an earlier draft of this study). Given the fact that kabbalists universally accepted the Galenic idea that semen originates in the brain, these two processes are virtually identical. Self-contemplation and auto-sexual arousal are two sides of the same coin.

179. See reference to Liebes cited above, n. 174.

180. Zak, "Doctrine of *Ṣimṣum*," p. 226 n. 79, remarks that in at least one passage (cf. *Shiʿur Qomah*, sec. 29, fols. 42d–43b) Cordovero's usage of the word does have overt sexual connotations. However, in that particular passage this term has such connotations in an explicit manner only when the union of the *Shekhinah* is discussed. Nevertheless, it is fairly reasonable to conclude that such a connotation is implied as well in the following language of Cordovero (ibid., 43a–b): "It says, 'I will walk [in your midst]' (Lev. 26:12), for the Agent exists [literally, "stands"] by Himself, i.e., this matter of the journey (*ṭiyyul*) is something that applies to Him alone so that He will participate in the secret of the unity, the disclosure of the light of the Ein-Sof to His creatures. Therefore, it says that He took delight in himself (*mishtaʿasheʿa be-ʿaṣmo*) and not in something outside of Him. Rather He went and took delight in Himself." It is likely that the words "He took delight in Himself" influenced the later formulations in the Lurianic sources. See ibid., sec. 10, 13b–c. Cf. idem, *Pardes Rimmonim* (Jerusalem, 1962), 8:19, 50d–51a. The erotic connotations of the myth of the Infinite delighting in himself or in the Torah prior to creation are discussed further by Zak in a chapter on the myth of Torah in a forthcoming book on Cordovero's kabbalah. (I thank the author for sending me a xerox copy of this chapter.) Also relevant are the comments of Y. Liebes, "Towards a Study of the Author of *Emek ha-Melekh*: His Personality, Writings and Kabbalah," *Jerusalem Studies in Jewish Thought* 11 (1993):117–20 (in Hebrew), a study that appeared long after this chapter was completed. For a different approach, see N. Yosha, *Myth and Metaphor: Abraham Cohen Herrera's Philosophic Interpretation of Lurianic Kabbalah* (Jerusalem, 1994), pp. 197–200 (in Hebrew). According to Yosha, the erotic connotation attributed

to the *shaʿashuʿa* is an innovation of Herrera. My opinion is in accord with those scholars who have argued that this notion already assumed a sexual connotation in Cordoverian and Lurianic texts. On the sexual implications of the walking motif, see E. R. Wolfson, "Walking as a Sacred Duty: Theological Transformation of Social Reality in Early Hasidism" in *Along the Path: Studies in Kabbalistic Myth, Symbolism, and Hermeneutics* (Albany, 1995). The underlying symbolic rationale for this connotation is the phallic interpretation of the feet; see Wolfson, "Images of God's Feet," pp. 145–46, 162–73.

181. The erotic quality of shaking, especially in the context of a recommended prayer gesture, is explicit in later Hasidic teachings attributed to the Besht as well as to some of the early polemic literature against the Hasidim. See the relevant discussion in L. Jacobs, *Hasidic Prayer* (New York, 1972), reprinted in *Essential Papers on Hasidism: Origins to the Present,* ed. G. D. Hundert (New York, 1991), pp. 346–57; and D. Biale, *Eros and the Jews: From Biblical Israel to Contemporary America* (New York, 1992), p. 144. Another motif that may be relevant in this context is the image of God's shaking his head to express his approval or acceptance of human supplication. Cf. B. Berakhot 3a, 7a, and the utilization of this aggadic motif in the German Pietistic *Shir ha-Kavod* in *Shire ha-Yiḥud we-ha-Kavod,* ed. A. M. Haberman (Jerusalem, 1948), p. 51. The Sarugian doctrine of *malbush* has been discussed by several scholars. See, most recently, Idel, *Golem,* pp. 148–54, 268–70, and idem, "Between the Kabbalah of Jerusalem and the Kabbalah of R. Israel Sarug (Sources for the Doctrine of Malbush of R. Israel Sarug)," *Shalem* 6 (1992): 165–73 (in Hebrew).

182. See, e.g., MS Oxford, Bodleian Library 1958, fol. 96a. Cf. *Shaʿar Maʾamere Rashbi,* 28a: "I have already written above that inscription (*gelifaʾ*) [signifies] that He makes a vessel (*bet qibbul*) in the manner of male and female." The act of engraving involves masculine and feminine, the writing and that which receives it.

183. Some texts in the *Zohar* explicitly characterize the activity of the *boṣinaʾ de-qardinutaʾ* in terms of judgment or even the catharsis of evil. See esp. *Zohar* 2:254b; 3:292b (*ʾIdraʾ Zuṭaʾ*). This line of thinking is developed by later kabbalists, especially in the Lurianic material. Cf. *ʿEṣ Ḥayyim* 29:7, 24b.

184. Mention should be made of the expression *menaʿaneʿa qol,* to trill with one's voice, in T. Sanhedrin 12:10, connected especially to the recitation of Song of Songs. It is also of interest to note that Cordovero employs the language of shaking or stirring the letters of Torah when one studies Scripture below; see, e.g., unpublished section of *ʾElimah Rabbati,* MS New York, Jewish Theological Seminary of America Mic. 2174, fol. 165a. While the shaking in this context does not involve an act of writing, it is nevertheless instructive that the reading of letters is referred to in this way by Cordovero. On the expression "quivering of the word" (*niʿanuʿa ha-teivah*) used with reference to the concretization of divine speech in the air at Sinai, see the comment attributed to Saadiah Gaon in Recanaṭi, *Perush ʿal ha-Torah,* 26a.

185. *Gan ha-Melekh,* MS Oxford, Bodleian Library 1586, fol. 2a.

186. Literally, "From that delight of part of Himself to Himself" (*me-ʾoto ha-shaʿashuʿa me-ḥelqe ʿaṣmo ʾel ʿaṣmo*). It appears to me that the meaning of this difficult phrase is self-delight.

187. *Limmude ʾAṣilut,* 21d–22a. Cf. *Shever Yosef* printed in Delmedigo, *Maṣref la-Ḥokhmah,* 60a; Bachrach, *ʿEmeq ha-Melekh,* 1:2, 2a–c; and see Lipiner, *Metaphysics of the Hebrew Alphabet,* pp. 6–7.

188. The zoharic explanation reflects a theosophic reworking of the position attributed to Aqiva in *Mekhiltaʾ de-Rabbi Ishmael,* ed. H. S. Horovitz and I. A. Rabin (Jerusalem, 1970), Baḥodesh, 9, p. 235: "'All the people saw the voices.' . . . R. Aqiva said: They saw and heard that which is visible. They saw the word of fire come forth from the mouth of God and hewn on the tablets."

189. On the image of the letters flying from the stone tablets, cf. B. Pesaḥim 87b, and *Exodus Rabbah* 46:1. On the letters flying from the burning Torah scroll, cf. B. ʿAvodah Zarah 18a.

190. On the gender quality of letters in the *Zohar,* see Wolfson, "Letter Symbolism and Merkavah Imagery," pp. 216–19.

191. On the connection of the spark and the letter *waw,* see above, n. 124.

192. That is, the particle *ʾet* is interpreted as referring to the Hebrew letters, for it comprises the first and the last of them, the *ʾalef* and the *taw.*

193. *Zohar Ḥadash,* 41b–c.

194. See Matt, *Zohar,* p. 249.

195. Cf. the comment of Judah Ḥayyat in his commentary *Minḥat Yehudah* in *Maʿarekhet ha-ʾElohut,* 144a–b:

> One must examine the words "nothing but a voice" [in the verse "You heard the sound of words but perceived no shape—nothing but a voice"] (Deut. 4:12). Is not vision inappropriate for a voice? Moreover, it is not a kind of image that it should say "nothing but a voice!" From the force of this question it is necessary to say that they also saw the voice of the image (*qol temunah*), and the image that all of Israel comprehended at the event of Mt. Sinai was not an image of a human but the image of letters (*temunat ha-ʾotiyyot*) from which were produced the voice (*qol*) and speech (*dibbur*). I have already informed you that they are living, divine potencies. . . . With respect to all the other commandments they heard that speech (*ha-dibbur*) itself and they saw with their eyes the letters of that speech for they were inscribed and hewn like flames of fire, as it says, "The voice of the Lord kindles flames of fire" (Ps. 29:7), and they would see them with their eyes. Therefore the verse says "And all the people saw the voices" (Exod. 20:15).

Ḥayyat then refers to *Tiqqune Zohar* 38, a passage that utilizes the aggadic motif of angels created from the voice of God. These angels, then, are constituted by the Hebrew letters, as Ḥayyat comments: "I have already informed you that the letters are living, divine potencies and they themselves are angels." The linguistic understanding of angelic beings is shared by many Jewish mystics; I hope to elaborate on this motif in a separate study.

196. MS Oxford, Bodleian Library 1581, fol. 59b.

197. E. R. Wolfson, "Circumcision, Vision of God, and Textual Interpretation: From Midrashic Trope to Mystical Symbol," *History of Religions* 27 (1987): 189–215, esp. 198–206, and idem, "Circumcision and the Divine Name," pp. 97–106.

198. See J. Derrida, "Shibboleth," in *Midrash and Literature*, ed. G. Hartman and S. Budick (New Haven and London, 1986), pp. 307–47, and D. Levin, *The Body's Recollection of Being: Phenomenological Psychology and the Deconstruction of Nihilism* (London, 1985), p. 202. On the eroticism of writing/reading see R. Barthes, *The Pleasure of the Text*, trans. R. Miller (New York, 1975), and V. B. Leitch, *Deconstructive Criticism: An Advanced Introduction* (New York, 1983), pp. 102–15.

199. *Maḥzor Vitry*, p. 628.

200. *Maḥshevot Haruṣ*, 57d. On the phallic nature of the *qolmos*, cf. *Tiqqune Zohar* 55, 89a.

201. A typical formulation of the philosophical (or, more precisely, Neoplatonic) understanding of the Ein-Sof is found in Scholem, *Major Trends*, p. 12. Scholem writes that this designation "reveals the impersonal character of this aspect of the hidden God from the standpoint of man." See op. cit., pp. 208–9, 214, 217; idem, *Kabbalah*, pp. 88–89; idem, *Origins*, pp. 265–72, 431–44; idem, "La Lutte entre le Dieu de Plotin et la Bible dans la kabbale ancienne," in *Le Nom de Dieu et les symboles de Dieu dans la mystique juive*, trans. M. Hayoun and G. Vajda (Paris, 1983), pp. 17–53; idem, *On the Mystical Shape*, pp. 38, 159; and Tishby, *Wisdom of the Zohar*, pp. 229–55, esp. pp. 234–35. On pp. 242–46 Tishby discusses the effort of some kabbalists to attenuate the radical nature of Neoplatonic negative theology by blurring the ontic distinction between Ein-Sof and *Keter*, the first of the gradations. Even so, it is clear from Tishby's discussion that he maintained a strictly philosophical approach to the Infinite. A more mythical orientation can be found in Liebes, *Studies in Jewish Myth and Jewish Messianism*, pp. 81–84. Mention should also be made of the research of Moshe Idel on the kabbalistic idea of the supernal anthropomorphic figure above the standard sefirotic pleroma that is itself constituted by ten static potencies or essences. In some cases this upper anthropomorphic form is even identified as Ein-Sof. See M. Idel, "The *Sefirot* above the *Sefirot*," *Tarbiz* 51 (1982): 239–80 (in Hebrew); idem, "The Image of Adam above the *Sefirot*," *Da^cat* 4 (1980): 41–55 (in Hebrew); and "Kabbalistic Materials from the School of R. David ben Yehudah he-Ḥasid," *Jerusalem Studies in Jewish Thought* 2 (1982/83):169–207, esp. 173 (in Hebrew). On the positive, anthropo-

morphic conception of Ein-Sof, see also M. Idel, "Jewish Kabbalah and Platonism in the Middle Ages and Renaissance," in *Neoplatonism and Jewish Thought,* ed. L. E. Goodman (Albany, 1992), pp. 338–43, and E. R. Wolfson, "Negative Theology and Positive Assertion in the Early Kabbalah," *Daᶜat* 32–33 (1994): v–xxii (English section). See also Meroz, "Early Lurianic Compositions," pp. 314–15.

202. See my study referred to above at end of n. 2.

203. See Laqueur, *Making Sex,* pp. 63–148.

4. Crossing Gender Boundaries in Kabbalistic Ritual and Myth

1. See C. W. Bynum, "Introduction: The Complexity of Symbols," in *Gender and Religion: On the Complexity of Symbols,* ed. C. W. Bynum, S. Harrell, and P. Richman (Boston, 1986), p. 7, and J. Epstein and K. Straub, "Introduction: The Guarded Body," in *Body Guards: The Cultural Politics of Gender Ambiguity* (New York and London, 1991), p. 3.

2. See E. R. Wolfson, "Woman—The Feminine as Other: Some Philosophical Reflections on the Divine Androgyne in Theosophic Kabbalah," in *The Other in Jewish Thought and History: Constructions of Jewish Culture and Identity,* ed. L. Silberstein and R. Cohn (New York, 1994), pp. 166–204. See also idem, "Erasing the Erasure/ Gender and the Writing of God's Body in Kabbalistic Symbolism," in this volume. In those studies, as well as here, I do not deny that some kabbalists describe the Infinite (Ein-Sof) in terms that would suggest a transcendence of gender. I contend, however, that the neuter Infinite reflects an attempt to portray the kabbalistic myth in philosophically acceptable terms. I do not consider the philosophical transformation of the myth in political terms as a kind of intellectual dishonesty or acquiescence. On the contrary, theosophic kabbalists of the Middle Ages were living in environments that incorporated to one degree or another philosophical modes of religious discourse. The main point, however, is that alongside these more speculative formulations is a deep structured myth predicated on a gendered Infinite as I have argued at length in the aforementioned studies. The personal character of Ein-Sof in kabbalistic writings has been emphasized recently by a number of scholars. See references in "Erasing the Erasure," p. 194 n. 201.

3. To be more precise, the kabbalists generally read the Priestly version of the creation of man and woman (especially as mediated through the rabbinic conception of the androgyne) in light of the Yahwistic version. That is, there is no appreciable difference in orientation between the two creation accounts. On the contrary, the secondary status accorded the woman in the Yahwistic version is used to interpret the ostensibly more egalitarian approach of the Priestly version. For discussion of the two creation narratives from the vantage point of human sexuality and gender, see P. A. Bird, "Sexual

Differentiation and Divine Image in the Genesis Creation Texts," in *Image of God and Gender Models in Judaeo-Christian Tradition,* ed. K. E. Børresen (Oslo, 1991), pp. 11–34. On the appropriation of the Yahwistic account in Christian literature in the patristic and medieval periods, see R. Howard Bloch, *Medieval Misogyny and the Invention of Western Romantic Love* (Chicago and London, 1991), pp. 22–29.

4. See I. Tishby, *The Wisdom of the Zohar,* trans. D. Goldstein (Oxford, 1989), p. 289. Tishby notes that the feminine *Shekhinah,* the last of the ten *sefirot,* is not to be regarded as a "second person" but rather as the "completion of the male image." Tishby nevertheless speaks of the "harmonious partnership of male and female" and thus does not appreciate the full extent of the androcentric representation of the female in kabbalistic symbolism.

5. MS New York, Jewish Theological Seminary of America Mic. 2194, fols. 25a–b.

6. It is of interest to note that in the diagram accompanying this text (MS New York, Jewish Theological Seminary of America Mic. 2194, fol. 25a) the sefirotic potencies are configured in a shape that resembles that of a penis extended upward. The significance of this graphic depiction is that the *sefirot* collectively constitute one phallic entity. No independent place is accorded the feminine. Cf. the depiction of the *sefirot* in the shape of a phallus in the version of the anonymous thirteenth-century *Sefer ha-Yiḥud* in MS Vatican, Biblioteca Apostolica ebr. 236, fol. 174a. Interestingly, the Infinite is represented by a black circle that crowns a line extending upward from the first *sefirah* designated as *ᶜAyin.* It is hardly coincidental that the black circle resembles the corona of the penis. Cf. MS Vatican, Biblioteca Apostolica ebr. 274, fol. 167a. According to the drawing of the sefirotic hypostases in this manuscript, there is similarly one form that constitutes a phallic representation of the divine. The feminine, or the last of the emanations, is depicted as the foot of this one form rather than a separate entity. It is also noteworthy that the first of the emanations is portrayed as the head of the penis, thus lending credence to my conjecture concerning an upper phallus. What is here graphically represented is expressed in other kabbalistic documents. See, e.g., the phallic description of *Keter* in the anonymous commentary on the *sefirot* in MS New York, Jewish Theological Seminary of America Mic. 1805, fol. 15b. See below, n. 85. The phallic character of *Keter* is highlighted in the Idrot sections of the *Zohar.* See, e.g., the description of the skull (*gulgaltaʾ*) in *Zohar* 2:128b–130a, 135b–136a (*ʾIdraʾ Rabbaʾ*) and the description of the thirteen adornments of the beard of *ʾArikh ʾAnpin* in ibid., 130b–134b. For parallel discussions see *Zohar* 3:288a–289b, 292b–293b (*ʾIdraʾ Zuṭaʾ*). In particular, the image of the oil overflowing from the curls of the beard has a strikingly phallic connotation. See ibid., 139a where the homoerotic implication of this symbolism is evident: "When the holy flowing oil goes down from the supernal glorious beard of the Holy Ancient One, who is concealed and hidden from everything, to the beard of *Zeᶜeir ʾAnpin,* his beard is arrayed in nine adornments." The homoerotic element seems also to be implied in the depiction of the ocular gaze in ibid., 128b: "When *Zeᶜeir ʾAnpin* looks at [*ʾArikh ʾAnpin*] everything below is arrayed, and his countenances extend and spread

out at that time, but not all the time as [is the case with] *ʿAtiqaʾ*." The extension of the face is a euphemism for the elongated phallus. See ibid., 133b: "When the two apples are revealed *Zeʿeir ʾAnpin* appears to be happy and all the lights below are joyous." It appears that in that context the apples symbolically represent the testicles. (See below, nn. 154 and 156.) The phallic signification may also underlie the designation of the beard of *ʾArikh ʾAnpin* as *mazzal,* which is connected etymologically in the kabbalistic imagination with the root *nzl,* to overflow. Cf. ibid. 134a and 289a–b. (The kabbalistic symbolism was no doubt informed by the fact that in earlier rabbinic sources the word *zaqan,* "beard," was used euphemistically to refer to the *membrum virile.* Cf. M. Sanhedrin 8:1, 8; Niddah 10:11; P. Yevamot 10:17, 11c; Ketuvot 4:5, 28d; B. Yevamot 80a–b, 88a, Ketuvot 27b, Sanhedrin 68b, 69a, 71b, Niddah 52a.)The phallic implications of many of these images are developed along similar, but not always identical, lines in the writings of other kabbalists who may have been involved in the zoharic circle, e.g., Joseph of Hamadan, especially his *Sefer Tashaq* and a fragment of an Aramaic text extant in MS Mussajoff 134, fols. 124a–131b, David ben Yehudah he-Ḥasid, especially in *Sefer ha-Gevul,* his translation of and commentary on a section of the *ʾIdraʾ Rabbaʾ* (on the phallic nature of *Keter,* cf. *The Book of Mirrors: Sefer Marʾot ha-Ẓoveʾot by R. David ben Yehudah he-Ḥasid,* ed. D. C. Matt [Chico, Calif., 1982], pp. 94, 220), and Joseph Gikatilla, especially in his *Sod Yod-Gimmel Middot ha-Noveʿot min ha-Keter ʿElyon* (published by G. Scholem, *Kitve Yad ba-Qabbalah* [Jerusalem, 1930], pp. 219–25, and see esp. 221–22). See Y. Liebes, *Studies in the Zohar,* trans. A. Schwartz, S. Nakache, and P. Peli (Albany, 1993), pp. 103–34. The phallic character of the uppermost aspect of God according to the symbolism of the Idrot is depicted iconically in *Sefer ha-Gevul.* To mention a few salient examples from two manuscript versions that I examined: In MS New York, Jewish Theological Seminary of America Mic. 2193, fol. 2b, there is a depiction of the skull (*gulgolet*) that extends downward from the supernal crown (*keter ʿelyon*) through the path (*netiv*) to the world of the righteous (*ʿolam ha-ṣaddiqim*). The shape of this diagram is that of a phallus pointing downward for the flow of semen goes from top to bottom. In the same manuscript, fol. 4a, *ʾArikh ʾAnpin* and *Zeʿeir ʾAnpin* are configured in the shape of a phallus pointing upward. The head of the phallus, or the corona, is labeled *ʾArikh ʾAnpin* and the base of the phallus consists of the thirty-two paths of *Zeʿeir ʾAnpin.* Cf. *Sefer ha-Gevul,* MS New York, Jewish Theological Seminary of America Mic. 2197, fols. 6b, 8b, 9a, 13a, 16b, 20b, 30a.

7. MS Oxford, Bodleian Library 1565, fol. 15b; see also MS New York, Jewish Theological Seminary of America Mic. 1777, fol. 15a.

8. On the shift in meaning of these terms in Joseph of Hamadan as compared to the zoharic literature, see M. Idel, *Kabbalah: New Perspectives* (New Haven and London, 1988), pp. 134–35; Liebes, *Studies in the Zohar,* pp. 105–7; and Ch. Mopsik, *Les Grands textes de la Cabale: les rites qui font dieu* (Paris, 1992), p. 214 n. 34.

9. See M. Idel, "Additional Fragments from the Writings of Joseph of Hamadan," *Daʿat* 21 (1988): 47–55 (in Hebrew). Joseph of Hamadan was especially fond of the image of the cherubim, which he uses constantly to relate

the erotic dynamic between the ninth and the tenth gradations. Moreover, one finds in his writings graphic descriptions of the female anatomy that go beyond what one finds even in the more recondite strata of zoharic literature. See, e.g., J. Zwelling, "Joseph of Hamadan's *Sefer Tashak*: Critical Text Edition with Introduction," (Ph.D. dissertation, Brandeis University, 1975), pp. 123–24, 296ff.

10. "Joseph of Hamadan's *Sefer Tashak*," p. 152. On the masculine and the feminine symbolism connected respectively with *gimmel* and *dalet*, see ibid., pp. 147–48.

11. The androgynous quality of the phallus is also alluded to in the remarks of Joseph of Hamadan that the *gimmel* symbolizes both the masculine King (pp. 148–49) and the Matrona sitting upon a throne (p. 150). It is of interest to note the following observation of Joseph of Hamadan in his commentary on the *sefirot*, MS Oxford, Bodleian Library 1678, fol. 66b: "This attribute [*Ḥokhmah*] forever overflows, for from the side of *Binah* and onwards there is masculinity and femininity, emanating from one side and receiving from another side. But [in] the attribute of *Ḥokhmah* everything is conjoined to one another, and masculinity and femininity are not yet discernible, i.e., it is not known in what side it emanates and in what side it receives. Therefore this attribute does not emanate and receive but rather only emanates." (See ibid., fols. 67a–b, where *Binah* is likewise described as comprising masculinity and femininity, bestowing and receiving, and is called "androgynous"). Even though gender is said not to apply to *Ḥokhmah*, the latter is described as overflowing or emanating, traits that are valorized as decidedly masculine. One may conclude, therefore, that the aspect of the Godhead beyond sexual differentiation is still characterized in essentially male terms. See below, n. 17. Concerning this work of Joseph of Hamadan, see M. Idel, "The Commentary on the Ten *Sefirot* and Fragments from the Writings of R. Joseph of Hamadan," *Alei Sefer* 6–7 (1979): 74–84 (in Hebrew). The unisexual character of the divine anthropos is affirmed in slightly different imagery by Joseph of Hamadan in *Sefer Tashak*, p. 136: "When the holy name YHWH appears, the head of the Holy One, blessed be He, and all of the holy body are manifest, and the Matrona is His crown." The feminine aspect of the Godhead is identified as the crown of the masculine form (symbolized by the Tetragrammaton). The eschatological application of this model is evident in ibid., p. 145: "In the days of King Messiah when the Holy One, blessed be He, will build his Temple, He will be crowned in His crowns and He will sit on the throne of His royalty. He will be pefected from all the holy sides like the letter *gimmel*, which has a crown and a throne." The portrait painted by Joseph of Hamadan of the coronated king sitting on his throne is meant to convey the reintegration of the feminine—manifest in the double aspect of crown and throne—to the masculine. Hence, God is symbolically represented by the *gimmel*, which comprises the three elements of the crown, the body, and the throne. It is likely, moreover, that this letter stands for the *gid*, or the phallus. The eschatological future, therefore, is marked by the reconstitution of the androgynous phallus. Cf. ibid., pp. 151–52. The conception of the male androgyne

is also affirmed in the following passage of Joseph of Hamadan, ibid., pp. 161–62: "Therefore these four letters [YHWH] join together. The *yod* is the image of the head of the Holy One, blessed be He; the *he*ʾ is the right arm and the [right] side of the body; the *waw* is the body in its entirety, the thighs, the feet, the knees, and the holy phallus; and the *he*ʾ is the left arm and the *Shekhinah*."

12. Conversely, the mystical significance of the commandment forbidding illicit sexual relationships turns on the presumption that these relations result in the separation of the masculine and the feminine potencies of the divine. See Joseph of Hamadan, *Sefer Ṭaʿame ha-Miṣwot*, negative commandments (no. 30), MS Paris, Bibliothéque Nationale 817, fol. 155a: "They are called *ʿarayot* because the attribute of *Ṣaddiq* is contained in the attribute of *Malkhut* and the attribute of *Malkhut* in the *Ṣaddiq* like a flame bound to the coal, and so too the rest of the attributes. Thus 'the Lord shall be one and His name one' (Zech. 14:9). The one who transgresses any of the illicit sexual acts discloses [the nakedness of] *Ḥokhmah* in relation to *Binah* and thereby separates these two attributes, and similarly between *Ṣaddiq* and *Malkhut*." The image from *Sefer Yeṣirah* of the flame bound to the coal is used repeatedly by Joseph of Hamadan to depict the union of the masculine and the feminine, specifically *Yesod* and *Shekhinah*. Cf. "Joseph of Hamadan's *Sefer Tashak*," pp. 37, 55, 66, 72, 93.

13. "Joseph of Hamadan's *Sefer Tashak*," pp. 22–23.

14. Cf. ibid., pp. 257–58: "Therefore the Torah said, 'You shall not wear cloth combining wool and linen' (Deut. 22:11), for these are the garments of the Matrona, and one is forbidden to wear them, as it is written, 'for you must not worship any other god' (Exod. 34:14), this corresponds to the Matrona. He who wears the garments of Matrona seems as if he worships her, and thus it is written, 'You shall not wear cloth combining wool and linen.' And this is the secret of 'a man shall not wear woman's clothing' (Deut. 22:5), this refers to the Matrona, and a person should not wear her garments, which are a mixture of wool and linen." A similar explanation of this prohibition is given by Joseph of Hamadan in his *Sefer Ṭaʿame ha-Miṣwot*, negative commandments, MS Paris, Bibliothéque Nationale héb. 817, fol. 145a. For his more general explanation of idolatry as the spiritual and psychological reification of the feminine, cf. "Joseph of Hamadan's *Sefer Tashak*," p. 274, and *Sefer Ṭaʿame ha-Miṣwot*, negative commandments, MS Pairs, Bibliothéque Nationale héb. 817, fol. 141b: "Know that this matter 'You shall have no other gods besides Me' (Exod. 20:3) corresponds to *Zeʿeir ʾAnpin*, the attribute of *Malkhut*, which is the secret of the Bride. One should not separate her from the Bridegroom who is the King, Lord of the Hosts, and one should not make of her an independent form or an independent god. One should not cut the shoots." In the continuation of this text (fols. 141b–42a) Joseph of Hamadan discusses the prohibition of making idols, which he explains kabbalistically in terms of the same phenomenon of separating the masculine and the feminine potencies in the Godhead. This is precisely how kabbalists explained the major transgressions recorded in the Bible. Examples of this are, Adam and Eve eating the

fruit of the Tree of Knowledge, the drunkeness of Noah, the construction of the Tower of Babel, and the worshiping of the Golden Calf. All of these sins, and indeed the very nature of sin in general, involve the separation of the male and the female that results from reifying the female as an autonomous potency.

15. Cf. Exod. 25:18.

16. MS Vatican, Biblioteca Apostolica ebr. 504, fol. 312b. See also fol. 308b.

17. MS Vatican, Biblioteca Apostolica ebr. 236, fol. 168a.

18. See E. R. Wolfson, "Left Contained in the Right: A Study in Zoharic Hermeneutics," *AJS Review* 11 (1986): 27–52. In accordance with another ontological principle articulated by the kabbalists, each attribute is contained in and interacts with its opposite. It is thus possible to speak of the containment of the right in the left just as one can speak of the containment of the left in the right. See, e.g., Jacob ben Sheshet's reflection in *Sefer ha-ʾEmunah we-ha-Biṭṭahon* on why the divine names sometimes have feminine verbs and sometimes masculine:

> The reason for this is that even though there is a distinction in names between the attribute of judgment and the attribute of mercy, everything that is in the one is in the other. Therefore, the attribute of judgment changes into the attribute of mercy and the attribute of mercy into the attribute of judgment . . . for if the attributes were not all contained one in the other one could not be changed into the other. . . . These names sometimes are in the masculine form and sometimes in the feminine. The Holy One, blessed be He, is unified in all of them (*meyuḥad be-khullan*) and all of them are unified in Him (*we-khullan meyuḥadim bo*).

Cf. *Kitve Ramban*, ed. C. D. Chavel (Jerusalem, 1964), 2:359. There is, however, a qualitative difference between the containment of the left in the right and the right in the left, for in both cases the distinctive character of the left is altered by its containment in the right.

19. See, e.g., *Zohar* 3:59b. Cf. the description of the *Shekhinah* in the commentary on the *sefirot* in MS New York, Jewish Theological Seminary of America Mic. 1805, fol. 16b: "If, God forbid, she is separated from the [phallic] All, then 'The Lord has a sword; it is sated with blood' (Isa. 34:6). She is aroused to judge the world by harsh punishments and severe judgments."

20. The biblical text here reads "him" but I have translated the passage as it appears in the manuscript citation.

21. MS Oxford, Bodleian Library 1923, fol. 93a.

22. In some kabbalistic sources, including the *Zohar*, one finds a retrieval of the ancient myth of parthenogenesis involving the primal splitting of the cosmic egg that gives birth by fission rather than through union. See Y.

Liebes, *Studies in Jewish Myth and Jewish Messianism,* trans. B. Stein (Albany, 1993), pp. 65–92, esp. 82–88. In the relevant kabbalistic sources, however, the primordial cleft is not a splitting of the mother as one finds in the ancient myths (see N. Loraux, "What is a Goddess?" in *A History of Women in the West: I. From Ancient Goddesses to Christian Saints,* ed. P. Schmitt Pantel and trans. A. Goldhammer [Cambridge, Mass., and London, 1992], pp. 38–39), but rather the rupture of the male androgyne into a father and a mother who then procreate through union. The privileging of the male gender in the first of the emanations that is above sexual differentiation is evident, e.g., in "Joseph of Hamadan's *Sefer Tashak,*" p. 73, where it is stated that from *Keter* "judgment and mercy separate but he, blessed be he, is entirely merciful." In light of the correlation of mercy and masculinity, one must assume that the kabbalistic symbolism implies the masculine character of the Godhead even in an ontological state that precedes the duality of male and female. See above, n. 10.

23. MS Oxford, Bodleian Library 1782, fol. 14a. See ibid., fol. 2b: "All of the power of the female and the essence of her lights and potencies are all hidden within *Zeᶜeir ᵓAnpin* in the manner that the female is the fulfilment of *Zeᶜeir ᵓAnpin.*"

24. *Sefer ha-Bahir,* ed. R. Margaliot (Jerusalem, 1978), § 61. For a more extended discussion of this passage, see E. R. Wolfson, "The Tree That Is All: Jewish-Christian Roots of a Kabbalistic Symbol in *Sefer ha-Bahir,*" *Journal of Jewish Thought and Philosophy* 3 (1993): 70–71.

25. *Sefer ha-Bahir,* §§ 83–84.

26. I have followed the reading in MS Munich 209, fol. 19a, *melakhim,* as opposed to the printed text (see following note), *malᵓakhim,* "angels."

27. *Sefer ha-Bahir,* §§ 72–73.

28. *Origins,* p. 174. See G. Scholem, *On the Mystical Shape of the Godhead,* trans. J. Neugroschel and ed. J. Chipman (New York, 1991), p. 176.

29. The interpretation I have proposed is further confirmation of my thesis set forth in "The Tree That Is All" that the idea of the androgynous phallus belongs to the final redactional stage of the *Bahir* in Provence. It is interesting that in *Sefer ha-Bahir,* §§ 91–93, the reference to the crown that is made of the precious stone is immediately followed by a discussion of the blue in the fringe garment that culminates with the description of the two signs (*simanim*), one belonging to the king and the other to his daughter. The blue of the fringe garment is the seal (*ḥotam*) of God that comprises two elements, the masculine and the feminine. It seems fairly obvious that in this context as well the symbolic allusion is to the bisexual phallus.

30. Cf. *Sefer ha-Bahir,* §§ 155, 159, and Scholem, *Origins,* p. 154.

31. See, by contrast, Scholem, *On the Mystical Shape,* p. 196, who refers to the relevant bahiric passage and suggests that it indicates that time flows from the primal time gathered in the feminine *Shekhinah.* Scholem thus

compares this to an Indian symbol that the idea of femininity produces the motion of time. In my opinion, it is the masculine potency, and more specifically the phallic impulse, that is the ground of time in kabbalistic symbolism, the feminine element being linked to space. For a preliminary discussion, see E. R. Wolfson, "From Sealed Book to Open Text: Time, Memory, and Narrativity in Kabbalistic Hermeneutics," in *Critical Jewish Hermeneutics*, ed. S. Kepnes (New York, 1995). The linkage of time and the masculine gender is underscored in the following comment of Ḥayyim Vital, *Shaʿar Maʾamere Rashbi* (Jerusalem, 1898), 2d: "Another reason [for the rabbinic ruling that women are exempt from positive commandments that are time-bound] can be explained from what I have informed you [regarding the fact] that *Nuqbaʾ di-Zeʿeir ʾAnpin* emanated from the back of *Zeʿeir ʾAnpin*, from the chest and below, and there they are joined together. This place is called 'time' (*zeman*) because 'time' is a word that applies to the reality of day and night, and you know that *Zeʿeir ʾAnpin* is called day and his *Nuqbaʾ* is called night. The positive commandments correspond to the 248 limbs. Therefore, all the commandments that are attached to the place that was mentioned, which is called 'time' and which is from the chest and below, are called positive commandments that are time-bound, for there is participation of the male and female who are called 'day' and 'night.' Since the man has already performed the commandment whose source is there, there is no need for the woman to perform it as well, for she is contained in him at the moment that he performs this commandment. Her 248 limbs are contained in his limbs and from him she is made and all of her anatomy is established." Cf. parallel in Ḥayyim Vital, *Sefer Ṭaʿame ha-Miṣwot* (Jerusalem, 1963), p. 35. Even though the aspect of time comprises both masculine and feminine, day and night, it is obvious that the latter is contained in the former. The concept of time expressed here is another example of the myth of the androgynous phallus. It is my intention to write a full study on the phenomenology of time in kabbalistic sources.

32. Cf. *Genesis Rabbah* 35:2, pp. 328–29.

33. Thus see, e.g., Joseph of Hamadan's commentary on the *sefirot*, MS Oxford, Bodleian Library 1628, fol. 69b, where, in line with earlier sources, the *Shekhinah* is referred to explicitly as the "corona of the phallus of the pure and holy supernal form." On the other hand, there are many passages where Joseph of Hamadan describes the *Shekhinah* as the independent force, usually depicted as the bride, that receives the seminal overflow from the phallic *Yesod*, frequently characterized as the golden bowl that pours forth fine oil. Cf. MS Oxford, Bodleian Library 1628, fol. 72a: "The tenth *sefirah* is the attribute of *Malkhut*, the secret of the woman, for the nine upper *sefirot* are the form of a male." Cf. M. Meier, "A Critical Edition of the *Sefer Ṭaʿamey ha-Miẓwoth* ('Book of Reasons of the Commandments') Attributed to Isaac Ibn Farhi/Section I—Positive Commandments/With Introduction and Notes" (Ph.D. dissertation, Brandeis University, 1974), p. 243: "Therefore, the phallus above (*berit shel maʿalah*) pours forth the good oil upon the Bride, the Community of Israel, and from there the blessing comes to the world." See ibid., pp. 140, 265–66, 274, 344; "Joseph of Hamadan's *Sefer Tashak*," pp. 93, 101,

226, 234, 250–51; MS Mussajoff 134, fol. 124b. Needless to say, many other textual illustrations could have been adduced. From one vantage point these symbolic portrayals are contradictory, for how could the feminine be both the corona of the penis and the independent entity (symbolized as the bride or second cherub) that receives the semen from the male (the bridegroom or the first cherub). From another perspective the opposing views are dialectically resolved. That is, the reception of the semen transforms the female into a male and thus there is a symbolic equivalence between the two: the female cherub that receives the semen from the male cherub is transformed into the corona of the penis. Joseph of Hamadan thus concludes the aforementioned commentary on the *sefirah* of *Malkhut* by saying that the aggadic statement regarding God's wearing phylacteries applies to this attribute; see MS Oxford, Bodleian Library 1628, fol. 72b. In what sense can this image be applied to the *Shekhinah*? Obviously, from a normative halakhic perspective one would not expect the female aspect of God to be so envisioned. I submit, therefore, that the reference to the phylacteries must be decoded as an allusion to the crown, and the latter signifies the corona of the phallus, an appropriate symbol of the *Shekhinah*.

34. "Joseph of Hamadan's *Sefer Tashak*," p. 68. It must be noted that on occasion Joseph of Hamadan emphasizes the androgynous nature of the *Shekhinah*. Cf. p. 97:

> Certainly the *Shekhinah*, the Bride and Community of Israel, sits beneath the shade of the Bridegroom, for everything is one, blessed be He. And in relation to us it is male, as the verse says, "The Lord is mindful of us, He will bless us," *yhwh zekharanu yevarekh* (Ps. 115:12). This corresponds to the *Shekhinah* who is male (*zakhar*) in relation to us . . . and in relation to the attribute above female.

See ibid., p. 356: "This alludes to the Matrona who is [sometimes] called male and sometimes female, in relation to the Holy One, blessed be He, she receives and in relation to us she overflows." And p. 436: "This alludes to the Matrona who is the secret of the androgyne, male and female, sometimes she is called male and sometimes she is called female." In similiar, although not exactly identical, terms the zoharic authorship emphasizes the androgynous nature of the *Shekhinah*. See. e.g., *Zohar* 1:232a, noted by Scholem, *On the Mystical Shape*, p. 186. See also Tishby, *Wisdom of the Zohar*, p. 379. Finally, I note that on occasion Joseph of Hamadan, in line with other kabbalists, interprets the rainbow as a phallic symbol. Cf. his commentary on the *sefirot* in MS Oxford, Bodleian Library 1628, fol. 72a. In the context of explaining the ninth of the *sefirot*, *Yesod*, he writes: "Its color is like that of the rainbow that is seen in the cloud. Therefore the [rabbis], blessed be their memory, said [B. Ḥagigah 16a], 'he who looks at the rainbow does not show respect to his Creator and it would have been better for him not to have come into this world,' for he is looking at the phallus of the Holy One, blessed be He (*she-mistakkel bi-verito shel ha-qadosh barukh hu*ʾ)." Cf. Joseph of Hamadan's formulation in MS

Jerusalem, Mussajoff 134, fol. 124b: "It has been taught that from that holy penis (*ʾammataʾ qaddishaʾ*) a myriad of the worlds are suspended in the opening of the penis (*pumeih de-ʾammaʾ*), and this is the holy covenant (*beritaʾ qaddishaʾ*) that is revealed in a cloud on a rainy day, and all of those colors that are in it are seen in the holy covenant." The point is reiterated in the continuation of this text: "All the colors of those holy ones that are seen in the cloud on a rainy day are engraved in the holy covenant, and from there the Sabbath has been given to Israel. . . . Therefore the rabbis, blessed be their memory, said [B. Ketubot 62b] that the [appropriate] time for scholars to perform marital intercourse is on Friday evening because the Holy One, blessed be He, reveals that holy covenant. Therefore we are circumcised because the Holy One, blessed be He, sanctifies that holy covenant, which is circumcised." See ibid., fol. 128b. The androgynous character of the symbol of the rainbow allows Joseph of Hamadan to apply this symbol to the masculine *Yesod* and to the feminine *Malkhut*. In the final analysis, however, the *membrum virile* is the locus of both male and female aspects. On the symbol of the rainbow in kabbalistic sources, see E. R. Wolfson, *Through a Speculum That Shines: Vision and Imagination in Medieval Jewish Mysticism* (Princeton, 1994), pp. 334 n. 30 and 337–38 n. 40.

35. *Genesis Rabbah* 21:9, p. 203.

36. MS Paris, Bibliothéque Nationale héb. 680, fol. 164b. This passage appears in the concluding section of a commentary on the account of creation in the book of Genesis attributed to the Catalonian kabbalist Joseph bar Samuel. This commentary is printed in Jacob ben Sheshet, *Sefer Meshiv Devarim Nekhoḥim*, ed. G. Vajda (Jerusalem, 1968), pp. 193–96 (see p. 11 n. 3 where the Paris manuscript is mentioned) and in Isaac of Acre, *Sefer Meʾirat ʿEinayim*, ed. A. Goldreich (Jerusalem, 1981), pp. 16–17. The passage that I have translated, however, is not found in either of the aforementioned versions.

37. In other kabbalistic sources the image of the fiery sword, or the "sword that wreaks vengeance for the covenant" (Lev. 26:25), is applied to the feminine Presence on account of the fact that she is a manifestation of divine judgment. See, e.g., *Zohar* 1:66b, 240b; 2:26a; Tishby, *Wisdom of the Zohar*, p. 1365; and Joseph Gikatilla, *Shaʿare ʾOrah*, ed. J. Ben-Shlomo (Jerusalem, 1981), 1:71; *Maʿarekhet ha-ʾElohut* (Ferrara, 1558), ch. 4, 86b–87a.

38. *Sefer Tashak*, pp. 13–14.

39. For discussion of this phenomenon in Western culture, see T. Laqueur, *Making Sex: Body and Gender from the Greeks to Freud* (Cambridge, Mass., and London, 1990). For a different approach to that of Laqueur, see J. Cadden, *Meaning of Sex Difference in the Middle Ages: Medicine, Science, and Culture* (Cambridge and New York, 1993).

40. See E. R. Wolfson, "Circumcision, Vision of God, and Textual Interpretation: From Midrashic Trope to Mystical Symbol," *History of Religions* 27 (1987): 189–215, and idem, "Circumcision and the Divine Name: A Study in the Transmission of Esoteric Doctrine," *Jewish Quarterly Review* 78 (1987): 77–112.

41. MS Paris, Bibliothéque Nationale héb. 843, fol. 39b.

42. See, e.g., *Zohar* 1:162a. For other references to this motif, see Wolfson, "Circumcision, Vision of God, and Textual Interpretation," p. 205 n. 53, to which many more sources could be added. On the phallic character of the *Shekhinah* as the *ʿaṭeret berit,* the corona of the phallus, cf. *Sefer ha-Peliʾah* (Korets, 1784), pt. 2, 54c–d: "*Yesod* is between the thighs . . . and corresponding to *Yesod* in the physical man is the penis that stands between the thighs. Therefore it is called *Yesod*. . . . *ʿAṭarah* is the end of the supernal edifice (*sof ha-binyan le-maʿalah*). Thus, corresponding to it is the corona of the penis (*ha-ʿaṭarah shel ha-maʿor*), which is the end of the person." In the continuation of this passage (55a) the anonymous kabbalist notes that the prohibition of looking at either the priest's hands or the rainbow is related to the sin of focusing on the *Shekhinah* in isolation from the other (masculine) *sefirot.* The spiritual valorization of the feminine is dependent on contextualizing the female in the male organ.

43. See *Zohar* 1:96b; 2:60b; and Tishby, *Wisdom of the Zohar,* pp. 1364–65.

44. MSS Vatican, Biblioteca Apostolica ebr. 283, fol. 51a, and Munich, Bayerische Staatsbibliothek 56, fol. 193b. Cf. *Shaʿare ʾOrah,* 1:114–17.

45. *Zohar* 1:246a. Cf. ibid., 2:137a.

46. *Zohar* 1:246a–b.

47. For discussion of this terminology, see G. Scholem, "On the Development of the Concept of Worlds in the Early Kabbalah," *Tarbiz* 3 (1931): 39–41 (in Hebrew).

48. Cf. the description of the *Shekhinah* in *Zohar* 3:142a (*ʾIdraʾ Rabbaʾ*) and the description of *Binah* in Moses de León, *Sheqel ha-Qodesh,* ed. A. W. Greenup (London, 1911), p. 29. Needless to say, the characterization of the feminine as essentially a vessel to contain the male is a much older trope in Jewish sources. Cf. the talmudic passage discussed at the end of n. 61, below.

49. See, e.g., *Zohar* 1:162a–b.

50. Cf. *Pesiqtaʾ Rabbati,* ed. M. Friedmann (Vienna, 1880), 5, 22b; *Tanḥumaʾ,* Nasso, 18; and *Numbers Rabbah* 12:12.

51. "Joseph of Hamadan's *Sefer Tashak,*" p. 13.

52. Even the mythic portrayal of the feminine Presence as the attribute of judgment is colored by a phallocentric orientation. That is, the descriptions of the Presence as a warrior or as one who wields a sword suggest a phallic understanding of judgment as an active force.

53. See Scholem, *Origins,* p. 142. A similar position is taken by Ch. Mopsik, *Lettre sur la sainteté: Le secret de la relation entre l'homme et la femme dans la cabale* (Paris, 1986), pp. 324–25 n. 218, and M. Idel, "Sexual Metaphors and Praxis in the Kabbalah," in *The Jewish Family: Metaphor and Memory,* ed. D. Kraemer (New York and Oxford, 1989), p. 211. Mopsik has reiterated his position most recently in *Le Secret du marriage de David et*

Bethsabée (Paris, 1994), pp. 16–25. In that context Mopsik explicates the nature of the androgyne in kabbalistic symbolism in light of the pseudo-Clementine *Homily* 14 (see pp. 24–25). According to Mopsik, the ancient Judeo-Christian text posits an idea of dual unity, i.e., a bisexual unity in which both genders are affirmed. Mopsik contrasts this text with the conception of the androgyne in other Greco-Roman sources that entail the "neutralization of sexual difference." In my view the kabbalistic understanding of the androgyne implies precisely such a neutralization of sexual differentiation. See also the formulation of Liebes, *Studies in the Zohar*, p. 106: "the dual sexuality of the divinity is the very foundation of all the doctrine of the Kabbala." To evaluate this statement more precisely one must take into consideration the cultural construction of gender in the relevant sources. When that is done it becomes evident that the feminine is part of the masculine, and hence the dual sexuality of the divinity is reduced to one sex that comprises two elements, the merciful male and the judgmental female. The kabbalistic orientation is close to the view expressed in various alchemical tracts, reflected in the psychological theory of Jung. See E. Zolla, *The Androgyne Reconciliation of Male and Female* (New York, 1981).

54. See A. J. Klijn, "The 'Single One' in the Gospel of Thomas," *Journal of Biblical Literature* 81 (1962): 271–78; M. W. Meyer, "Making Mary Male: The Categories 'Male' and 'Female' in the Gospel of Thomas," *New Testament Studies* 31 (1985): 554–70; P. Brown, *The Body and Society: Men, Women, and Sexual Renunciation in Early Christianity* (New York, 1988), pp. 103–21; and K. Vogt, " 'Becoming Male': A Gnostic and Early Christian Metaphor," in *Image of God and Gender Models*, pp. 172–87. On the myth of the androgyne in ancient Greco-Roman literature, see M. Delcourt, *Hermaphrodite: mythes et rites de la bisexualité dans l'antiquité classique* (Paris, 1958); and L. Brisson, "Neutrum utrumque: La bisexualité dans l'antiquité gréco-romaine," in *L'Androgyne* (Paris, 1986), pp. 27–61.

55. See the summary account given by C. W. Bynum, " '. . . And Woman His Humanity': Female Imagery in the Religious Writing of the Later Middle Ages," in *Gender and Religion: On the Complexity of Symbols*, p. 257: "Male and female were contrasted and asymmetrically valued as intellect/body, active/passive, rational/irrational, reason/emotion, self-control/lust, judgment/mercy, and order/disorder."

56. See *Zohar* 1:49b.

57. See ibid. 3:163b.

58. See, e.g., ibid. 3:145b. For a different approach, see Mopsik, *Lettre sur la sainteté*, pp. 214–15. Mopsik emphasizes that according to the kabbalists the eschaton signifies the restoration of the equality between the two sexes and the end of the domination of one over the other.

59. B. Qiddushin 2b.

60. MS Jerusalem, Sassoon 993, p. 48.

61. K. von Kellenbach, "Anti-Judaism in Christian-Rooted Feminist Writings: An Analysis of Major U.S. American and West German Feminist Theologians" (Ph.D. dissertation, Temple University, 1990), p. 207, remarks that Augustine "grants woman humanity as long as she is joined by a man, 'so the whole substance may be one image.' Marriage becomes a prerequisite for women's humanity. A single woman remains essentially incomplete. The male, on the other hand, represents the divine by himself." The passage is cited in D. Boyarin, *Carnal Israel: Reading Sex in Talmudic Culture* (Berkeley, Los Angeles, and Oxford, 1993), p. 43 n. 25. Conceptually, this description of Augustine is applicable to the kabbalistic sources and, I believe, the earlier rabbinic sources as well. While it is true that in the rabbinic materials we find evidence for the idea that sexual union restores the image of the original androgyne, and perhaps also the divine image in which this androgyne was created, it is nevertheless the case that the female is essentially incomplete without her being joined to the male, whereas the male has a sense of independent completeness, or, to put the matter somewhat differently, the perfection of both the male and female is judged from the vantage point of the male. The fact of the matter is, moreover, that the theological pronouncements of the rabbis generally and predominantly involve an imaging of God as exclusively male. This fact not only privileges the masculine but also suggests that the male alone can represent the *imago dei*. Lest I be misunderstood on this point, let me emphasize that I am not denying the presence in rabbinic texts of the view that the complete anthropos involves the union of male and female (cf. B. Yevamot 63a) nor the notion that without a wife a man is in a state of deficiency (cf. *Genesis Rabbah* 17:1, pp. 151–52). The issue is rather that through the union of male and female, the female completes the male by affording him the opportunity to engender new life. The completeness of the female, therefore, is obviously related to procreation, which must be seen as an androcentric value in rabbinic culture. Consider the following interpretation of "Then Adam said, This one at last is bone of my bones, and flesh of my flesh. This one shall be called woman, for from man was she taken" (Gen. 2:23) in *ʾAvot de-Rabbi Natan*, ed. S. Schechter (Vilna, 1887), version B, ch. 8, 12a: "[This time] the woman was created from man; from now on a man will take the daughter of his fellow and he is commanded to be fruitful and multiply." The author of this comment is dealing with the obvious empirical fact that every man is born of woman rather than the other way around as suggested by the myth of the primal Adam. See G. Anderson, "Celibacy or Consummation in the Garden? Reflections on Early Jewish and Christian Interpretations of the Garden of Eden," *Harvard Theological Review* 82 (1989): 125–26. From the midrashic reflection on the verse it follows that woman's role as the one who bears the child parallels her assumed original ontic status as being taken from man. That is to say, procreation is a reconstitution of the original androgynous state in which the female was contained in the male. Consider the statement attributed to R. Simlai in *Genesis Rabbah* 8:9, p. 63: "Originally [literally, in the past] Adam was created from the earth and Eve was created from Adam, but from that point on [it is said that man and woman were created] 'in our image and in our likeness,' for man is not [created] without woman nor woman

without man, and neither of them without the *Shekhinah*." In this particular setting the teaching of R. Simlai is presented as the internal interpretation of the key phrase in Gen. 1:26 that stands in marked contrast to the master's response to the query of the heretics (*minim*). It is significant that the divine likeness is connected with human procreation. (I owe this insight to David Aaron who has made this very point in "Imagery of the Divine and the Human: On the Mythology of Genesis Rabba 8 § 1," to be published in a forthcoming issue of the *Journal of Jewish Thought and Philosophy*.) As Theodor and Albeck note in their edition of *Genesis Rabbah*, the thematic import of R. Simlai's statement is analogous to the rabbinic teaching that there are three partners in the creation of every person, the biological parents and God. Cf. B. Qiddushin 30b. That the underlying intent of the statement attributed to Simlai is as I have explained is supported by a second context in *Genesis Rabbah* 22:2, p. 206, where the relevant comment is placed in the mouth of R. Ishmael who thus interprets the significance of the particle *ʾet* in the expression *wa-toʾmer qaniti ʾish ʾet yhwh*, "she said, 'I have gained a male child with the help of the Lord' " (Gen. 4:1): "[The significance of] *ʾet yhwh* is that originally Adam was created from the earth and Eve from Adam, but from that point on [it is written] 'in our image and in our likeness,' man is not [created] without woman nor woman without man, and neither of them without the *Shekhinah*." The divine likeness and image is connected to procreation, which in turn is a reconstitution of the originary state wherein the feminine was contained in the masculine. For a different reading of the rabbinic sources on the nature of the androgyne, see Boyarin, *Carnal Israel*, pp. 42–46. Finally, it is worth considering the statement in B. Sanhedrin 22b: "a woman is amorphous (*golem*) and she makes a covenant only with one who makes her into a vessel." Sex thus perfects the woman by giving her shape. Significantly, this transformation is depicted in covenantal terms. The making (or cutting) of the covenant is equivalent to the phallicization of the female through coitus.

62. The point is well documented in scholarly literature. See A. E. Waite, *The Holy Kabbalah* (Secaucus, N.J., 1975), pp. 377–405; Scholem, *Major Trends*, pp. 225–29; idem, *On the Mystical Shape*, pp. 183–85; Tishby, *Wisdom of the Zohar*, pp. 1355–79; Mopsik, *Lettre sur la sainteté*, pp. 45–163; and Idel, "Sexual Metaphor and Praxis," pp. 207–13. See also M. D. Georg Langer, *Die Erotik der Kabbala*, with introduction by P. Orban (Munich, 1989), pp. 41–57.

63. *Zohar* 3:37b. Many of the zoharic passages that I cite in my analysis of the kabbalistic understanding of sexual intercourse have been noted by Tishby, *Wisdom of the Zohar*, pp. 1357–60, and the accompanying notes. Needless to say, however, my way of interpreting the texts is radically different from that of Tishby. Thus, for example, after reviewing some of the relevant sources, Tishby commented: "These passages assign a very important role to the woman in marriage. She is depicted as occupying an exalted position, since she is a reflection of the Shekhinah and also enjoys her protection" (p. 1358). Although Tishby goes on to note the negative characterization of the feminine in terms of the demonic power, he does not fully appreciate the androcentric understanding of the feminine in kabbalistic symbolism. I have concluded on the basis of the very same passages that Tishby mentioned that

the role assigned to the woman is secondary and subservient to that of the male. The sacral character of carnal intercourse is to be judged exclusively from the vantage point of the man's obligation to procreate and thereby extend and increase the divine image in the world. It is true that the woman has an important role in human sexuality, but it can hardly be said that she occupies an exalted position. Such a claim simply neglects to take into account the sociocultural dimension of gender symbolism in the theosophic kabbalistic sources.

64. The androcentrism is also evident in another motif that recurs in zoharic literature; viz., by virtue of marriage and sexual intercourse the man cleaves to the Presence and is thus situated between two females (his earthly wife and the divine Presence) in the pattern of the sixth gradation, *Tif᾿eret,* who is lodged between *Binah* and *Malkhut.* For references see Tishby, *Wisdom of the Zohar,* pp. 1357–58.

65. See Ch. Mopsik, "The Body of Engenderment in the Hebrew Bible, the Rabbinic Tradition and the Kabbalah," in *Zone: Fragments for a History of the Human Body,* ed. M. Feher, R. Naddaff, and N. Tazi (New York, 1989), pp. 48–73.

66. This is the theosophic implication of the interpretation of "The Lord is great and much acclaimed in the city of our God" (Ps. 48:2) in *Zohar* 3:5a: "When is the Holy One, blessed be He, called great? When the Community of Israel is found together with Him. . . . It may be inferred that the King without the Matrona is not a King, and He is not great or glorious. Therefore, he who is not found as male and female, all praise is removed from him and he is not in the category of an anthropos." See as well *Zohar* 2:38b: "In the place where male and female are found, there is no praise except for the male."

67. The kabbalistic view is obviously based on the aggadic notion that the one who does not fulfill the obligation to procreate diminishes the divine image. Cf. B. Yevamot 63b; *Genesis Rabbah* 34:14, ed. Theodor-Albeck, p. 326, and other sources discussed there in n. 2.

68. *Zohar* 1:186b.

69. See *Zohar* 1:187a, and Tishby, *Wisdom of the Zohar,* p. 1362. For the most part the phenomenon of transmigration of the soul or metempsychosis is treated in zoharic passages as a punishment for the man who dies without having borne children. See Scholem, *On the Mystical Shape,* p. 209. Interestingly enough, according to ancient Mandaean lore, reincarnation is similarly viewed as punishment for childlessness. See E. S. Drower, *The Mandaeans of Iraq and Iran* (Leiden, 1962), p. 41. The similarity between the Mandaean and kabbalistic positions was noted by E. M. Yamauchi, *Gnostic Ethics and Mandaean Origins* (Harvard Theological Studies 24; Cambridge, 1970), p. 41 n. 193.

70. With respect to this understanding of sexuality the kabbalists follow the rabbinic tradition that likewise emphasizes the procreative aspect of sexual intercourse. See above, n. 61.

71. This designation of the *Shekhinah* is an abbreviated form of the expression used by Ezra of Gerona, *temunah ha-kolelet kol ha-temunot,* "the image that comprises all the images." See Tishby, *Wisdom of the Zohar,*

p. 1375 n. 63, and Y. Liebes, *Sections of the Zohar Lexcion* (Jerusalem, 1976), pp. 50–51 (in Hebrew).

72. *The Book of the Pomegranate: Moses de León's Sefer ha-Rimmon*, ed. E. R. Wolfson (Atlanta, 1988), p. 224 (Hebrew section; all subsequent references to this volume are to this part of the text). See ibid., pp. 241–42, and the passage from Joseph of Hamadan cited below in n. 85.

73. See Liebes, *Studies in the Zohar*, p. 187 n. 177.

74. Although not stated explicitly in the text, it is obvious that just as the male is entirely mercy the woman is entirely judgment. The union of the two results in the amelioration of the feminine by the masculine.

75. *Zohar* 3:296a (*ʾIdraʾ Zuṭaʾ*).

76. Ibid. The subordinate position accorded the woman is in evidence as well from *Zohar* 1:49a: "Come and see: when a woman is joined to her husband she is called by the name of her husband, *ʾish* and *ʾishah, ṣaddiq* and *ṣedeq*, he is dust and she is dust, he is *ṣevi* and she is *ṣeviyyah*."

77. *Zohar* 3:31a. This passage is cited by Scholem, *On the Mystical Shape*, p. 186, but as evidence to support the claim that there are active as well as passive elements in the *Shekhinah*. In my view, Scholem's reading misses the point of this text, which is to underscore that the feminine is contained in the male and ontically tranformed as a result of the sexual union. Hence, the active elements of the *Shekhinah* are in no way related to femininity, but derive rather from the masculine. The zoharic claim that the female is called by the name of the male signifies the ontological effacement of the feminine in the moment of coitus. See also *Zohar* 3:183b: "In the place where a male is found even the female entity is called masculine."

78. "Life" corresponds to the masculine, or more specifically the *semen virile*, and "place" to the feminine.

79. On the containment of the attribute of the night in that of the day, see *Zohar* 1:120b, and *Book of the Pomegranate*, p. 50.

80. *Zohar* 3:177b.

81. For discussion of this theme, see reference to my study above in n. 18.

82. *Zohar* 3:178a.

83. Ibid., 259b. See parallel in *Zohar Ḥadash*, ed. R. Margaliot (Jerusalem, 1978), 56c.

84. The use of eating as a metaphor for sexual intercourse is found already in rabbinic sources. See Boyarin, *Carnal Israel*, pp. 70–75, 116–17, 123. As Boyarin astutely notes, this metaphorical field is determined by the fact that in rabbinic thought the very essence of sexuality is procreation in an analogous fashion to eating, whose essence is the preservation of the life of the body.

85. The image of the chain (*shalshelet*) is used by Joseph of Hamadan to refer to the sefirotic pleroma on the whole. On the other hand, this image is used more specifically to refer to the aspect of the divine that corresponds to the phallus, which comprises all the divine potencies. See Meier, "A Critical Edition of the *Sefer Ṭaʿamey ha-Miẓwoth*," pp. 243–44, where the rite of circumcision is said to symbolize the "chain of the image (*shalshelet ha-demut*) that alludes to the glorious form corresponding to the face below." See ibid., p. 251, where the man who has no children is compared to "one who does not establish the image of the chain" (*demut ha-shalshelet*). Cf. pp. 140, 146, 152, 179, 252, 256, 262, 271, and "Joseph of Hamadan's *Sefer Tashak*," pp. 62, 72, 80, 81. In the latter instance, the beginning of the "holy and pure chain" of emanation, *Keter*, is described in the obviously phallic image of the "holy spring." It should be noted that on other occasions Joseph of Hamadan describes *Keter* as the skin that covers the head of the supernal form, an image that calls to mind that of the corona of the penis. Cf. "Joseph of Hamadan's *Sefer Tashak*," pp. 69, 104, 272. See ibid., p. 126, where the rabbinic custom of covering one's head is connected with the theosophic notion that God's head is covered. Cf. pp. 235–36 where the covering of the head of the Matrona—related to the bent shape of the letter *kaf*—is connected with the proper sexual modesty vis-à-vis the Holy King. The same symbolism is linked to the closed *mem* on p. 252. On Sabbath the Matrona embraces the Holy King and the head covering is pushed back so that her face is exposed. In the moment of sexual union the Matrona is represented by the final *kaf*, which is a straight and extended line. Cf. pp. 237–40. On pp. 297–98 the reason given for the woman's covering her head is to prevent the disclosure of the forces of judgment, which are linked to her hair. In the same context the reason given for why a woman cuts her hair when she is pure is to remove all impurity before she has sexual intercourse with her husband. Cf. pp. 298–99: "Each and every hair from those holy hairs of the Matrona are inscribed with names that are called other gods, and they arouse all kinds of magic and all kinds of sorcery." Cf. p. 301: "The holy hairs of the Matrona are harder than the hairs of the Holy One, blessed be He, because the skull of the Holy One, blessed be He, is completely merciful without any hairs of judgment from various sides; therefore it is soft. The skull of the Matrona has an aspect of judgment from various sides and thus [the hairs of Matrona] are harder and darker than the hairs of the Holy One, blessed be He." On the other hand, Joseph of Hamadan emphasizes the masculine, and indeed phallic, aspect of hair, which serves as a channel to transmit the flow of divine energy. Cf., e.g., pp. 298–300: "Through these holy hairs the holy dew descends from the head of *ʾArikh ʾAnpin* to the head of the Matrona . . . and she is sweetened. . . . These holy hairs of the Matrona are intertwined with the head of the Holy One, blessed be He. . . . The holy hairs of the Matrona are called the thread of mercy that the Holy One, blessed be He, extends to the righteous." Needless to say, many more examples from this text and other works of Joseph of Hamadan could be adduced. Liebes, *Studies in the Zohar*, pp. 124–25, contrasts this aspect of Joseph of Hamadan's writings with the zoharic view that relates the growing of hair to the augmentation of the forces of judgment and impurity. He did not,

however, take into account the passages that I mentioned that are much closer to the negative valorization of hair according to the *Zohar*. On the symbolic implication of the image of envelopping in Joseph of Hamadan, see reference in E. R. Wolfson, "The Image of Jacob Engraved upon the Throne: Further Speculation on the Esoteric Doctrine of the German Pietists," in *Along the Path: Studies in Kabbalistic Myth, Symbolism, and Hermeneutics* (Albany, 1995), p. 181 n. 353. Finally, mention should be made of the passage in "Joseph of Hamadan's *Sefer Tashak*," p. 132: "When the seventh millenium comes the holy name will not be seen except for the letter *yod*, and nothing will be seen except for the Supernal Crown that resembles the letter *yod*." It is evident from the context that the *yod* also symbolizes the sign of the covenant. It follows, therefore, that a connection is made between the *yod*, *Keter*, and the corona of the phallus.

86. "Joseph of Hamadan's *Sefer Tashak*," p. 51. Cf. Joseph of Hamadan's description of sexual copulation in Meier, "A Critical Edition of the *Sefer Ṭa*ᶜ*amey ha-Miẓwoth*," p. 243: "When a man unites with his wife and he enters the sign of the covenant in the attribute of judgment, the judgment is mixed with mercy (*mit*ᶜ*arev ha-din* ᶜ*im ha-raḥamim*), and this is the secret of the ᶜ*aravot*, and he sweetens the efflux from above and causes the unity of the Bridegroom and the Bride." On this symbolic connotation of the word ᶜ*aravot*, cf. ibid., pp. 133 and 137.

87. A similar point is made by Boyarin, *Carnal Israel*, pp. 75–76, with respect to rabbinic Judaism: "The commitment to coupling did not, however, imply any reduction of the radically unequal distribution of power that characterized virtually all of the societies of late antiquity. That inequality not only remained a fact of life for rabbinic Judaism but was confirmed in a whole conceptual apparatus, along with a complex tangle of emblematic stories, articulated in the talmudic literature."

88. This work has been the object of several scholarly discussions. See G. Scholem, "Did the Ramban Write the ʾ*Iggeret ha-Qodesh*?" *Kiryat Sefer* 21 (1944–45): 179–86 (in Hebrew), and the additional note of Scholem in *Kiryat Sefer* 22 (1945–46): 84; M. Harris, "Marriage as Metaphysics: A Study of the ʾ*Iggeret ha-Kodesh*," *Hebrew Union College Annual* 33 (1962): 197–220; *The Holy Letter: A Study on Medieval Jewish Sexual Morality*, ed. and trans. S. J. Cohen (New York, 1976), pp. 7–27; K. Guberman, "The Language of Love in Spanish Kabbalah: An Examination of the ʾ*Iggeret ha-Kodesh*," in *Approaches to Judaism in Medieval Times*, ed. D. R. Blumenthal (Chico, Calif., 1984), 1:53–95; and Mopsik, *Lettre sur la sainteté*. See also discussion of the epistle in D. Biale, *Eros and the Jews: From Biblical Israel to Contemporary America* (New York, 1992), pp. 102–9.

89. *Kitve Ramban*, ed. C. D. Chavel (Jerusalem, 1964), 2:331–35.

90. See Biale, *Eros and the Jews*, p. 107. While Biale duly notes the subordinate role of women in sexual intercourse according to the ʾ*Iggeret ha-Qodesh*, his statement that "[s]ince each partner is connected symbolically

with the male and female *sefirot*, the thought or intention of each is equally powerful" needs to be qualified in light of the explicit claims that women are never directly connected to the divine realm. The intention of the woman is vital, but not nearly as powerful as that of the man.

91. B. Berakhot 60a; Niddah 25b, 28a, 31a. The view of the rabbis reflects the Hippocratic and Galenic (as opposed to the Aristotelian) notion that both parents produce sperm. See C. W. Atkinson, *The Oldest Vocation: Christian Motherhood in the Middle Ages* (Ithaca and London, 1991), pp. 47–49.

92. *Kitve Ramban*, p. 336. Cf. Judah ben Solomon Campanton, *ʾArbaʿah Qinyyanim*, MS JTSA Mic. 2532, fol. 45a: "This actual matter you find [in the case of] Abraham and Sarah who gave birth in their good thought to Isaac who resembled his father, as it is written, 'Abraham gave birth to Isaac,' the expression 'gave birth' (*holid*) has the numerical value of resembled (*domeh*). Thus every man must sanctify himself in the time of intercourse." See ibid., fols. 49a–b.

93. *Kitve Ramban*, p. 334.

94. *Zohar* 3:81a–b. See Tishby, *Wisdom of the Zohar*, p. 1360.

95. My approach contrasts sharply with that of Scholem, who sees the active and the passive aspects as related to the feminine nature of the *Shekhinah*, the former consisting of the woman's capacity to give birth. See *On the Mystical Shape*, pp. 165, 174–75. I am suggesting, by contrast, that the gender of femininity is valorized exclusively as passive and that the more active role associated with the feminine is dependent upon the metamorphosis of the female into a male. See further discussion below on the kabbalistic symbol of the mother. However, in another passage (p. 183) Scholem takes a position closer to my own when he says that in the *Zohar* there is an attribution of "active and, in Kabbalistic terms, masculine aspects" to the lower *Shekhinah*, previously considered quintessentially feminine. See also p. 186, where Scholem speaks of the "active, masculine aspects" that are applied to the *Shekhinah* alongside the feminine symbols.

96. *Zohar* 1:122a. The masculine valence of the woman's ability to bear children is underscored in the following passage in Ḥayyim Vital, *ʿEṣ Ḥayyim* (Jerusalem, 1910), 39:7, 72b–c:

> It is known that when *Zeʿeir* and *Nuqbaʾ* copulate, he imparts the male waters and she imparts the female waters. It is known what the rabbis, blessed be their memory, said "a woman does not make a covenant except with he who makes her into a vessel" [B. Sanhedrin 22b]. The rabbis, blessed be their memory, also said that "a woman does not get pregnant from the first sexual intercourse" [B. Yevamot 34a]. . . . The explanation of these matters is as follows: it is known that *Nuqbaʾ* does not take any light except by means of *Zeʿeir ʾAnpin*, and it is known that the two crowns are in *Daʿat*, and they are called *Ḥesed* and *Gevurah*, and they

> are the forty-five-letter name and the fifty-two-letter name. Even though *Nuqba*ʾ was [attached] back-to-back with *Zeʿeir ʾAnpin*, she could not be perfected and become a configuration (*parṣuf*) until she received the crown of strengths, which are the five forces of strength. She does not take the five forces of strength by themselves but only their illumination as they pass through the hinder parts of *Zeʿeir ʾAnpin*. The five forces of strength descend after the completion of the [forces of] mercy, and they stand in the phallus of *Zeʿeir ʾAnpin*, and from there they transmit their illumination to *Nuqba*ʾ. These stand in her permanently and they are her life-force, and they are called the soul of *Malkhut*. Since her substance only comes to be from their illumination, she was not fit to give birth, for the female is only fit to give birth when she is complete, and if she is deficient she cannot give birth. All the perfection comes to be only when the five forces of strength, which are the fifty-two-letter name, are in her . . . for this is verily the soul of *Nuqba*ʾ. This is the reason why the woman does not get pregnant from the first sexual intercourse, for the first intercourse turns her into a vessel to receive the drop of semen, and after that vessel receives [the semen] from the first intercourse from that point on she can become pregnant and she receives the drop of semen in other copulations.

According to this passage, the soul of the female, which allows her to give birth, consists of the five forces of judgment that derive from the male and that are implanted in the female in the first act of coitus. That act transforms the female into a vessel, which is endowed with the task of receiving the seminal fluid. One will readily admit that the nature of the female is represented exclusively from the vantage point of the phallus. To highlight the extent to which the androcentric understanding of parturition informed the kabbalistic mentality, I will briefly analyze some key passages in an important treatise by the seventeenth-century Sabbatian theologian, Abraham Miguel Cardoso, *Derush ha-Shekhinah*. (I am currently preparing a full-length study on the role of the feminine in Cardoso's thought. What is presented here is a preliminary discussion of one aspect that is most relevant to the theme of the masculinization of childbirth.) On the one hand, Cardoso insists that the *Shekhinah* occupies a unique position because she alone is endowed with the capacity to create and thus she manifests the full intention of the first *sefirah*. On the other hand, Cardoso recognizes that the feminine cannot give birth without the masculine: "Certainly one will comprehend that there is no woman without a man, according to [the verse] 'for from man she was taken' (Gen. 2:23). Then you will discern the secret of divinity (*sod ha-ʾelohut*)" (MS New York, Jewish Theological Seminary of America Mic. 1677, fol. 2a). The secret of divinity, which Cardoso reiterates in many of his compositions, entails the androgynous nature of the Creator, who is distinguished from the hidden First Cause. Part and parcel of the theological secret is the acceptance of the ontically secondary status of the female as that which is taken from the male. Yet, in spite of this recognition, Cardoso attributes supreme value to the female. In fact, so enamored is Cardoso of the feminine that he even turns the biblical conception of the woman's derivative status into a positive:

> The intent of what we say that Eve was contained in Adam is that she was with him in order to emerge afterward in a complete disclosure. The Holy One, blessed be He, constructed the feminine from the rib [or side] of Adam. She is the last of all created beings and she comprises everything that was in Adam, and in addition she comprises the essential being of Adam for she was not made from the dust [of the earth] as he was but rather from the flesh and bone of Adam. . . . Thus the greatness of Eve over Adam is clarified, she comprises everything that he comprises and in her is the existence of the masculine for she is flesh of his flesh (MS New York, Jewish Theological Seminary of America Mic. 1677 fols. 5a–b).

In the final analysis, Cardoso cannot shed the androcentric bias of medieval kabbalah. The feminine is extolled as the creative force in the universe, but that power ultimately derives from the masculine.

> Eve was complete and she was called "woman" (*ʾishah*) since she was taken from the man (*ʾish*), and his being and his power are comprised in her. Therefore she is called *ʾishah* for she is ready to give birth. It is appropriate that each and every female is taken from the male . . . for a man imparts to her the spirit, which comprises his essence and his power, by means of the first intercourse, and through that his wife becomes a vessel that is suitable to bear sons and daughters. . . . When the female does not [carnally] know a male it is written in relation to her *naʿar*, but after she has had intercourse she is called *naʿarah*, for prior to the intercourse she is like a male who cannot give birth and after the intercourse she becomes a vessel and she is called *naʿarah*, the complete female that comprises the power of the male (*neqevah shelemah shekolelet koaḥ ha-zakhar*). The woman comprises the man, 'for from man she was taken' (Gen. 2:23), and they are one flesh and one substance. The blemish of one harms the other (ibid., fols. 8a–b).

The feminine becomes fully herself only after she has had intercourse with the male and she becomes a vessel to receive the semen. Cardoso falls short of explicitly affirming the gender transformation of the female to the male, but it is quite obvious that he locates the procreative power of the female in the male.

97. *Sefer ha-Bahir*, § 172.

98. Gen. 2:19.

99. Ibid. 2:25.

100. B. Yevamot 62b.

101. Ibid. 61b.

102. MS Vatican, Biblioteca Apostolica ebr. 236, fols. 76a–b. See also MS Parma, Biblioteca Palatina 2704 (De Rossi 68), fol. 87a.

103. Cf. *Zohar* 3:7a, discussed in Tishby, *Wisdom of the Zohar*, p. 1361.

104. See A. Preus, "Galen's Criticism of Aristotle's Conception Theory," *Journal of the History of Biology* 10 (1977): 65–85, and M. Boylan, "The Galenic and Hippocratic Challenge to Aristotle's Conception Theory," *Journal of the History of Biology* 17 (1984): 83–112.

105. *Zohar* 3:42b.

106. *On the Mystical Shape*, pp. 174–75.

107. Ibid., p. 176.

108. Ibid., p. 186.

109. Ibid., p. 187.

110. On portrayals of the uterus as the penis in Renaissance anatomical material, see evidence adduced by Laqueur, *Making Sex*, pp. 79–98. The kabbalistic transformation of motherhood into a masculine ideal is predicated on a one-sex model as well that viewed the female genitals as internal analogues to the male genitals. The womb, therefore, is characterized in terms of a penis-like extension.

111. On the androgynous character of the archetype of the Great Mother, see E. Neumann, *The Origins and History of Consiousness*, foreword C. G. Jung, and trans. R. F. C. Hull (Princeton, 1954), p. 46. On the phenomenon of the phallic mother, or the uroboric snake woman that combines begetting and childbearing, see idem, *The Great Mother: An Analysis of an Archetype*, trans. R. Manheim, 2nd ed. (Princeton, 1963), pp. 13, 170, 308–10.

112. G. Scholem, "Two Treatises of R. Moses de León" *Qoveṣ ʿal yad* 8 (1976): 375 (in Hebrew). Cf. *Zohar* 1:229a, and 3:78a.

113. *Book of the Pomegranate*, p. 229.

114. Ibid., p. 166. Cf. *Zohar* 1:59b–60a.

115. This is the technical expression used in some rabbinic sources to refer to the apostasy of Elisha ben Abuyah. For references and discussion, see D. J. Halperin, *The Merkabah in Rabbinic Literature* (New Haven, 1980), pp. 90–91.

116. Both words, *ʿeryah* and *ʿervah*, have the connotation of nakedness and can refer more specifically to the uncovering of the genitals.

117. G. Scholem, "The Commentary of R. Isaac of Acre on the First Chapter of *Sefer Yeṣirah*," *Kiryat Sefer* 31 (1955–56): 386 (in Hebrew).

118. See, e.g., *Zohar* 1:219a and *Book of the Pomegranate,* p. 138: "Behold I will reveal to you a true secret. Know that there is no male in Israel who is married that does not stand between two women, one hidden and the other revealed. When a man is married the *Shekhinah* above his head becomes in relation to him a hidden world, and his wife stands next to him in the matter that is revealed. Thus, he stands between two women, one hidden and the other revealed, to be in the pattern that is above." The biblical model recalled in this context is Jacob who stands between his two wives, Leah and Rachel, symbolically corresponding to *Binah* and *Malkhut.* See parallel in *Zohar* 1:50a, noted by Liebes, *Studies in the Zohar,* pp. 72–73. In line with the gender dynamic operative in this text, the upper female in relation to the male is a concealed world, and the lower female is the revealed world. The upper feminine, however, in this posture is valorized as male.

119. See *Zohar* 1:158a.

120. Ibid. 2:9a.

121. See ibid. 1:184a where the image of nursing from the mother's breast (cf. Song of Songs 8:1) is interpreted as a reference to the unity and love between *Yesod* and *Shekhinah.* In that context, therefore, breast-feeding assumes a sexual connotation. The breasts can also symbolize masculine and feminine potencies; cf. *Zohar* 1:44b and 2:253a (both interpreting Song of Songs 4:5). In the latter instance it is evident, moreover, that the divine name *shaddai,* etymologically connected to *shadayim,* "breasts" (on the possibility of this philological connection in the biblical text itself, see D. Biale, "The God with Breasts: El Shaddai in the Bible," *History of Religions* 20 [1982]: 240–56) signifies the phallic activity of the feminine potency that supplies sustenance for all things below her in accord with what she receives from the right side of mercy. See also *Zohar* 2:257a, where the celestial palace (*hekhal*) is called *ʾel shaddai* because it sustains the world like breasts and "God will fill it and establish it in the future, as it is written, 'That you may suck from her breast consolation to the full, that you may draw from her bosom glory to your delight' (Isa. 66:1). The breast of consolation and the splendor of her glory are all in this palace, and at that time it is written, 'Who would have said to Abraham that Sarah would suckle children!' (Gen. 21:7), for suckling is dependent upon Abraham." Hence, it is evident from this passage that nursing is valorized as a male trait, related specifically to the attribute of mercy personified in the figure of Abraham. The masculine valorization of nursing that one finds in kabbalistic literature should be contrasted with the application of the maternal imagery of breast-feeding to Jesus and the prelates that one finds in twelfth-century Cistercian devotional texts. See C. W. Bynum, *Jesus as Mother: Studies in the Spirituality of the High Middle Ages* (Berkeley, 1982), pp. 110–69. In the case of the Christian authors, there does not seem to be any transvaluation of the feminine into the masculine, but rather the appropriation of maternal metaphors—especially breasts and nurturing—to describe aspects of the relationship of Jesus and the prelates to individual souls. In the kabbalistic literature, by contrast, the application of the maternal images to God is

predicated on the gender transformation of the concept of motherhood. Images of giving birth and nursing are valenced as specifically phallic activities.

122. See Idel, *Kabbalah: New Perspectives*, p. 55.

123. *Zohar* 1:256b.

124. In the continuation of the zoharic text the growth of the breasts is linked more specifically to the righteous and meritorious activities of Israel. That is, when the Jewish people cleave to the Torah and go in a truthful path, then the *Shekhinah* is fortified like a wall and develops towering breasts. The allegorical depiction of Israel's deeds as the breasts of the *Shekhinah* is found as well in *Zohar* 2:80b. See also 1:45a, where the beauty of a woman is tied especially to her breasts.

125. The phallic signification of the mature breasts is evident as well in *Zohar* 3:296a (*ʾIdraʾ Zuṭaʾ*): "The beauty of the female is entirely from the beauty of the male. . . . This female [*Shekhinah*] is called the smaller wisdom in relation to the other one, and thus it is written, 'We have a little sister, whose breasts are not yet formed' (Song of Songs 8:8), for she tarries in the exile. 'We have a little sister,' certainly she appears as little, but she is big and great, for she is the completion of what she has received from everyone, as it is written, 'I am a wall, my breasts are like towers' (ibid., 10). 'My breasts' are filled to nurse all things. 'Like towers,' these are the great rivers that issue forth from the supernal mother." The phallic characterization of the breasts is drawn explicitly in Menaḥem Azariah of Fano, *Yonat ʾElem*, ch. 57, 45a:

> The blessings of the breasts that lactate milk according to the secret of "And the Lord passes," *wa-yaʿavor yhwh* (Exod. 34:6), for these [letters allude to] the 72 [letter-name, i.e., *ʿayin-bet*], the 216 [letters comprised in that name, i.e., *reish-yod-waw*], and 26 [the numerical value of YHWH]. In this manner [are the letters arranged]: the 72 on the right side of *Binah*, the 216 on the left side and YHWH in the middle. The numerical value of them all is equivalent to the sum of Shaddai [i.e., 72 + 216 + 26 = 314], which is from the word *shadayim*. . . . When the Mother nurses *Zeʿeir* and *Nuqbaʾ* [she] is called El Shaddai on account of the breasts (*shadayim*) that are in her median line.

The breasts, therefore, are aligned in the phallic position of the middle, and because of them the maternal potency of God assumes the name El Shaddai. Cf. the explanation of impregnation (*ʿibbur*) in the Lurianic text preserved in MS New York, Jewish Theological Seminary of America Mic. 2155, fol. 69a: "After birth [*Binah*] nursed him in the secret of the milk until he grew up and was weaned (cf. Gen. 21:8) and this is [the significance of] *ʾel ʿelyon gomel* [the supernal God bestows goodness] from the expression *wa-yigmol sheqedim* [it bore almonds] (Num. 17:23). During the time of the nursing she is called El Shaddai from the expression *shadayim*." Finally, let me note that the symbolic correlation of the penis and the breasts that I have delineated in kabbalistic literature represents the reverse of what one finds in Freudian psychoanalytic theory. That is, according to Freud, the penis becomes heir to the nipple of the mother's breast when sucking comes to an end. See *The Complete Introductory Lectures on Psychoanalysis,* trans. and ed. J. Stachey New York, 1965), p. 565. Although Freud evaluates the sexuality of the breast entirely from the vantage point of the penis, he does not, as the kabbalists, interpret the biological functions of the breasts in phallic terms.

126. *Zohar* 2:85b; cf. *Book of the Pomegranate,* p. 163. The nexus between the motif of returning and the role of *Binah* as that which overflows in blessings is underscored in the anonymous kabbalistic text, influenced by zoharic traditons and the writings of Moses de León, the *Sefer ha-Ne*ᶜ*elam,* MS Paris, Bibliothéque Nationale héb. 817, fol. 57a.

127. *Zohar* 3:15b. On the paradoxical nature of this passage, see the marginal notes in *Gershom Scholem's Annotated Zohar* (Jerusalem, 1992), p. 2232.

128. The nexus of repentance, Yom Kippur, and illicit sexual relations, especially uncovering the genitals of the father and the mother, in the zoharic text is evident as well in the following comment of Joseph of Hamadan in his commentary on the *sefirot,* MS Oxford, Bodleian Library 1628, fol. 67b:

> From there [*Binah*] begins the drawing-forth of the genitals (*yeniqat* ᶜ*arayot*), and thus on Yom Kippur we read at the time of Minḥah [the afternoon service] the matter of illicit sexual relations (ᶜ*arayot*), for they draw forth from the attribute of *Binah,* which is called *Teshuvah* in every place. On Yom Kippur we stand in the strength of *Teshuvah,* and you find that the beginning of the [section on] illicit sexual relations is "the nakedness of the father and mother" (Lev. 18:7), which is the attribute of *Binah* on account of the beginning of the secret of illicit sexual relations (*sitre* ᶜ*arayot*).

For a parallel to this explanation, cf. Joseph of Hamadan's *Sefer Ṭa*ᶜ*ame ha-Miṣwot,* positive commandments (no. 48) in Meier, "A Critical Edition of the *Sefer Ṭa*ᶜ*amey ha-Miẓwoth,*" p. 196: "We read the section on ᶜ*arayot* in the Minḥah prayer on Yom Kippur because we comprehend [at that time] the attribute of *Binah,* and from there we begin to draw forth the ᶜ*arayot,* the secret of the wife and her husband, the secret of unity." For a slightly different formulation, cf. "Joseph of Hamadan's *Sefer Tashak,*" p. 109, where it is emphasized that from *Binah* is the drawing-forth of the golden bowl (*yeniqat golat ha-zahav*), i.e., the phallus, that overflows to all the attributes. Cf. Joseph of Hamadan's *Sefer Ṭa*ᶜ*ame ha-Miṣwot,* negative commandments (no. 30), MS Paris, Bibliothéque Nationale héb. 817, fol. 155a, where a connection is made between the custom to read the section on ᶜ*arayot* during the afternoon service of Yom Kippur and the tannaitic treatment of illicit sexual relations as an esoteric discipline (according to M. Ḥagigah 2:1). In that context, moreover, Joseph of Hamadan offers a slightly different nuanced explanation for this commandment:

> Know that the matter of the ᶜarayot all relates to the fact that one should not make use of the sceptre of the glorious king, for he who has intercourse with his mother it is as if he actually had intercourse with the *Shekhinah* for she is the mother of all living things. Therefore, it is written [in Lev. 18:7] "your mother" twice, corresponding to the mother above and the mother below. Not for naught did the rabbis, blessed be their memory, say [B. Berakhot 57a], the one who has intercourse with his mother in a dream should anticipate understanding. . . . This is the attribute of *Binah* that is called mother. Therefore, he who has intercourse with his mother makes use of the sceptre of *Binah* who is called mother, and he who makes use [of the sceptre] of the glorious king is guilty of death. Therefore the Torah says, "Your father's nakedness and the nakedness of your mother, you shall not uncover," corresponding to *Ṣaddiq* and *Malkhut* who are called father and mother, and [the continuation of the verse, "she is your mother—you shall not uncover her nakedness"] corresponds to *Binah*.

According to an alternative symbolic explanation, on Yom Kippur there is a reunion of mother and daughter; i.e., *Binah* and *Malkhut* are conjoined in a union that has no precise analogue in the anthropological sphere. On the contrary, sexual relations between husband and wife are prohibited precisely because in the divine realm this mating occurs. Cf. *Book of the Pomegranate*, pp. 162–63, and *Sefer ha-Ne*ᶜ*elam*, MS Paris, Bibliothéque Nationale héb. 817, fol. 57b.

129. The complex symbolism and dialectic of concealment and disclosure are well captured in the following passage of Isaac Luria copied by Samuel Vital and printed in *Sha*ᶜ*ar Ma*ᵓ*amere Rashbi* (Jerusalem, 1898), 23b:

> Just as *Neṣaḥ, Hod,* and *Yesod* of the Mother are clothed in the head of *Ze*ᶜ*eir* ᵓ*Anpin*, so *Neṣaḥ, Hod,* and *Yesod* of *Ze*ᶜ*eir* ᵓ*Anpin* extend and enter into the point of Zion of the foundation of *Malkhut*, her femaleness [i.e., the uterus; cf. ibid., 28b], and they are joined in the secret of union. . . . Then the womb of the female of *Ze*ᶜ*eir* ᵓ*Anpin* that is below opens up, but she also is concealed and hidden. It follows that the beginning of that key is united with and is closed in relation to the Mother and its end is closed and united below with the Female. . . . Thus the two genitals, that of the Mother and that of the Daughter, are concealed, and then there are no complete judgments. But when, God forbid, Israel sin they cause the Mother to depart from her children and consequently the Mother removes her *Neṣaḥ, Hod,* and *Yesod* from the skull of *Ze*ᶜ*eir* ᵓ*Anpin*, and thus her foundation was revealed. This causes the *Ze*ᶜ*eir* ᵓ*Anpin* also to depart above and he is not with his Female. Consequently, the foundation of the Female was also revealed, and this is the matter of the uncovering of the geni-

tals. This causes the judgments of the Mother and Daughter to come forth from there and they extend below. . . . But you should know that when their wombs open up this is the secret of the opening of the womb (*peṭer reḥem*) at the time of childbirth, and then, by contrast, is the aspect of mercy and not the aspect of judgment. Understand this distinction.

130. With respect to this quality of motherhood, there is an obvious discrepancy between the social and the religious duties of the woman and the theosophic symbolism. That is, the symbolic valorization of the mother as masculine stands in marked contrast to the exclusive (secondary) social and religious role accorded the woman related to the biological functions of motherhood. This process is in contrast to that of Christianity in which the construction of spiritual motherhood (related to the ideology of monasticism) replaced biological motherhood as the most efficacious role of women. See Atkinson, *The Oldest Vocation*, pp. 64–100. The situation of Christianity is also to be distinguished from Judaism insofar as in the case of the former ideas about the motherhood of God were shaped around texts and rituals connected to the figure of Mary. See Atkinson, *The Oldest Vocation*, pp. 101–43, and S. Benko, *The Virgin Goddess: Studies in the Pagan and Christian Roots of Mariology* (Leiden, 1993).

131. See passages from Joseph of Hamadan cited above, n. 128.

132. *Zohar* 1:60a. In other contexts a distinction is made between *be᾿er* and *be᾿erah*, the former referring to the *Shekhinah* before she receives water from the masculine attribute of *Ḥesed* and the latter once she has received it. Cf. *Zohar* 3:183b. The former expression is used in particular in contexts that describe the relationship of Isaac, who represents the attribute of judgment, and the *Shekhinah*. Cf. *Zohar* 1:60b, 135b, and 3:103a, 115a, 156b.

133. See, e.g., *Zohar* 1:60b, 3:84a. The latter context is particularly interesting insofar as the topic of discussion is the gaze of the Holy One upon David: "When the Holy One, blessed be He, wants to have mercy upon the world He looks upon that David, and shines His face upon him, and he illuminates the worlds and has pity on the world. The beauty of this David illuminates all the worlds." It is possible that this passage implies an element of homoeroticism in the divine realm. That is, even though David is a standard symbol for the Presence, usually valorized as female, in this context the issue seems to be the masculine deity gazing upon the aspect that sustains the world. That aspect is the male dimension of the Presence, indeed the corona of the phallus. See *Zohar* 1:168a where there is a reworking of the older motif of God gazing upon the icon of Jacob and having pity upon the world. For discussion of this theme see my study "Image of Jacob Engraved upon the Throne."

134. *Zohar* 3:296a (*᾿Idra᾿ Zuṭa᾿*).

135. Ibid., 1:248b.

136. Ibid., 3:183b.

137. Ibid., 1:2a.

138. Cf. Exod. 23:17 (34:23): "Three times a year all your males shall appear before the Sovereign, the Lord," *shalosh peᶜamim ba-shanah yeraᵓeh kol zekhurkha ᵓel pene ᵓadon yhwh*. The meaning of this biblical idiom according to many kabbalists is linked to the phallomorphic gaze that binds God and the male mystic. That is, the divine phallus is the object of vision and the human phallus is the faculty of vision. See *Through a Speculum That Shines*, pp. 369–70. Cf. Abraham Azulai, *Ḥesed le-ᵓAvraham* (Bene-Beraq, 1986), § 33, 15b: "This is the secret of the verse, 'all your males shall appear before the Sovereign, the Lord,' for the male should imagine His form and His existence in the *Shekhinah* who is standing there. Even though the comprehension of God is in every place, nevertheless a person should not contemplate in order to engrave His image in the *Shekhinah* as He is seen in the sacred place." Azulai thus limits the imaginative visualization of God to the Temple, the *hagios topos*. From a philosophical perspective God is omnipresent and therefore he can be comprehended everywhere, but from a phenomenological perspective the iconic representation of God's image in the imagination should occur only within the spatial confines of the sacred space. The nature of that vision, moreover, entails contemplation of God's form within the *Shekhinah*. In my opinion, this relates to the fact that the *Shekhinah* is the *ᶜaṭeret berit*, the corona of the phallus. Hence, the divine form can be seen through the *Shekhinah*.

139. *Shaᶜar Maᵓamere Rashbi*, 7b. See R. Meroz, "Redemption in the Lurianic Teaching" (Ph.D. dissertation, Hebrew University, 1988), p. 125 (in Hebrew).

140. On the essential connection of masculinity and the face, see Vital, *ᶜEṣ Ḥayyim*, 31:5, 34c.

141. *Shaᶜar Maᵓamere Rashbi*, 28c.

142. For some references, see above, n. 129.

143. See, e.g., *Zohar* 1:38b: "It is written, 'A capable wife is a crown for her husband' (Prov. 12:4). The secret of faith entails that a man cleaves to his Master to fear him constantly without deviating to the right or left." The righteous person is portrayed as cleaving to the aspect of God depicted as the crown. It is evident that this refers to the *Shekhinah* (cf. *Zohar* 2:83b, and 3:42b, 96b, 72a, 82b, 136b, 178b, 230a), but precisely through this image the femininity of the *Shekhinah* is transposed into masculinity inasmuch as the crown signifies the corona of the penis.

144. See my study referred to above in n. 40 and the subsection "Crowning and Visionary Union with the Phallus," in chapter 7 of my monograph, *Through a Speculum That Shines*, pp. 357–68.

145. It is extremely difficult to assess whether these homoerotic tendencies were expressed in overt homosexual behavior. There is hardly any documentation outside the imaginative literature of the mystics to confirm homosexual practices. A similar theoretical question has been raised by various scholars in relation to the explicit homoerotic imagery used by Andalusian Hebrew poets: does this language signify that the poets actually practiced homosexuality? For representative treatments, see J. Schirmann, "The Ephebe in Medieval Hebrew Poetry," *Sefarad* 15 (1955): 55–68 (in Hebrew); N. Allony, "The Zevi in the Hebrew Poetry of Spain," *Sefarad* 23 (1963): 311–21 (in Hebrew); N. Roth, " 'Deal Gently with the Young Man': Love of Boys in Medieval Hebrew Poetry of Spain," *Speculum* 57 (1982): 33–59; J. Press, "What in the World Is the Sin If I Thrill to Your Beauty?: The Homosexual Love Poems of the Medieval Rabbis," *Mosaic* (1989):12–26; and R. P. Scheindlin, *Wine, Women, and Death: Medieval Hebrew Poems of the Good Life* (Philadelphia, 1986), pp. 82–83, 86–88. On sexual promiscuities and deviances from traditional norms in Jewish communities of Spain during the time of the flourishing of theosophic kabbalah, see Y. T. Assis, "Sexual Behaviour in Mediaeval Hispano-Jewish Society," in *Jewish History: Essays in Honour of Chimen Abramsky*, ed. A. Rapoport-Albert and S. J. Zipperstein (London, 1988), pp. 25–60. It is in order here to recall the observation of Biale, *Eros and the Jews*, p. 89, that the "mystics may have guarded against sexual license in this world by projecting it into a higher realm." Although in that context Biale does not refer to homosexuality amongst the kabbalists, it is instructive to expand his comments in this direction. On the possible intimation of latent homosexuality in the case of Joseph Karo, see Biale, p. 115. See also p. 147, where Biale discusses the homosexual innuendo of an anti-Hasidic author reflecting on the male fellowship of the Hasidic court. In sixteenth-century kabbalistic material, there are explicit penitential instructions for the sin of homosexuality. Cf. Eleazar Azikri, *Sefer Ḥaredim* (Jerusalem, 1966), p. 200, and *Shaʿar ha-Kelalim*, ch. 11, printed in Vital, *ʿEṣ Ḥayyim*, p. 18. The work is associated with three of Luria's disciples, Moses Yonah, Moses Najara, and Joseph Arzin. According to Y. Avivi, however, the text was authored by Ḥayyim Vital on the basis of compositions written by the aforementioned kabbalists. See Meroz, "Redemption in the Lurianic Teaching," pp. 90–91. Most striking is the fact that material related to homosexuality is found in esoteric works that were written only for circulation amongst a small elite, as we find in the *Kanfe Yonah* of Moses Yonah. See extended discussion in MS Jerusalem, Sassoon 993, pp. 208–17. Cf. printed version of Menaḥem Azariah of Fano, *Kanfe Yonah* (Korets, 1786), pt. 1, ch. 86, 30d; ch. 89, 31c–d; pt. 2, sec. 9, 39a–b. While there is still not enough evidence to document actual homosexuality, the need to incorporate in this work such a lengthy discussion about the theurgical ramification and ultimate rectification of this sin may be revealing. It is also of interest to note the following comment in a collection of Lurianic materials extant in MS Oxford, Bodleian Library 1782, fol. 177b: "The remedy (*tiqqun*) for homosexuality was given by the rabbi, blessed be his memory [i.e., the Ari] to three people but it is not known if that remedy has the same effect for all Jews." This passage clearly indicates that the discussions about homosexuality in the relevant

Lurianic texts were not simply theoretical but had practical applications. Still, the Lurianic kabbalists, in consonance with earlier sources, uphold heterosexuality as the only legitimate and authorized form of sexual behavior. All forms of deviant sexuality outside the relationship of husband and wife are considered detrimental inasmuch as such actions create a division above between male and female. It is for that reason that homosexuality, celibacy, and onanism are all demonized in kabbalistic literature. See Liebes, *Studies in the Zohar*, pp. 67–74, and idem, "'Two Young Roes of a Doe': The Secret Sermon of Isaac Luria before His Death," *Jerusalem Studies in Jewish Thought* 10 (1992): 163–64 (in Hebrew).

146. For such an approach in twelfth-century Cistercian literature, see Bynum, *Jesus as Mother*, pp. 161–62.

147. In this context it is also relevant to note that kabbalistic authors, especially in the *Zohar* and subsequent texts influenced by it, viewed masturbation and nocturnal emission as cardinal sins, for the male semen is spilled without any female receptacle to hold it. My suggestion that the peak mystical experience of union is in fact a reconstitution of the androgynous phallus does not suggest in any way a legitimation of onanism. The imaging of divine sexuality, reflecting the accepted sexual practices below, is based on the union of male and female. The issue is, however, the gender valence accorded the female in light of an androcentric and monistic ontology. What would be considered illicit sexuality in the anthropological sphere is thus transferred as the mythical structure operative in the divine sphere.

148. See the subsection "Mystical Fellowship as Constitution of the Divine Face," in *Through a Speculum That Shines*, pp. 368–77.

149. "Joseph of Hamadan's *Sefer Tashak*," p. 154.

150. B. Sanhedrin 111b.

151. "Joseph of Hamadan's *Sefer Tashak*," pp. 154–55. The phallic nature of the breasts seems to be implied in ibid., p. 280. In that context the letter *ṣaddi*, which symbolizes the attribute of the phallic *Ṣaddiq*, is applied to the "apples of the Matrona," which clearly represent the breasts. See n. 156, below.

152. Cf. the description of letter *pe* in ibid., p. 272: "The *yod* in the middle alludes to the head of the Holy One, blessed be He, and the circle that surrounds it is the secret of the knot of the phylacteries and the praying shawl (*tallit*) of the Holy One, blessed be He, above. . . . Moreover, the secret of this letter *pe* [entails] the circle that surrounds the *yod* within it, which is the Supernal Crown (*keter ᶜelyon*) that emerges from the tip of the *yod* . . . and this is the secret of the membrane that surrounds the holy head." On the image of *Keter* as the membrane that covers the head, which I assume corresponds to the corona of the penis, see n. 85, above. On the depiction of the feminine as a half-circle, or the letter *kaf*, cf. ibid., pp. 236–37. When the feminine unites with the masculine the circle becomes full and the *kaf* is

transformed into a *samekh*; cf. p. 265. The crown is also associated with a circle in the depiction of the letter *qof* in ibid., pp. 282–83. In fact, this letter symbolizes the coronation of the souls of the righteous who are represented by the line that is encircled by the crown. On the image of the *Shekhinah* as the centerpoint of the circle whence all things derive their sustenance, see, e.g., *Zohar* 1:229a–b. In that context it seems that the point in the middle of the circle, identified as the holy of holies, *qodesh qedashim*, symbolically corresponds to the clitoris, the erectile organ of the vulva that is homologous to the penis. See, however, *Zohar* 3:296b (*ʾIdraʾ Zuṭaʾ*) where it appears that the holy of holies symbolically corresponds to the vagina in which the head of the penis enters, the latter depicted as the High Priest who alone has access to the inner sanctum of the Temple. Concerning this passage, see Liebes, *Studies in the Zohar*, pp. 63–64. On the phallic description of the *Shekhinah* as the point in the middle of the circle, see especially *Book of the Pomegranate*, p. 333, where Moses de León writes: "The foundation stone whence the world is established stands in the middle. Indeed, the secret of the lower point is in the middle . . . for just as King Solomon, the secret of the median line, stands in the middle between the upper and lower waters, so too the secret of the lower point stands in the middle. When she stands in the middle she ascends in holiness." The image of ascent here signifies the transformation of the female aspect of the *Shekhinah* into the masculine. It is in light of this transformation that the lower point is the foundation stone that sustains all existence. Precisely such a dynamic underlies the following passage in a Lurianic text in MS Oxford, Bodleian Library 1741, fol. 128a:

> *Malkhut* is the secret of the point beneath *Yesod* for she was there from the time that the point came forth. When *Malkhut* ascends to receive the light that is in *Yesod* she is the single attribute comprised of ten (*middah ʾaḥat kelulah mi-yod*). When she ascends to *Neṣaḥ* and *Hod* she becomes a distinct configuration (*parṣuf ʾeḥad*). When she ascends to the chest she receives the aspects of *Keter* and she becomes a complete configuration (*parṣuf shalem*) and she is called "my sister, my beloved" (Song of Songs 5:2).

The feminine *Malkhut* becomes a complete configuration only when she ascends to the chest of the masculine and receives the aspects of *Keter*, the divine crown. Although it is not stated explicitly, I presume that this signifies the transformation of the feminine point into a crown, and more specifically the corona of the male organ. Ironically enough, it is in this posture that the description of the female beloved of Song of Songs is applied to *Malkhut*. The phallic character of the symbol of the point for *Shekhinah* is even more emphatically expressed in another work of Moses de León. Cf. J. Wijnhoven, "*Sefer ha-Mishkal*: Text and Study" (Ph.D. dissertation, Brandeis University, 1964), p. 110: "The last point is the secret of the holy phallus (*sod berit ha-qodesh*) and she stands amongst her hosts like the secret of the mid-point . . . within the circle." Cf. also passage from Moses de León's commentary on Ezekiel's vision of the chariot, MS New York, Jewish Theological Seminary of America Mic. 1805, fol. 20b, cited and discussed in Wolfson, "Woman—The Feminine as Other," pp. 199–200 n. 61.

153. On the image of the *Shekhinah* as the half-moon with a dot in the middle, cf. "Joseph of Hamadan's *Sefer Tashak*," p. 134. In that context, moreover, the connection is made between that image and the head of the court who sat with seventy members of Sanhedrin. It is evident from that passage as well that the *yod* is the corona of the penis. Cf. ibid., pp. 167–68.

154. The motif of the holy apples is employed in zoharic literature as well to refer to the three central gradations that correspond to the patriarchs. Cf. *Zohar* 2:207b. In the singular the apple can symbolize the sixth gradation, *Tif᾿eret*, which corresponds to the Holy One, blessed be He, or the divine son. Cf. *Zohar* 3:74a, 286b. Mention should also be made of a common designation of the *Shekhinah* in zoharic literature as the orchard of the holy apples. Cf. *Zohar* 1:142b, 147b, 224b; 2:12b, 60b, 84b, 88a; and 3:84a, 128b, 271a (*Piqqudin*), 292b (*᾿Idra᾿ Zuṭa᾿*). It is possible that in some contexts the image of the apples refers anatomically to the testicles. Cf. *Zohar* 2:15b, 141a (*᾿Idra᾿ Rabba᾿*). See n. 156, below.

155. "Joseph of Hamadan's *Sefer Tashak*," p. 123.

156. The gender transformation is implied in "Joseph of Hamadan's *Sefer Tashak*," p. 323: "King Solomon, may peace be upon him, said in his wisdom, 'I am a wall, my breasts are like towers' (Song of Songs 8:10), this alludes to the breasts of the Matrona that are like towers, and from these holy apples of the Matrona the righteous in the Garden of Eden and the holy angels are nourished. . . . From these breasts of the Matrona the upper and lower beings are sustained, and the holy angels and souls of the righteous draw forth from there honey and milk. Thus it is written, 'Honey and milk are under your tongue' (ibid., 4:11)." Consider Hamadan's statement on p. 124: "Those who do not nurse from the breasts of the mother nurse from the breasts of the Holy One, blessed be He. All the prophets and pious ones suck from the holy apples in the world-to-come and they are illuminated by those holy hairs that surround the holy apples." The homoerotic element here is quite evident: the prophets and the pious suck directly from the breasts of the male aspect of the divine. Although in the physical world the breasts of the woman are generally larger than those of a man (see p. 123), in the spiritual realm, designated the "world-to-come," the traditional eschatological term employed by the rabbis, it is a greater level to be nursed by the breasts of the masculine. From the context, moreover, it is clear that this sucking is the physical depiction of the spiritual state of God teaching Torah to the righteous. It is possible that in these examples the "holy apples" of the male potency symbolically represent the testicles, which are the masculine counterpart to the breasts. Precisely such a point is made by Joseph of Hamadan in the text preserved in MS Jerusalem, Mussajoff 134, fol. 124a: "It has been taught: the secret of hidden secrets concerning these holy apples of the body of the holy King, and they are like breasts. Those holy apples of the holy King

produce honey, and from the breasts of the Matrona milk is produced, as it is written, 'Honey and milk are under your tongue.' Whoever studies Torah in this world merits in his portion [in the world-to-come] to suck honey from the breasts of the holy King and milk from the breasts of the Matrona." That the holy apples of the male refer to the testicles is stated explicitly in another passage from the same composition, fol. 125a: "It has been taught: from the penis hang two apples and hanging on those [apples] are the holy hairs. . . . Therefore, those holy apples, from which are hanging those holy hairs, are like the holy skull (*moḥa*ʾ *qaddisha*ʾ) that has two membranes, the upper membrane and the lower membrane, for it is the skull for the lower ones, *Neṣaḥ* and *Hod*, for from there *Ze*ʿ*eir* ʾ*Anpin* receives and from there the upper and lower beings are blessed." The two apples thus symbolize the testicles, which correspond to *Neṣaḥ* and *Hod*, also identified as the "feet of the Holy One, blessed be He." (On fol. 130b *Neṣaḥ* and *Hod* are identified as the kidneys of the divine anthropos, but on fol. 131a they are again designated the "holy feet of the Holy One, blessed be He.") In an astonishing exegetical turn, Joseph of Hamadan interprets the first letter of Scripture, the enlarged *bet*, as a reference to these two potencies, the source of the dual Torah and the source of this world and of the world-to-come.

157. "Joseph of Hamadan's *Sefer Tashak*,", pp. 174–75. The homoerotic aspect of the mystics' communion with God is strikingly evident in the following comment of Joseph of Hamadan in MS Jerusalem, Mussajoff 134, fol. 128a: "It is written, 'And the enlightened will shine [like the splendor of the sky]' (Dan. 12:3), because they derive pleasure from the holy body (*gufa*ʾ *qaddisha*ʾ) of the Holy One, blessed be He, and they are illuminated by Him and cleave to Him, as it is written, 'and to Him shall you cleave,' verily to Him, blessed be He, and to His light." I suggest that in this passage, as is the case in other kabbalistic documents (see Liebes, *Sections of the Zohar Lexcion*, pp. 170, 178, 258–60) the word "body" signifies the male organ (cf. MS Jerusalem, Mussajoff 134, fol. 129a). It follows, therefore, that according to Joseph of Hamadan's interpretation of the critical verse from Daniel, the mystics in particular take joy in and cleave to the divine phallus.

158. See P. Berakhot 9:3, 14a, and *Genesis Rabbah* 13:13, p. 122.

159. See A. Altmann, "Gnostic Themes in Rabbinic Cosmology," in *Essays in Honour of the Very Rev. Dr. J. H. Hertz, Chief Rabbi . . . on the Occasion of His Seventieth Birthday*, ed. I. Epstein, E. Levine, and C. Roth (London, n.d.), pp. 23–24.

160. See Scholem, *On the Mystical Shape*, pp. 187–88, and Liebes, *Studies in the Zohar*, pp. 53, 185 n. 157. Although Scholem duly noted that the concept of the female waters involved the active force of the feminine, his attempt to distinguish between the zoharic and the Lurianic usage of this motif cannot be upheld. The developments that occur in the Lurianic material must be seen as exegetical transformations of the earlier passages occasioned by distinctive psychological orientations.

161. *Zohar* 1:29b.

162. Ibid., 1:60b.

163. Ibid., 1:153b.

164. Concerning this theme see E. R. Wolfson, "Forms of Visionary Ascent as Ecstatic Experience in the Zoharic Literature," in *Gershom Scholem's Major Trends in Jewish Mysticism 50 Years After*, ed. J. Dan and P. Schäfer (Tübingen, 1993), pp. 209–35.

165. *Zohar* 1:135a.

166. See E. R. Wolfson, "Images of God's Feet: Some Observations on the Divine Body in Judaism," in *People of the Body: Jewish and Judaism from an Embodied Perspective*, ed. H. Eilberg-Schwartz (Albany, 1992), pp. 143–81, and idem, "Walking as a Sacred Duty: Theological Transformation of Social Reality in Early Hasidism," in *Along the Path: Studies in Kabbalistic Myth, Symbolism, and Hermeneutics* (Albany, 1995), pp. 240–41 n. 111.

167. Cf. *Zohar* 2:127a, where the *Shekhinah* is described as the Garden of Eden that God planted "for the sake of His pleasure and His desire to take delight in it with the souls of the righteous." Cf. *Zohar* 3:79b: "Praiseworthy are the righteous for several supernal secrets are hidden for them in that world, and the Holy One, blessed be He, takes delight in them in that world." Needless to say, many more examples that depict God's taking delight with the souls of the righteous could have been cited. The significant point for this study is that the righteous are generally described in these contexts as being crowned in the Garden of Eden, a symbolic reference to the *Shekhinah*. I do not think it is incorrect to suggest that the implicit ontic significance of this symbol is that the righteous constitute the crown itself, i.e., the corona of the penis with which God takes delight.

168. For Luria's own reformulation of the zoharic conception, cf. *Shaʿar Maʾamere Rashbi* 29a and 30c. The mystical transformation of the male worshipers into the female waters through prayer is affirmed by other sixteenth-century Safedian kabbalists. Cf. Moses Cordovero, *Tefillah le-Mosheh* (Prezmysl, 1932), 69b and 112b, and idem, *Pardes Rimmonim* (Jerusalem, 1962), 8:19, 50d. The transformative quality of the supplication prayer in the thought of Cordovero and Luria has been discussed by M. Fishbane, *The Kiss of God: Spiritual and Mystical Death in Judaism* (Seattle and London, 1994), pp. 111–15. On the significance of the symbol of the male and the female waters in the various stages of the development of Lurianic kabbalah, see Meroz, "Redemption in the Lurianic Teaching," pp. 150–51, 167, 220–22, 230, 258–59, 262–63, 282–87. See also Y. Avivi, *The Kabbalah of the Gra* (Jerusalem, 1993), pp. 44–45 (in Hebrew); Y. Jacobson, "The Aspect of the Feminine in the Lurianic Kabbalah," in *Gershom Scholem's Major Trends in Jewish Mysticism 50 Years After*, ed. J. Dan and P. Schäfer (Tübingen, 1993), p. 255.

169. A *locus classicus* for the ritual of closing the eyes during prayer in kabbalistic literature is *Zohar* 3:260b, where it is connected specifically with

the prohibition of looking at the *Shekhinah.* Regarding this gesture during prayer, see E. Zimmer, "Poses and Postures during Prayer," *Sidra* 5 (1989): 92–94. On shutting the eyes as a contemplative technique in kabbalistic sources, see also M. Idel, *Studies in Ecstatic Kabbalah* (Albany, 1988), pp. 134–36. For discussion of some of the relevant sources and the reverberation of this motif in Hasidic texts, see Z. Gries, *Conduct Literature (Regimen Vitae): Its History and Place in the Life of Beshtian Hasidism* (Jerusalem, 1989), pp. 220–22 (in Hebrew).

170. *Zohar* 2:95a, 98b–99a.

171. *Sha*ʿ*ar ha-Kawwanot* (Jerusalem, 1963), 21c; cf. *Peri* ʿ*Eṣ Ḥayyim* (Jerusalem, 1980), p. 168.

172. *Sha*ʿ*ar ha-Kawwanot,* 20c. Cf. ʿ*Eṣ Ḥayyim* 39:7, 72c: "This is the secret of the unity of the reading of the *Shema*ʿ in truth, for it is already known that it is the aspect of the union of the Father and Mother in order to give *Ze*ʿ*eir* and *Nuqba*ʾ new consciousness (*moḥin ḥadashim*) so that they too will be able to unite to produce other children." Cf. Y. Avivi, "R. Joseph ibn Tabul's Sermons on the *Kawwanot,*" in *Studies in Memory of the Rishon le-Zion R. Yitzhak Nissim,* ed. M. Benayahu (Jerusalem, 1985), 4:82–83 (in Hebrew).

173. Cf. ʿ*Eṣ Ḥayyim,* 29:2, 84a, and *Sha*ʿ*ar Ma*ʾ*amere Rashbi,* 53a–b. See also *Sha*ʿ*ar ha-Kelalim,* ch. 1, p. 10.

174. Cf. ʿ*Eṣ Ḥayyim* 39:1, 65a; 49:1, 112d, and *Qehillat Ya*ʿ*aqov* (Jerusalem, 1992), p. 3.

175. *Sha*ʿ*ar Ma*ʾ*amere Rashbi,* 26b; Meroz, "Redemption in the Lurianic Teaching," pp. 258–59.

176. Cf. *Zohar* 3:120b–21a, 195b. See also *Zohar* 2:200b; *Zohar Ḥadash* 42a; *Book of the Pomegranate,* pp. 83–84; and Liebes, *Studies in the Zohar,* pp. 52–53.

177. On the death of the righteous providing the female waters that serve as a stimulus for the union above, cf. Ḥayyim Vital, *Sha*ʿ*ar ha-Gilgulim* (Jerusalem, 1981), ch. 24, pp. 176–77, and see further references below in n. 186.

178. Cf. the marginal note of Jacob Ẓemaḥ in Ḥayyim Vital, *Mavo*ʾ *She*ʿ*arim* (Jerusalem, 1892), 2:2.6, 8c. According to that passage the eyes are said to correspond to the consciousness of Knowledge that is in the head (*moaḥ ha-da*ʿ*at she-ba-ro*ʾ*sh*). Here too one sees the specific linkage of the eyes to a masculine potency, albeit displaced from the genital region of the body to the cranium. In that context the zoharic reference to the beautiful maiden without eyes is also mentioned.

179. *Sha*ʿ*ar ha-Kawwanot,* 59c.

180. In the Lurianic material one can still find evidence for the more standard kabbalistic approach to the closing of the eyes as a technique to

enhance mental concentration. See, e.g., *Shaʿar Ruaḥ ha-Qodesh* (Jerusalem, 1874), 42d, 46d; *Shaʿar ha-Kawwanot,* 4a (regarding Luria's own practice of shutting his eyes during the private and public recitation of the Eighteen Benedictions).

181. *Shaʿar Maʾamere Rashbi,* 29a.

182. The point is underscored with respect to the righteous in the following Lurianic text extant in MS Oxford-Bodleian 1551, fol. 135b: "The secret of the female waters is the merit of our prayers. . . . And also the souls of the righteous that ascend . . . they arouse these male waters, i.e., the consciousness (*moḥin*) of *Zeʿeir* and his *Nuqbaʾ*. After they arouse the male waters of *Zeʿeir* they too are called female waters in relation to the *ʾAbbaʾ* and *ʾImmaʾ*, *Yisraʾel Sabbaʾ* and *Tevunah,* which are also joined together." The principle is stated by Vital in *ʿEṣ Ḥayyim* 39:1, 66c: "When *miṣwot* and good deeds are found in Israel, through them *Zeʿeir* and *Nuqbaʾ* can unite face-to-face, and by means of them she can raise the female waters toward the male waters in the masculine. But if, God forbid, there is no merit in Israel, there is no power in the *Nuqbaʾ di-Zeʿeir ʾAnpin* to raise her female waters to her husband, for it is known that the female waters do not rise except by means of the lower souls."

183. See above, n. 91.

184. *Shaʿar ha-Kawwanot,* 46d.

185. In this context, then, the female waters comprise demonic forces, aspects of judgment, that need to be purified. Cf. *Kanfe Yonah,* MS Jerusalem, Sassoon 993, pp. 23–24, 26–27; *Shaʿar ha-Kelalim,* ch. 1, p. 10; Joseph ibn Ṭabul, *Kawwanat Beriʾat ha-ʿOlam,* MS Columbia x893/M6862, fols. 95b–96a, 114b (concerning this composition, see Meroz, "Redemption in the Lurianic Kabbalah," pp. 81–82); *ʿEṣ Ḥayyim* 39:1–2, 65a–68a; and *Mavoʾ Sheʿarim,* 2:3:9, 16d–17d. See I. Tishby, *The Doctrine of Evil and the 'Kelippah' in Lurianic Kabbalah* (Jerusalem, 1942), pp. 89–90 (in Hebrew), and Meroz, op. cit., pp. 262–63, 282–87.

186. *ʿEṣ Ḥayyim* 29:3, 21d. Cf. *Shaʿar Maʾamere Rashbi,* 17d–18a. According to that complex passage, *Zeʿeir ʾAnpin* constitutes the female waters also identified as the encompassing light (*ʾor ha-maqif*). The male is contained in the female in the secret of impregnation (*sod ha-ʿibbur*). This containment signifies the masculinization of the feminine rather than the feminization of the masculine.

187. *ʿEṣ Ḥayyim* 39:11, 76a. See Meroz, "Redemption in the Lurianic Teaching," pp. 177–78.

188. *ʿEṣ Ḥayyim* 10:3, 49a–b. A parallel to this passage is found in *Mavoʾ Sheʿarim,* 2:3:2, 12c. The latter source is cited by Jacobson, "Aspect of the Feminine," p. 251.

189. *ʿEṣ Ḥayyim,* 10:3, 48d.

190. Ibid., 49a–b.

191. *Sha ʿar ha-Haqdamot* (Jerusalem, 1909), 28c.

192. *Mavoʾ Sheʿarim*, 2:3:2, 12a. See Meroz, "Redemption in the Lurianic Teaching," pp. 244–45.

193. *ʿEṣ Ḥayyim*, 10:3, 48d.

194. *Sha ʿar ha-Kawwanot*, 18d; cf. parallel in *Peri ʿEṣ Ḥayyim*, p. 158.

195. Cf. M. Niddah 9:8.

196. *ʿEṣ Ḥayyim* 1:1, 14c.

197. *Sha ʿar ha-Kawwanot*, 105c.

198. *Yonat ʾElem*, ch. 29, 24a–b. Cf. Moses Yonah, *Kanfe Yonah*, MS Jerusalem, Sassoon 993, p. 35: "The point of *Malkhut* is now in the place of the head of *ʾArikh ʾAnpin*, for this place is her root and source. . . . Insofar as her place is in the head of *ʾArikh ʾAnpin*, we have the power through our good actions and our prayers that we pray with intention to raise *Malkhut* above until the place of the head of *ʾArikh ʾAnpin* . . . since this was the place where she was in the beginning." The elevation of *Malkhut* to the head of *ʾArikh ʾAnpin* through pious behavior is a prolepsis of the final *tiqqun*, which involves the restoration of the feminine to the masculine. The depiction of the *Shekhinah* as the corona of the phallus of Ein-Sof is expressed in earlier kabbalistic sources, which no doubt served as the basis for the Lurianic material. Consider, for example, *Tiqqune Zohar* 10, 24b: "When [the *Shekhinah*] ascends to Ein-Sof, she is the *yod* in the head of the *ʾalef*. Through what does she ascend? Through the middle column, which is a *waw*. [She is] the diadem on his head when she ascends. . . . It is said concerning her, 'a capable wife is a crown for her husband' (Prov. 12:4)." The ascent of the *Shekhinah* to Ein-Sof through *Tifʾeret* results in her transformation into the *yod* in the head of the *ʾalef*, which must be understood as the corona of the phallus. On the masculine character of *Keter* and the need to masculinize the feminine or left side, see Nathan of Gaza, "Derush ha-Taninim," in *Be-ʿIqvot Mashiaḥ*, ed. G. Scholem (Jerusalem, 1934), p. 25. On the one hand, Nathan categorically rejects the attribution of the feminine at the highest levels of the divine. Thus he states that there is no aspect of the feminine in *Keter* and therefore there is no blessing. On the other hand, he affirms precisely such an aspect, but he attempts to transform the gender dialectically from feminine to masculine. "You already know that the left side that is in *Keter* is the feminine, and the feminine is always forming, and by means of her three drops emerge, and each drop [divides] into three drops so there are the nine channels that are the vessels. . . . The drops come out from the phallus of Understanding (*yesod de-Binah*) from the right side, for since she is the feminine she brings forth from the right side in order to be contained in the secret of the male." It is of interest to note that in the same work Nathan portrays Sabbatai Ṣevi as the feet of God (based on Exod. 24:10), which in turn are identified as the "corona of the phallus of the Father" (*ʿateret yesod ʾabbaʾ*). When this aspect of the divine ascends it assumes the position of the diadem on the head of the

masculine potency (*ʿaṭeret baʿlah,* according to the locution of Prov. 12:4). The messianic figure is thus portrayed as the corona of the phallus that rises until it becomes ontically integrated into the highest realms of the Godhead. Cf. "Derush ha-Taninim," p. 16. Alternatively, Nathan relates that the revelation of the Messiah represents the restoration of the feminine to the masculine. Cf. ibid., p. 20:

> The root of the King Messiah is in the corona of the phallus of the Father (*ʿaṭeret yesod ʾabbaʾ*) . . . and the Messiah, son of David . . . his place is in *ʿAṭarah,* he is in the corona of the phallus of *Zeʿeir* (*ʿaṭeret yesod di-zeʿeir*). Therefore it says concerning him, "The crown was taken from the head of their king [and it was placed on David's head]" (2 Sam. 12:30) . . . and it says, "Mordecai left the king's presence in royal robes [of blue and white] with a magnificent crown gold" (Esther 8:15). "Mordecai left," this is the secret of the phallus of the Father (*yesod ʾabbaʾ*) that protrudes. It says a "crown of gold" (*ʿaṭeret zahav*) . . . for when the phallus of the Father goes out he takes the crown of gold . . . and when that phallus projects he contains that crown in him, according to the secret of [the verse] "I have set my bow in the clouds" (Gen. 9:13).

This text affirms the structural dynamic that I discussed in the body of the chapter: the messianic moment is marked not by the sacred union of a man and a woman, but rather by the reintegration of the feminine to the masculine, symbolically portrayed by the corona of the extended phallus. I have elaborated on this theme in a lecture, "The Rite of Sabbatai Ṣevi Coronation and Sabbatian Myth," delivered at a conference on "Myth and Ritual in Judaism," sponsored by the Skirball Department of Hebrew and Judaic Studies, New York University, October 23–24, 1994.

199. *Devarim Neḥmadim,* cited in *ʾImre Pineḥas ha-Shalem,* ed. Y. Frankel (Jerusalem, 1988), p. 41. See ibid., pp. 5–6.

◆ BIBLIOGRAPHY ◆
OF SECONDARY SOURCES

Alter, R. *Necessary Angels: Tradition and Modernity in Kafka, Benjamin, and Scholem.* Cambridge, Mass., 1991.

Altmann, A. "Gnostic Themes in Rabbinic Cosmology." In *Essays In honour of the Very Rev. Dr. J. H. Hertz, Chief Rabbi . . . On the Occasion of His Seventieth Birthday,* edited by I. Epstein, E. Levine, and C. Roth, 19–32. London, n.d.

———. *Studies in Religious Philosophy and Mysticism.* Ithaca, 1969.

Aminoff, I. "The Figures of Esau and the Kingdom of Edom in Palestinian Midrashic-Talmudic Literature in the Tannaitic and Amoraic Periods." Ph.D. dissertation, Melbourne University, 1981.

Anderson, G. "Celibacy or Consummation in the Garden? Reflections on Early Jewish and Christian Interpretations of the Garden of Eden." *Harvard Theological Review* 82 (1989): 121–48.

Assis, Y. "Sexual Behaviour in Mediaeval Hispano-Jewish Society." In *Jewish History: Essays in Honour of Chimen Abramsky,* edited by A. Rapoport-Albert and S. J. Zipperstein, 25–60. London, 1988.

Atkinson, C. W. *The Oldest Vocation: Christian Motherhood in the Middle Ages.* Ithaca and London, 1991.

Avivi, Y. *The Kabbalah of the Gra.* Jerusalem, 1993. In Hebrew.

Baer, Y. *A History of Jews in Christian Spain.* Translated by L. Schoffmann, 2 vols. Philadelphia, 1978.

Barthes, R. *The Pleasure of the Text.* Translated by R. Miller. New York, 1975.

Benko, S. *The Virgin Goddess: Studies in the Pagan and Christian Roots of Mariology.* Leiden, 1993.

Ben-Shlomo, J. *The Mystical Theology of Moses Cordovero.* Jerusalem, 1965. In Hebrew.

Biale, D. *Eros and the Jews: From Biblical Israel to Contemporary America.* New York, 1992.

———. *Gershom Scholem Kabbalah and Counter-History.* Cambridge, Mass. and London, 1979.

———. "The God with Breasts: El Shaddai in the Bible." *History of Religions* 20 (1982): 240–56.

Bird, P. A. "Sexual Differentiation and Divine Image in the Genesis Creation Texts." In *Image of God and Gender Models in Judaeo-Christian Tradition,* edited by K. E. Børresen, 11–34. Oslo, 1991.

Blau, L. *Das Altjüdische Zauberwesen.* Budapest, 1898.

Bloch, R. H. *Medieval Misogyny and the Invention of Western Romantic Love.* Chicago and London, 1991.

Borgen, P. *Bread from Heaven: An Exegetical Study of the Concept of Manna in the Gospel of John and the Writings of Philo.* Leiden, 1965.

———. "Paul Preaches Circumcision and Pleases Men." In *Paul and Paulinism: Essays in Honour of C. K. Barrett,* edited by M. D. Hooker and S. G. Wilson, 37–46. London, 1982.

Boyarin, D. *Carnal Israel: Reading Sex in Talmudic Culture.* Berkeley, Los Angeles, and Oxford, 1993.

Boylan, M. "The Galenic and Hippocratic Challenge to Aristotle's Conception Theory." *Journal of the History of Biology* 17 (1984): 83–112.

Bozarth-Campbell, A. *The Word's Body: An Incarnational Aesthetic of Interpretation.* University, Alabama, 1979.

Brandon, S. G. F. *Creation Legends of the Ancient Near East.* London, 1963.

Brisson, L. "Neutrum utrumque: La bisexualité dans l'antiquité gréco-romaine." In *L'Androgyne,* 27–61. Paris, 1986.

Brown, P. *The Body and Society: Men, Women, and Sexual Renunciation in Early Christianity*. New York, 1988.

Bynum, C. W. "'. . . And Woman His Humanity': Female Imagery in the Religious Writing of the Later Middle Ages." In *Gender and Religion: On the Complexity of Symbols*, edited by C. W. Bynum, S. Harrell, and P. Richman, 257–88. Boston, 1986.

———. "Introduction: The Complexity of Symbols." In *Gender and Religion: On the Complexity of Symbols*, edited by C. W. Bynum, S. Harrell, and P. Richman, 1–20. Boston, 1986.

———. *Jesus as Mother: Studies in the Spirituality of the High Middle Ages*. Berkeley, 1982.

Cadden, J. *Meaning of Sex Difference in the Middle Ages: Medicine, Science, and Culture*. Cambridge and New York, 1993.

Carruthers, M. *The Book of Memory: A Study of Memory in Medieval Culture*. Cambridge and New York, 1990.

Clark, R. T. R. *Myth and Symbol in Ancient Egypt*. London, 1959.

Cohen, G. D. "Esau as a Symbol in Early Medieval Thought." In *Jewish Medieval and Renaissance Studies*, edited by A. Altmann, 19–48. Cambridge, Mass., 1967.

Cohen, J. *"Be Fertile and Increase, Fill the Earth and Master It": The Ancient and Medieval Career of a Biblical Text*. Ithaca and London, 1989.

———. "Rationales for Conjugal Sex in RaABaD's *Ba'alei ha-nefesh*." *Jewish History* 6 (1992): 65–78.

Cohen-Alloro, D. *The Secret of the Garment in the Zohar*. Jerusalem, 1987. In Hebrew.

Conzelmann, H. "The Mother of Wisdom." In *The Future of Our Religious Past*, edited by J. M. Robinson, 230–43. New York, 1971.

Corbin, H. *Face de Dieu, face de l'homme: Herméneutique et soufisme*. Paris, 1983.

———. *Temple and Contemplation*. Translated by P. Sherrard with the assistance of L. Sherrard. London, 1986.

Dan, J. *The Esoteric Theology of German Pietism*. Jerusalem, 1968. In Hebrew.

———. *Hebrew Ethical and Homiletical Literature.* Jerusalem, 1975. In Hebrew.

Daniélou, J. *Théologie du Judéo-Christianisme,* 2nd edition. Paris, 1991.

Delcourt, M. *Hermaphrodite: mythes et rites de la bisexualité dans l'antiquité classique.* Paris, 1958.

Delling, G. "The 'One Who Sees God' in Philo." In *Nourished with Peace: Studies in Hellenistic Judaism in Memory of Samuel Sandmel,* edited by F. Greenspahn, E. Hilgert, and B. Mack, 27–49. Chico, Ca., 1984.

Derrida, J. *Glas.* Paris, 1974.

———. *Of Grammatology.* Translated by G. Chakravorty Spivak. Baltimore and London, 1976.

———. "Shibboleth." In *Midrash and Literature,* edited by G. Hartman and S. Budick, 307–47. New Haven, 1986.

———. *Writing and Difference.* Translated by A. Bass. Chicago and London, 1978.

Dilcher, G. "Oralität, Verschriftlichung und Wandlungen der Normstruktur in den Stadtrechten des 12. und 13. Jahrhunderts." In *Pragmatische Schriftlichkeit im Mittelalter: Erscheinungsformen und Entwicklungsstufen,* edited by H. Keller, K. Grubmüller and N. Staubach, 9–19. Munich, 1992.

Drower, E. S. *The Mandaeans of Iraq and Iran.* Leiden, 1962.

Dubois, P. *Sowing the Body: Psychoanalysis and Ancient Representations of Women.* Chicago and London, 1988.

Elior, R. "The Metaphorical Relation between God and Man and the Significance of the Visionary Reality in Lurianic Kabbalah." *Jerusalem Studies in Jewish Thought* 10 (1992): 47–58. In Hebrew.

Eppel, R. "Les tables de la Loi et les tables célestes." *Revue d'Histoire et de Philosophie Religieuse* 17 (1937): 401–12.

Eppel R. and H. Bietenhard. *Die himmlische Welt im Urchristentum und Spät judentum.* Tübingen, 1951.

Epstein, J. and K. Straub, "Introduction: The Guarded Body." In *Body Guards: The Cultural Politics of Gender Ambiguity,* 1–28. New York and London, 1991.

Farber, A. "The Concept of the Merkabah in Thirteenth-Century Jewish Esotericism—'Sod ha-ʾEgoz' and Its Development." Ph.D. dissertation, Hebrew University, 1986. In Hebrew.

———. "On the Sources of Rabbi Moses de León's Early Kabbalistic System." In *Studies in Jewish Mysticism, Philosophy and Ethical Literature,* edited by J. Dan and J. Hacker, 67–96. In Hebrew.

Fenton, P. "La Hierarchie des saints dans la mystique juive et dans la mystique islamique." In *ʿAlei Shefer: Studies in the Literature of Jewish Thought Presented to Rabbi Dr. Alexandre Safran,* edited by M. Ḥallamish, 49–73. Bar-Ilan, 1990.

Fiorenza, E. S. "Wisdom Mythology and Christological Hymns." In *Aspects of Wisdom in Judaism and Early Christianity,* edited by R. Wilkens, 29–33. Notre Dame, 1975.

Fischel, H. A. "The Transformation of Wisdom in the World of Midrash." In *Aspects of Wisdom in Judaism and Early Christianity,* edited by R. Wilkens, 70–82. Notre Dame, 1975.

Fishbane, M. *The Kiss of God: Spiritual and Mystical Death in Judaism.* Seattle and London, 1994.

Fishman, T. "A Kabbalistic Perspective on Gender-Specific Commandments: On the Interplay of Symbols and Society." *AJS Review* 17 (1992):199–245.

Fleischer, E. *Hebrew Liturgical Poetry in the Middle Ages.* Jerusalem, 1975. In Hebrew.

Fossum, J. E. *The Name of God and the Angel of the Lord.* Tübingen, 1985.

Freud, S. *The Complete Introductory Lectures on Psychoanalysis,* translated and edited by J. Strachey. New York, 1966.

———. *The Interpretation of Dreams,* translated and edited by J. Strachey. New York, 1965.

Gershenzon, S. "The Circle Metaphor in Leone Ebreo's *Dialoghi D'Amore.*" *Daʿat* 29 (1992): v–xvii. English section.

Ginsburg, E. K. *The Sabbath in the Classical Kabbalah.* Albany, 1989.

Ginzberg, L. *The Legends of the Jews.* Philadephia, 1968.

Glück, H. *Schrift und Schriftlichkeit: Eine sprach-und Kulturwissenschaftiche Studie.* Stuttgart, 1987.

Goldberg, H. E. "Torah and Children: Some Symbolic Aspects of the Reproduction of Jews and Judaism." In *Judaism Viewed from Within and from Without: Anthropological Studies,* edited by H. E. Goldberg, 111–18. Albany, 1987.

Goldziher, I. "Mélanges Judéo-Arabes." *Revue des études juives* 50 (1905):188–90.

Gottlieb, E. *The Kabbalah in the Writings of R. Baḥya ben Asher ibn Halawa*. Jerusalem, 1970. In Hebrew.

———. *Studies in the Kabbala Literature*. Edited by J. Hacker. Tel-Aviv, 1976. In Hebrew.

Graham, W. A. *Beyond the Written Word: Oral Aspects of Scripture in the History of Religion*. Cambridge and New York, 1987.

Grant, R. M. "The Mystery of Marriage in the Gospel of Philip." *Vigiliae Christianae* 15 (1961):129–40.

Green, A. "Bride, Spouse, Daughter: Images of the Feminine in Classical Jewish Sources." In *On Being a Jewish Feminist*, edited by S. Heschel, 248–60. New York, 1983.

Gries, Z. *Conduct Literature (Regimen Vitae): Its History and Place in the Life of Beshtian Hasidism*. Jerusalem, 1989. In Hebrew.

Grözinger, K. E. "The Names of God and Their Celestial Powers: Their Function and Meaning in Hekhalot Literature." *Jerusalem Studies in Jewish Thought* 6:1–2 (1987): 53–69. English section.

Gruenwald, I. "A Preliminary Critical Edition of Sefer Yeẓira." *Israel Oriental Studies* 1 (1971): 132–77.

———. "Some Critical Notes on the First Part of Sefer Yeẓira." *Revue des études juives* 132 (1973): 475–512.

Guberman, K. "The Language of Love in Spanish Kabbalah: An Examination of the ʾ*Iggeret ha-Kodesh*." In *Approaches to Judaism in Medieval Times*, edited by D. R. Blumenthal, 1:53–95. Chico, Calif., 1984.

Halperin, D. J. "A Sexual Image in Hekhalot Rabbati and Its Implications." *Jerusalem Studies in Jewish Thought* 6:1–2 (1987): 117–32. English section.

———. *The Faces of the Chariot: Early Jewish Responses to Ezekiel's Vision*. Tübingen, 1988.

———. *The Merkabah in Rabbinic Literature*. New Haven, 1980.

Handelman, S. *The Slayers of Moses: The Emergence of Rabbinic Interpretation in Modern Literary Theory*. Albany, 1982.

Hanna, J. L. *Dance, Sex and Gender: Signs of Identity, Dominance, Defiance, and Desire*. Chicago and London, 1988.

Harpham, G. *The Ascetic Imperative in Culture and Criticism*. Chicago and London, 1987.

Harris, M. "Marriage as Metaphysics: A Study of the ʾ*Iggeret ha-Kodesh.*" *Hebrew Union College Annual* 33 (1962):197–220.

Harris, R. *The Origin of Writing.* La Salle, 1986.

———. "Quelques réflexions sur la tyrannie de l'alphabet." In *L'écriture: le cerveau, l'œil et la main,* edited by C. Sirat, J. Irigoin, and E. Poulle. Brepols, Turnhout, 1990.

Hayman, P. "Was God a Magician? Sefer Yeṣira and Jewish Magic." *Journal of Jewish Studies* 40 (1989): 225–37.

Hecht, R. "The Exegetical Contexts of Philo's Interpretation of Circumcision." In *Nourished with Peace: Studies in Hellenistic Judaism in Memory of Samuel Sandmel,* edited by F. Greenspahn, E. Hilgert, and B. Mack, 51–79. Chico, Calif., 1984.

Hengel, M. *Judaism and Hellenism: Studies in Their Encounter in Palestine During the Early Hellenistic Period.* Translated by J. Bowden, 2 vols. Philadelphia, 1974.

Holdrege, B. A. *Veda and Torah: Transcending the Textuality of Scripture.* Albany, 1995.

Huss, B. "The Doctrine of *Sefirot* in the *Ketem Paz* of Simeon Lavi." *Peʿamim* 43 (1990):51–84. In Hebrew.

———. "*Genizat Ha-Or* in Simeon Lavi's *Ketem Paz* and the Lurianic Doctrine of *Ẓimẓum.*" *Jerusalem Studies in Jewish Thought* 10 (1992): 341–62. In Hebrew.

Idel, M. "Additional Fragments from the Writings of R. Joseph of Hamadan." *Daʿat* 21 (1988): 47–55. In Hebrew.

———. "Between the Kabbalah of Jerusalem and the Kabbalah of R. Israel Sarug (Sources for the Doctrine of Malbush of R. Israel Sarug)," *Shalem* 6 (1992): 165–73. In Hebrew.

———. "The Commentary on the Ten *Sefirot* and Fragments from the Writings of R. Joseph of Hamadan," *Alei Sefer* 6–7 (1979): 74–84. In Hebrew.

———. "The Concept of Torah in the Hekhalot and Its Metamorphosis in the Kabbalah." *Jerusalem Studies in Jewish Thought* 1 (1981): 23–84. In Hebrew.

———. *Golem: Jewish Magical and Mystical Traditions on the Artificial Anthropoid.* Albany, 1990.

———. "The Image of Adam above the *Sefirot.*" *Daʿat* 4 (1980): 41–55. In Hebrew.

———. "Infinities of Torah in Kabbalah." In *Midrash and Literature,* edited by G. Hartman and S. Budick, 141–57. New Haven and London, 1986.

———. "Jewish Kabbalah and Platonism in the Middle Ages and Renaissance." In *Neoplatonism and Jewish Thought,* edited by L. E. Goodman, 319–51. Albany, 1992.

———. "Judah Moscato: A Late Renaissance Jewish Preacher." In *Preachers of the Italian Ghetto,* edited by D. B. Ruderman. Berkeley, 1992.

———. *Kabbalah: New Perspectives.* New Haven and London, 1988.

———. "Kabbalistic Materials from the School of R. David ben Yehudah he-Ḥasid," *Jerusalem Studies in Jewish Thought* 2 (1982–83):169–207. In Hebrew.

———. *Language, Torah, and Hermeneutics in Abraham Abulafia.* Albany, 1989.

———. "Maimonides and Kabbalah." In *Studies in Maimonides,* edited by I. Twersky, 31–81. Cambridge, Mass., and London, 1991.

———. "Métaphores et pratiques sexueles dans la cabale." In Ch. Mopsik, *Lettre sur la sainteté: le secret de la relation entre l'homme et la femme dans la cabale,* 329–58. Paris, 1986. English version in *The Jewish Family: Metaphor and Memory,* edited by D. Kraemer, 197–224. New York and Oxford, 1989.

———. *The Mystical Experience in Abraham Abulafia.* Albany, 1988.

———. "On the Concept *Ẓimẓum* in Kabbalah and Its Research." *Jerusalem Studies in Jewish Thought* 10 (1992): 59–112. In Hebrew.

———. "Reification of Language in Jewish Mysticism." In *Mysticism and Language,* edited by S. T. Katz, 42–79. New York and Oxford, 1992.

———. "The *Sefirot* above the *Sefirot.*" *Tarbiz* 51 (1982): 239–80. In Hebrew.

———. *Studies in Ecstatic Kabbalah.* Albany, 1988.

———. "We Have No Kabbalistic Tradition on This." In *Rabbi Moses Naḥmanides: Explorations in His Religious and Literary Virtuosity,* edited by I. Twersky, 51–73. Cambridge, Mass., 1983.

Izutsu, T. *God and Man in the Koran: Semantics of the Koranic Weltanschauung.* Tokyo, 1964.

Jacobs, L. *Hasidic Prayer.* New York, 1972.

Jacobson, Y. "The Aspect of the Feminine in the Lurianic Kabbalah." In *Gershom Scholem's Major Trends in Jewish Mysticism 50 Years After,* edited by J. Dan and P. Schäfer, 239–55. Tübingen, 1993.

Jaffee, M. S. "How Much 'Orality' in Oral Torah? New Perspectives on the Composition and Transmission of Early Rabbinic Tradition." *Shofar* 10 (1992): 53–72.

Janowitz, N. *The Poetics of Ascent: Theories of Language in a Rabbinic Ascent Text.* Albany, 1989.

Jay, M. *Downcast Eyes: The Denigration of Vision in Twentieth-Century French Thought.* Berkeley, Los Angeles, and London, 1993.

Jellinek, A. *Philosophie und Kabbala.* Leipzig, 1854.

Jospe, R. "The Superiority of Oral Over Written Communication: Judah Ha-Levi's *Kuzari* and Modern Jewish Thought." In *From Ancient Israel to Modern Judaism Intellect in Quest of Understanding: Essays in Honor of Marvin Fox,* edited by J. Neusner, E. S. Frerichs, and N. M. Sarna, 3:127–55. Atlanta, 1989.

Kallus, M. "Two Mid-Thirteenth Century Texts from the ᶜIyyun Circle." M.A. thesis, Hebrew University, 1992.

Kelber, W. H. *The Oral and the Written Gospel: The Hermeneutics of Speaking and Writing in the Synoptic Tradition, Mark, Paul, and Q.* Philadelphia, 1983.

Keller, H. "Pragmatische Schriftlichkeit im Mittelalter. Erscheinungsformen und Entwicklungsstufen. Einführung zum Kooquium in Münster, 17–19, Mai 1989." In *Pragmatische Schriftlichkeit im Mittelalter: Erscheinungsformen und Entwicklungsstufen,* edited by H. Keller, K. Grubmüller, and N. Staubach. Munich, 1992.

Kirshenblatt-Gimblett, B. "The Cut That Binds: The Western Ashkenazic Torah Binder as Nexus between Circumcision and Torah." In *Celebration: Studies in Festivity and Ritual,* edited by V. Turner, 136–46. Washington, D.C., 1982.

Klijn, A. J. "The 'Single One' in the Gospel of Thomas." *Journal of Biblical Literature* 81 (1962): 271–78.

Koep, L. *Das himmlische Buch in Antike und Christentum.* Bonn, 1952.

Krell, D. F. *Of Memory, Reminiscence, and Writing: On the Verge.* Bloomington and Indianapolis, 1990.

Landshuth, L. *ʿAmude ha-ʿAvodah Reshimat Roshe ha-Payyṭanim u-Meʿaṭ mi-Toldotehem ʿal Seder ʾAlfaʾ Betaʾ ʿim Mispar Piyyuṭehem ha-Nimṣaʾim be-Sifre Tefillot.* Berlin, 1857.

Lang, B. *Wisdom and the Book of Proverbs: An Israelite Goddess Redefined.* New York, 1986.

Langer, G. *Die Erotik der Kabbala.* Preface by P. Orban. Munich, 1989.

Laporte, J. "Philo in the Tradition of Biblical Wisdom Literature." In *Aspects of Wisdom in Judaism and Early Christianity,* edited by R. Wilkens. Notre Dame, 1975.

Laqueur, W. *Making Sex: Body and Gender from the Greeks to Freud.* Cambridge, Mass., 1990.

Leitch, V. B. *Deconstructive Criticism: An Advanced Introduction.* New York, 1983.

Leupin, A. *Barbarolexis Medieval Writing and Sexuality.* Translated by K. M. Cooper. Cambridge, Mass., and London, 1989.

Levin, D. M. *The Body's Recollection of Being: Phenomenological Psychology and the Deconstruction of Nihilism.* London, 1985.

Liebes, Y. "The Messiah of the Zohar." In *The Messianic Idea in Jewish Thought: A Study Conference in Honour of the Eightieth Birthday of Gershom Scholem,* 87–236. Jerusalem, 1982. In Hebrew.

———. "Rabbi Solomon Ibn Gabirol's Use of Sefer Yeṣira and a Commentary on the Poem 'I Love Thee,' " *Jerusalem Studies in Jewish Thought* 6:3–4 (1987): 73–124. In Hebrew.

———. *Sections of the Zohar Lexicon.* Jerusalem, 1976. In Hebrew.

———. *Studies in Jewish Myth and Jewish Messianism.* Translated by B. Stein. Albany, 1992.

———. *Studies in the Zohar.* Translated by A. Schwartz, S. Nakache, and P. Peli. Albany, 1993.

———. "Towards a Study of the Author of *Emek ha-Melekh*: His Personality, Writings and Kabbalah," *Jerusalem Studies in Jewish Thought* 11 (1993):101–37. In Hebrew.

———. "Tsaddiq Yesod Olam—A Sabbatian Myth." *Daʿat* 1 (1978): 73–120. In Hebrew.

———. " 'Two Young Roes of a Doe': The Secret Sermon of Isaac Luria before His Death." *Jerusalem Studies in Jewish Thought* 10 (1992): 113–69. In Hebrew.

Lipiner, E. *The Metaphysics of the Hebrew Alphabet.* Jerusalem, 1989. In Hebrew.

Loraux, N. "What Is a Goddess?" In *A History of Women in the West: I. From Ancient Goddesses to Christian Saints,* edited by P. Schmitt Pantel and translated by A. Goldhammer, 11–44. Cambridge, Mass., and London, 1992.

Lorry, P. *Alchemie et mystique en terre d'Islam.* Paris, 1989.

Mack, B. L. *Logos und Sophia.* Göttingen, 1977.

MacRae, G. "The Jewish Background of the Gnostic Sophia Myth." *Novum Testamentum* 12 (1970): 86–101.

Marcovich, M. "The Wedding Hymn of Acta Thomae," *Illinois Classical Studies* 6 (1981): 367–85, reprinted in *Studies in Graeco-Roman Religions and Gnosticism,* 156–73. Leiden, 1988.

Martin, H.-J. *Histoire et pouvoirs de l'écrit.* Avec la collaboration de B. Delmas, préface de Pierre Chauni de l'Institut. Paris, 1988.

Matt, D. *Zohar: The Book of Enlightenment.* New York, 1983.

Meroz, R. "Early Lurianic Compositions." In *Massuʾot: Studies in Kabbalistic Literature and Jewish Philosophy in Memory of Prof. Ephraim Gottlieb,* edited by M. Oron and A. Goldreich, 311–38. Jerusalem, 1994. In Hebrew.

———. "Redemption in the Lurianic Teaching." Ph.D. dissertation, Hebrew University, 1988. In Hebrew.

———. "R. Yisrael Sarug—Luria's Disciple: A Research Controversy Reconsidered." *Daʿat* 28 (1992): 41–50. In Hebrew.

Meyer, M. W. "Making Mary Male: The Categories 'Male' and 'Female' in the Gospel of Thomas." *New Testament Studies* 31 (1985): 554–70.

Meyer, R. *Tradition und Neuschöpfung im antiken Judentum.* Tübingen, 1965.

Miller, J. *Measures of Wisdom: The Cosmic Dance in Classical and Christian Antiquity.* Toronto, 1986.

Mollenkott, V. R. *The Divine Feminine.* New York, 1983.

Mopsik, Ch. "The Body of Engenderment in the Hebrew Bible, the Rabbinic Tradition and the Kabbalah." In *Zone: Fragments for a History of the Human Body,* edited by M. Feher, R. Naddaff, and N. Tazi, 48–73. New York, 1989.

———. *Le Secret du marriage de David et Bethsabée.* Paris, 1994.

———. *Les Grands textes de la Cabale: les rites qui font dieu.* Paris, 1992.

———. *Lettre sur la sainteté: le secret de la relation entre l'homme et la femme dans la cabale.* Paris, 1986.

Mordell, P. *The Origin of Letters and Numerals according to the Sefer Yeẓirah.* Philadelphia, 1914.

Neumann, E. *The Great Mother: An Analysis of an Archetype.* Translated by R. Manheim, 2nd ed. Princeton, 1963.

———. *The Origins and History of Consiousness.* Foreword by C. G. Jung and translated by R. F. C. Hull. Princeton, 1954.

Neusner, J. *Midrash in Context.* Philadelphia, 1984.

———. *Torah: From Scroll to Symbol in Formative Judaism.* Philadelphia, 1985.

Nickelsburg, G. W. E. "Stories of Biblical and Early Post-Biblical Times." In *Jewish Writings of the Second Temple Period,* edited by M. E. Stone. Philadelphia, 1984.

Ong, W. J. *Ora'ity and Literacy: The Technologizing of the Word.* London, 1982.

———. *The Presence of the Word: Some Prolegomena for Cultural and Religious History.* Minneapolis, 1967.

Oron, M. "The Narrative of the Letters and Its Source: A Study of a Zoharic Midrash on the Letters of the Alphabet." In *Studies in Jewish Mysticism, Philosophy and Ethical Literature Presented to Isaiah Tishby on His Seventy-Fifth Birthday,* edited by J. Dan and J. Hacker, 97–109. Jerusalem, 1986. In Hebrew.

Pachter, M. "Circles and Straightness: A History of an Idea." *Daʿat* 18 (1987): 59–90. In Hebrew.

Parks, W. "The Textualization of Orality in Literary Criticism." In *Vox intexta: Orality and Textuality in the Middle Ages,* edited by A. N. Doane and C. B. Pasternack, 46–61. Madison, 1991.

Partner, N. F. "No Sex, No Gender." In *Studying Medieval Women: Sex, Gender, Feminism,* edited by N. F. Partner, 117–41. Cambridge, Mass., 1993.

Preus, A. "Galen's Criticism of Aristotle's Conception Theory." *Journal of the History of Biology* 10 (1977): 65–85.

Reeves, J. C. *Jewish Lore in Manichaean Cosmogony: Studies in the Book of Giants Traditions.* Cincinnati, 1992.

Reif, S. C. "Aspects of Medieval Jewish Literacy." In *The Uses of Literacy in Early Mediaeval Europe*, edited by R. McKitterick, 134–55. Cambridge and New York, 1990.

Robb, K., ed. *Language and Thought in Early Greek Philosophy.* La Salle, 1983.

Robinson, J. M. "Jesus as Sophos and Sophia." In *Aspects of Wisdom in Judaism and Early Christianity*, edited by R. Wilkens, 1–16. Notre Dame, 1975.

Roth, N. " 'Deal Gently with the Young Man': Love of Boys in Medieval Hebrew Poetry of Spain." *Speculum* 57 (1982): 33–59.

Saperstein, M. *Decoding the Rabbis: A Thirteenth-Century Commentary on the Aggadah.* Cambridge, Mass., 1980.

Schäfer, P., ed. *Geniza-Fragmente zur Hekhalot-Literature.* Tübingen, 1984.

———. ed. *Synopse zur Hekhalot-Literatur.* Tübingen, 1982.

Schatz Uffenheimer, R. *Hasidism as Mysticism: Quietistic Elements in Eighteenth Century Hasidic Thought.* Translated by J. Chipman. Princeton, 1993.

Schechter, S. *Aspects of Rabbinic Theology.* New York, 1961.

Scheindlin, R. P. *Wine, Women, and Death: Medieval Hebrew Poems of the Good Life.* Philadelphia, 1986.

Schiffman, L. H. *Who Was a Jew? Rabbinic and Halakhic Perspectives on the Jewish-Christian Schism.* Hoboken, N.J., 1985.

Schiffman, L. H. and M. D. Swartz, *Hebrew and Aramaic Incantation Texts from the Cairo Genizah.* Sheffield, 1992.

Schimmel, A. *Mystical Dimensions of Islam.* Chapel Hill, N.C., 1975.

Scholem, G. "The Authentic Writings of the Ari in Kabbalah," *Kiryat Sefer* 19 (1942): 184–99. In Hebrew.

———. "Colours and Their Symbolism in Jewish Tradition and Mysticism." *Diogenes* 109 (1980): 64–76.

———. *Das Buch Bahir.* Leipzig, 1923.

———. "Did the Ramban Write the *ʾIggeret ha-Qodesh?*" *Kiryat Sefer* 21 (1944–45): 179–86. In Hebrew.

———. *Explications and Implications: Writings on Jewish Heritage and Renaissance.* Edited by A. Shapira, 2 vols. Tel-Aviv, 1989. In Hebrew.

———. *Jewish Gnosticism, Merkabah Mysticism and Talmudic Tradition.* New York, 1965.

———. *Kabbalah.* Jerusalem, 1974.

———. *The Kabbalah in Provence,* edited by R. Schatz. Jerusalem, 1970. In Hebrew.

———. *The Kabbalah of Sefer Temunah and R. Abraham Abulafiah,* edited by J. Ben-Shlomo. Jerusalem, 1987. In Hebrew.

———. *Kitve Yad ba-Qabbalah.* Jerusalem, 1930.

———. "La Lutte entre le Dieu de Plotin et la Bible dans la kabbale ancienne." In *Le Nom de Dieu et les symboles de Dieu dans la mystique juive.* Translated by M. Hayoun and G. Vajda, 17–53. Paris, 1983.

———. *Major Trends in Jewish Mysticism.* New York, 1954.

———. "Meqorotav shel maᶜaseh R. Gadiʾel ha-Tinoq be-Sifrut ha-Qabbalah." In *Le-ʾAgnon Shai,* edited by D. Sadan and E. E. Urbach, 289–305. Jerusalem, 1959.

———. "The Name of God and the Linguistic Theory of the Kabbala." *Diogenes* 79 (1972): 59–80; *Diogenes* 80 (1972):164–94.

———. "On the Devlopment of the Concept of Worlds in the Early Kabbalah." *Tarbiz* 3 (1931): 33–66. In Hebrew.

———. *On the Kabbalah and Its Symbolism.* Translated by R. Manheim. New York, 1969.

———. *On the Mystical Shape of the Godhead.* Translated by J. Neugroschel and edited by J. Chipman. New York, 1991.

———. *Origins of the Kabbalah.* Translated by A. Arkush and edited R. J. Zwi Werblowsky. Princeton, 1987.

———. *Reshit ha-Qabbalah.* Tel-Aviv, 1948.

Scholes, R. *Semiotics and Interpretation.* New Haven and London, 1982.

Sirat, C. *La lettre hébraïque et sa signification.* Avec L. Avrin. Paris and Jerusalem, 1981.

———. "Par l'oreille et par l'œil: La Bible hébraïque et les livres qui la portent." In *The Frank Talmage Memorial Volume*, edited by B. Walfish, 1:233–49. Haifa, 1993.

Slomovic, E. "Patterns of Midrashic Impact on the Rabbinic Midrashic Tale." *Journal for the Study of Judaism* 19 (1988): 76–83.

Smalley, B. *The Study of the Bible in the Middle Ages*. Notre Dame, 1964.

Smith, J. Z. "Fences and Neighbors." In *Approaches to Ancient Judaism*, edited by W. S. Green, 2:9–15. Chico, Calif., 1980.

Sperber, D. "On Sealing the Abysses." *Journal of Semitic Studies* 11 (1966):168–74.

Stern, M. *Greek and Latin Authors on Jews and Judaism*. 3 vols. Jerusalem, 1976–1980.

Stock, B. *The Implications of Literacy: Written Language and Models of Interpretation in the Eleventh and Twelfth Centuries*. Princeton, 1983.

———. *Listening for the Text: On the Uses of the Past*. Baltimore and London, 1990.

Suleiman, S. R. "(Re)Writing the Body: The Politics and Poetics of Female Eroticism." In *The Female Body in Western Culture: Contemporary Perspectives*, edited by S. R. Suleiman, 7–29. Cambridge, Mass., and London, 1985.

Talmage, F. "Apples of Gold: The Inner Meaning of Sacred Texts in Medieval Judaism." In *Jewish Spirituality from the Bible through the Middle Ages*, edited by A. Green, 313–55. New York, 1986.

Tishby, I. *The Doctrine of Evil and the 'Kelippah' in Lurianic Kabbalah*. Jerusalem, 1942. In Hebrew.

———. " 'The Holy One, blessed be He, the Torah, and Israel are One': The Source of a Saying in the Commentary of Ramhal on the Idra Rabba." *Kiryat Sefer* 50 (1975): 480–92, 668–74. In Hebrew.

———. *The Wisdom of the Zohar*. Translated by D. Goldstein. Oxford, 1989.

Urbach, E. E. *The Sages: Their Concepts and Beliefs*. Jerusalem, 1978. In Hebrew.

Verman, M. *The Books of Contemplation: Medieval Jewish Mystical Sources.* Albany, 1992.

———. "Classifying the Ḥug ha-Iyyun." In the *Proceedings of the Tenth World Congress of Jerusalem Studies,* Division C, Volume 1: Jewish Thought and Literature (1990): 57–64.

Vermes, G. *Scripture and Tradition in Judaism.* Leiden, 1983.

Vogt, K. " 'Becoming Male': A Gnostic and Early Christian Metaphor." In *Image of God and Gender Models in Judaeo-Christian Tradition,* edited by K. E. Børresen, 172–87. Oslo, 1991.

Waite, A. E. *The Holy Kabbalah.* Introduction by K. Rexroth. Secaucus, N.J., 1975.

Wasserstrom, S. "Sefer Yeṣira and Early Islam: A Reappraisal." *Journal of Jewish Thought and Philosophy* 3 (1993): 1–30.

Weigle, M. *Creation and Procreation: Feminist Reflections on Mythologies of Cosmogony and Parturition.* Philadelphia, 1989.

Weiss, J. *Studies in Eastern European Jewish Mysticism,* edited by D. Goldstein. Oxford, 1985.

Werblowsky, R. J. Zwi. *Joseph Karo: Lawyer and Mystic.* Philadelphia, 1977.

Widengren, G. *The Ascension of the Apostle and the Heavenly Book.* Upsala, 1950.

Wijnhoven, J. "The Zohar and the Proselyte." In *Texts and Responses: Studies Presented to Nahum N. Glatzer on the Occasion of His Seventieth Birthday,* edited by M. Fishbane and P. Flohr, 269–332. Leiden, 1975.

Wilckens, U. *Weisheit und Torheit.* Tübingen, 1959.

Wirszubski, Ch. *Pico della Mirandola's Encounter with Jewish Mysticism.* Cambridge, Mass., and London, 1989.

Wolfson, E. R. *Along the Path: Studies in Kabbalistic Myth, Symbolism, and Hermeneutics.* Albany, 1995.

———. "Anthropomorphic Imagery and Letter Symbolism in the *Zohar.*" *Jerusalem Studies in Jewish Thought* 8 (1989): 85–111. In Hebrew.

———. "Beautiful Maiden without Eyes: *Peshaṭ* and *Sod* in Zoharic Hermeneutics." In *The Midrashic Imagination,* edited by M. Fishbane, 155–203. Albany, 1993.

———. ed. *The Book of the Pomegranate: Moses de León's Sefer ha-Rimmon.* Atlanta, 1988.

———. "Circumcision and the Divine Name: A Study in the Transmission of Esoteric Doctrine." *Jewish Quarterly Review* 78 (1987): 77–112.

———. "Circumcision, Vision of God, and Textual Interpretation: From Midrashic Trope to Mystical Symbol." *History of Religions* 27 (1987): 189–215.

———. "Effacer l'effacement/ sexe et ecriture du corps divin dans le symbolisme kabbalistique." Translated by J.-C. Attias. In *Tranmission et passages en monde juif,* ed. E. Benbassa. Paris, 1995.

———. "Forms of Visionary Ascent as Ecstatic Experience in the Zoharic Literature." In *Gershom Scholem's Major Trends in Jewish Mysticism 50 Years After,* edited by J. Dan and P. Schäfer, 209–35. Tübingen, 1993.

———. "From Sealed Book to Open Text: Time, Memory, and Narrativity in Kabbalistic Hermeneutics." In *Critical Jewish Hermeneutics,* edited by S. Kepnes. New York, 1995.

———. "God, the Demiurge and the Intellect: On the Usage of the Word *Kol* in Abraham ibn Ezra." *Revue des études juives* 149 (1990): 77–111.

———. "The Hermeneutics of Visionary Experience: Revelation and Interpretation in the *Zohar.*" *Religion* 18 (1988): 311–45.

———. "Images of God's Feet: Some Observations on the Divine Body in Judaism." In *People of the Body: Jews and Judaism from an Embodied Perspective,* edited by H. Eilberg-Schwartz, 143–81. Albany, 1992.

———. "Left Contained in the Right: A Study in Zoharic Hermeneutics." *AJS Review* 11 (1986): 27–52.

———. "Letter Symbolism and Merkavah Imagery in the *Zohar.*" In *ᶜAlei Shefer: Studies in the Literature of Jewish Thought Presented to Rabbi Dr. Alexandre Safran,* edited by M. Ḥallamish, 195–236. Bar-Ilan, 1990.

———. "Merkavah Traditions in Philosophical Garb: Judah Halevi Reconsidered." *Proceedings of the American Academy of Jewish Research* 57 (1989): 179–242.

———. "Meṭaṭron and Shiᶜur Qomah in the Writings of Ḥaside Ashkenaz," to be published in the proceedings of the conference Mystik, Magie und Kabbala im Aschkenasischen Judentum, December 9–11, 1991, edited by K. E. Grözinger.

———. "Mystical Rationalization of the Commandments in *Sefer ha-Rimmon*." *Hebrew Union College Annual* 59 (1988): 217–51.

———. "The Mystical Significance of Torah Study in German Pietism." *Jewish Quarterly Review* 84 (1993): 43–78.

———. "Negative Theology and Positive Assertion in the Early Kabbalah." *Daᶜat* 32–33 (1994): v–xxii. English section.

———. "The Theosophy of Shabbetai Donnolo, with Special Emphasis on the Doctrine of *Sefirot* in His *Sefer Ḥakhmoni*." *Jewish History* 6 (1992): 281–316.

———. *Through a Speculum That Shines: Vision and Imagination in Medieval Jewish Mysticism*. Princeton, 1994.

———. "The Tree That is All: Jewish-Christian Roots of a Kabbalistic Symbol in *Sefer ha-Bahir*." *Journal of Jewish Thought and Philosophy* 3 (1993): 31–76.

———. "Woman—The Feminine as Other in Theosophic Kabbalah: Some Philosophical Observations on the Divine Androgyne." In *The Other in Jewish Thought and History: Constructions of Jewish Identity and Culture*, edited by L. Silberstein and R. Cohn, 166–204. New York, 1994.

Wolfson, H. A. *Philo: Foundations of Religious Philosophy in Judaism, Christianity and Islam*. 2 vols. Cambridge, Mass., 1947.

Yaari, A. *Toledot Ḥag Simḥat Torah*. Jerusalem, 1964.

Yamauchi, E. M. *Gnostic Ethics and Mandaean Origins*. Harvard Theological Studies 24. Cambridge, Mass., 1970.

Yohsa, N. *Myth and Metaphor: Abraham Cohen Herrera's Philosophic Interpretation of Lurianic Kabbalah*. Jerusalem, 1994. In Hebrew.

Zak, B. "The Doctrine of *Ṣimṣum* of R. Moses Cordovero." *Tarbiz* 58 (1989): 207–37. In Hebrew.

———. "More on the Evolution of the Saying, 'The Holy One, blessed be He, the Torah, and Israel are One,' " *Kiryat Sefer* 57 (1982): 179–84. In Hebrew.

Zimmer, E. "Poses and Postures during Prayer." *Sidra* 5 (1989): 89–130. In Hebrew.

Zolla, E. *The Androgyne Reconciliation of Male and Female.* New York, 1981.

Zumthor, P. *La Lettre et la voix. De la'Littérature' médiévale.* Paris, 1987.

Zunz, L. *Literaturgeschichte der synagogalen Poesie.* Berlin, 1865.

◆ INDEX ◆

References to contemporary scholars are limited to occurrences of their names in the main body of the text.